MULTICULTURAL TEACHING

A Handbook of Activities, Information, and Resources

THIRD EDITION

Pamela L. Tiedt

University of California, Berkeley

Iris M. Tiedt

Moorhead State University

Allyn and Bacon

Boston   London   Sydney   Toronto

Copyright © 1990, 1986, 1979 by Allyn and Bacon
A Division of Simon & Schuster, Inc.
160 Gould Street
Needham Heights, Massachusetts 02194

Series Editor: Sean W. Wakely
Senior Editorial Assistant: Carolyn O'Sullivan
Cover Administrator: Linda Dickinson
Manufacturing Buyer: Tamara McCracken
Production Coordinator: Superscript Associates
Editorial-Production Service: TKM Productions
Cover Designer: Susan Slovinsky

Library of Congress Cataloging-in-Publication Data

Tiedt, Pamela L.
    Multicultural teaching : a handbook of activities, information, and resources / Pamela L. Tiedt, Iris M. Tiedt. — 3rd ed.
        p.   cm.
    Includes bibliographies and index.
    ISBN 0-205-12214-0
    1. Intercultural education—United States.   2. Cross-cultural orientation—United States.   I. Tiedt, Iris M.   II. Title.
LC1099.3.T54   1989
372.6′044—dc20   89-15124
                                                        CIP

Printed in the United States of America
10 9 8 7 6 5 4   93 92 91

Contents

Preface

We are excited about sharing this third edition of *Multicultural Teaching* with teachers and future teachers because we feel that multicultural education is integral to teaching and learning at all levels.

We find it especially enlightening to observe the evolution of our own thinking as it is revealed in the three editions of this book. Our perspective has changed along these lines:

1. Our reason for creating the book in 1979 was that we wanted teachers to recognize the need for multicultural understandings for all students. We wanted to critique the "melting-pot theory," to suggest ways of making students aware of diversity as something to be valued, and to encourage teachers to include multicultural objectives throughout all instruction.
2. The 1986 edition strengthened the above ideas with particular emphasis on multicultural teaching across the curriculum. Two chapters were added to address ways of integrating instruction in reading and language arts and social studies classes. The recommended approach was student-centered, with chapters on self-esteem and student language.
3. This third edition marks a major change in the authors' thinking as we strive to clarify definitions within multicultural education. Special attention is given to *culture* and the fact that every student grows up a member of a particular culture. This cultural background is a part of a student's prior knowledge, and it influences his or her response to schooling. The diverse cultural backgrounds of our students must be considered as we plan learning experiences that will enable students to achieve to their fullest potential.

Consistent across the three editions has been a driving assumption that multicultural understandings are fundamental to the education of all children, not only children from minority backgrounds but also those from white middle-class families. Recognition of the many cultures within any classroom provides the foundation for true multiculturalism. From this base, students can experience empathy for other individuals and groups that they encounter. Therein lies the hope for world harmony and peaceful coexistence in this global village.

A second assumption is that all of education is inherently *multicultural,* for it is delivered by and addressed to individuals who represent varied cultures. Recognizing our individual biases, their sources, and how they affect our thinking is a first step toward multicultural understanding. Multicultural teaching is exciting then for both teacher and student, for it invites the honest exchange of views on real issues that may be controversial. When emotions and deep-seated beliefs enter the classroom, students become involved; learning takes place.

A final assumption is that multicultural education is basic. It is an integral part of the curriculum, not a separate course or a series of varied discrete activities added to an existing prescribed curriculum. Multicultural teaching presupposes a climate in which students can dare to question, venture to take risks, and to learn from each other. Multicultural education is not limited to information presented within the covers of a textbook nor is it confined within the school walls.

As we open the door to multicultural thinking, we can create new roles for ourselves in the classroom. We can step down from the podium to engage in the discovery process with our students. We can begin to see the classroom as a center of inquiry in which we collaborate with our students. Our goal, then, is to empower students to think, to perform as active learners, as they construct their own meaning from the world around them.

We hope that we have been able to share ideas in *Multicultural Teaching* that will encourage you to join in this challenging endeavor.

Special thanks are due to the reviewers: Ryan Collay, University of Oregon; Mary Cordier, Western Michigan University; Lee Manning, Columbia College; and Rudy Serrano, California State University, Bakersfield.

P.L.T.
I.M.T.

NEVER JUDGE
ANOTHER MAN
UNTIL YOU HAVE
WALKED
A MILE IN HIS
MOCCASINS.
NORTH AMERICAN INDIAN PROVERB
Cole

1

Education for Multicultural Understanding

Up until now, multicultural education has been too much dual cultural education. . . . Multiculturalism must be seen to embrace the whole of humankind. From a strategic point of view, this maturing of multicultural education through cooperative pluralism *represents an opportunity of joining with other groups and other movements designed to assist the human race to live together in understanding, appreciation, and peace.*[1]

John I. Goodlad

Preview

After reading this chapter, you should be able to:

- Explain the need for multicultural education.
- Identify changes in thinking about cultural pluralism in the United States.
- Define multicultural education.
- Use pertinent terms accurately.
- Summarize a rationale for multicultural teaching.
- Discuss current issues related to multiculturalism.

The United States houses a diverse population. Historically, we can trace the origins of this diversity, beginning with the Native American tribes that lived on the land before visitors from Europe "discovered" them and the North American continent. The people who immigrated then came from various European countries — England, France, Germany, Italy, Spain. At the same, too, we must remember that immigration was taking place along the western coast as Russian hunters reached out into the vast territory that is now Alaska. Immigration continued with people coming to the New World for many different reasons — religious persecution, exploration, and wealth. Thousands were brought forcibly as slaves. Today's immigrants include Vietnamese, Latin Americans, Filipinos, and Ethiopians, among others. The history of this country clearly identifies our roots — the origins of the diverse individuals that make up our population today.

Not only are we diverse in origin, but we differ in many other ways. All of us can be identified by gender; we are men or women who have needs and expectations based on our sex. We can also be categorized by age, with all of us moving in turn from the youngest group to the elderly, changing our perspectives as we mature. Along the way, we identify with many different groups based on family, language, national origins, race, and beliefs. We also group ourselves according to interests and concerns — musicians, students, parents, disabled, unemployed, Democrats, conservationists — many times belonging to several groups at any one time. Membership in such groups changes and varies in length of time. Belonging to such groups shapes our identities and our ways of thinking.

Yet each one of us is unique. Out of all the diverse factors that influence our growth, beginning with the accident of birth, we are shaped by knowledge, experience, values, and attitudes. Each of us internalizes a unique self-culture from which we operate. Recognizing this I-Culture, our individual biases and their origins, is the first step toward achieving empathy for others, which is the overall goal of multicultural education.

These three paragraphs summarize the stance from which we are writing this book. As we move forward through the chapters that follow, we hope to explicate these views and to suggest methods of integrating multicultural concepts into all of education.

Establishing a Foundation for Multicultural Education

To begin our dialogue about multicultural education, we want to address the essential assumptions that undergird the presentation in this book. In this section we will discuss the following questions:

Is there a need for multicultural education?
How do we define multicultural education?
How does multicultural education fit in the schools?
What are the expected outcomes for multicultural education?

The Need for Multicultural Education

The recognition of diverse needs within our population is evident in the many groups that surface, carrying such acronyms as NAACP, CIO, NOW, AMA, POW, OWL, MADD, and NEA. The recognition of cultures within our population and the need for greater understanding across these cultures has increased, appearing under various titles ranging from Affirmative Action, to Women's Studies, to Early Childhood Education, to AIDS Education. Multicultural education pertains to all of these efforts and more.

Race riots, the Ku Klux Klan, anti-Semitism, rape, and child abuse are not occurences of the past. Fear and ignorance still lead individuals or groups to perform atrocities against other human beings. As summarized in the introductory paragraphs of this chapter, almost all of us are children of immigrants from other lands. Young people, who will soon become our country's adult citizens, need to learn broad concepts of cultural difference and respect for the diversity of our population. These diversities are derived from gender, age, national origins, language backgrounds, religious beliefs, politics, the work world, physical and mental abilities, and experiences.

We believe that our ways of thinking about the other members of the U.S. population are also shaped by education—in the home, in the school, and in the larger societal context. Through education we can broaden our awareness of other people, their needs, and their hopes and dreams. Educators need to lead the way toward breaking down the kind of stereotyped thinking that can lead to dissension and war. A humane approach to education threaded through the total curriculum presented over twelve or more years may eventually lead to a truly democratic society. The intent of this book is to suggest ways of delivering this message of empathy and esteem to students of all ages in all classrooms.

Defining Multicultural Education

Multicultural education has been the source of controversy and confusion. Defined geographically, it has led to studies of other countries and the concept of the earth as a global village. Focus on ethnic studies has brought an awareness of literature and folklore specific to groups that speak the same language or share a religious belief. Concern for the needs of all people has expanded to include newly recognized groups, for example, the disabled and the elderly. Multicultural education must include these themes along with others. As we strive to define multicultural education and multicultural teaching, we need to focus first on defining culture. From that base, we can move to the broader concepts inherent in multiculturalism.

The key to defining multicultural education lies in the root word *culture*. Culture connotes a complex integrated system of belief and behavior that may be both rational and nonrational. Each one of us is born into a culture. Our beliefs derive from these ethnic and family backgrounds, but they continue to be shaped by all of our experiences after birth. For the most part, family attitudes, language, and other behaviors are internalized without question. It is only when we encounter other cultures that we begin to observe differences, to wonder, and to ask questions.

Each of us can map the influence that have shaped our individual culture – the kids we went to school with, the various places we have lived or traveled to, the person we married or lived with, the people with whom we have worked. Your individual culture reflects the culture of your family, but it is not identical to the culture of any other member of the family. As we map cultural influences, we must consider the many groups to which we belong or have belonged and the many people with whom we have interacted; and we will identify our individual concerns and interests. Each of us can create a cultural map similar to that completed here for Carlita:

Notice that Carlita, a twenty-year-old woman attending college in San Diego, is greatly influenced by her family, some of whom still live in Mexico. She acknowledges the influence particularly of her oldest brother, who serves as the head of the family now that her father is dead. Carlita adheres to the tenents of the Catholic church as she has been taught since birth. However, education is causing her to question some basic assumptions of both family and church. She is moving ahead with career plans. We could predict that her individual culture will continue to change as she encounters other career-oriented women and moves up the career ladder in her profession.

Multicultural Education in the Schools

Education begins at the home – a personal individualized kind of coaching in the context of family to which the child responds eagerly and enthusiastically. In this setting, language acquisition occurs naturally and children acquire numerous concepts and many of the values and attitudes that stay with them for life. On the other hand, we have long realized that home schooling is limited and insufficient to meet the needs of a complex technological society. Children need more than the home can offer. Thus, we have established a vast system of schools to educate our children in the broad knowledge base that some allude to as "cultural literacy." Certainly the curriculum covers a breadth and universality of knowledge that few parents could provide. The school also serves as a place where students are further socialized as they interact with other students and work under the tutelage of the adults who present what society judges to be most important for children to know at that particular time.

A major aim of schooling is to dispel ignorance. We do not fear that which we understand, whether it is higher mathematics, the Amish community's lifestyle, or the history of Korean Americans. Therefore, as we focus on multicultural concepts, we feel that it is essential that young children and older students first learn to understand their own individual cultures. Based on a strong sense of worth and self-esteem, they can then begin to understand and to accept the cultures of others. Thus, we can combat stereotyping and prejudice, which have only negative effects on our national welfare.

Building on this understanding of the diverse members of the population in the United States, we should be able to extend our empathy readily to persons living in other countries. Without full understanding, people who speak a different language and display different values often appear threatening. However, with a knowledge base of understanding, when we meet people from, for example, Japan, we see them as warm, friendly human beings. Lack of understanding on both sides can lead to conflict and violence. Multicultural education, in its broadest application, should lead to world harmony. "Multicultural education is the generic term for broadly-based programs that confront ethnocentric or exclusionary educational practices and programs. Its intent is to foster understanding and respect for ethnic and miniority groups."[2] Thus, multicultural education includes a wide variety of concerns.

Within the school curriculum, multicultural education is ideally integrated across disciplines, not taught as one specialized course or a series of courses focused on special needs or interests. Such an approach recognizes the contributions of women in history, includes literature by and about Black Americans in English language arts, and discusses the rights of the disabled in a speech class. Organized around broad themes, inquiry leads students to comprehend the diversity of our population and to appreciate the role of each group in enriching the societal milieu we share.

Goals and Outcomes of a Multicultural Education Program

As already stated, the overall goal of multicultural education is world harmony, the understanding that will enable us to coexist in the world with diverse people. Without true understanding from all sides, we will inevitably have wars. More specifically, the primary aim of multicultural teaching is to develop awareness of all the people who make up the United States as human beings with similar needs and aspirations. Furthermore, our students need to be aware that we exist in an interdependent world and that we cannot possibly ignore the problems faced by other people, for example in Laos or Afghanistan.

The general outcomes expected from a multicultural program can be stated from many different perspectives. Because we advocate a student-centered approach to curriculum and instruction, we will state the outcomes in terms of student performance. Through multicultural education, we intend that students will learn to:

- Display a positive feeling of self-esteem; be aware of the characteristics of their own individual cultures.
- Extend this right to self-esteem to others; compare their individual cultures to those of others.
- Identify different cultural groups in their community and the United States and describe the similarities and differences of these groups; learn that *different* is not synonymous with *deficient*.
- Discuss stereotyped thinking and how it leads to prejudice; apply critical skills to solve such problems in the school and community and consider how this process might extend to solving worldwide conflicts of interest.

As we plan for multicultural education in our schools, we need to recognize that true understanding—empathy—does not happen overnight. "In the long run, intercultural skills are not 'pushbutton' substitutes for understanding. Communication strategies are never mechanistic, artificial ways around loving, warm personal involvement with people and the hard work to make relationships work."[3]

Summary

Multicultural education aims at awareness of the diversity that is characteristic of our national population and the source of that diversity. It begins with helping each student to identify a personal culture and to build his or her self-esteem. From this base, students can extend their learning to include knowledge of diverse cultures and the contributions that members of different cultural groups have made to the growth of the United States. Such understandings form the basis for a humane education, extending over twelve or more years, that has the possibility of educating students to participate in creating a truly democratic society that contributes to world harmony.

HOW NATIONAL THINKING CHANGED

National thinking has changed in many respects since the first settlement of Jamestown in 1607. Historically, we can note the controversy and the shaping of the thinking that led to the Revolutionary War and the beginning of the United States. Historically, too, we can trace the evolution of thinking that led to the freeing of the slaves. In this section, we will address the thinking that has moved us to our present conception of multicultural education as we advocate presenting it in the schools today. We will examine legislation that led to the current position and also clarify the terminology related to multicultural education and the ethnic groups involved.

Equality for all Americans—whatever their race, sex, age, national origin, or language—is a major concern in the whole of American society today. Legislation has been pased to provide equal opportunity for education. Efforts have been made to eliminate discriminatory practices in the work world, including equal pay for equal work. Women and members of minority groups are holding more responsible political positions. Yet we must continue to solve problems daily to ensure that every American can feel equally valued.

These changing attitudes have a direct effect on practice in the schools. All students have a right to equality of education, so textbooks, terminology, and teaching practices must change to reflect that goal. This background information will enable you to work more effectively with multicultural education.

Rethinking the Melting-Pot Theory

During the first half of this century, the aim of the schools was to assimilate all children into the American culture as quickly as possible. Children were expected to forget their native languages and to learn to speak and write English, the accepted language of the nation, the language of business and society. Metaphorically, the United States was seen as a hugh melting pot into which all diverse people were dumped to melt away the differences, thereby creating people who were very much alike.

The term *melting pot* came from a play by that name which was written by Israel Zangwill in 1909. The following quotation illustrates the prevailing American nationalist sentiment that created the image of a homogeneous culture.

> America is God's Crucible, the great Melting Pot where all the races of Europe are melting and reforming! Here you stand, good folk, think I, when I see them at Ellis Island, here you stand in your fifty groups with your fifty languages and histories, and your fifty hatreds and rivalries, but you won't be long like that, brothers, for these are the fires of God. A fig for your feuds and vendettas! Germans and Frenchmen, Irishmen and Englishmen, Jews and Russians— into the Crucible with you all! God is making the American . . . The real American has not yet arrived. He is only in the Crucible, I tell you—he will be the fusion of all races, the coming superman.[4]

The melting-pot theory is inappropriate today because the presence of cultural diversity is recognized as a strength, not a weakness. This country is not perceived today as a melting pot but rather a tossed salad, with various groups contributing to the national culture while maintaining their distinct identity. As a result, individuals can be proud of their ethnic heritage instead of ashamed of their differences.

Language is a crucial aspect of this concern for preserving the heritage of different groups. Pressure to include languages beside English in the school curriculum comes from members of many groups who feel that their language is an essential part of their culture. In addition, others have pointed out the students' rights to their own language and have identified the close tie between valuing one's language and self-esteem. The chart on page 8 summarizes the evolution of thinking about language in the United States during the twentieth century.

Emergence of Multicultural Education

Many laws and court decisions paved the way for bilingual education and the current trend toward multicultural teaching. If we examine legislation and court cases, we see the same evolution of theory and philosophy regarding the rights of the

EVOLUTION OF THINKING
ABOUT LANGUAGE IN THE UNITED STATES

Prior to 1914
Many community schools existed to teach a specific language, such as German. Saturday classes were common.

1918
World War I brought about reactions against Germany and a resurgence of patriotic feeling; use of "English only" in schools legislated in many states.

1945
World War II led to realization of need for knowledge of foreign languages; teaching of foreign languages in schools encouraged.

1953
UNESCO published a monograph advocating use of the mother tongue to teach students; not widely accepted in the United States.

1958
Russian launching of Sputnik frightened U.S. leaders who turned to schools. National Defense Education Act (NDEA) passed to help U.S. schools keep up with Russian education. Aid given to promote key subject areas including teaching of foreign languages.

1963
Dade County, Florida, initiated bilingual program for Spanish-speaking Cuban children coming to Miami. Interest spread to other states.

1965
Elementary and Secondary Education Act (ESEA): Funds granted to schools to upgrade education in many areas including English instruction (modern grammar, linguistics).

1968
Bilingual Education Act: Title VII of ESEA promoted bilingual programs in schools.

1971
Massachusetts Bilingual Education Act: Massachusetts was first state to pass law mandating bilingual education for non-English-speaking children (NES). Other states followed.

1973
Bilingual Education Reform Act: Updated 1968 law; mandated language instruction as well as study of history and culture in bilingual programs.

1974
U.S. Supreme Court Decision: *Lau* v. *Nichols* — NES students have a legal right to bilingual instruction as part of "equal educational opportunity." Aspira Consent Decree class action suit on behalf of Puerto Rican children resulted in New York City Board of Education agreeing to provide instruction in students' native languages.

1981
Senator S. I. Hayakawa first introduced a Constitutional Amendment to declare English the official language of the United States. (Defeated)

1984
California voters passed bill to publish ballots and other election material only in English.

1984–85
Illinois, Indiana, Kentucky, Nebraska, and Virginia passed resolutions declaring English as their official state language.

individual that we have already discussed related specifically to language. Contemporary court decisions have in certain instances overthrown earlier legislation related, for example, to human rights and equality of educational opportunity. Today there is a strong push toward multicultural approaches to teaching at all levels.

What are the issues involved? Legal actions affecting the education of minorities, persons of varied cultural backgrounds, and the economically disadvantaged are all relevant. The chronology of such events might rightly begin with the benchmark case of *Brown* v. *Topeka Board of Education.* In 1954 this Supreme Court decision stated that segregated schools are unequal. State laws providing separate schools for black and white students were declared unconstitutional.

Following this decision came legislation establishing the U.S. Commission on Civil Rights in 1957. This independent, bipartisan agency was charged to "Investigate complaints alleging denial of the right to vote by reason of race, color, religion, sex, or national origin, or by reason of fraudulent practices."

The commission published *A Better Chance to Learn: Bilingual-Bicultural Education,* a report designed for educators as a "means for equalizing educational opportunity for language minority students." This overview, published in 1975, summarizes efforts to help students in school who speak languages other than English. This agency sees language and culture as basic considerations in providing equal rights.

In 1968 the Bilingual Education Act (BEA) was passed as Title VII of the Elementary and Secondary Education Act. The intent of this law was clarified by President Lyndon B. Johnson:

> This bill authorizes a new effort to prevent dropouts; new programs for handicapped children; new planning help for rural schools. It also contains a special provision establishing bilingual education programs for children whose first language is not English. Thousands of children of Latin descent, young Indians, and others will get a better start — a better chance — in school . . .

Efforts to enforce such legislation also appeared. The Office of Civil Rights Guidelines, for example, indicated that affirmative efforts to give special training for NES students were required as a condition to receiving federal aid to public schools in 1970. The text read:

> Where inability to speak and understand the English language excludes national origin-minority group children from effective participation in the education program offered by a school district, the district must take affirmative steps to rectify the language deficiency in order to open its instructional program to these students.

A related issue is the treatment of women in the United States. In 1972, Title IX, an amendment to the Civil Rights Act, stated, "No person in the United States shall, on the basis of sex, be excluded from participation in, be denied the benefits of, or be subjected to discrimination under any education program or activity receiving federal financial assistance."

The most significant case related to multicultural/bilingual education, however, is *Lau* v. *Nichols,* a Supreme Court case that is pressuring all school districts to provide for linguistic and cultural diversity. In 1974 it charged a school district as follows:

> The failure of the San Francisco school system to provide English language instruction to approximately 1,800 students of Chinese ancestry who do not speak English, or to provide them with other adequate instructional procedures, denies them a meaningful opportunity to participate in the public educational program and thus violates . . . the Civil Rights Act of 1964. . . .

This class-action suit against the San Francisco Unified School District led to a decision that school districts must provide education in languages that meet the needs of students who attend the school. Thus began plans to teach students in their native language, whether it be Yupik or Tagalog, and provide ESL programs specifically designed for each group.

These laws stressed human rights and the need for bilingual education. Out of this thrust came multicultural approaches to teaching that recognized the need for awareness of our culturally diverse society. Teachers in bilingual classrooms are asked to present both linguistic and cultural instruction. Social studies classes must today present multicultural perspectives of sociology and history. Language arts instructors are expected to enrich their classrooms with multicultural literature and language information.

Legislation and court decisions reflect the thinking of our times. It is important to realize, on the other hand, that laws alone do not effect change. What you do in your classroom may, however, serve to break down stereotypes, promote multicultural understanding, and make a crucial difference in the personal development of many individual students. This book is designed to provide activities, information, and resources that will aid you in reaching those goals.

Changes in Terminology Reflect Thinking

As our national attitudes have changed, so has terminology. We need to clarify our use of terms such as *culture, class, ethnic group, identity group,* and *race* as we begin our study of multicultural education.

Culture is a totality of values, beliefs, and behaviors common to a large group of people. A culture may include shared language and folklore, ideas and thinking patterns, communication styles—the "truths" accepted by members of the group. Members of this culture "speak the same language" so they understand the allusion and humor, and they have similiar expectations for the good life.

At the same time, however, as members of a cultural group interact with the larger society, they become aware of different ways of behaving, different expectations, and they may change individually or collectively. Within a culture, subcultures may evolve as groups of people change sufficiently to be identifiable.

An example of a large complex cultural group is those individuals around the world who believe in Judaism. Although they share a common religion, two divisions of belief developed—the Ashkenazic who speak Yiddish and the Shephardic who speak Ladino. Jews can also trace their ethnic roots to specific nations. Within the United States we can identify Reform, Conservative, and Orthodox subgroups of the Jewish culture.

Used in this anthropological sense that is appropriate for multicultural education, *culture* has no social standing. All cultures are distinctive with identifiable differences, but they are equally acceptable. We need to be aware, however, of other connotations that have been associated with the word *culture*. This term has been attached to a number of categories of activities or knowledge, for example, "pop culture" or the "culture of poverty." Such loosely construed use of this term is confusing. A literary or elitist use assumes that wealthier, better educated persons have more "culture" than do poor, uneducated people. This definition equates culture with knowledge of the arts and literature. Operating from the anthropological sense, we would not say, "He is a very cultured man." In this text we acknowledge that all people have a culture, and we judge all cultures as being equally valid and having equal worth. All of us are acculturated or socialized to live appropriately within a particular culture from birth. Much of our learning is the result of socialization or cultural conditioning.

Class, on the other hand, does connote status in the society. Social class is closely associated with socioeconomic status (SES). We sometimes think of the United States as a "classless" society because these strata are not clearly defined, and it is possible for persons to move from one class to another. Yet, there are distinctions based on wealth, education, and the kind of work one does. These distinctions may be revealed through aesthetic tastes, linguistic characteristics, and privilege as well as opportunity. Interesting studies have been made of different groupings, for example, those who drink Pouilly Fuisse, attend the symphony, and read *The New Yorker,* and those who drink Miller Lite, attend the local football games, and read *People Magazine.* There is an ever-widening gap between the upper-middle class and those who live in poverty. As teachers, we need to be aware of our stereotyped expectations and attitudes toward children that may be based on difference in class, for example, poor children who come to school in less attractive clothing are not as bright as well-dressed, more advantaged children and thus cannot learn more advanced thinking skills.

Ethnicity is an umbrella term that has been used to include varied groupings based on national or linguistic backgrounds as well as religion, class, and regional identification. The origin of this term is the Greek *ethnos,* which means *nation.* This term is often used inaccurately to refer to members of all minority groups within the society. The term *ethnocentrism* refers to the centrality of dominance of the national group identity that may limit an individual's perspective. Ethnic studies may focus on national origins, but they have also often included Black Studies programs. *Ethnography* is the study of groups; this term is used to describe a kind of qualitative research that observes group interaction and effects.

The use of the word *ethnic* needs to be clarified. An example of a large ethnic group in the United States is comprised of Mexican Americans who share a complex culture. This group is often subsumed within the category, Hispanic, although not all Mexicans originated from Hispanic roots, speaking the language of Spain. See the discussion under the heading of Group Names.

Identity groups are people who share interests, concerns, or roles and "speak the language" common to that group. Members may share attitudes and needs and work toward a cause. They may share special skills and behaviors that bring them together for learning or performance events. Identity groups may be based on vocational or professional roles. We all belong to many identity groups. A culture is a more broadly encompassing identity group. (Note, however, that an identity group is not a culture as we have identified it above.) The Woman's Movement grew out of the needs of an identity group. The disabled are now speaking as a group to achieve equity and to fight discrimination. Identity groups do effect change.

Race is another term that has been inappropriately used and needs to be defined technically. Race is not synonymous with nationality, a language spoken, or a culture. It is incorrect, therefore, to speak of the Jewish race, the English-speaking race, or the Negro race. For many years it was the practice to identify three races: European (white), African (black), and Asian (yellow). As scientific information about blood types grew, a number of major races have been identified. Sometimes called geographical races, nine groups are identified as follows:

- African (Negroid) – Collection of related persons living south of the Sahara. Black Americans are mostly of this origin.
- American Indian (Amerindian or American Mongoloid) – Related to the Asian geographical race. Only group in the Western hemisphere for many years.
- Asian (Mongoloid) – Persons in continental Asia except for those in South Asia and the Middle East; includes Japan, Taiwan, the Philippines, and Indonesia.
- Australian (Australian aborigine or Australoid) – A group of people in Australia.
- European (Caucasoid) – Located in Europe, the Middle East, and north of the Sahara. Includes persons living on other continents.
- Indian – Persons in South Asian from the Himalayas to the Indian Ocean.
- Melanesian (Melanesian-Papuan) – Dark-skinned persons living in New Britain, New Guinea, and the Solomon Islands.
- Micronesian – Dark-skinned persons living on islands in the Pacific: Carolines, Gilberts, Marianas, and Marshalls.
- Polynesian – Many persons living in the Pacific Islands such as Hawaii, Easter Island, and the Ellice Islands.

Group names have changed periodically. As changes have been made, there has been controversy about which terms are acceptable. More militant members of ethnic groups have at times preferred one term while less militant members of the same group use another. Such terms as *Chicano, Mexican American,* and *Hispanic,* for example, are widely used today, and each has its own rationale.

Teachers must be aware of changing terminology. We demonstrate our awareness of how thinking has changed by our own use of appropriate terms. The once widely accepted term *culturally disadvantaged,* for example, is no longer acceptable because many people are aware of its loaded implications. We recognize that all groups have cultures that are unique, and, at the same time, have much in common. *Disadvantaged* is an evaluative term that assumes a standard against which all cultures are judged and has led to the assumption that minority groups do not have a culture of their own. Following is a brief discussion of terminology that may need clarification.

Asian Americans. The more specific terms *Chinese Americans* or *Japanese Americans* are acceptable, too. The use of *Oriental* has fallen into disrepute because it connotes stereotyped views, for example, "the inscrutable Oriental."

Black Americans. Many Blacks accept the term *Negro,* which is the Spanish word for black. Others who wish to stress their African origins prefer *Afro-American*. In general, *Black American* or *Afro-American* is acceptable. Certainly, such derogatory terms as *colored, darky, nigger,* and so on are not acceptable.

Hispanics. The term *Chicano* was adopted by leaders who wished to stress that they are developing a unique culture in this country. The term *Mexican American* is preferred by some groups. At times there are references to the *brown movement,* but the term is not widely used.

Native Americans. The terms *Amerindian, Indian,* and *Native American* are used. The only problem with using *Native American* is that it is nonspecific, including many Indian tribes as well as a number of Eskimo groups. If possible, it is preferable to designated a specific tribe, such as Hopi or Aleut.

Capitalization of terms can be a problem. Frequently people express confusion about how to handle the capitalization of ethnic terms, particularly those that include the world *black*. There clearly is a need for some logical consistency. It is also important to respect the wishes of the persons involved. Taking these points into consideration, we have decided on the following practices.

Since many Blacks prefer to substitute that term for Negroes, we capitalize both negroes and/or Blacks as names for a distinct group. The singular forms would also then be capitalized as proper nouns, Negro and Black.

The term *Black American* is analogous to *Irish American* and *Jewish American* and is capitalized in similar fashion. Black is not capitalized, however, when used as an ordinary adjective as in black car, black man, and black child. The word *chicano* would follow the same pattern, as in Chicanos and chicano child.

Summary

In general, national thinking, exemplified by legislation and judicial decision, has changed to reflect greater insight and human practices that accept all of our citizens as having equal worth. Educators emphasize self-esteem—the bottom line for all students—and political leaders are moving to provide equity for all citizens of the

United States. Yet, pockets of ignorance continue to exist, and deep-seated prejudices surface unexpectedly from even the highly educated. We need to clarify our thinking, revealed by our use of terms, as we move ever onward toward multicultural understanding.

PLANNING FOR MULTICULTURAL EDUCATION

An education that is multicultural is comprehensive and fundamental to all educational endeavors. Given an understanding of the nature of human differences and the realization that individuals approach concepts from their own perspectives, advocates of education that is multicultural are consistent in their belief that respect for diversity and individual difference is the concept's central ingredient.[5]

All people in the United States need multicultural education, and we recognize that the learning of such concepts must begin during the early years. If schools are to promote multicultural understanding, then we need to begin by training teachers. Both preservice and inservice education is needed to prepare teachers to present multicultural concepts to K–12 students. Ideally, multicultural concepts will thread through all of teacher education. Multicultural education will appear in foundations courses, psychology and assessment courses, and all courses focusing on methods and materials of teaching.

In the same way, multicultural concepts will thread through the total K–12 curriculum. Students will constantly be reminded of the achievements of diverse members of our population, and they will continue to learn new ways of thinking that avoid the two-dimensional stereotype that is exemplified by a good-bad or right-wrong distinction.

Both teachers and students will learn to:

- Explain the rationale for including multicultural education in the K–12 curriculum.
- Outline changing thinking about groups within the U.S. population (e.g., assimilation, acculturation).
- Discuss the needs of major racial, ethnic, and identity groups in the population.
- Define terms relevant to multicultural education.
- Selet instructional materials to use in K–12 classrooms.
- Design lessons that teach multicultural concepts within the context of varied subject areas of instruction.
- Develop a unit of study focusing on a group or issue.
- Describe the history of various groups within the United States.
- Explain the conflict and tension that might develop as groups shift in power and numbers or as they move.

This brief overview gives you a sense of the scope and sequence we have chosen to follow in presenting the complex topic of multicultural education. You can readily perceive the flow of our thinking about the topic. Following this introductory chapter, we focus on the teaching/learning process and how it applies to implementing a Multicultural Education Program in K–12 classrooms. The chapters that follow explore in detail specific aspects of multicultural education: self-esteem, language, and group identity. Two chapters focus on teaching multicultural concepts within the context of other subjects of study, and one chapter spells out a myriad of activities organized around the calendar—an easy way for the busy teacher to introduce multicultural concepts into the classroom. The final chapter brings us full circle to reflect on what has been presented in the whole text. And last, an extensive bibliography appears in the Appendix that provides teachers with a variety of titles to search out when planning units of study.

REFLECTIONS

Multicultural education must be broadened to include cultural understandings for all educated persons. Recognizing that our membership in a group provides identity, we hope that we can develop group pride without chauvinism.[6] Diversity does not mean divisiveness. We believe that we can avoid the segregation that strengthens group identity to the exclusion of others as we work to dispel the stereotyped thinking that derives from fear and leads to prejudice. Such understanding begins with awareness of self and leads to recognizing the needs of others.

APPLICATIONS

Now that you have completed this first chapter, it is important to begin applying what you have learned. Prepare now to share the concepts and perceptions presented with young learners.

1. In his book, *Cultural Literacy,* E. D. Hirsch makes the following statements:

> Multicultural education should not be the primary goal of education even though it promotes tolerance and provides an informed perspective.
> . . . The acculturative responsibility of the schools is primary and fundamental. To teach the ways of one's own community has always been and still remains the essence of the education of our children, who enter neither a narrow tribal cultural nor a transcendent world culture, but a national literate culture.[7]

Write a brief statement about your response to Hirsch's observations. Save this statement to review at the end of this class. It will be interesting to see how your thinking may change.

2. How do Hirsch's comments compare with the following by Richard Garcia?

> Synergism—shared, collective, regenerating energy—should be the rallying cry rather than rampant competition for limited resources.[8]

Break into small groups of four or five people. Discuss this quotation and how it relates to multicultural education. Share your conclusions with the whole group.

3. Begin browsing through the extensive bibliography of multicultural literature presented in the Appendix beginning on page 343. Select several books that you would like to obtain from the library. Begin a card file as you record the following information for each book that you read.

> Author
> Title
> Grade level (approximate)
> Short summary
> Ideas for using with a class

You will learn more about working with such literature in the following chapters, but it is important to begin getting acquainted with multicultural literature as soon as possible because there is much to explore.

4. Work with other members of your group to begin a multicultural survey of your community. Decide how you can ascertain the various ethnic and racial groups represented in the area. Begin collecting such data in a class book called Our Multicultural Community. Practicing teachers can survey their individual schools and/or districts.

Endnotes

1. John I. Goodlad. From a speech at the Center for Educational Renewal, University of Washington, 1986.
2. Ricardo Garcia. *Education for Pluralism: Global Roots Stew*. Phi Delta Kappa, 1981, p. 15.
3. Carley H. Dodd. *Dynamics of Intercultural Communication*. Brown, 1987.
4. Israel Zangwill. *The Melting Pot* (play). 1909.
5. Carl A. Grant, ed. *Sifting and Winnowing: An Exploration of the Relationships between Multicultural Education and CBTE*. Teacher Corp Associates, University of Wisconsin, 1975.
6. Garcia, p. 26.
7. E. D. Hirsch. *Cultural Literacy: What Every American Needs to Know*. Houghton, 1987, p. 18.
8. Garcia, p. 11.

Resources

Thomas J. Archdeacon. *Becoming American: An Ethnic History*. Macmillan, 1983.

James A. Banks. *Multiethnic Education: Theory and Practice*. 2nd ed. Allyn & Bacon, 1988.

"Dealing with Diversity: At Risk Students." *Educational Leadership, 46*, 5 (February 1989).

Ricardo L. Garcia. *Education for Cultural Pluralism: Global Roots Stew*. Phi Delta Kappa, 1981.

E. D. Hirsch. *Cultural Literary: What Every American Needs to Know.* Houghton, 1987.

William W. Purkey and John M. Novak. *Inviting School Success: A Self-Concept Approach to Teaching and Learning.* Wadsworth, 1984.

Robert E. Slavin. *Effective Programs for Students at Risk.* Allyn and Bacon, 1989.

Iris McClellan Tiedt et al. *Reading/Thinking/Writing: A Holistic Language and Literacy Program for the K–8 Classroom.* Allyn and Bacon, 1989.

CHILDREN LEARN WHAT THEY LIVE

If a child lives with criticism,
    He learns to condemn.
If a child lives with hostility,
    He learns to fight.
If a child lives with ridicule,
    He learns to be shy.
If a child lives with tolerance,
    He learns to be patient.
If a child lives with encouragement,
    He learns confidence.
If a child lives with praise,
    He learns to appreciate.
If a child lives with fairness,
    He learns justice.
If a child lives with security,
    He learns to have faith.
If a child lives with approval,
    He learns to like himself.
If a child lives with acceptance and friendship,
    He learns to find love in the world.

2

Teaching for Multicultural Understanding

Education enables individuals to come into full possession of all their powers.

John Dewey

Preview

After reading this chapter, you should be able to:

- Plan a multicultural program for your classroom.
- Identify values and attitudes that are part of the "hidden curriculum."
- Select teaching strategies that support the concepts of equity and express value for diversity.
- Plan direct teaching experiences for students in K–12 classrooms to break down stereotypes or to promote respect for diversity.
- Design lessons that lead students to think critically about what they observe, hear, or read related to multicultural concepts.

An effective multicultural education program displays the same quality indicators as those of any school program. The key elements are the teacher's delivery, the students' involvement in learning, and a curriculum based on sound theory. We begin this chapter by summarizing these aspects of the program.

In addition, we present a lesson model designed to engage students in performing various kinds of thinking skills as they deal with multicultural content. We also describe several basic teaching methods that are recommended for work in any content area with suggested applications for multicultural education.

PLANNING FOR MULTICULTURAL EDUCATION

> There is an acute need . . . to assure that educational programs reflect the best knowledge available on education that is multicultural, and that this knowledge is ingrained throughout our educational programs.[1]

Multicultural education is best threaded through the total curriculum in an elementary school self-contained classroom. To have the greatest effect, it must be included in the objectives of every middle or secondary school classroom. Therefore, careful planning and evaluation of programs are required. Both planning and evaluation involve teachers and administrators at all levels as they specify outcomes and select activities and materials for instruction. In this section we will explore the following topics with specific attention to planning and evaluation:

Establishing a knowledge base for the program (curriculum)
Describing the teacher's role (delivery system)
Considering the students' needs (learning)

ESTABLISHING A KNOWLEDGE BASE FOR INSTRUCTION: CURRICULUM

The knowledge base selected for multicultural education may duplicate some aspects of the knowledge base recommended for teaching and learning in any subject area. The knowledge base will be the same, furthermore, if the program is designed for delivery in a single classroom or is part of a schoolwide effort. In addition, the knowledge base we identify should be sufficiently broad enough to cover K–12 levels in a well-articulated districtwide program. We begin with identifying a knowledge base that will be shared by all participating teachers. What will students learn?

We perceive multicultural education as a thread that weaves through the total curriculum; it is not a single syllabus for a class taught in ninth grade or a unit of study presented in grades 3 and 6. Threading multicultural concepts throughout the K–12 curriculum is admittedly more difficult than teaching a single class, but we feel that this approach is infinitely more meaningful. We also want to avoid learning lists of unrelated information in an effort to make students culturally literate. Rather, our aim is to empower our students to become "culturally thoughtful."

Our scope and sequence for multicultural education begins with the outcomes we expect students to achieve. Outcomes assessment, then, will inform us and the students of the intent of the program and, referred to periodically, will help us assess progress toward the established objectives.

What are we trying to achieve? What should students be able to do? How will their thinking be affected? We need to consider both cognitive objectives and affective objectives as we design a multicultural education curriculum. The matrix on the opposite page provides a useful framework with which to begin. Teacher educators might substitute appropriate areas of study or courses across the top of the chart.

Involving all faculty members in identifying competencies for the multicultural program will ensure that each person assumes responsibility for the success of the program. As already pointed out, objectives must be both affective and cognitive, and they must not only cross the total curriculum but permeate deeply into the very practices that we carry out as we teach. Objectives will be written in active terms that engage students in:

acting out	defining	observing	solving
analyzing	describing	recalling	stating
applying	explaining	reciting	visualizing
comparing	identifying	retelling	writing
deciding	listing		

The overall goal of the multicultural program has been expressed in our definition of multicultural education. We want to increase student self-esteem, understanding and appreciation of others in our society, and deepen concern for the needs of all people in the United States and in the world. The objectives we write will focus on the subject area we are teaching but will also include those that lead directly to this multicultural goal. The end result will be better instruction in all areas of the curriculum.

The planning matrix on page 22 is designed to assist a faculty in identifying competencies for a multicultural program. The matrix gives you a feeling for the breadth of this subject. We must identify the concepts and values that we want to teach, the skills that must be developed, and the desired behaviors that we want to effect. We need to consider these factors for each curriculum area—reading, oral and written language, mathematics, social studies, science, and so on. Many of the objectives for multicultural education are the same ones we would write for teaching in general.

It is not difficult to incorporate multicultural objectives, both affective and cognitive, and to reflect sound theory and practice in the list of aims for any class. A science teacher, for example, might include the following objectives for a study of animals:

Students will:

- Keep a learning log summarizing what they learn each day (reinforces learning; individualized).

A PLANNING MATRIX FOR MULTICULTURAL COMPETENCIES

Kind of Learning	Topic	Academic Activities										Other Activities			
		Reading	Oral, written language	Mathematics	Social studies	Science	Health	Foreign language	Art, music, drama, dance	Physical education	Practical arts, vocations	Co-curricular	Staff development	Administrative	Community
I. Understand concepts	A. Self B. Life-style C. Culture D. Changes in individuals and groups E. Cultural contact as agent in change F. Personal heritage G. Similarities/differences among individuals and groups H. Competence I. Occupational diversity J. Stereotypes/prejudice/discrimination														
II. Acquire values	A. Self-esteem B. Appreciation of self and others C. Respect for values/dignity/worth of self and others D. Respect for similarities/differences E. Acceptance of cultural pluralism F. Acceptance of diversity of life-styles G. Desire to bring about equity/reduce stereotypes H. Positive attitude toward school and life														
III. Develop skills	A. Analyzing influence of heritage B. Analyzing similarities/differences C. Distinguishing between myths/stereotypes and facts D. Recognizing prejudiced behavior E. Identifying biases in media F. Interpreting personal heritage G. Clarifying personal values H. Using skills of conflict resolution														
IV. Demonstrate behaviors, personal and social	A. Working to reduce inequities B. Confronting prejudiced behavior C. Cooperating with diverse others D. Using community persons as resources E. Using persons in school as resources F. Working to resolve conflicts G. Participating/involving others in life of school H. Using interpersonal skills														

State of California. *Planning for Multicultural Education as a Part of School Improvement.* Sacramento, CA: California State Department of Public Instruction, 1979, p. 26.

- Identify stereotypes that we associate with specific animals (introduces concept in nonthreatening context).
- Compile information to support or disprove one specific stereotype (the scientific method).
- Discuss stereotyped thinking in general (transfer of knowledge).
- Recognize the need to support generalizations with scientific facts (inquiry method; thinking skills).

Objectives that promote self-esteem and the appreciation of others can be inserted into the list of behavioral objectives for every instructional area. Consider how these objectives could fit into a reading lesson or a social studies unit.

Students will:

- List their own personal strengths.
- Identify areas in which they need to grow.

Students will:

- Express positive feelings for other students.
- Work cooperatively in group situations to help each other.

Students will:

- Learn facts about their family origins.
- Identify the many groups to which they belong.
- List ethnic groups in the community.
- Act out folktales from selected ethnic groups.

Students will:

- Describe the contributions made by diverse groups to our pluralistic society.
- Define such terms as *racism* and *sexism*.
- Discuss the importance of understanding among the people of the world in order to achieve world peace.

It is unlikely that any one of these objectives will be fully achieved in one lesson, thus we need to think also in terms of how these objectives can be introduced and reinforced at different levels over a period of time. We need to plan a Spiral Curriculum that moves upward from the bottom line of self-esteem with wide unpredictable swings. Like a star atop a Christmas tree, world peace is placed at the top of the spiral.

Curriculum consists of more than overt messages given in lectures and textbooks. It also includes the hidden or covert curriculum that is seldom recognized and almost never assessed. Consider what students learn in these classrooms.

Motherly Mrs. McIntyre loves children and loves to teach first-grade reading. She always brags to the principal about the wonderful readers in her Great Books group and has one of them read aloud when he visits the classroom. (How do the less able students feel? What knowledge are they internalizing?)

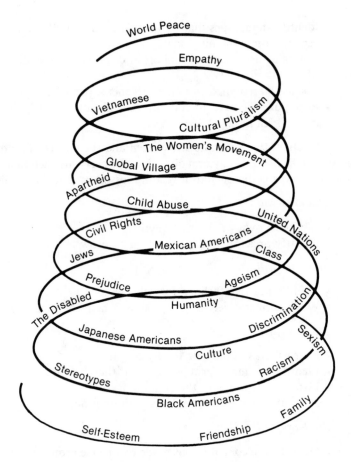

A Spiral Curriculum for Multicultural Education

Jim Melville teaches seventh-grade language arts. He reads aloud to his students and brings in piles of books from the library. He tells students that he always picks out books about boys because he knows boys hate stories about girls but girls enjoy the adventure stories about boys. (How might this practice affect the self-esteem of girls in this classroom? What are the boys and girls learning?)

High school history teacher, Donna Fosdick, has regular celebrations to remember the events of Pearl Harbor Day, Martin Luther King's birthday, and Cinco de Mayo. She comments that she can't afford more time from the curriculum for these extra observances. (Is there more to understanding other cultures than just observing these few holidays? What do students learn from hearing this attitude expressed? What are they failing to learn?)

We need to think of a curriculum that crosses the many disciplines that we teach. We need to design a curriculum that achieves cultural literacy in its broadest sense.

This literacy must encompass comprehension and changes in thinking that are revealed through clearly demonstrated understanding and empathy for others.

Summary

The multicultural curriculum begins with a study of self as students become aware of their own cultural backgrounds, their beliefs and attitudes, their eating habits, and other ways of behaving. Building from a sense of their own self-worth, students can then begin to compare and contrast their cultural identities with those of others in the classroom. Thus, guided by a knowledgeable teacher, they begin to discover that diversity is fascinating, not threatening. The curriculum presented, both overt and hidden, leads students toward an understanding of others that may enable them to share the world in peace.

DESCRIBING THE TEACHER'S ROLE: DELIVERY SYSTEM

Ernest Boyer states: "I'm convinced the time has come to . . . focus on the leadership of the principal, the renewal of the teachers, and above all, the dignity and potential of every student.[2] Any multicultural program should plan for the effective presentation of the curriculum. We need to make certain that teachers and administrators are well-informed and that their knowledge is accurate and up-to-date, but a well-planned delivery system is also crucial if learning is to take place. Teachers need to know how to use the best of teaching strategies—questioning, cooperative learning, engaging students in active hands-on learning activities. They need to select methods and materials that will involve students in thinking about real issues that affect their daily lives.

After a beginning list of competencies has been compiled, specific plans should be made for implementing the program in each classroom. The teacher is the key to the success or failure of any program so what you do in your own classroom every day is of primary importance.

From the moment students enter the classroom they begin learning. The climate of the room, the way you treat students, the language you speak—all serve as models for student behavior. Fair evaluation, recognition of individual needs, a clear sense of liking projected to students as you work with them will demonstrate what you want to teach. Your role calls for you to select the best teaching methods, to choose the materials you will use wisely, and to communicate to parents. Good teaching is student-centered.

Teachers who respect students select teaching methods that treat students fairly. For example, teachers would not use sarcasm as a way of putting students down, recognizing that the person who resorts to sarcastic comments to children is an insecure adult. Respect for students is shown in the acceptance of their idiosyncracies and recognition of their needs as growing young people. The teacher should have reasonable expectations of students and understand how to motivate their participation in language activities.

Evaluation of student performance is a particularly sensitive aspect of teaching. As we consider "putting grades on report cards," we should be aware that students see us as "putting grades on them," which can be very threatening, indeed. As we plan for evaluation, we should keep the following guidelines in mind:

1. *Grading.*   Don't put grades on everything a student does. Have many short writing and speaking activities that are not graded, but shared with other students or perhaps placed in a class collection that students can read at their leisure.

2. *Writing in all subject areas.*   Never grade the first draft of a student's writing. Periodically have students revise a selection that will be published in some way (on the bulletin board, in a class book, in the newspaper). Tell the students that you will put a grade on this work. (See Chapter 7.)

3. *Establishing criteria.*   Always make your criteria clear for grades you give. What does a student have to do to receive an A, B, or C? Talk with students about the characteristics of outstanding work, average work, and poor work as you make a specific assignment, and show them examples.

4. *Self-evaluation.*   As much as possible, have students check their own work. Provide answer sheets so they can discover mistakes immediately. Stress reading items over again as needed, and correcting errors. If you eliminate yourself from this kind of "grading," you cease to be the ogre who has all the "right" answers.

5. *Individual conferences.*   Have a short conference with each student once a week, if possible. Five minutes of individual attention does a lot for children who need support. This is a good time for examining children's writing or talking about the library book they are currently reading.

6. *Send a commendation to parents.*   Several times during the year, send a letter to each parent commending at least one thing their child has accomplished. Children will be glad to take a Good Work Letter home. Be sure to write this letter in the language of the home, even if you have to prepare several translations.

7. *Accentuate the positive!*   Focus on what students accomplish, not what they fail to achieve or the mistakes they make. Compare:

> Wow, you spelled thirteen words out of fifteen correctly!
> Too bad, you missed two words out of fifteen today.

Choose instructional techniques that allow for individual differences and ones that add a spark of excitement to classroom activities. Avoid fill-in-the-blank workbooks or dittoed sheets in favor of activities that engage students in listening, speaking, reading, writing, and thinking — active involvement that results in learning across the curriculum. Read journals and attend current workshops to discover innovative strategies that will make teaching more fun and effective, for example:

1. Employ clustering to assess students' knowledge of a new topic (see p. 194).
2. Assign an I-Search paper to show students how to find out what they really want to know (see p. 233).
3. Organize focused learning centers that engage students in "doing" (see p. 235).
4. Use a learning log or process journal to record student thinking, questions, and reactions.

You do not have to be bilingual in order to introduce concepts about various languages and dialects in your classroom. It is important that students become aware, for example, of the wide variety of languages that the U.S. population uses daily across the country. Even though you may have a bilingual program in your school, it probably deals with only one of those languages. It is important for children and teachers to recognize that English is not the only language spoken in the United States.

If you are a monolingual teacher, you can bring in speakers of varied !anguages to broaden student perspectives. Not only will visitors introduce different languages, but they can also share ideas and values from other cultures. Your role can be to facilitate this kind of interaction, to explore the resources of your community, and to plan learning experiences designed to teach children about the multilingual/ multicultural nature of our population. If you are fluent in a second language, or even if you know a little about another language, you can share your knowledge. Naturally we do not expect children to become bilingual by brief exposures to phrases in several languages, but learning to say *tovarishch* (Russian — friend), *hasta luego!* (Spanish — So long!), or *gesundheit!* (German — To your good health!) opens doors to new knowledge that can be fascinating to young language learners and exposes them to multicultural concepts.

Sharing stories from different cultures also offers a way of expanding student horizons. Folklore from Russia (discover the wicked Baba Yaga), Native American Indians (laugh over the antics of Coyote the Trickster), Black Africa (look for Anansi the Spider), or lore from the American West (Pecos Bill and Paul Bunyan) can be enjoyed equally by students and teachers.

Summary

Research tells us that good teaching is not teacher-dominated. Effective teachers will plan integrated studies that engage students in actively reading and writing about the Civil War as they also learn about the plight of the Africans brought forcibly to the United States. Students will engage in inquiry as they search for information to share with their study group. The effective teacher is enthusiastic about the content to be studied, but he or she is also caring about the needs of the learners who are spending considerable time in the classroom. Good teaching is reflective as teachers think consciously about what is happening and how teaching and learning can be improved in an ongoing process of development.

CONSIDERING THE NEEDS OF
STUDENTS: LEARNING

Our intent in developing multicultural education at K–12 levels is to have an impact on student thinking. We want learning to take place that will result in changing behaviors. Therefore, it is important that we consider the students in our classrooms in terms of their physical and psychological needs as well as the values and culture they bring to the classroom—their prior knowledge and experience. This awareness will help us in delivering our curriculum effectively.

Student-centered instruction recognizes student learning as the ultimate aim of education. We want students to be self-motivated learners, to inquire and to discover, and also to question established practices or assumptions. At the same time, students need to be aware of the responsibilities that are directly related to choice and decision making. The following proposed "Bill of Rights for Children: An Education Charter for the Decade of the Child" was drafted by Thomas Sobol, Commissioner of Education in New York State.[3]

All children have the right to:

- A healthy, secure, nurturing infancy and early childhood;
- A free, sound, basic education;
- An education appropriate for his or her needs;
- An education which respects each student's culture, race, socioeconomic background, and home language;
- Schools and educational programs which are effective;
- Educational programs which prepare them for jobs, for college, for family life, and for citizenship in a democracy;
- The resources needed to secure their educational rights;
- Education in school buildings which are clean, safe, and in good repair;
- Pursuance of their education without fear;
- An education which involves responsibilities as well as rights.

Multicultural education in the schools is designed for students. It begins rightfully with each student's concept of self and expands in ever-widening circles to understanding of others. It leads students to move from focus on self to involvement and consideration of others. Eventually, multicultural education engages students in the larger issues and problems of the world, as depicted in the diagram on the following page.

The nation is finally realizing the economic importance of saving "at-risk" students—those students who drop out of school as soon as possible. Since these students form a kind of identity group and many of them tend to be members of minority groups, it seems appropriate to address this problem in a book on multicultural education. For too long we have failed to solve the problem of reaching these students, intervening in the early years, providing models with whom they could identify. Our teaching has been inappropriate, failing to recognize that "at-risk students need to learn higher order thinking such as problem solving, not just basic skills that may keep them dependent thinkers all their lives."[4] Multicultural approaches to

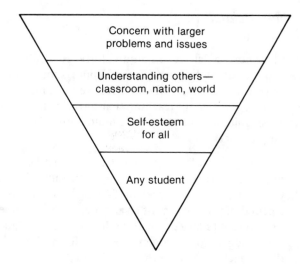

education may have something to offer these students as we deliberately select literature with which they can find a common bond and make a sincere effort to provide equity in the classroom. We must recognize that the welfare of at-risk students today will have economic consequences for all of us in the next century.

Summary

A sound multicultural education program depends on careful planning across levels and across subject areas. The quality indicators of an effective program include:

1. Content that makes interdisciplinary and multicultural connections
2. Teachers who recognize the need for multicultural education, who are involved in the planning, and who are willing to learn with their students
3. Students who are self-motivated learners concerned about their own rights as well as the rights of others

TEACHING MULTICULTURAL CONCEPTS EFFECTIVELY

In the preceding section of this chapter, we discussed the curriculum, the role of the teacher, and the needs of students. In this section we will focus more directly on teaching and how we can present multicultural concepts effectively. We will address specifically:

Research findings related to multicultural teaching

A sound lesson model that promotes student success

Selected teaching strategies that support student learning and that demonstrate multicultural concepts

Research Findings Related to Multicultural Teaching

As we consider how to deliver this multicultural curriculum, we need to clarify what we know about teaching that specifically supports multicultural education. Because this is not a text that focuses only on effective teaching, we will identify just a few of the influential ideas about teaching that have the most promise in enabling us to be successful in guiding students toward multicultural understandings. Research tells us, for example, that:

1. Teaching is not "telling." The learner must be actively engaged in inquiring, in constructing his or her own meaning, if learning is to take place.[5]
2. Cultural literacy is more than learning lists. Such learning accumulates over a period of years and must be acquired within a context that enables students to integrate knowledge with understanding. Broad humanistic studies will lead students to encounter factual information and to give it meaning by fitting each piece into the big picture.[6]
3. All students come to school with a vast store of knowledge. The five-year-old brings a wealth of information based on his or her individual culture and experiences he or she has had during this long period of rapid learning. We need to recognize this prior knowledge as we introduce new concepts, helping the student become aware of how the new knowledge is related to what is already known.[7]
4. Teacher attitudes and expectations of how students can or will do affects how children perform in school.[8,9]

Because teachers' attitudes and expectations are so fundamental to effective multicultural education, we share the results of two major studies. The Shipman study focuses on children entering school. The Rosenthal/Jacobson study focuses on children in the upper elementary grades.

The Shipman Study

Young children approach life eagerly, positively, no matter what their backgrounds. Self-confidently they reach out to learn. They work hard to learn, for example, the complexities of language and how to function in their social environment — family, neighborhood, and school. What happens in school has a significant effect on the development of this natural potentiality to learn. Teacher expectations directly influence children's performance. For children from low-income homes or from minority ethnic groups, this effect can be adverse.

A six-year study of children from low-income homes by Virginia Shipman and others investigated "how home and school work together to influence the child's development."[10] Findings reported in 1976 reveal:

1. "Disadvantaged" and middle-class children enter school with the same average level of self-esteem.
2. After three years of schooling, children from low-income homes experience

a significant drop in level of self-esteem compared to children from middle-class homes.

3. Although there is a loss of self-confidence, children from low-income homes still feel positive at this stage rather than negative about their ability to take care of themselves.

The Shipman study clarifies the characteristics of children from low-income homes. Studying more than 1,000 children from 1969–1975, she found that these children:

1. Enter school with as broad a range of abilities as any other group.
2. Have as much self-esteem as children from other groups.
3. Come from homes containing the same range of positive and negative influences on learning as do middle-class children.

These findings should help teachers rid themselves of the misconceptions that low socioeconomic status automatically means little value for learning. They also emphasize the need for viewing each child as an individual.

What does this study tell us about the process of schooling? The implications of this study for the classroom relate to teacher expectations for children from low-income homes. Shipman notes, "It gets down to what happens in the classroom between the teacher and the child—how much encouragement that child is given, how much stimulation and warmth." Teachers who have low expectations for students may have an adverse effect on children's performance.[11]

Teacher expectations based on income level or cultural background are not the only factors affecting student performance. Teachers need to consider the advantages the English-speaking child has on entering most U.S. schools compared to the NES child.

English-speaking child	*Non-English-speaking child*
1. Language used is familiar.	1. Language used is strange.
2. Teaching materials are presented in English, and the child learns to read English.	2. Child is expected to use materials presented in English; child may be illiterate in his or her native language.
3. Child's self-esteem is supported by successful experiences in school.	3. Child feels unhappy, is unsuccessful in school, and cannot wait to go home.
4. He or she graduates from high school and may enter college.	4. He or she drops out of school as soon as possible.*

We need to be aware of these differences in how children may regard the school

*Note that these findings tend to polarize characteristics in a way that may support stereotypes. We need to be aware, for example, that NES students from higher socioeconomic backgrounds or high prestige groups may perform very well.

experience. The role of the teacher should be to minimize the ways the NES students feel at a disadvantage, for language is closely allied with the students' self-concept. (The activities in Chapter 3 also support the development of positive self-concepts.)

Children who have experienced failure and frustration may perceive themselves as having limited ability or little chance of success and may not even try a task before saying "I can't." They have internalized a negative perception of themselves, and this attitude will influence their whole approach to life. This child needs to be revitalized and reassured. Our task is not easy even if we begin working with a young child at the age of four or five; it becomes increasingly difficult as the child grows older.

The Rosenthal/Jacobson Study

Another well-known study that suggests possible effects of teacher expectations on student performance was published under the title *Pygmalion in the Classroom* by Robert Rosenthal and Lenore Jacobson.[12] Twenty percent of the children in an elementary school in northern California were identified to teachers as having great potential for intellectual growth. Actually, these children's names were selected at random, so they had no greater potential than any other random group in the school. The teachers, however, perceived the children as having great potential and this belief seemed to color their expectations for these children. After eight months in the classroom, this group made significant gains in IQ scores compared to the children who had not been singled out. Apparently, the teachers' attitudes and expectations, although never explicitly verbalized, were communicated to the children. The teachers' expectations served as a self-fulfilling prophecy: *teachers expected the children to succeed and they did.*

Many things influence a teacher's expectations. Labels such as *slow, learning disabled,* and *mentally retarded* written in a cumulative folder are dangerous if they provide a set of expectations that actually limits the possibilities for children. Test scores can have the same limiting effect. Skin color, socioeconomic level, or a child's surname are other determinants of limited expectations. If children are to succeed, we must be aware of the damaging effect of such subtle expectations. Teachers need to avoid using labels, and work hard to project honest appreciation of student achievements. Teachers should consider test scores as only one piece of evidence, relying on their own observations of a child's abilities and performance.

Summary

Research findings support our recognition that effective multicultural teaching is student-centered rather than teacher-dominated. The teacher does not abdicate his or her position but rather plans quality learning activities that engage students in active, hands-on experiences and builds in success so that students develop self-esteem. The teacher models appreciation for diversity by building on students' prior knowledge and making clear expectations that are realistic for each student's abilities. Learning experiences are designed to promote student interaction and to generate inquiry and thinking that are expressed through talking and writing. The total effort aims toward achieving broad cultural literacy for all.

A Sound Lesson Model

In planning any lesson it is important to think through the entire process. First of all, what are your objectives for teaching the lesson? What do you want students to be able to do? Remember that objectives can, and should, be both affective and cognitive. The following lesson model begins with stating the objectives.

Next you begin thinking about how you can reach these objectives. What procedures will you use? What materials — films, books, pictures, records, objects — will help you stimulate student learning? Then determine what students will do in response to the stimulus. Plan an active, hands-on experience — something the students *can* do (realistic expectations). Next comes the followup. What do students do after participating in the learning activity? How do they share the results? Finally, but not to be forgotten, how will you know they have met the objectives you specified? Evaluation techniques will range from acting out to telling to writing, but they involve a performance by the student (not limited to the commonly used paper and pencil test).

By following this model, you will plan a theoretically sound learning experience

---

**DESIGNING A LESSON:
THE SAFE MODEL FORM**

Title of lesson: _____

Grade levels intended for: _____

Objective(s): (What will students do?)
1. _____
2. _____
3. _____

Brief description:

_____
_____
_____
_____
_____

Procedures:
STIMULUS (Tell the teacher-reader what to do using specific material.)

ACTIVITY (What will students do? Include suggestions to teacher.)

FOLLOWUP (Individual, pairs, small group, large group — suggestions.)

EVALUATION (Criteria for success of lesson based on objective(s).)

---

for children. The acronym SAFE will help you remember to incorporate all four parts to produce an effective lesson that you and your students will enjoy:

Stimulus
Activity
Followup
Evaluation

A Sample Lesson Following the Model

SAFE Lesson 1:   A Biographical Sketch

Level of Difficulty: Grades 7–12

Outcomes:

Students will:

1. Read a short biographical sketch of a minority author.
2. Analyze the quality of the writing.
3. Identify the features of a biographical sketch.
4. Compose a biographical sketch following the model.
5. Share information about minority authors and their writings.

Procedures:

This lesson should be developed over a period of several days. Duplicate copies of the following biographical sketch of Alex Haley:

Introducing Alex Haley

Alex Palmer Haley is the well-known author of *Roots: The Saga of an American Family,* which was published in 1976 and made into a stirring film that was presented on television to millions of Americans. Born August 11, 1921, in Ithaca, New York, Alex Haley was the son of a professor and a teacher.

Alex Haley served as a journalist in the U.S. Coast Guard. He tells of writing love letters for his fellow seamen who weren't particularly good at writing. He won their admiration and gratitude (and earned considerable money, too) by creating romantic letters that ensured that the men's sweethearts were waiting when they returned to port.

Haley soon decided that he wanted to concentrate on writing full-time. After struggling for a number of years to earn a living as a writer, he finally succeeded by working with the author of *The Autobiography of Malcom X,* which appeared in 1965.

But it was *Roots* that brought Haley real acclaim. Recognizing this unique contribution to American literature, the noted writer, James Baldwin, writes:

Roots is a study of continuities, of consequence, of how a people perpetuate themselves, how each generation helps to doom, or helps to liberate, the coming one—the action of love, or the absence of love, in time. It suggests, with great power, how each of us, however unconsciously, can't but be the vehicle of history which has produced us. Well, we can perish in this vehicle, children, or we can move on up the road.

After 12 years of painstaking genealogical research, Haley collected the life story of seven generations of his family in the United States and several more generations in a village on the Gambia River in West Africa. He presents these authentic facts in a fictionalized story, a form he calls "faction," a delicate combination of fact and fiction which allows him to flesh out these ancestral characters, to include their thoughts and emotions. The resulting novel has touched the lives of millions of readers in a way that a scholarly report would never have achieved. As Haley knows, "When you start talking about family, about lineage and ancestry, you are talking about every person on earth."

Stimulus

Have students read the sketch of Haley's life. Tell the students this form of writing is called a biographical sketch. Ask students to note and then discuss particular words they find interesting. Identify collectively and list on the board the features of a well-written biographical sketch, for example:

Tells where and when the person was born.
Makes clear why the person is known.
Uses a quotation from the person about his or her work.

Tell students that they are going to write a biographical sketch about any minority (broadly interpreted) writer whose work they have read or want to read. (You may brainstorm a list of recommended authors on the board, such as Toni Morrison, Lillian Hellman, Laurence Yep, Virginia Hamilton, Isaac B. Singer, Richard Wright, Richard Rodrigues.) They may begin with an encyclopedia entry, but they are to use other resources, too. You may wish to specify that they locate at least two sources other than the encyclopedia.

Activity

Take students to the library where they can locate the encyclopedias, check out books by the author selected, and locate other sources of information. Point out *Current Biography* and *Contemporary Authors*. Students should take notes from resources they cannot check out. For homework, they are to begin the first draft of the biographical sketch to present in class on the following day.

Followup

On the next day review the features of a biographical sketch and make any additions recommended. Then have students work in pairs as they read the first drafts of the sketches and check their writing together against the list of features. The partners should work cooperatively to suggest revisions that will strengthen each paper. You may wish to use another day for working in groups of five or six students as a broader audience responds to second drafts prepared as homework.

Evaluation

The aim is to communicate to an audience with clear expository prose that is interesting to read. Students can evaluate the finished products as Grabs Me! (5 points), So-So (3 points), and Not So Hot (1 point). Students should be permitted to improve their writing in order to gain more points. Cooperative learning techniques used in groups can assist each student in achieving the top score. Note that this teaching strategy aims to develop self-esteem by facilitating success. All students are learning to collaborate to reach a goal.

The polished biographical sketches are published in a class book entitled Authors We Have Known. Students may refer to this book when they are selecting books to read. The collection can be added to by including book reviews (see page 194). Note that students are learning about the contributions of members of diverse cultures to what we call "American literature." They learn about these authors as people, and they are introduced to literature they may be motivated to read based on a classmate's recommendation.

Summary

In planning any lesson it is essential to include a warm-up period that prepares students to succeed at the task they are to undertake. Directions must be clear and resources must be readily available. Students need adequate time and formative evaluation to help them complete the task. Cooperative learning techniques enable students to learn from each other. With guidance, students can learn to work successfully with these peer-learning strategies. As students work in pairs and small groups, they have an opportunity to get acquainted and to help one another succeed. Such understandings and ways of behaving undergird multicultural teaching, but we recognize that they are esential components of all effective teaching.

Selected Teaching Strategies

Methods of instruction are as important as the content listed in the curriculum. As we consider just how multicultural concepts will be introduced to students, we need to think not only about what is to be taught, but also how students will be engaged in active learning that requires analysis, evaluation, and reflection. The same effective strategies can be used in delivering the multicultural curriculum, whether lessons are closely tied to the social studies program or taught within the context of the English language arts program with a strong emphasis on literature by and about members of various cultures.

In this section we present several recommended teaching strategies that will benefit students in any classroom no matter what the subject or level of instruction:

> Reading literature aloud to a class
> Brainstorming ideas about a problem or topic
> Teaching around a theme or developing a unit of study

Reading Literature Aloud to a Class

Reading aloud to students is an outstanding method of assuring that even less able readers have an opportunity to know good literature. Begin by presenting the book, short story, article, or poetry as writing done by another human being with whom students can enter into a transaction. The aim of the transaction is to construct meaning collaboratively. All we have are the words before us that an author wrote and our own ideas, so encourage students to ask questions about what the author might be saying and also about their responses to these ideas. (Avoid being the teacher who has all the "right" answers that you expect students to know.)

Use reading aloud as a method of engaging students at all levels and in all subject areas with the ideas presented in books. As you read essays written by biologist Lewis Thomas, a picture book by Byrd Baylor, or the poetry of Langston Hughes, students are learning:

1. *What book language sounds like.*   Remember that written language is a different dialect from that spoken by your students. More formal, usually written in the standard English dialect, book language is what they will gradually learn to write. It is not the familiar language that they speak with their family and friends. Before they can be expected to produce this written dialect, they need to hear it, to begin acquiring that dialect of English in much the same manner that they earlier acquired the ability to speak English.

2. *Forms that writing can take.*   As students listen to language or read it, they also gain knowledge of the forms (schemata) through which they can express their ideas. Through listening to novels or short stories, for example, students are developing a "sense of story." They are learning how an author engages characters in dialogue and how character traits are revealed through behavior. They are introduced to such concepts as theme, setting, and plot development. Sharing other forms — haiku, song lyrics, an editorial, a letter of complaint — helps students learn how to write those forms.

3. *Grammatical structures.*   As students listen to good writing, they hear a variety of sentence structures. They hear sentences composed of varied combinations of clauses, phrases, and strings of words. They are adding to and reinforcing their knowledge of English grammar as they listen to the opening sentences that William Saroyan wrote for *The Human Comedy*, speaking in the third person of the omniscient author:

   > The little boy named Ulysses Macauley one day stood over the new gopher hole in the backyard of his house on Santa Clara Avenue in Ithaca, California. The gopher of this hole pushed up fresh moist dirt and peeked out at the boy, who was certainly a stranger but perhaps not an enemy. Before this miracle had been fully enjoyed by the boy, one of the birds of Ithaca flew into the old walnut tree in the backyard and after settling itself on a branch broke into rapture, moving the boy's fascination from the earth to the tree.

4. *Feelings, ideas, content.*   A good book presents interesting content, vicarious experiences, and ideas that students can talk and write about. The characters share emotions with which they can identify. Students gain insight into the lives of others and begin to understand the concepts of diversity and universality applied to the people with whom they inhabit the earth.

5. *The sound of fluent reading — intonation.* As you read, students hear what fluent reading sounds like. They hear the accents and pauses, the intonation that a good reader uses automatically. They can talk about the meaning that intonation adds to language. They are learning to enjoy reading and talking about good books together.

6. *The joy of reading; what books have to offer.* Less able readers may be hearing a book that they could not read independently whereas able readers are often motivated to read a book that you have shared. All enjoy the experience of sharing an engaging story, laughing together, or even sharing the vicarious experience of death. The students are developing positive attitudes toward reading through your enthusiastic sharing.

Every piece of literature — every example of writing — that we share through reading aloud teaches students more about language and literature. Your reading aloud, however, offers additional assets as a teaching strategy of which you should be aware. One important advantage is that reading an article, a short story, or the chapter of a book means that *the whole class has a body of shared content that all can respond to immediately.* Your teaching is not hampered by students who have not read the assignment or completed their homework. Nor do you have to locate a class set of books. Reading aloud is *efficient and economical.*

Furthermore, reading aloud is *very enjoyable.* A sense of *camaraderie* develops through this shared experience — a *rapport* between you and your students that benefits the total learning program you present.

Choosing multicultural literature that supports instruction in the subject you are teaching adds the opportunity to deal with breaking down stereotypes and adding to student knowledge of people from diverse cultures. The following are representative of the multicultural fiction and nonfiction you might choose to read aloud and to talk about:

Grades K-3

The Snowy Day (Ezra Jack Keats)
Sam, Bangs, and Moonshine (Evaline Ness)
The Happy Owls (Celestino Piatti)
Crow Boy (Taro Yashima)

Grades 4-7

Dragonwings (Laurence Yep)
The House of Wings (Betsy Byars)
Ishi (Theodora Kroeber)
Where the Lilies Bloom (Vera and Bill Cleaver)

Grades 8–12

Black Boy (Richard Wright)
The Pigman (Paul Zindel)
I Know Why the Caged Bird Sings (Maya Angelou)
Living by the Word (Alice Walker)
Hunger by Memory (Richard Rodriguez)

Brainstorming Ideas about a Problem or Topic

Brainstorming is an accepted technique for collectively generating solutions to a problem. The traditional rules include:

1. Ideas are suggested and listed without evaluation, critical analysis, or even comment.
2. Usually even wild ideas can be expected in the spontaneity that evolves when you suspend judgment. Practical considerations are not important at this point. The process should stimulate creativity.
3. At this stage, the quantity of ideas counts, not quality. All ideas should be expressed, not screened out by any individual. Suggesting a quantity of ideas will increase the likelihood of generating outstanding ones.
4. Encourage piggybacking, building on the ideas of other group members, whenever appropriate, pooling creativity. Students should be free to build onto ideas or to make interesting combinations of various suggestions.
5. Focus on a single problem or issue. Don't skip around or try to brainstorm a complex, multiple problem.
6. Establish a congenial, relaxed, cooperative climate.
7. Make sure that all members, no matter how shy and reluctant to contribute, get their ideas heard.
8. Record *all* ideas.

Followup Activities:

1. Review the list of ideas, selecting the top 5, 10 (any appropriate number) to discuss further in terms of practicality. Have small groups discuss each one in detail. Have each group present the pros and cons of that idea for consideration.
2. Vote on the top 2 or 3 ideas to try. Place them in order of priority according to your purpose or need.
3. Begin implementing the ideas in order.

Multicultural topics lend themselves to such brainstorming techniques. Invite students to suggest alternative solutions or ideas about such questions as:

- How can we help students who are having trouble getting along in school ("at risk")?
- Why should we be concerned about what is happening in Israel or Afghanistan?

- How have Afro-Americans contributed to the development of the United States?
- What would be appropriate behavior if someone called you an insulting name? What might you do if you witnessed such behavior?

Brainstorming helps students share ideas and structure their thoughts. Such exercises help groups reach consensus. Variations on this approach to brainstorming are:

Clustering (illustrated in the next section)
Mapping (see page 129)
Venn diagram (see page 232)

Such brainstorming techniques facilitate expressing thinking through speaking or writing. All can be used with groups or can be done individually before beginning to write.

Teaching around a Theme or Unit

Focusing units of study on broad themes provides perhaps the best way of integrating factual knowledge with the understanding that we prize. You might develop such a study by beginning with:

A novel *(Sounder; The Sign of the Beaver)*
A current event (Apartheid, the PLO, discrimination suit)
A broad topic (Love, Conflict, Aging)
An ethnic group (The Acadians, Hawaiians)
A picture book *(Katie-Bo: An Adoption Story)*
A biography *(Nelson Mandela; Cesar Chavez)*

We can begin a unit of study by clustering ideas around the topic to be studied. The example presented here is based on reading a novel, *The Return of the Indian* by Lynne Reid Banks (Doubleday, 1986). As the teacher reads this novel (sequel to the popular *Indian in the Cupboard*), students begin constructing a web of ideas about Indians and Indian life they derive from the book. Students add to the large network of ideas daily as they read together. When the book is completed, the collection of ideas looks like that shown on the following page.

Notice how the ideas develop in clusters of related ideas or categories. In this case reading the novel and clustering the ideas presented by the author leads to a broader study of American Indians. Reading this novel is motivating to students who become involved with the characters and the action. They can depict scenes on a large floor map as they follow the events in the story. To provide accuracy, small groups can research the history and geography related to this novel. Through this study, students should gain insight into the plight of the Indians and the historical significance of the battles between the Redcoats and the French.

Students will be stimulated to read other fiction and nonfiction about native Americans and the part they played in the early settlement of this country. For example, almost all will want to read the book that preceded this one, *Indian in the*

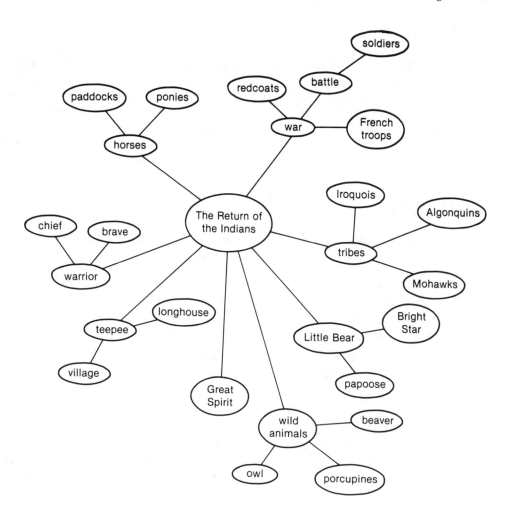

Cupboard. Refer to the extensive bibliography that begins on page 343 for additional literature to develop this unit. Other sample units of study begin on pages 248 and 316.

Summary

Methods of instruction are crucial to the success of any learning experiences. How we engage students in learning influences the involvement and interest. Reading literature aloud is an excellent way of using good books to support instruction. Brainstorming engages students in collaborative thinking. Integrating learning activities around a theme helps students make connections. These three strategies are examples of useful instructional techniques that can be used with any content matter and at all grade levels.

REFLECTIONS

Teaching for multicultural understanding requires a well-planned curriculum based on expected outcomes. The teacher's role in delivering this curriculum is to guide student inquiries and to serve as facilitator and resource person. The student learner also plays an active part in initiating avenues of inquiry in conjunction with a group of fellow researchers. The best of methodologies and resources must be selected as we develop an integrated humanistic study that furthers multicultural understanding.

APPLICATIONS

Try the following activities as you prepare to work with multicultural education at the primary, middle school, or high school level.

1. Begin a resource file in which to place the materials you collect related to multicultural studies. This file will complement your file of cards recording books you have read. Use a large cardboard carton that will hold standard file folders. Make folders for such topics as:

   Mexico and Mexican Americans
   China and Chinese Americans
   Our Community
   Africa

   Continue to add folders as you learn more about this broad subject. Watch for informative articles, news items, and pictures related to topics that you will talk about in your classroom. Begin sending for free travel posters and other materials that will increase your multicultural knowledge base as you grow professionally. Include items that will help students understand the concepts you want to teach.

2. Select a topic, book, or group that you would like to study. Plan a unit of study following the procedures described at the end of this chapter. As this project grows, you may need a whole box to hold this unit and the realia (musical instruments, toys, statues) you collect.

3. Plan a lesson that introduces another form of writing based on selections from multicultural literature. Follow the model presented in this chapter as you carefully design the prewriting activities to build in success. Involve students in the followup editing activities as well as in the final evaluation.

Endnotes

1. Eugene E. Eubanks, President, American Association of Colleges of Teacher Education.

2. Ernest Boyer. "On the High School Curriculum: A Conversation with Ernest Boyer." *Educational Leadership, 46,* 1 (September 1988): 4–9.

3. Thomas Sobol. Commissioner of Education, New York State Department of Education, undated.

4. Barbara Z. Presseisen. *Teaching Thinking and At-Risk Students: Understanding the Problem.* Research for Better Schools. 444 N. Third St., Philadelphia PA 19123.

5. James R. Squire, ed. *The Dynamics of Language Learning: Research in Reading and English.* National Council of Teachers of English, 1987.

6. E. D. Hirsch, Jr. *Cultural Literacy: What Every American Needs to Know.* Houghton Mifflin, 1987.

7. Iris M. Tiedt et al. *Teaching Thinking in K–12 Classrooms.* Allyn and Bacon, 1989.

8. Virginia Shipman et al. *Young Children and Their First School Experiences.* Educational Testing Service, 1976.

9. Robert Rosenthal and Lenore Jacobson. *Pygmalion in the Classroom.* Holt, 1968.

10. Shipman et al. *Young Children.*

11. Ibid.

12. Iris M. Tiedt et al. *Reading/Thinking/Writing: A Holistic Language and Literacy Program.* Allyn and Bacon, 1989, pp. 72–74.

Resources

Richard Abrahamson, and Betty Carter, eds. *Books for You: A Booklist for Senior High Students.* Committee on the Senior High School Booklist. NCTE, 1988.

Arthur Combs. *A Personal Approach to Teaching: Beliefs that Make a Difference.* Allyn and Bacon, 1982.

Arthur Combs and Donald Avila. *Helping Relationships: Basic Concepts for the Helping Professions,* 3rd ed. Allyn and Bacon, 1985.

E. D. Hirsch, Jr. *Cultural Literacy: What Every American Needs to Know.* Houghton, 1987.

Mary H. Sasse. "Literature in a Multiethnic Culture." In *Literature in the Classroom: Readers, Texts, and Contexts.* National Council of Teachers of English, 1988, pp. 167–178.

Donald A. Schon. *Educating the Reflective Practitioner.* Jossey-Bass, 1987.

John Sikula, ed. *Action in Teacher Education.* The Association of Teacher Education, 1988.

Iris M. Tiedt. *Writing: From Topic to Evaluation.* Allyn and Bacon, 1989.

Iris M. Tiedt et al. *Reading/Thinking/Writing: A Holistic Language and Literacy Program.* Allyn and Bacon, 1989.

Iris M. Tiedt et al. *Teaching Thinking in K–12 Classrooms.* Allyn and Bacon, 1989.

Eileen Tway and Mary Lou White. "Literature and International Understanding." In *Literature in the Classroom: Readers, Texts, and Contexts.* National Council of Teachers of English, 1988, pp. 179–194.

Behavior is a mirror, in which everyone shows his image.

- Johann von Goethe

3

Promoting Self-Esteem

Love and self-worth are so intertwined that they may properly be related through the use of the term identity. *Thus we may say that the single basic need that people have is the requirement for an identity; the belief that we are someone in distinction to others, and that the someone is important and worthwhile. Then* love *and* self-worth *may be considered the two pathways that mankind has discovered that lead to a successful identity.*[1]

William Glasser

Preview

After reading this chapter, you should be able to show students:

- How they are important as individuals.
- That each student has a culture.
- Ways that culture influences us.
- That it is okay to be different.

As young language learners, children are absorbed in the difficult task of figuring out the world around them. They put tremendous amounts of energy into picking up new information and applying what they've learned in varied situations. But when they approach school age, something changes.

Most children arrive at school with positive feelings about themselves and their ability to achieve. After a few years of schooling, however, many begin to say "I'm not good at this" or "I can't learn that." Why does this happen and what can we do about it? Where is the spirit, enthusiasm, and curiosity with which the young child first approached the task of language learning?

In teaching, we need to consider how the student perceives the world of the classroom. We can help students begin to reflect on themselves, their characteristics, and how they are like and unlike others. Then, as they see the differences among individuals, we can show them how such differences are part of establishing an identity, rather than a source of shame. When we make the classroom a safe place for students to find out who they are and who they can be, we are creating the foundation for their future self-respect as well as respect for others. In addition, as students begin to share basic features of their identity, they are building an understanding of Culture: what it is, where it comes from, and how it varies. Ultimately, we want students to be able to take pride in the sources and symbols of their identity, as individuals and as members of a group, and to see diversity as an asset in the world in which they live.

BEGIN WITH THE STUDENT

All students possess a culture that plays a large part in how they view the world and how they operate in the school setting. This culture includes rules of behavior that may be explicitly taught in the home or by family members, but it also includes values and attitudes that are implicit in the environment—such as approaches to learning new skills or patterns of motivation. These attitudes are absorbed by children without conscious effort as they grow up in a particular setting.

Even you, the teacher, approach teaching from the perspective of a particular culture, which affects your expectations for student success or failure and your picture of appropriate teacher and student roles. An education that is multicultural, however, aims to provide many opportunities for students to express themselves in varied ways. And success in school is redefined, thus, so that *all* students have a chance to receive positive attention and be successful.

Special Recognition

In a large class, inevitably some students receive more attention (positive or negative) than others. Keep a copy of your class list handy and glance at it often, especially during transitions between activities. Check to see that you have had some contact with each student in the class—a quick compliment or even a friendly, personal smile. Through recognizing each student as an individual, you provide an opening for further discussion. Also, you may see that someone needs help or reassurance.

Listen to the students. Is someone more quiet than usual? Or is someone talking more than normal? Often these are signals that something is troubling the student. You can take the student aside later for a private chat or offer a special reward or activity that can serve as a pat on the back.

Tell students what you like about their work. Too often, most of the feedback students receive on their efforts is negative. We tend to see the errors students make rather than their successes. Remember to acknowledge what students have accomplished. Be sincere and be specific.

Special Days

Students' birthdays offer an opportunity to recognize students as individuals. On your class calendar, list the birthdays that will occur that month. Let the birthday student chose a special treat for that day, such as:

- Wear a special hat
- Choose a game for everyone to play
- Teach the class a poem
- Distribute papers or books for the teacher
- Use her or his favorite color on the bulletin board

Another way of recognizing a student is to have everyone in the class brainstorm what they like about that person. These comments can be written down and collected in a book for the student to take home. The students can also make up a song about that person and sing it, perhaps to the tune of "Happy Birthday."

Ask students how birthdays are celebrated in their families. Do they have any special customs or ceremonies? Suggest that there are many different ways to honor someone on their special day.

Although most students enjoy being the center of attention for a day, many may also be shy or embarrassed by the publicity. Monitor your birthday activities to make sure that the student feels like an important part of the class and not the brunt of a joke.

The "Me" Collage

Have students clip magazines and prepare a collage that reveals things about their lives. Talk about the things they might include, for example:

- Birthplace—picture, part of a map
- Baby pictures
- Things they like—food, sports
- Their family—people pets
- Where they have lived or traveled

Words as well as pictures can be included to help tell others in the classroom more about themselves. Clippings are pasted on a large piece of colored construction paper or cardboard. A frame can be attached after the collage is completed.

Have students write a brief biographical description that can be attached to the collage or read aloud to the class. These collages make interesting displays for Open House when parents visit the school. Record each student's presentation of the biographical sketch that accompanies his or her collage. Play the tape continuously as parents visit the classroom. Post an order of the presentations on the board so people can tell when their child will be heard.

A Story to Discuss

Read the following story about French poet Jean Cocteau to the students. Follow up with a discussion about why diversity is better than unformity.

There's Nobody Like You!

The French poet Jean Cocteau found out early in life why diversity is better than uniformity.

As a young man, M. Cocteau was designing a stage set which required a tree as background. He spent night after night in the theater basement cutting out individual leaves for his creation.

Then a wealthy friend, whose father owned a factory, approached him with another idea.

"Give me the design of that leaf," he said, "and in three days you will have thousands of them here."

After his friend's return, they pasted the multitude of identical leaves onto the branches.

The result, M. Cocteau recalled, was "the most boring package of flat, uninteresting forms one can see."

At last he understood why each leaf of a tree and each man in the world are different from any other.

— *Christopher News Notes,* no. 187, May 1971

It's Okay to Be Afraid

Introduce the subject of being afraid by reading a book such as *There's a Nightmare in My Closet* by Mercer Mayer (Dial). Then ask the students to write a sentence or two about something of which they are really afraid. You participate, too. With no names attached, each paper is folded up tight and put in a box. You might say:

Now that you have your fear written on paper, I want you to fold it up tight and put it in this box. (Collect everyone's fears.) Here we have everybody's fears collected in a box. Sometimes the things we're afraid of are only fearsome because we can't talk about them. We keep them hidden inside us. Today we're going to bring some of these fears out in the sunshine where we can look at them. I'm going to ask somebody to pick up one of these fears and read it out loud. If the one that's drawn is yours, you don't have to tell anyone because your name isn't on the paper.

Discuss the fear that is drawn from the box: "How many of you have been afraid of the dark when you go to bed? What did you do about it?" Repeat this activity as long as the group is interested. Then set the box aside for further discussion the next day.

Open-Ended Writing

Provide open-ended sentences for students to complete either orally or in writing. The following ideas help children probe their feelings and express them with little fear of sharing:

- I feel really happy when . . .
- When I get big, I am going to . . .
- Once I got really scared because . . .
- When I'm all alone, I pretend . . .
- I get really mad when . . .

Taking Care of Yourself

Ask children, "Can you usually take care of yourself?" For preschool and primary grade children, ask the question orally to each individually. For students in third grade or older, more accurate results will be obtained through individual questioning. You might achieve a different objective by preparing this question on an assessment sheet to move the child beyond consideration of the question asked.

Can you usually take care of yourself? Yes _____
No _____
Tell about a time when you were able to take care of yourself.
_____
_____
_____

After students have written their responses, encourage them to share the responses with others. This type of sharing is supportive; in this case it should reinforce feelings of strength.

In the Shipman study[2] fewer than one-third of the questioned third graders answered "Yes" (25.5 percent low income; 29.5 percent more affluent). Clearly we need to teach all students to feel secure in their ability to cope.

Feeling Inadequate

To help children talk about their feelings of inadequacy, follow up the previous discussion with this direction: "Tell about a time when you were not able to take care of yourself. How did you feel? What happened?" Encourage students to share. Tell them of a time you felt inadequate. Talk about what they could do now, if something similar happened. Share solutions.

Therapeutic Writing

An excellent way to promote writing that supports student self-esteem is to encourage free writing in a journal. Journals can be kept in spiral-bound notebooks or they can be made of sheets of composition paper stapled together. Schedule a specific time for daily writing in student journals, and continue this daily writing for at least three weeks. The journals should be kept in the classroom so that each child has his or her journal on hand at the scheduled time. We recommend that you, too, write in a journal to demonstrate the value of this activity and to have entries to share periodically. Journal writing should never be graded or corrected. At times, students may select an entry to share, but the privacy of this personal writing must be assured.

The journal provides a means of getting to know your students. This personal writing proves therapeutic for students who may never have anyone they can tell about their feelings, impressions, or even such overwhelming experiences as child abuse.

At all times, students should feel free to write about something important to them. However, you may want to suggest a topic each day for those who need an idea. Use some of the following topics for journal writing.

- Friends are important
- A time when I felt sad
- Some of my favorite things are . . .

Before you embark on this activity, recognize that students may write about painful or intimate topics. Decide in advance how you might handle some unpleasant or upsetting discussions. When you read student journals, always allow students the option of keeping their writing private. If you share writing with the class or in small groups, don't force students who are reluctant to contribute.

My Lifeline

Have students draw a series of mountain peaks across a sheet of paper. Tell them that this line represents their life. What are the big peaks in their life? What are the smaller peaks? Have them identify the peaks in their lifetime as they write on each mountain.

This idea can be extended by describing their usual daily existence across the base of the mountains. A few fantasies can be added on clouds: "Someday I'd like to . . . ."

Curriculum Materials

A number of commercial materials have been produced specifically to meet the needs of children in developing self-esteem. You might want to examine the following:

> *About Me: A Curriculum for a Developing Self.* Harold Wells and John T. Canfield. Encyclopedia Britannica, 425 N. Michigan Ave., Chicago, IL 60611. For grades four to six. Titles include: *I Know Who I Am, I Know My Strengths, I Can Set and Achieve Goals, I Try to Be Myself, I Am in Charge of Becoming Myself.*

> *I Have Feelings.* Terry Berger. Behavioral Publications, 2852 Broadway, New York, NY 10025. Ages four to nine. Covers seventeen different feelings, both good and bad, such as anger, sorrow, joy, and grief.

WHAT IS AN IDENTITY?

All classrooms are heterogeneous classrooms; skin color, for example, is not the only measure of student diversity. All students experience a kind of "culture-shock" when they first enter school. At home, they have been someone's son or daughter, sister or brother, friend or relative. They have an identity; they know "who" they are. At home and in the community they are members of a particular group. They know what is expected of them—when to talk and when to be silent, how to be respectful, and how to get along with their peers.

But suddenly at school, the rules change. The student is only a name on a tag, someone sitting at a particular desk, or a name on a school file. The teacher asks questions when he or she already knows the answer to them. Students are supposed to raise their hand when they want to speak. Even when they don't know the answer, they are expected to respond with something. And they're not allowed to help each other figure out the answers. The available identities seem to be Good Student or Bad Student; Good Reader or Bad Reader; Fast or Slow.

For some students, the contrast between the home culture and the school expectations is never resolved. They find few routes to school success and may drop out of school in response to increasing experiences of failure. In many classrooms only students who do well on multiple-choice standardized tests are labeled "good students"; the others are "bad students" by default. This "bad student" label often hides students whose accomplishments and abilities simply are not recognized by the schools.

When teachers learn to look more closely at the students they see everyday, they can come to know these students as individuals who are also part of a culture.

By allowing students to bring parts of their culture into the school, they can help students find their way both as members of a culture and as students. The following activities lead to this goal.

The Color of Me

Cut a number of strips of paper in a variety of colors, for instance, red, yellow, green, blue, purple, orange, brown, gray, black, and white. For a class of thirty, you may need twenty pieces of each color.

Ask the children to close their eyes. Then say, "Imagine that you are looking at a painting of yourself. What color would you be? If you could choose one color, what color would you choose to be you?" Have children come to the table on which the colored strips of paper are spread out to choose the color with which they identify. Divide into small groups to talk about the colors selected and what they mean to each person.

Writing Personal Essays

Have each child mount the strip of paper chosen in the preceding activity on a sheet of composition paper. The students can explain why they see themselves as this color by writing a short personal essay beginning with these words: "I think I am _____ because . . . ."

This is a very revealing step toward self-awareness and it will provide insight into the child's self-perception. This is not the type of writing to display on the wall, but children may voluntarily share their writing in small groups. Be careful not to make evaluative comments, saying only perhaps, "Thank you for sharing, Paulie." Such open disclosures are healthy for all students and should be encouraged, but never forced.

I Am a Hamburger

Children can become more aware of themselves by selecting other things with which they identify. In addition to color, have children answer these kinds of questions: What food are you? What kind of car are you? What kind of building are you?

After each person has answered the questions on paper, have the children talk about the questions in small groups where each person can participate directly. Although the choices are revealing in many ways, usually people are not threatened by this neutral approach. Sometimes this occasions laughter as children share the humor of someone's choice. Like most people, children enjoy talking about themselves. They may contribute such metaphoric ideas as these:

- Jose: I think I'm a peanut because you have to crack me open to find out what's good inside.
- Kelly: I'm a big office building because I like to be in charge and to be where the action is.
- Sara: I'm a little red sports car, snappy with a lot of get up and go!

What I Like about My Life

Encourage children to talk about what they like about their lives and what they do not like. Ask the following questions:

- Can you think of somebody who has a worse life than you?
- Name one thing you think is really great about your life.
- If you could change one thing in your life, what would you change?

Follow this discussion by writing a poem.

WRITE A POEM

Write about something important to you—love, music, sister, time, food, flying, whatever.
Follow this pattern:

> Line 1: 1 word—the subject
> Line 2: 2 words—describe the subject
> Line 3: 3 words—express a feeling
> Line 4: 4 words—describe an action
> Line 5: 1 word—refer to the subject

Give Yourself a Present

If you could give yourself a present, what would you choose? This question should start a lively discussion. After students have talked about their ideas, ask them to write about the present they would choose. Ask them to describe the present and tell why they selected that particular thing.

Which Would You Rather Be?

Provide a list of characteristics from which students select those they would most like to have. Each student gets a copy to mark individually. Before they mark their papers, discuss the meaning of each item. (See the form below).

WHAT KIND OF PERSON WOULD YOU LIKE TO BE?

Mark 1 before the word that is most important to you. Mark 2 before the next most important, and so on. The number 14 will mark the thing that is least important to you. I would like to be:

_____	Polite	_____	Loving
_____	Dependable	_____	Creative
_____	Hard-working	_____	Brave
_____	Cheerful	_____	Capable
_____	Neat	_____	Respectful
_____	Helpful to others	_____	Truthful
_____	Smart	_____	Open-minded

After papers are marked (with no names attached), have students tally the results on the board. This can be done with students keeping their own papers. Simply tally the number of children who marked 1, 2, or 3 for each item. Then tally the number who marked 12, 13, or 14 for each item. This gives you an indication of the high-valued and low-valued items as well as those that were not considered important. Discuss the results for a very provocative interchange.

Friendship Is . . .

Read poems to students from the collection *I Like You, If You Like Me: Poems of Friendship* (edited by Myra Cohn Livingston, McElderry Book, 1987). Students can talk about friendship as a class. Then have each student write a story, create a poem, or draw a picture. Their work can be collected into a book entitled "Friendship Is . . . ." Students will enjoy sharing their ideas with others.

Values and Proverbs

Initiate a discussion on differences in values by writing on the chalkboard a proverb such as: *Finders keepers; losers weepers.* Ask students what this means to them. In what situation might they use this proverb? What kind of behavior does it justify? Do they agree with the ideas in this proverb?

Have students generate a list of related proverbs, in English or other languages. Students from different backgrounds can describe their culture's attitude toward possessions.

Favorite Foods

Start a discussion about foods and different customs by asking students what they eat for breakfast. Write some of the different responses on the board. Why does this variety exist? Some students may have invented unique breakfast menus, whereas others eat foods that are representative of a particular culture. What do they consider a "typical" American breakfast? Is that what they eat? Would they like to eat a "different" kind of breakfast? Why or why not?

Use this discussion to talk about eating habits as an example of a custom, based on a culture. Students can begin to see themselves as inheritors of a cultural tradition, and other students as representatives of different cultural traditions. You can also point out examples of cross-cultural borrowing, as students suggest foods they like that have come from other cultures.

Students will be curious to find out what the other students in the class eat everyday and whether there are any differences or similarities between them. Have students keep a log of what and when they eat in one day, including snacks, then share this list with the class. What differences do they notice? What similarities? Does everybody eat exactly the same foods at the same time? Why not? Discuss influences on variation such as individual taste, family customs, cultural background, and examples set by other people.

You can develop a unit on nutrition based on this information. In presenting the food groups and nutritional needs, focus on the ways different groups meet the same dietary requirements.

As Others See Us

Talk about "special" days with students. What are some holidays or other significant days that they and their families celebrate? What are their favorite special days? Why?

What if a new person came into the class or arrived in this country and didn't know about these holidays, how would the students explain these days? Have each student choose a special day to write about. They must describe it to someone who doesn't know anything about the day or American customs.

Read some of the descriptions to the class and discuss them. Did the writers include all the necessary information? Did they have difficulty describing something they know so well?

You can explore similar topics with students. What else should new people know? How can students help others adjust to a new environment? Perhaps students can prepare a list or description of classroom rules or procedures.

For Fun

Another demonstration of ways that culture affects us is in our choice of what we do for fun. Lead students in a discussion of what they do outside of school. Do some students play different games or participate in different activities? If students mention activities that you or others don't know, encourage them to explain these to the class. You might have some students teach the class new games, for example, jump rope songs.

What games do students play at recess? Does everyone know the same games? Some students may be less familiar with the recess routine. Have students explain the rules for the common recess games so that all can participate in these activities if they wish. Help students see that although some students may not know the games that are valued at recess or after school, everyone has something to contribute.

BUILD PRIDE IN GROUP MEMBERSHIP

When students are allowed to bring elements of their culture into the classroom, they develop self-esteem as they build pride in their identity as a member of a particular group. When they see their individual differences are valued in the classroom, they are encouraged to take a risky step of trying new ideas and skills and to see mistakes as a step on the road to learning. And when they can build on their strengths as competent members of a culture, they are able to achieve greater success in school. Our task as teachers is to provide varied opportunities for success so that students can make these connections.

We All Belong to Many Groups

Ask students to list on a sheet of paper all the groups they belong to. After they have had time to write a number of ideas, ask each person to tell one group they belong to; encourage them to share different ideas as much as possible. As new ideas are suggested, have students add to their individual lists. Then ask children to draw pictures of themselves and to list all the groups they belong to. Display these pictures on the wall. Then they can be bound in a class book: Room 15, the Class of 1996.

Sue Wong is . . .
  a girl
  a daughter
  a member of the Wong family
  a Californian
  a San Franciscan
  a member of this class
  a twelve-year-old
  a Chinese-American
  a U.S. citizen

Family Comes First

Today many people are searching for their roots. They interview older members of the family, pore over old photographs, and spend hours reading records in courthouse and libraries. Eventually, they compile enough information to begin drawing a family tree showing the interrelationships of large numbers of people. Children will enjoy studying their personal origins with the interest and help of their families.

Begin with simple discussions of the children's names and how they feel about them. Later, develop an interview sheet on which students can record information they gain by talking with their parents and grandparents. Before beginning this unit of study, write a letter of explanation to parents, stressing the basic skills that students are learning as they gather and record information. Each student may prepare a bound book about his or her family to share as a holiday gift.

My Name

Talk about names with the children. Discuss how they feel about their first names, how their names were chosen, and what names mean.

Have the children make designs based on their first names. Color the name designs for display on the bulletin board. This design makes a good cover for a personal collection of writing.

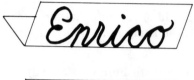

Choosing Names

Ask children how they got their first names. Are they named after someone, perhaps an aunt or grandfather? Perhaps someone has a family name, like Jamison, or an invented name composed of both parent's names, such as Rayella. You might discuss how they feel about their names. Ask them to write about one of these topics:

- I like my first name because _____.
- I wish I could change my first name because _____.
- If I could choose a name for myself, it would be _____ because_____.
- If I had a baby, I would name it _____ because _____.

Naming Customs

Talk about different customs of naming children. Children will be interested in knowing about the use of the names of saints by Catholic families or the Jewish practice of naming children after dead relatives. Ask the children to share information from their personal experience. You might read the first few pages of *Roots* (Doubleday, 1976) in which Alex Haley describes the naming of Kunta Kinte.

What People Call You

Observe that some families use pet names or nicknames. Others scorn the use of nicknames. In the South, children are commonly called by both the first and middle names, for example, James Leroy or Nancy Kathryn. Ask students: "What does your mother call you? How about your friends?" Discuss what the children like to be called. Ask them what they would like you to call them in school. Practice pronouncing these names as the children do until you can say them easily.

One Name in Many Languages

Students will be interested, too, in discovering that the same name is used in many languages. One illustration is the name John, which can be found in a variety of languages:

John (English)	Jan (Northern Europe, Holland)	Johan (Norwegian)
Ian (Scotch)	Juan (Spanish)	Johannes (German)
Ivan (Russian)	Shane (Irish)	Sean (Irish)
Iban (Basque)	Evan (Welsh)	Yohanna (Arabic)
Jannis (Greek)	Giovanni (Italian)	
Jean (French)	Hans (German)	

See if the students can discover the equivalent in other languages of such names as Peter, James, David, William, Mary, Rose, and Helen.

Surnames

Discuss surnames. What are they? Where do they come from? Have children state their surnames as you write them on the board. Observe the variety of names in the classroom. Some are long and some are short. Some have only one syllable (Wong) and others contain several syllables (Asakura, Rodríguez, Anderson).

Use surnames in classroom learning experiences. Have students line up alphabetically for lunch. Younger students can line up according to the first letter only, while older students can check the second and third letters as needed for more precise order.

Discuss the characteristics of surnames. "Mc" and "Mac" names originated in Ireland and Scotland, for example. Let students make generalizations about the names represented in their classroom, such as:

- We have many Spanish names:
  Castañeda
  Chávez
  Feliciano
  Vásquez
- Chinese names are short:
  Wang
  Lee
  Ching
- Many Vietnamese people have the same last name, but aren't related:
  Nguyen
  Ng
  Huynh

Family Names in Different Cultures

Different cultures have different rules for last names or family names. In English-speaking countries, most children take the last name of the father. Some countries use both the mother's and father's names (this custom is growing in the United States). Other countries give different forms of the father's first and last names to male and female children.

In Spanish, for example, a person's surname consists of the father's family name followed by the mother's family name.

Teresa	Pérez	Gutiérrez
	(father)	(mother)
Carlos	Chávez	Martínez
	(father)	(mother)

Sometimes the word *y* (and) is inserted between the surnames of the father and mother, for example: Juan López y Benavente. Juan would be called Señor López, however, and his name would be under L in the telephone directory. Likewise, Teresa and Carlos would be listed as:

Pérez Gutiérrez, Teresa
Chavez Martínez, Carlos

Origins of Names

Family names are interesting to children when they discover the meanings that lie behind them. They can easily see that those names that have "son" or "sen" at the end carry the meaning "son of"; for example, Anderson, Christianson, Petersen, and Williamson. One of the most common names is Johnson, son of John. Endings that mean *son of* in other languages include *ez* (Spanish), *tse* (Chinese), *wicz* (Polish), and *ov* (Russian and other Slavic languages).

Rodriguez (or Rodrigues) = son of Rodrigo (Roger)
Ivanov = son of Ivan (John)

Many last names are associated with a person's line of work; for instance, Carpenter, Farmer, Baker, Miller, and Smith (blacksmith). Characteristics of a person often led to the use of other names, such as Young, Black, Long, White, and Little.

For names of foreign origin, use a dictionary for that language. Set out on a discovery trip that all can participate in as they help each other find the origins of their family names.

A Study of Names

If students become especially interested in names, you might want to begin a more extensive study of American names. Look for the following books that provide information about the meanings of common names and their origins:

Eloise Lambert and Mario Pei. *Our Names: Where They Came From and What They Mean*. Lothrop, 1960.

C. M. Mathews. *How Surnames Began*. Lutterworth Press, 1967.

Young students will appreciate the following book:

Mary Lee and Richard Lee, *Last Names First — and Some First Names Too.* Westminster Press, 1985.

Family Roots

Students can ask their families about family history and write the information on a chart.

My Family			
	Name	Birthplace	Date
Mother			
Father			
Brothers			
Sisters			
	Mother's Family Name	Birthplace	Date
Mother			
Father			
Brothers			
Sisters			
	Father's Family Name	Birthplace	Date
Mother			
Father			
Brothers			
Sisters			

A Family Tree

Children can construct a family tree using the information they collected from the previous activity. They should interview their parents and grandparents to discover as much as possible about the family.

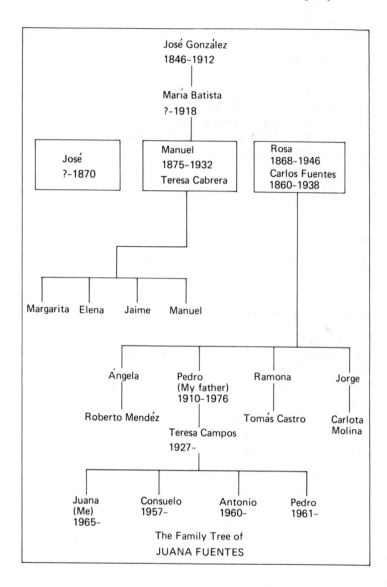

José González
1846–1912

María Batista
?–1918

| José
?–1870 | Manuel
1875–1932
Teresa Cabrera | Rosa
1868–1946
Carlos Fuentes
1860–1938 |

Margarita Elena Jaime Manuel

Ángela Pedro
(My father)
1910–1976 Ramona Jorge

Roberto Mendéz Tomás Castro Carlota
Molina

Teresa Campos
1927–

Juana
(Me)
1965– Consuelo
1957– Antonio
1960– Pedro
1961–

The Family Tree of
JUANA FUENTES

When introducing this kind of activity, be aware that some parents might be offended by what they perceive as an invasion of privacy. Therefore, it is important to discuss the project in the classroom first so children have a clear sense of your intent, namely, developing *pride in the family,* the importance of remembering our ancestors, our *roots.* You might, for example, tell the group something of your own origins. Parents who saw the televised version of *Roots* will be especially interested in this project.

What Is Genealogy?

Introduce the big word *genealogy* (notice the spelling), which means the study of lineage, family history. Many people trace their family history as a matter of pride. Today there are societies focusing on such study. Discuss lineal descent, which is important in royal families such as in England. Students might find out the order of succession following Queen Elizabeth II to the British throne.

An interesting book for upper elementary and junior high students is *Who Do You Think You Are? Digging for Your Family Roots* by Suzanne Hilton (Westminster Press, 1976).

Task Cards for Primary Children

Suggestions throughout this book can be adapted for various levels. Page 63 shows two sample ideas adapted specifically for primary grades.

Other Sources of Cultural Identity: Food

One area where ethnic diversity has been much appreciated is food. Food habits and the preparation of traditional dishes are central to the identity of a culture and they linger long after other cultural characteristics are lost. Food is also a subject that breaks down barriers between members of different cultures because sharing food is such a positive experience.

Teachers can present food from different cultures as a year-long theme, in a special unit, or as a follow-up activity to another unit (such as a study of *haiku* poetry). The concepts that can be developed from studying food in other cultures are:

- People of all groups have a contribution to make.
- People are more alike than they are different.
- Differences in customs and attitudes can be an asset to society.
- Prejudice and stereotyping is usually based on lack of information.
- Understanding others will enrich our own lives.

Snacks—A Universal Food

Everybody loves snacks. Have students conduct a survey to find out which snacks are most popular. Brainstorm as a class to determine what questions you will ask (What do you eat? How many? Where? Favorite?) and who you will ask (other classes, friends, family). Ask students to write their predictions for the results of the survey. Develop a form to record results and set a deadline for reporting back. When you have assembled a quantity of data, discuss how to organize it in an easy-to-understand way. Finally, when you have analyzed the data and compared your predictions against the conclusions, write a report for the school newspaper or make copies for the school.

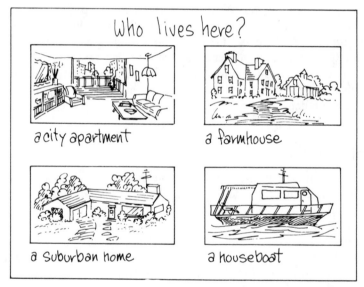

Class Recipe Book

Collect recipes to be duplicated and made into a collection for each student to take home. Students can bring in recipes for their favorite foods or a special dish from their family or culture. Each student can explain his or her recipe and talk about the preparation and ingredients. If possible, invite a parent or a member of the family to come to the class and show everyone how to make one of these dishes. (You might even ask students to bring in samples of their favorite foods.)

Class work with recipes leads naturally to a study of measurement (weight, mass) and the mathematics of conversion. Students can practice measuring with different instruments and multiplying quantities for larger groups. Students may also want to investigate the scientific questions of cooking; for example, how food changes from raw to cooked.

International Foods

When we borrow a food from another country we often borrow the name for it, too. See how many foods the students can name that come from different countries. What countries are these from?

sauerkraut	spaghetti	enchiladas	macaroni
tortillas	quiche	wontons	croissant

The Origin of "American" Foods

Students can investigate the origin of such typically American foods as pizza, hot dogs, and hamburgers. Where do noodles come from? (The Italians got them from China.) What common foods come from the New World (and hence were unknown in Europe before then)? (Tomato, potato, chocolate.) Do students know that the tomato used to be considered poisonous when raw?

Another area for students to research is the variety of regional names for food items. One popular sandwich is called a hoagy, grinder, submarine, poor boy, or Dagwood, depending on where you live. Where does the word *sandwich* come from?

Food Prejudices

People in most cultures have strong ideas about which foods are considered acceptable for eating and which are not. For example, many people in the United States turn up their noses at foods that are delicacies in other countries, such as snails and frog's legs. Likewise, people in other countries think the American custom of eating corn on the cob is disgusting because to them, that food is fit only for pigs. Sometimes, just altering the name can change people's williness to try new foods. People who would never eat squid may try *calamari* (Italian for squid).

Children are notoriously reluctant to try new foods. Have students investigate their own food prejudices. Select several unusual foods (you can find imported canned foods at most supermarkets). Tell the students the name of each food or show them the labels. Have them write a short description/reaction to the idea of eating the food. Then have them taste each food, blindfolded, and write down their impressions without identifying the food.

Afterwards, discuss the difference in reactions. Would they have ordered any of the foods in a restaurant or tried them at home? Did they react more positively when they didn't know what they were tasting? What difference does being able to see the food make? Are they more likely now to try something new? Why or why not?

REFLECTIONS

In this chapter, we have argued that a multicultural approach to teaching must be based on the student's self-esteem. We must support the student's strengths in order for the student to be able to learn. Students come to school already members of a culture and proficient in many aspects of that culture. When we encourage students to build a strong sense of identity founded on this culture, we help them make the bridge to success in school. Part of going to school is finding out who you are, and a large part of who you are is the culture you are born into and the culture you carry around with you. We can help students discover their individual and cultural identity and learn to value these parts of themselves.

APPLICATIONS

1. Reflect on who you are and what factors have contributed to your identity. Sit with a pen and paper and write for five minutes about your identity. Just write whatever comes to mind; keep the pen moving and don't stop to analyze it yet. Now read over what you wrote. What aspects of identity did you include? What influences on identity are reflected in your response?

2. What is culture? Look up several definitions in different dictionaries. How would you explain culture to your students? Contrast the anthropological concept of culture with the literary approach to "high culture."

3. Begin keeping a journal in which you can write responses to your reading in this book and others. How do you feel about what you write? How do you feel about sharing your writing? Pick a selection and talk about what you wrote in small groups.

4. Construct a family tree for your family (or part of it). How far back can you go? When did your ancestors come to this country? Do you know why they came? Who in your family can you ask for more information? Are there family stories or traditions that have been handed down about certain members of the family? If your grandparents, for example, come from different countries or different backgrounds, how did they meet? What influences brought these different people together?

Endnotes

1. William Glasser. *Schools without Failure*. Harper and Row, 1969.
2. Virginia Shipman et al. *Young Children and Their First School Experiences*. Educational Testing Service, 1976.

Resources

Anti-Defamation League of B'nai B'rith. *Individual Differences.*

_____. *The Wonderful World of Difference.*

Alphonse Bisignano. *Cooking the Italian Way.* Lerner, 1982.

California State Department of Education. *Beyond Language: Social and Cultural Factors in Schooling Language Minority Students.* 1986.

Courtney Cazden. *Classroom Discourse: The Language of Teaching and Learning.* Heinemann, 1988.

Haim Ginott. *Teacher and Child.* Macmillan, 1972.

Thomas Gordon. *T.E.T.: Teacher Effectiveness Training.* Wyden, 1974.

Shirley Brice Heath. *Ways with Words: Language, Life, and Work in Communities and Classrooms.* Cambridge, 1983.

Milton Meltzer. *A Book about Names.* Crowell, 1985.

James Moffett and Betty Wagner. *Student-Centered Language Arts and Reading: Grades K–12,* 2nd ed. Houghton Mifflin, 1976.

Danuta Zamojska-Hutchins. *Cooking the Polish Way.* Lerner, 1984.

He has a right
to criticize
who has a heart
to help.

Abraham Lincoln

4

Developing a Feeling of Connectedness

Men and women are not only themselves; they are also the region in which they were born, the city apartment or farm in which they learned to walk, the games they played as children, the old wives' tales they overheard, the food they ate, the schools they attended, the sports they followed, the poems they read, and the God they believed in.[1]

W. Somerset Maugham

Preview

After reading this chapter, you should be able to show students:

- How the contributions of each individual are essential to the success of the group.
- That the way language is used can affect other people.
- How to recognize and combat stereotypes.

The classroom of students and teacher is a community of its own, and good teachers recognize the need to build a community spirit that will help students works together. The premise of the multicultural approach to teaching and learning is that students will learn best when they learn to work together. Because "everybody is smarter than anybody," teachers need to consider patterns of classroom organization that permit varied options for instruction, from whole class to small group, pairs, and individual work.

The difficulties of working with diversity are not eradicated just by proclaiming respect for and appreciation of diversity, however. We need to work hard to educate students about the dangers of stereotyping and how misleading our concepts and our language can be. For example, when students grow up surrounded by language and images that communicate the message that Black is bad/dangerous/wrong, our job as responsible teachers is to help students spot these traps and learn how to combat their powerful influences.

Within the classroom, we can draw students' attention to their judgments and expectations that are based on stereotyping and on assumptions of homogeneity. By providing experiences in working with other students who are both similar and different, everyone will learn strategies for working cooperatively and benefiting from everyone's strengths. Learning to work together is the second fundamental aspect of education that is truly multicultural.

BUILDING A POSITIVE CLASSROOM CLIMATE

No matter how different the neighborhoods are that your students go home to, they are all in one classroom and you can use that physical fact to build a classroom community. However, a community spirit does not arise purely from the presence of many people in the same room. You need to plan specific activities that will lead students to feel that they belong together, that they have a shared history and, therefore, shared goals. From the beginning of the school year, to welcoming new arrivals and helping them fit in smoothly, the teacher's role is central to the development of a community spirit.

The first days with a new group of children establishes the climate that will affect each child's sense of well-being. Activities that help children get acquainted through nonthreatening shared experiences ensure a comfortable, accepting atmosphere. Notice that these suggested strategies are short and they allow for individual differences in ability.

Communicating a Sense of Belonging

The teacher plays a crucial role in welcoming children to school. We need to extend a welcome to each child, making each one feel at ease in the classroom. This is important at the beginning of the school year, particularly for children entering school for the first time. It is even more important for children who enter a classroom after the year has already begun, for children (as well as adults) experience great difficulty breaking into a group that has already been formed. The following activities are designed to make children feel a sense of belonging, of being "wanted."

Welcoming the Child

Make a welcome message as clear as possible by displaying the word on a bulletin board. (If you have Spanish-speaking children in the classroom, use the word *Bienvenido*. For French, use *Bienvenue*.)

A Welcome Wagon in Your School

Challenge a group of older students to organize a Welcome Wagon that would assume responsibility for personally and officially welcoming newcomers to the school. Students of all levels could be part of this team effort. Encourage students to brain-storm possibilities for making students feel at home in their new surroundings. They might ask themselves: "What would make me feel good about coming to a new school?" Ideas include:

- Introduce the student to several children who live near him or her.
- Meet the child at the principal's office to express a welcome and to introduce him or her to the classroom teacher.
- Give the newcomer a small gift, such as a welcome card made by students or a flower to pin on (if everyone knows this symbol, they can be encouraged to smile their own welcome or to say "Hello").

The Meaning of Welcome

Talk about the word *welcome* as a way of drawing students' attention to the meaning of the display. For younger students, talk about what the word means: "What do we mean when we tell someone 'You're welcome' after someone thanks us for some-thing?" Children might note that *welcome* is a friendly expression; it conveys pleasure, gladness, and friendship. The discussion might add a special dimension to the use of this simple expression that we say without thinking.

Older students might compile a list of expressions that include the word *welcome*, for example:

- *Welcome,* stranger!
- Give someone a warm *welcome*
- Wear out one's *welcome*
- Put out the *welcome* mat

They might be interested, too, in knowing the origins of this word, which comes from the Scandinavian languages and appears in Icelandic as *velkominn*.

Ten Things about Me

A good activity for the beginning of the year is to ask each student to write ten things about himself or herself. Students can list anything, for example:

Reggie Davis

I get up at 5:30 each morning to deliver papers.
I live next to Julie and Carl.
My favorite food is fried chicken and mashed potatoes.

Introducing

Students can exchange the lists they wrote in the previous activity. Working in small groups, each person then introduces the student whose paper he or she received. The student introducing Reggie might say:

I'd like you to meet Reggie Davis. He gets up at 5:30 every morning to deliver newspapers. Just imagine! I'm still sleeping at that time. His favorite food is fried chicken and mashed potatoes . . . .

A Class Directory

Type a list of the students' names to give to the children in your room. You may include their addresses, birthdays, or other information that might interest the children as they become acquainted. They will be highly motivated to read this directory even though names of students and streets may be difficult.

Have students introduce themselves according to this listing. They may simply say: "I am Juana Rodríguez. I live on Fairglen Avenue." Or they might add other information, such as what they like to do on Saturday or where they were born. Ask the students what they would like to know about each other and what each is willing to share.

Perception of Others

A group that has been together for a period of time will benefit from sharing their perceptions of each other. Prepare a chart on which students record information. Give each child a copy of this chart, which he or she completes for everyone in the group. Then the group shares their perceptions. One person volunteers to begin: "I see myself as orange because I'm always active. I see myself as a burrito because I'm 'full of beans' and I'm a little plump but not too much. I see myself as a pickup truck because I'm pretty practical and not fussy. I see myself as a house in the middle of the woods because I like to be alone outdoors."

Going around the circle, each person then tells the items he or she has written in the columns for this person. Naturally they will differ, but the items selected and the reasons given provide interesting insights that add to each person's understanding of his or her own self.

	Color	Food	Car	Building
Joe				
Terry				
Sara				
Linda				
Juanita				
Felipe				

If you are working with a small group of students, include your own name on the chart. The students will be interested in how you perceive them, and their perceptions of you will be enlightening.

STRATEGIES FOR GOOD INTERPERSONAL RELATIONS

Most students need a lot of help with strategies for getting along well with others, particularly with other students who are different from them. Working together doesn't come easily. Again, the teacher has an important role to play in setting up the situations in which students are expected to work cooperatively. Discussion of ground rules and brainstorming, prior to engaging in a task, help set a positive atmosphere. Teacher monitoring for conflict and problem resolution is essential to the success of small group work to support students until they have worked out and practiced their own strategies.

A Discussion of Arguments

What do people argue or fight about? Ask students to suggest areas where children and parents might disagree. Is it ever possible that both sides could be right? Does the biggest (or oldest or strongest) person always win?

Develop an analogy with a baseball game. Have students describe an argument and a baseball game. Write the characteristics on the board. Then ask students: "How is an argument like a baseball game?" Possible answers include:

- You make points off each other.
- One side wins.
- People get more and more involved.

Then ask them: "How is an argument different from a baseball game?" Possible answers include:

- You're not always on the same side.
- There's no umpire to make sure you fight fair.
- Both sides aren't evenly matched.

Although students may take time to warm up, they will enjoy this challenge as long as you reinforce the idea that there are no right or wrong answers.

Sharing Problems

After discussing situations that can lead to conflict, students may want to write their own examples of problems. These can be used for a finish-the-story activity (other students write an ending), creative drama (students act out the situation for the class to watch and comment on), or roleplay (students take on the roles involved and develop them out of their own experience).

Playing a Part

By roleplaying, students can experience potential sources of conflict and ways to reach an agreement in a nonthreatening way. Have the class generate a list of topics or situations. Even the shyest students will participate and contribute when they lose themselves in acting out the part of another person. The following are some guidelines to setting up a successful roleplay.

1. Use props such as hats or masks to help students assume their roles.
2. Set a time limit. Keep roleplays short at first.
3. Assign students to partners or groups so that they don't always work with friends.
4. Give them an explicit, detailed situation or explanation to get started. Or have them draw the plot elements (Who, What, Where) out of a box.
5. Start with focused sessions before you try open-ended, more complex situations.
6. Consider the best arrangement of the classroom and decide in advance where to place students.
7. Encourage all communication and praise originality.

Sample Topics for Roleplay

Roleplay offers students a chance to think about and identify with the point of view of another person. Here are topics that will stimulate heated discussion and involvement.

- Would you tell on a friend if you saw her break something but she told the teacher she didn't do it?
- All the other kids get a larger allowance than you. Could you convince your parents to raise it?

- If you're at a friend's house and you forget the time and you get home really late, what would your parents (mother, father, guardian) say?
- Your parents only allow you to watch TV certain hours but you want to watch this particular show. Could you persuade them to change the rules, even if it is a school night?
- What if you borrow your friend's bike and then someone steals it? What should you say or do?
- All the other kids are calling the new student names. Would you join in? What would you do?
- The teacher asked the students to bring $4.00 for the class picnic. Your mother says she can't afford it but you're too embarrassed to tell the teacher. What should you do?

Cartooning

Many cartoons or comic strips derive their humor from depicting familiar or stereotypic conflicts between friends, parents and children, men and women, or workers and bosses. Take a comic strip or cartoon that students are familiar with and duplicate it, painting out the dialogue. Discuss the situation with students. What do they think is going on? What clues are there in the setting? Can they relate the situation to their own lives? Have they ever experienced anything similar?

Have students individually or in small groups write a dialogue to fit the situation. They can then read the dialogue to the class or act it out. The point is to encourage a variety of solutions to this "problem." More advanced students may be challenged if you leave in one side of the conversation and have them write the other side.

Student Advice Column

Often students are burdened by problems or conflicts with parents and friends because they think they are the only ones who have these problems. Once students begin to feel safe discussing their problems, they will realize that most people share their concerns.

Begin a personal advice service in the class by having everyone write letters describing real or imaginary problems. To preserve anonymity, you can put all the letters in a box, or choose one person to type the letters, which will be shared with the class. Have everyone contribute suggestions and advice about one problem. This can be written as a letter (in response) and posted on the bulletin board along with the original request for advice. If students are interested, you can assign a different student every week to be responsible for the "advice column." Questions in the letters can focus not only on interpersonal conflict but also on local issues or larger concerns.

Cooperation

Talk about ways we depend on other people. What would we do without people in the helping professions — firefighters, police, nurses, doctors? Bring an article from the newspaper about people helping one another to share with the class.

Students also help each other. Discuss the importance of assisting other people in school or at home. Have students answer the following questions.

- How do you help your family?
- How do your family and neighbors help each other?
- How does a friend help you?
- How can students help each other at school?

Differences in answers may show up some of the cultural diversity in what is considered *acceptable* helping behavior. Sometimes, "helping" someone can get you into trouble, like helping with the answers on a test. Students can discuss these differences and develop a list of acceptable helping behaviors for the classroom.

Using the information on the list, prepare a chart for the classroom so that all students understand the rules and new students will be able to fit in easily.

Learning from Others

Students in school sometimes feel terribly ignorant because there's so much for them to learn. However, they don't realize the wealth of knowledge and skills they already possess. Brainstorm a list of what the students in the classroom know how to do. All of them speak at least one language, for example. Some may play different sports, ride a bicycle, or play an instrument. Help students think of what to include to show how smart they all are together. Make sure that everyone has at least one item listed.

Develop a chart of the skills and abilities of the students, with a list of student names and a place to sign up for peer tutoring if anyone wants to learn something about that subject. A good student who wants help with English (or math or science) can ask someone who is good at that subject for assistance. Or a student may be interested in another student's hobby, like bird-watching or stamp collecting. Provide a short period (perhaps after lunch) for the groups to get together and set up trial meetings. After several weeks, check to see if students are still meeting. At this point, students may have questions about different ways to explain ideas and teach other people. The class can discuss the experience and suggest effective ways to peer tutor.

Cooperative Learning

Many teachers are implementing plans for small group learning that are cooperatively rather than competitively based. In cooperative learning, students are assigned to teams composed of heterogeneous skills and ability levels. All the members of the team get credit for the work done by the team, but their grade is based on improvement, not a curve. Each student is responsible for knowing all the information prepared or studied by other team members.

The key to effective use of cooperative learning in the classroom is a plan for appropriate recognition and reward for individual and team work. Although the teams can compete against each other, students are more comfortable learning from one another since they know the grade is based only on their own improvement. Students often lack experience in working effectively in groups, so the teacher must provide guidelines to make sure that no one in the group is being exploited.

In cooperative learning, students will learn to appreciate the different skills of others and the value of these skills. Because they are assigned to work with students they may not know, they will learn about people from different backgrounds. They will learn how to depend on others, learn from others, stand up for themselves, and handle disagreements.

For further information, see:

Eliot Aronson, *Jigsaw Classroom.* Sage, 1987.

David Johnson et al. *Circles of Learning: Cooperation in the Classroom.* ASCD, 1984.

Shlomo Sharan et al., eds. *Cooperation in Education.* Brigham Young University Press, 1980.

Robert Slavin. *Cooperative Learning.* Longman, 1983.

Reading Aloud

Read books aloud occasionally about students who have problems. Talk about the characters and their problems with the group. Books you might use include:

Primary

Joseph Kraus. *Leo, the Late Bloomer.* Windmill, 1971. A little tiger is slow about doing things, but he finally "blooms."

Cindy Wheeler. *Marmalade's Nap.* Knopf, 1983. A cat tries to find a quiet place to snooze.

John Steptoe. *Stevie.* Harper & Row, 1969. A young black boy resents having Stevie in his home but misses him when he is gone.

Charlotte Zolotow. *A Father Like That.* Harper & Row, 1971. A story of a small boy without a father.

Charlotte Zolotow. *The Quarreling Book.* Harper & Row, 1963. A chain of reactions begins when Father forgets to kiss Mother good-bye.

Taro Yashima. *Crow Boy.* Viking, 1955. A young Japanese boy feels rejected at school until an understanding teacher helps.

Paul Zindel. *I Love My Mother.* Harper & Row, 1972. A boy shares his feelings with his mother.

Brinton Turkel. *The Adventures of Obadiah.* Viking, 1972. A young Quaker boy living in colonial Nantucket faces the problem of lying; see other books about Obadiah.

Diane Stanley. *The Conversation Club.* Macmillan, 1983. Peter Fieldmouse is welcomed to a new neighborhood.

Upper Elementary

Eleanor Clymer. *The Horse in the Attic.* Bradbury, 1983. Caroline's family moves to a house that contains a mystery.

Maia Wojciechowska. *Shadow of a Bull.* Atheneum, 1964. The son of a great Spanish bullfighter fears being a coward.

Yoshiko Uchida. *Journey to Topaz; A Story of the Japanese-American Evacuation.* Scribner's, 1971. Yuki and her family were interned in Utah during World War II.

Virginia Sorenson. *Plain Girl.* Harcourt Brace Jovanovich, 1955. An Amish girl learns to think for herself.

Emily C. Neville. *Berries Goodman.* Harper & Row, 1965. Two city boys learn the meaning of prejudice, in this case, against Jews.

Jean Little. *Kate.* Harper & Row, 1971. In this sequel to *Look Through My Window,* Kate learns to value her Jewish heritage.

Joseph Krumgold. *And Now Miguel.* Crowell, 1953. This is a moving story of New Mexican sheepherders and Miguel's problems of growing up.

Janet Lunn. *The Root Cellar.* Scribner, 1983. An unhappy orphan discovers an exciting fantasy world.

Mildred Taylor. *The Friendship.* Dial, 1987. Two friends are divided by racial prejudice in a pain-filled story.

Mildred Taylor. *The Gold Cadillac.* Dial, 1987. On a trip to the South in the 1950s, a family encounters racial prejudice.

LEARNING TO QUESTION
STEREOTYPES AND EXPECTATIONS

A normal part of the learning process is being able to make generalizations based on a few examples. The ease with which little children learn to produce sentences they have never heard before is an example of the power of such generalizations. But most of the generalizations that are made about people tend to be stereotypes, because they constrain the enormous diversity of humanity into little boxes. The result is dehumanizing: all people with glasses are "brains," athletes (or "jocks") are stupid, and blondes are "dumb." Independent of any statistical reality for the association, the existence of these stereotypes means that any individual who appears to fit into one of the categories is judged accordingly, without a chance to provide his or her own evidence. (There may actually be brainy people who wear glasses, but there are also people who wear glasses who are not so smart.) People who perceive the world according to stereotypes are prevented from assimilating new, contradictory evidence. And people who belong to stereotyped groups (probably all of us fit somewhere) find their options limited by other people's expectations.

The most insidious, dangerous stereotyping is racial, religious, or ethnic prejudice. Most often based on "received information," this prejudice is difficult to combat because it is irrational and illogical. Early education that provides experience with people from different backgrounds and training in recognizing and overcoming stereotyping is the only way to prevent this prejudice from taking hold. Stereotyping and prejudice are impossible to avoid; the teacher's role is to help students develop strategies to deal with these issues when they encounter them.

Establishing a Baseline

Stereotypes are often based on lack of information. Before beginning a unit of study, take time to find out what students know or think they know about the subject. Brainstorm ideas, phrases, sentences, and feelings with the class and keep a record of what the students produce. This simple preassessment can be used to design exercises or activities based on student misconceptions or ignorance. It can also serve to test what students have learned by the end of the unit. You can use the same brainstorming technique and compare the two lists, or you can present the first list as a question-and-answer or true-false exercise to show change.

Animals – A Neglected Group

We have developed surprisingly rigid ideas about most common animals, and children learn this quite young. Have students verbalize these stereotypes by describing the following animals in one or two words: mouse, fox, deer. Where do these ideas come from? Have they ever seen one of the animals? If a student has had a mouse as a pet, he or she may give specific examples to contradict the general statements made by others.

Focus on one animal, such as the wolf. Have students describe this animal. Record what they say in writing or on a cassette. Then read a story that portrays a sympathetic picture of the wolf, such as *The Friendly Wolf* by Dorothy and Paul Goble, *Mowgli and His Brothers* by Rudyard Kipling, or *Julie and the Wolves* by Jean Craighead George.

After completing the story(ies), ask students to comment about what wolves are like. Record this session also. Play the first recording for the class. Has there been a change of opinion? Why?

Recent studies of wolf behavior in the wild have demonstrated that the wolf's reputation for being a "rapacious killer" is unfounded. In fact, wolves seem to be similar to dogs in many ways, including sociability, lack of aggression, and family loyalty. Yet the image from "Little Red Riding Hood" remains. Challenge this picture by having students rewrite the story from the wolf's point of view. All we know is Little Red Riding Hood's side. What if she were wrong? What might have happened, according to the wolf? Or students could write the grandmother's experience. What really happened to her? Discuss several different solutions offered, stressing the idea that there is not a "correct" answer.

Color Associations

Talk about the associations we have with colors. Ask: "What do you think of when you think *red*?" List the ideas on the board, for instance: fire, anger, burning, blood.

Then discuss how children feel about red. Is it a *good* color? They may, for example, conclude that red is not a good color, but it is exciting or it signals danger.

Follow this discussion by thinking about our use of the word *red* in expressions in our language. List the ideas:

- To get red with anger
- Blood red, as red as blood
- To be a Red (Communist)

Small Group Exploration of Color

Have the class break into groups of five or six and ask each group to explore one specific color. They can collect ideas related to these topics:

- Things associated with the color
- Kinds of feelings associated with the color
- Expressions using this color

The object of this exploration is to demonstrate that we have developed stereotyped ideas about color. What do we mean when we say, for example, "I am blue"?

- Blue is sad. (I am blue.)
- Yellow means cowardice. (I am yellow.)
- Green means young or unskilled. (I am green.)

Ask students to consider how these stereotyped ideas might have developed. If there are students in the class from different backgrounds, they may have very different associations with these colors. Discuss how such stereotypes can vary from culture to culture.

If White Means Good, Then Black Means . . .

Children quickly learn to make the association between white = good, and black = evil, and to transfer this association to people. The many references in our society that represent black as evil or bad serve to reinforce this association. Help students become more aware of how their attitudes are conditioned by discussing expressions that include black. List examples given by students. How many of them are positive, how many negative?

blackmail	black eye	blackhead	black market
black flag	black lie	black-hearted	black mark
black rage	black mood	black magic	black humor
blackball	blackout	black sheep	in the black
Black Death	in black and white	blacken	black depression

What does black mean in each of these expressions? What does black mean when we are talking about a person's skin color? Does the word *black* used in *Black Power* and *Black is beautiful* have any connection with the expressions listed? These are important questions for students to discuss in order to eliminate the stereotype that black is bad.

What Does Stereotype Mean?

Now that students have seen for themselves examples of stereotypes and how they color our thinking, you can talk about the term itself and what it means. Do they know *stereo* from *stereophonic*? Or *stereoscopic*? They probably associate *stereo* with two (speakers, pictures) but actually it refers to the three-dimensional quality obtained by using two speakers for sound or two pictures for vision. How is this related to *stereotype*? Have students look up the word, preferably in different dictionaries, and compare definitions. Can they see the connection between *stereo* and *stereotype*? (A stereotype reduces the complex, multidimensional nature of human beings, or other things, to a single statement, image, or attitude.)

After completing a unit on stereotypes, have students write their own definitions of *stereotype*. Collect these in a book and discuss.

Sex Stereotypes

Ask students to make individual lists of characteristics of men and women. After each has had time to write a number of items, ask each one to contribute something to add to a class compilation of these characteristics. The list may include items like this:

Men	*Women*
Don't cry	Cook meals for family
Play sports	Wear makeup
Support the family	Giggle a lot
Fix things around the house	Do the grocery shopping

Discuss the items on the list to find out if all men or all women do these things. Do women do some of the things on the men's list and do men do some of the things on the women's list? Have students respond from their personal experience. Afterwards, have students rewrite each item as a sentence with an adverb such as *usually, frequently, always, never, sometimes, rarely,* etc., such as:

- Men often play sports.
- Women usually cook meals for the family.

Role Reversals

Have the students divide into pairs. Ask them to pretend to be a couple having dinner together. If possible, have the boys play the woman's role and the girls play the man's role. Set a time limit for the conversation (five to ten minutes). Then discuss how the students felt. Was it easy to switch roles? What was different? Do men and women talk differently?

Doctors and Other "Wise Men"

Students have been filled with extremely rigid ideas about men and women and the stereotypical occupations for each. Test their awareness of one common stereotype by asking them to draw a picture of a doctor. After they have completed their drawings, talk about the similarities and differences among the drawings. What conclusion can they reach about the image of a doctor? (Talk about characteristics of race, sex, dress, age, etc.) Now ask them to describe their own doctor. Do the pictures they drew match the doctors they know, or do the pictures represent a generalized idea, a stereotype? Where do students think this idea comes from if not from their experience? Can they think of other ways they might be influenced?

You can try the same activity with other occupations usually associated with a particular group, such as airline pilots, school teachers, ballet dancers, etc. After several of these exercises, students will become more aware of and less susceptible to expressing these generalizations or stereotypes. From these concrete and familiar examples, you can move to more abstract discussion and criticism.

Sexism in Books

Frequently you will find examples of stereotyped thinking about sex roles in children's books. It is impractical to remove all such books from the library, but we should help students read critically. An example of such stereotyping is found in *Sylvester and the Magic Pebble* by William Steig (Simon & Schuster, 1969). The mother donkey wears an apron and plays the "helpless female"; father donkey is strong and sits smoking his pipe and reading the evening paper while mother sweeps under his feet. A positive approach to such stereotyped thinking is recognition of such writing as a "period piece" that would not be written today.

Share with students books that portray more realistic pictures of men and women. Old favorites that are outstanding include *Madeline* by Ludwig Bemelmans and *Pippi Longstocking* by Astrid Lindgren. New books that you will enjoy sharing include:

> Barbara Cohen and Bahija Lovejoy. *Seven Daughters and Seven Sons.* Atheneum, 1982.
>
> Ellen Emerson White. *The President's Daughter.* Avon, 1984.
>
> Jay Williams. *Petronella.* Parents, 1974.
>
> Vera and Bill Cleaver. *Where the Lilies Bloom.* Lippincott, 1967.
>
> Jean Craighead George. *Julie and the Wolves.* Harper & Row, 1972.
>
> Norma Klein. *Mom, the Wolf Man and Me.* Avon, 1974.
>
> Myra Cohn Livingston. *Poems for Mothers.* Holiday, 1988.

Especially good for primary grades are the following:

Vera Williams. *Something Special for Me*. Greenwillow, 1983.
Eve Mirriam. *Mommies at Work*. Knopf, 1955.
Norma Klein. *Girls Can Be Anything*. Dutton, 1973.
Marge Blaine. *The Terrible Thing That Happened at Our House*. Parents, 1975.

Sexism and Toys

Even children's toys perpetuate ideas of sex role stereotypes. Ask students to list examples of boys' toys and girls' toys. What kinds of toys are considered suitable for boys? For girls? Might girls want to play with toys that are supposed to be for boys? Or boys play with girls' toys? What would happen? (Who has the most interesting, inventive toys?) This discussion should result in increased crossing of the conventional "girls' toys" and "boys' toys" lines and decreased negative response to behavior that does not fit sex role stereotypes.

Students can also investigate use of sex role stereotypes in the marketing of toys. Look at TV commercials, illustrations used in the packaging, and the names given to toys. Can you tell which group the toys are intended for? Why would manufacturers choose to do this? If students study examples of stereotyping, they may want to write letters to the manufacturers, explaining their investigation and their findings. They can also make recommendations for changes to the manufacturer.

Families Differ

Discuss the topic: What is a typical family? Students will probably arrive at the stereotyped perception of a family as a mother, father, and two children. They may even feel that the boy is the older of the two children.

Is this what families are really like? How many families represented in the classroom consist of two parents and two children? What other arrangements do the children know about? List them on the board.

Father   Mother   One Child
Father   Mother   More than Two Children
Mother   One Child
Grandmother   Three Children
Father   Two Children
Father   Mother   One Child   Grandfather

The point of this discussion is to show children that families differ. It also opens up an opportunity for students to talk about their own families, something about which they may have felt uncomfortable. It helps to know that other parents have been divorced or that someone else's parent may have died.

Topics that are related that can be discussed without evaluation include:

- Some mothers work and some do not.
- Sometimes relatives live together.

- What constitutes a family?
- Some children are adopted.

Books about Different Family Arrangements

Children's books are helpful in exposing children to different family arrangements. It is helpful for all children to have a broadened perspective of this institution which is rapidly changing in our society. Here are a few titles that you might want to order for your library:

Primary Grades

Meredith Tax and Marilyn Hafner. *Families*. Little, Brown, 1981. Examples of different families.

Paul Zindel. *I Love My Mother*. Harper & Row, 1975. Mother and boy.

Joan Lexau. *Me Day*. Dial, 1971. Young black boy visits with divorced father.

Lucille Chifton. *Everett Anderson's Nine Months Long*. Holt, 1987. Everett's mother has remarried and is going to have a baby. Look for other stories about Everett.

Upper Elementary

Brenda Wilkinson. *Ludell*. Harper & Row, 1975. Grandmother and fifth-grade girl; unwed mother does not live with them.

Margaret Storey. *The Family Tree*. Nelson, 1973. Orphaned girl lives with older male cousin.

Zilpha K. Snyder. *The Witches of Worm*. Atheneum, 1972. Twelve-year-old girl and divorced mother.

Rose Blue. *A Month of Sundays*. Watts, 1972. Boy and divorced mother.

Charlotte Anker. *Last Night I Saw Andromeda*. Walck, 1975. Eleven-year-old girl and mother; father visits.

Reading such stories as part of your regular time for reading aloud to the class will be helpful to students and may open up topics for discussion. Before selecting a book to read aloud, it is important, of course, that you read it first.

Images of Native Americans

Students are surrounded by negative and inaccurate images of Native Americans or Indians. Many materials used in schools reinforce this and are demeaning to Indians. You may have Native American students in your class who find it convenient to pass as Hispanic or Anglo since they often have Spanish or French last names.

Talk about the ideas students have about Native Americans. Brainstorm a list on the board or on a chart of all the information students can think of. They will probably reflect the common stereotypes of Native Americans as savages, fighters, or primitives. They may mention rain dances or tom-tom drums. Many may think the Native Americans had no language other than grunts or gestures.

Use this list to investigate the reality of Native American life and the rich range of variation. Look at the Native American groups that used to live in your area. What happened to them? What were they like? Research the present situation for Native Americans. Check the stereotypes against the facts. How would Native Americans feel if someone said these things about them? Would they be insulted?

Discuss the stereotypes that students had. Do they still think these are true? Talk about where they got their stereotyped information and compare it to their current study. Why do most people still hold the same old inaccurate, insulting ideas?

Use this technique to deal with stereotypes about any group represented in the classroom. The best way to handle omnipresent stereotyping is to confront it directly, identify it as stereotyping, present facts that contradict stereotypes, and model recognition and acceptance of diversity.

Evaluating Books for Children

How can you evaluate literature for use in the classroom? We need to examine books in terms of (1) realistic portrayals of members of ethnic groups, (2) inclusion of a fair representation of persons that make up our society, and (3) an honest attempt to break down existing stereotypes and prejudices.

You can construct your own checklist especially designed to fit your own purposes. You can also guide students in developing a checklist and in applying this instrument. A simple checklist might look something like this:

Book Title _____

Author _____ Publisher _____ Year _____

Illustrator _____ Pages _____

	Positive images of:			Negative images of:
Story	*Art*		*Story*	*Art*
_____	_____ women		_____	_____ women
_____	_____ men		_____	_____ men
_____	_____ aged persons		_____	_____ aged persons
_____	_____ ethnic groups (list below)		_____	_____ ethnic groups (list below)

This checklist notes only what is present. The lack of checkmarks means, therefore, that there was nothing offensive, but neither was there a positive effort to combat stereotypes.

Comparing Evaluations of Books

Students can compare their evaluation of specific books with evaluations that have been published. The Council on Interracial Books for Children, for example, has published *Human Values in Children's Books*, in which they analyze contemporary books. Older students could easily read this report and discuss the evaluation. Here are sample evaluations* for (1) a book ranked outstanding, *Ludell*, and (2) a book that was severely criticized, *Three Fools and a Horse*:

Ludell

Brenda Wilkinson. Harper and Row, 1975. Grades 5-up.

In this sensitive and powerful novel, the positive and the negative sides of growing up in a rural southern Black community are revealed through the eyes of fifth-grader Ludell. The place is Waycross, Georgia, in the 1950s where Ludell Wilson lives with her grandmother ("Mama"). Next door is the Johnson crew: Mrs. Johnson, sixteen-year-old Mattie and her child, Ruthie Mae (Ludell's best friend), Willie, Hawk and Cathy.

Ludell's keen perceptions expose the harsh underside of life in Waycross—the poverty, the selfishness and unconcern of her teachers in the segregated school she attends, the constant reminders that both Mama and Mrs. Johnson work as maids in white people's homes. Whenever racism and oppression are manifest, it is commented upon and clearly defined.

Each experience, whether humorous or tragic, contributes to Ludell's growing awareness of herself and of others. The reader can sense that one day her aspirations will lead her to seek a life outside of Waycross and to exercise more control over her destiny.

Author Wilkinson effectively captures the subtle nuances of Black southern dialect and draws readers inside the Black experience. In addition she provides a truly positive role model for young Black readers. Ludell has a keen sense of who she is, shares with those less fortunate than herself and is shown overcoming adversities in her life.

	ART	WORDS		ART	WORDS		ART	WORDS	N.A.
anti-Racist		✓	non-Racist			Racist — omission / commission			
anti-Sexist			non-Sexist		✓	Sexist			
anti-Elitist		✓	non-Elitist			Elitist			
anti-Materialist			non-Materialist		✓	Materialist			
anti-Individualist		✓	non-Individualist			Individualist			
anti-Ageist			non-Ageist		✓	Ageist			
anti-Conformist			non-Conformist		✓	Conformist			
anti-Escapist		✓	non-Escapist			Escapist			
Builds positive image of females/minorities		✓	Builds negative image of females/minorities				Excellent	Good	Fair	Poor
Inspires action vs. oppression			Culturally authentic		✓	Literary quality		✓ (Good)	
						Art quality			

*Source: Adapted from *Human Values in Children's Books*. Council on Interracial Books for Children, Inc., 1841 Broadway, New York, NY.

Three Fools and a Horse

Betty Baker. Illus. by Glen Rounds. Macmillan, Grades 3–up.

The Foolish People were an imaginary group invented by the Apaches as an object of humor. *Three Fools and a Horse* chronicles the misadventures of three of the Foolish People of Two Dog Mountain — Little Fool, Fat Fool and Fool About. The trio decide they must have one of the horses of the "flat land men" (Plains Indians) in order to be "big men, the biggest men of the Foolish People." Little Fool challenges one of the flat land men to a horse race (Little Fool has no horse). Surprisingly, he wins the race and the horse. Unexpected consequences follow from the Fools' attempt to ride horseback.

Native American folk stories should be tole by Native Americans, not appropriated from "folklore and anthropology magazines" and then vulgarized by whites. Ms. Baker has no business writing about the Foolish People if their stories are going to be, as they have been in this book, "combined, slightly changed and much elaborated. . . ." The Apache's Foolish People stories are entertaining in their own context, and their misrepresentation here is unethical and racist. Both the Fools (portrayed as ugly and self-seeking) and the Plains Indians (equally ugly and ridiculous) are maligned. The flat land people are differentiated in looks from the Fools only by the addition of leggings, braids, feathers and hook noses.

Though the author claims these stories taught moral lessons to Apache children her book strongly reinforces the "heap dumb Injun" stereotype.

	ART	WORDS		ART	WORDS		ART	WORDS	N.A.
anti-Racist			non-Racist			Racist — omission			
						commission	✓	✓	
anti-Sexist			non-Sexist			Sexist			✓
anti-Elitist			non-Elitist	✓	✓	Elitist			
anti-Materialist			non-Materialist	✓	✓	Materialist			
anti-Individualist			non-Individualist	✓	✓	Individualist			
anti-Ageist			non-Ageist			Ageist			✓
anti-Conformist			non-Conformist	✓	✓	Conformist			
anti-Escapist			non-Escapist	✓	✓	Escapist			
Builds positive image of females/minorities			Builds negative image of females/minorities	✓	✓		Excellent	Good	Fair	Poor
Inspires action vs. oppression			Culturally authentic			Literary quality		✓		
						Art quality		✓		

Types of Stereotypes

Discuss the categories listed in the preceding evaluation. Ask students to think of an example of each of the types: Racist, Sexist, Elitist, Materialist, Individualist, Ageist, Conformist, Escapist. Can students define these terms? Why would we want to rate books along these lines? What do these terms have in common? Have students bring in their own books and talk about the presence or absence of these features. Discuss with the class what N.A. means (Not applicable—used on the preceding checklist).

THE FIRST AMERICANS

One might say that the Native Americans are the only true Americans because all the other groups came from another country. When we talk about multicultural issues, we often ask how long ago your family immigrated, or what countries your family came from. But these questions don't fit the Native Americans—one of the most neglected of the major groups in this country.

Too many people have had their ideas of Indians fixed by Western films, and they would have trouble accepting an Indian who didn't live in a tepee, ride a horse, wear a headdress, or speak broken English. Yet today, even after years of reservation living, economic hardship, and poor education, some tribes have been able to maintain their cultural identity. This identity is based on the cultural traditions handed down through the tribe, and since not all tribes lived in tepees or rode horses, the tribe should be the group that we study or refer to when we talk about Native Americans in school.

In this section we present a variety of activities to use in introducing the study of Native Americans. These suggestions illustrate only the range of activities possible. From the ideas presented here, you can go on to develop a unit of your own that is more representative of the tribes and the history of your particular region.

Saturate Your Classroom

An exciting way to develop a study like this is to turn your whole classroom into a learning center focused on Native Americans. Talk with your students as you plan together to saturate your classroom with another culture. There are several ways you might organize this operation, for instance:

Plan A.   Imagine that the whole classroom is an Indian campground with a campfire in the middle. Move desks to the outer edges in the "trees." Designate certain areas of the classroom for specific activities, such as the horse corral or the chief's tepee. Students will then decide on what tribe they will be, where they will be located geographically, and what the habits of these Indians were.

Plan B.   Divide the class into several tribes; the number depends on the amount of space available. Each tribe is located in a specific part of the classroom where they can develop a home typical of the tribe they select. They need to read to discover facts about how the tribe lived and how it got along with other tribes.

Starting Out

Before beginning a study of Indians in the United States, use some means of assessing student information and attitudes. This will provide an interesting and instructive comparison at the end of the study. Try some of these ideas:

- Have each student draw a picture of an Indian engaged in some activity.
- Ask students to complete this sentence at least three times: An Indian . . .
- Ask students to list as many Indian tribes as they can.

Put these sheets away until the study is completed. After the study you might have the students repeat the same activities. Then compare the results.

Native Americans

Draw a large outline map of the United States on which to locate the various groups of Indian tribes. They can be grouped as follows according to similar modes of living:

Eastern Woodland Area   Algonquin, Delaware, Iroquois, Massachuset, Mohawk, Mohegan, Narraganset, Onandaga, Penobscot, Powhatan, Tuscarora, Passamaquoddy, Pawtuket, Tippecanoe, Wampanoag, Wyandot

Great Lakes Woodland Area   Chippewa/Ojibwa, Huron, Illinois, Kickapoo, Miami, Oneida, Ottawa, Potawatomi, Sauk and Fox, Seneca, Shawnee, Winnebago

Southeastern Area   Catawba, Cherokee, Creek, Lumbi, Natchez, Seminole, Yuchi

North Central Plains Area   Arapaho, Arikara, Assiniboin, Blackfeet, Cheyenne, Cree, Crow, Gros Ventre, Mandan, Pawnee, Shoshone, Sioux/Dakota

South Central Plains Area   Caddo, Chickasaw, Choctaw, Comanche, Iowa, Kaw/Kansa, Kiowa, Omaha, Osage, Ponca, Quapaw

Southwest Area   Apache, Hopi, Maricopa, Navajo, Papago, Pima, Pueblo, Zuñi

California Area   Chumash, Hoopa, Maidu, Mission, Modoc, Mohave, Mono, Pit River, Pomo, Tule River, Wailaki, Yahi, Yokuts, Yuma, Yurok

Northwestern Plateau Area   Bannock, Cayuse, Coeur D'Alene, Colville, Flathead, Kalispel, Klamath, Kootenai, Nez Percé, Paiute, Puyallup, Spokane, Ute, Walla-walla, Wasco, Washoe, Yakima, Nisqually

Northwest Pacific Coast Area   Aleuts, Eskimo, Haida, Lummi, Makah, Muckleshoot, Nootka, Quinault, Salish, Shoalwater, Snohomish, Suquamish, Tlingit

Speakers of Indian Languages

The following chart shows languages that are still spoken today. Many historical Indian tribes were wiped out (particularly in New England) and other groups have no one left who remembers the native language. Figures are listed only where there are more than 1000 speakers. Inuit (Eskimo) languages are grouped together.

Language	Number of Speakers	Location
Navaho	almost 100,000	Arizona, New Mexico, Utah, Colorado
Ojibwa-Ottawa-Algonquin-Salteaux	40,000–50,000	Montana, North Dakota, Minnesota, Wisconsin, Michigan, Canada (Sask., Man., Ont., Que.)
Cree	30,000–40,000	Montana, Canada
Eskimo	15,882	Alaska
Papago	11,000	Arizona
Teton	10,000–15,000	Colorado
Apache	10,100–14,000 includes: San Carlos (8,000–10,000) Mescalero (1,000–1,500) Jicarilla (1,000–1,500) Chiricahua (100–1,000)	 Arizona New Mexico New Mexico Arizona, New Mexico
Cherokee	10,000	(North Carolina)
Muskogee (Creek)	7,000–8,000	(Escambia Co., Alabama)
Keres	7,000	New Mexico Rio Grande pueblos
Choctaw	6,722	Oklahoma (near Philadelphia, Miss.)
Blackfoot-Piegan-Blood	5,000–6,000	Montana, Canada (Alta.)
Shoshone-Gosiute	5,000	California, Nevada, Idaho, Oregon, Wyoming
Hopi	4,800	Northeast Arizona
Cheyenne	under 4,000	Oklahoma, Montana
Yuman	3,900	Arizona, California
Zuni	3,500	West New Mexico
Santee	3,000–5,000	Washington
Tiwa	3,000	New Mexico
Yaqui	3,000	Arizona
Crow	3,000	Montana
Chickasaw	2,000–3,000	Oklahoma
Sahaptin	2,750	
Tewa	under 2,500	New Mexico, Arizona
Ute	2,000–4,000	(Colorado, Utah)
Seneca	2,000–3,000	New York, Canada (Ont.) (Erie, Chautauqua, Cattaraugus, Genesee Co., N.Y.)
Northern Paiute-Bannock-Snake	2,000	N. Paiute—East California, Nevada; Bannock—Idaho; Snake—East Oregon
Kiowa	2,000	Oklahoma
Pima	2,000	Arizona
Comanche	1,500	Oklahoma
Towa	1,200	New Mexico

Arapaho-Atsina-Nawathinehena	1,000–3,000	Wyoming, Oklahoma
Winnebago	1,000–2,000	Nebraska, Wisconsin
Oneida	1,000–2,000	New York, Canada (Ont.), (Onondaga Co., N.Y.)
Tlingit	1,000–2,000	Southeast Alaska
Mohawk	1,000–2,000	New York, Canada (Ont., Que.) (Franklin and St. Lawrence Co., N.Y.)
Assiniboin	1,000–2,000	Montana
Yankton	1,000–1,200	Nebraska
Aleut	1,000–1,200	Alaska
Omaha	1,000 +	Nebraska
Cayuga	1,000 +	(Erie, Chautauqua, Cattaraugus, Onondaga Co., N.Y.)
Fox-Sauk	1,000	Oklahoma
Flathead-Pend d'Oreille-Kalispel-Spokan	600–1,200	Montana, Washington

SOURCE: C. F. and F. M. Voegelin, "Languages of the World: Native American Fascicle One." *Locations in parentheses, except for Canadian provinces, from Department of the Interior, Bureau of Indian Affairs.* Indians of the Lower Plateau, Indians of the Gulf States, Indians of the Great Lakes Area, Indians of the Eastern Seaboard.

English Words from Native American Languages

Words borrowed into English show how much the first settlers owed the Native Americans they encountered. Most words come from the Algonquin languages, spoken along the East Coast. Can students guess what these words were borrowed as? Develop a chart to show the relationship.

chitmunk	(chipmunk)	paccan	(pecan)
aroughcoun	(raccoon)	pasimenan	(persimmon)
squnk	(skunk)	msickquatash	(succotash)
ochek	(woodchuck)	askootasquash	(squash)
musquash	(muskrat)	wikawam	(wigwam)
moos	(moose)	tamahak	(tomahawk)
aposoun	(opossum)	mohkussin	(moccasin)
pawcohiccora	(hickory)		

Gifts from the Native Americans

Students will be interested in learning of the many things we gained from the Native Americans. They knew the best trails and ways of traveling across the country by canoe and by snowshoe. They invented hammocks. The Native Americans were the first, too, to grow and use tobacco and rubber. They introduced white settlers to the following foods that we use today:

corn	tomatoes	chicle (for chewing gum)	grits
sweet potatoes	vanilla	beans	hominy
peppers	avocados	chocolate	popcorn
pineapples	peanuts	maple sugar	succotash
squash			

Have several students prepare an illustrated chart of these foods. You may experiment with preparing hominy or grits, dishes that are easy to make in the classroom.

Hermina Poatgieter's book, *Indian Legacy; Native American Influences on World Life and Culture* (Messner, 1981), provides more information about what we learned from the Indians.

Native American Place Names

Many state names, such as Massachusetts, originated in Native American languages. Names of many rivers, such as the Ohio and Mississippi, and names of cities, such as Pontiac, Michigan, and Chicago, Illinois, also originated from Native American languages.

Prepare a map on which to locate Native American names. Include a chart to explain what the names mean and where they come from.

Native American Folklore

Folklore from the various Native American tribes is an excellent source for storytelling activities. Explore some of the following:

John Bierhorst (retold by). *Doctor Coyote*. Macmillan, 1987.

Jane Curry. *Back in the Beforetime: Tales of the California Indians*. McElderry Books, 1987.

Paul Goble (retold by). *Star Boy*. Bradbury, 1983.

Christie Harris. *The Trouble with Adventurers*. Atheneum, 1982.

George Bird Grinnell, collector, John Bierhorst, editor. *The Whistling Skeleton; American Indian Tales of the Supernatural*. Four Winds, 1982.

Alice Marriott and Carol Rachlin. *American Indian Mythology*. Crowell, 1968.

Alice Marriott and Carol Rachlin. *Winter-telling Tales*. Crowell, 1969.

A useful bibliography is *Folklore of the North American Indians,* compiled by Judith Ullom, for sale by the Superintendent of Documents, U.S. Government Printing Office. This annotated bibliography comes out of the Children's Book Section of the Library of Congress.

Writing Folktales

Many of the Native American folktales are "pourquoi" tales, stories that answer "why" something happened, for example:

- Why the rabbit has a short tail
- Why the sun rises in the east and sets in the west
- Why the moon is a full circle at times and only a sliver or crescent at others.

These stories represent attempts to explain things that are important to people. Read aloud a number of pourquoi tales, such as the following:

Gail Robinson (retold by). *Raven, the Trickster: Legends of the North American Indians.* Atheneum, 1982.

Henry Chafetz. *Thunderbird and Other Stories.* Pantheon, 1964.

Jane Louise Curry (retold by). *Down from the Lonely Mountain.* Harcourt, 1965.

Then have children use this pattern to tell or write their own pourquoi tales. Collect them on a tape or in a book of tales to be shared with others.

Making Navaho Fry Bread

Create a learning center at which children can take turns making a semiauthentic version of fry bread. (Teacher supervision is necessary for this activity.)

Directions
Fill the electric skillet half full of oil. Turn on high to heat.

Measure into bowl:

4 C flour	1 tsp. salt
3 tsp. baking powder	1½ C water

Gradually add the water as you stir.

Knead the dough until it does not stick to your hands. Add a little more flour as needed. Divide the dough into small balls. Then flatten them until thin and make a hole in the center like a doughnut. Slide into hot oil. Fry on each side until light brown. Remove and drain on layer of paper towels. Eat while warm.

Sports from the Native Americans

Many of the sports we know today originated in games the Native Americans first played. They played shinny, a game with a puck that was played on ice, similar to ice hockey. Native American children played such games as hide and seek, follow-the-leader, crack-the-whip, prisoner's base, and blindman's bluff. They also had games not unlike hopscotch, marbles, and jack straws.

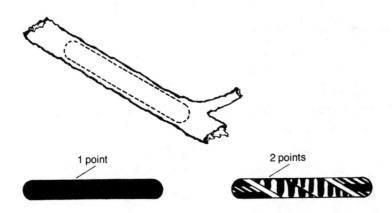

For more information about Native American sports and how to play them, look for *Sports & Games the Indians Gave Us* by Alex Whitney (McKay, 1977). This author shows children how to make gaming equipment for use in the games described. Stick dice are easy to make, for example. Use a stick about one-half inch wide and four inches long. With a knife round off the ends of the stick. Paint one side red and paint a multicolor design on the other side. With the red side counting as one point and the design as two, see who can get twenty points first.

A Weaving Center

Weaving is an art that has been practiced by many cultures. You may wish to construct one or two large looms on which students can create a decorative piece of cloth cooperatively. Students can create miniature looms on which they can work individually. Directions given are for the large loom, but small looms can be made in similar fashion.

Obtain two lightweight logs about five feet long. Cut off any branches, but leave the rough ends sticking out. Suspend one log from the ceiling to simulate the limb of a tree. The second log is then suspended from the first by rough rope as shown here:

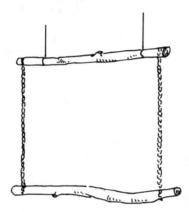

If suspending the log from the ceiling is not possible in your classroom, fasten four logs together with rope to form a loom frame, as shown here:

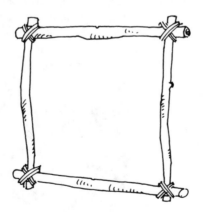

Thread the loom with heavy rug yarn choosing natural colors as much as possible rather than the bright, artificial colors. Using black or beige, loop the yarn around the log to keep it from sliding, thus:

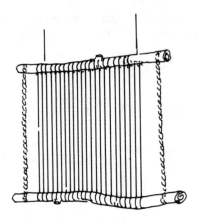

Students can make wooden shuttles of flat pieces of wood. They can alternate colors to form stripes of varied widths.

Native American Masks

Begin a study of masks by showing the excellent film, *The Loon's Necklace* (Britannica Films, 11 minutes), a legend told by the artful filming of authentic masks from a museum.

Students can create their own masks from heavy cardboard. Folding the cardboard in half makes it fit the child's face more closely. A piece of elastic holds it securely in place.

The shape of the mask and the way the eyes are developed serve to suggest the person or animal. It is not necessary, however, to be overly realistic. Masks can then be used to tell folktales, perhaps the pourquoi tales the children have written.

A good resource for making masks is *Creative Masks for Stage and School* by Joan Peters and Anna Sutcliffe (Plays, Inc., 1975).

Native American Poetry

Share these poems with the children in your room. Because they are short, you might print one or two on posters for display in the classroom.

Song of Failure

A wolf
I considered myself,
But the owls are hooting
and the night
I fear.
  — Teton Sioux

Spring Song

As my eyes search the prairie,
I feel the summer in the spring.
  — Chippewa

Glyph

Truly buzzards
Around my sky are circling!
For my soul festers,
And an odor of corruption
Betrays me to disaster.
Meanness, betrayal and spite
Come flockwise,
To make me aware
Of sickness and death within me.
My sky is full of the dreadful sound
Of the wings of unsuccesses.
  — Washoe-Paiute

May I Walk

On the trail marked with pollen may I walk,
With grasshoppers about my feet may I walk,
With dew about my feet may I walk,
With beauty may I walk,
With beauty before me, may I walk,
With beauty behind me, may I walk,
With beauty above me, may I walk,
With beauty under me, may I walk,
With beauty all around me, may I walk,
In old age wandering on a trail of beauty, lively, may I walk,
In old age wandering on a trail of beauty, living again, may I walk,
It is finished in beauty.
  — Navajo

Child's Night Song
Very much, very much,
I of the owl am afraid,
Sitting alone in the wigwam.
— Chippewa

SOURCE: *Reading Ideas,* May 1978.

Children Write Poetry

After reading the anonymous Native American poems, encourage children to write similar poetry. Discuss the kinds of topics a Native American child might present in poetry and why. Notice that the out-of-doors is present in each of the poems. Animals are included in several of the poems. Observe, too, that there is no rhyming in this poetry so the stress is on the ideas expressed. Here is a poem that one child wrote which you might find useful as an example:

> As I walk in the woods,
> I feel the eyes of the forest around me.
> — *Danny Richards*

An excellent collection of poetry written by young Native Americans is *The Whispering Wind* edited by Terry Allen (Doubleday, 1972). Included in the collection is poetry that would be suitable for all age levels.

More Books about Native Americans

As you develop this study, the following references and children's books will be helpful:

Betty Baker. *A Stranger and Afraid.* Macmillan, 1972.

_____. *And One Was a Wooden Indian.* Macmillan, 1970.

Byrd Baylor. *Moon Song. Scribner, 1982.*

John Bierhorst, ed. The Sacred Path: Spells, Prayers, and Power Songs of the American Indians. Morrow, 1983.

Dee Brown. *Bury My Heart at Wounded Knee: An Indian History of the American West.* Holt, Rinehart and Winston, 1970.

Eth Clifford. *The Year of the Three-Legged Deer.* Houghton Mifflin, 1972.

Margaret Embry. *Shadi.* Holiday House, 1971.

Hazel Fredericksen. *He-Who-Runs-Far.* Young Scott Books, 1970.

Jean Craighead George. *Water Sky.* Harper, 1987.

Lynne Gessner. *Lightning Slinger.* Funk and Wagnalls, 1968.

Dorothy Goble and Paul Goble. *The Friendly Wolf.* Bradbury, 1974.

————. *Horse Raid.* Bradbury, 1973.

Daniel Jacobson. *Indians of North America.* Watts, 1983.

Harry C. James. *Ovada: An Indian Boy of the Grand Canyon.* Ward Ritchie Press, 1969.

Evelyn Sibley Lampman. *Half Breed.* Doubleday, 1967.

————. *The Year of Small Shadow.* Harcourt Brace Jovanovich, 1971.

Gerald McDermott. *Arrow to the Sun.* Viking, 1975.

Scott O'Dell. *Island of the Blue Dolphins.* Houghton Mifflin, 1960.

————. *Sing Down the Moon.* Houghton Mifflin, 1970.

Alice Osinski. *The Navajo.* Children's Press, 1987.

————. *The Chippewa.* Children's Press, 1987.

Jean Rogers. *Goodbye My Island.* Greenwillow, 1983.

Anne Siberell. *Whale in the Sky.* Dutton, 1982.

Ann Tomchek. *The Hopi.* Children's Press, 1987.

Mary Townsend. "Taking Off the War Bonnet: American Indian Literature." *Language Arts* (March 1976): 236–244.

M. J. Wheeler. *First Came the Indians.* Atheneum, 1983.

Barbara Williams. *The Secret Name.* Harcourt Brace Jovanovich, 1972.

Carter Wilson. *On Firm Ice.* Crowell, 1968.

A Mural of Native American Life

After students have gained information through reading and discussing topics related to Native American life, have them plan a large mural to which each one can contribute. The space of the mural might be considered similar to the map of the United States. Roughly, then, space could be allocated to activities associated with the Plains Indians, those of the Southwest, the Pacific Northwest, and so on. Sketch this plan on the chalkboard.

Bring in books with pictures that suggest scenes to be included. Crayons can be used for the figures and the background can be painted in with pale brown tempera or light green, as appropriate.

When the mural is completed, display it in the school hall or a room where all can see it.

An All-School Assembly

Plan a school assembly to share the results of your study. Let students discuss various ways they can present an informative and entertaining program. Consider some of the following activities:

- An introduction (the purpose of your study and some of the things you learned).
- Presentation of the mural with an explanation of the many Native American tribes in what is now the United States.
- Reader's theater presentation of Native American folklore which might include music or drum beating.
- Demonstration of Native American sports, dances, etc.
- Creative dramatization of a Native American story.
- An invitation to visit your room to see the things you have made.

Sources of Information

Collect pictures for display in the classroom. Two good sources are:

Society for Visual Education, 1345 Diversey Parkway, Chicago, IL 60614.

Arizona Highways, 2039 W. Lewis, Phoenix, AZ 85009.

Sources of recordings are:

Folkways/Scholastic Records, 50 W. 44th St., New York, NY 10036.

Music Division, Library of Congress, Washington, D.C. 20540.

A variety of information can be obtained from these sources:

The American Indian Museum of Natural History, Central Park West and 79th Street, New York, NY 10024.

Bureau of Indian Affairs, Department of Interior, Washington, D.C. 20242. Ask for their list of penpals.

Museum of the American Indian, Broadway at 155th St., New York, NY 10032.

Also refer to sources listed in the Appendix.

REFLECTIONS

Interpersonal relations is the second major leg of multicultural teaching after self-esteem. In this chapter, we have argued for helping students learn how to work together and how to fight the stereotypes that surround them and make it difficult to work with others. Teachers are crucial in this process: students need teacher support and encouragement to find strategies to resolve conflicts and work constructively. But basic to the multicultural approach to education is the assumption that we need each other yet we need to maintain our differences.

APPLICATIONS

1. How influential is our language in creating and maintaining stereotypes and prejudices? Pick a group that you belong to, such as:

   student   athlete
   parent   blonde
   male   bespectacled
   female   musician

   What phrases or descriptions are associated with the group you selected? Do they carry positive or negative connotations? How do they make you feel when somebody uses them? What effect might these words have on children's ideas about you? Discuss your results in small groups. Would you want to change some of the language used?

2. Begin to collect a picture file. Look for pictures of men, women, boys, and girls who represent a variety of ethnic and racial backgrounds and who are engaged in both common and unusual activities. Mount them on cardboard with a plastic overlay for protection, then group them according to subject or possible use. Is it easy to find pictorial representations of all groups in our society (or in the world), in all occupations? Which groups are rarely depicted? What impression do students receive who seldom see pictures of people like themselves or their family? Write two lesson plans using your picture file.

3. Using the evaluation form given in the chapter (or one of your own), select ten children's books (fiction and nonfiction) to evaluate for race, age, sex, or other stereotypes. Decide how you would use each book to promote awareness and acceptance of diversity. What would you do with books such as *Huckleberry Finn* or *Dr. Doolittle* that some have condemned for their racism? How could you use each book to discuss the destructiveness of stereotyping? Develop two lesson plans about books that present subtle or overt stereotyped images and thinking. Select two books that have been criticized for racism or sexism and develop a lesson plan that uses each book to teach critical thinking.

Endnote

1. W. Somerset Maugham. *The Razor's Edge.* Doubleday, 1944.

Resources

Deborah Byrnes. *"Teacher, They Called Me a _____!" Prejudice and Discrimination in the Classroom*. Anti-Defamation League of B'nai B'rith, 1988. (823 United Nations Plaza, New York 10017)

Candy Carter, ed. *There Are So Many Things I Wish I'd Asked My Father*. Learning Opportunities. (Box 2466, Truckee, CA 95734)

Interracial Books for Children Bulletin. The Council on Interracial Books for Children.

Northwest Regional Educational Laboratory Center for Sex Equity, comp. *Bibliography of Nonsexist Supplementary Books (K–12)*. Oryx Press, 1984.

E. Pepitone, ed. *Children in Cooperation and Competition*. Heath, 1980.

R. E. Slavin. *Cooperative Learning*. Longman, 1983.

Christine Sleeter and Carl Grant. *Making Choices for Multicultural Education: Five Approaches to Race, Class, and Gender*. Merrill, 1988.

Sharon Whitney. *The Equal Rights Amendment: The History and the Movement*. Watts, 1984.

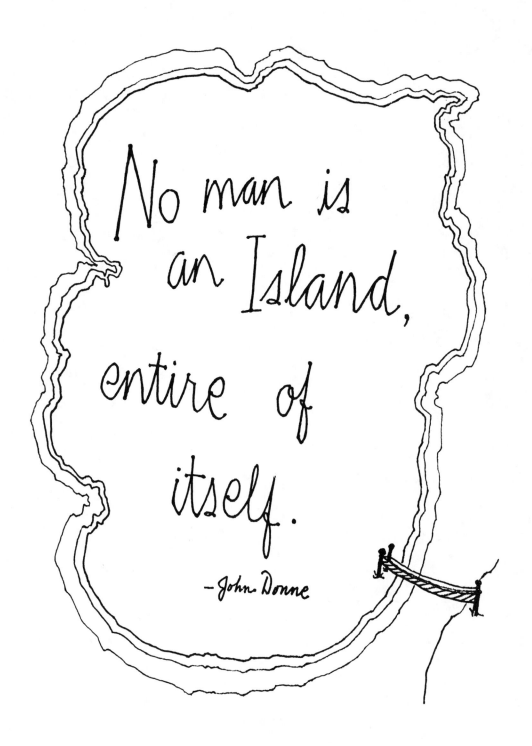

No man is an Island, entire of itself.

—John Donne

5

Expanding Our Horizons

America cannot be an ostrich with its head in the sand.[1]

Woodrow Wilson

Preview

After reading this chapter, you should be able to show students:

- How their community is made up of different groups and what those groups have contributed.
- The many different groups in the country, how these groups have been treated, and the consequences of this treatment.
- How to understand that people in other countries are like us and although there are differences in expression, there are universals of human culture.
- How all of us need and depend on other people.

In the preceding chapters, we have looked at how students learn who they are and where they fit in the classroom community. Now we move beyond the horizons of the school to the neighborhood, the country, and the globe to show students how their immediate world is tied to the larger world around them. In fact, each classroom is a larger universe in microcosm, as each child comes to school from a family that has connections to other groups, other regions, perhaps even other countries. And within the familiar community that children grow up in are groups that have had different histories within the United States, influenced by such factors as the country they came from, when they arrived, and the reasons for the immigration. Some children may have been born in other countries, but even those born here do not have to go far back in their family history to find relatives and ancestors born elsewhere.

EXPLORING YOUR COMMUNITY

Schools used to belong to the community in which they were located. Children walked to school, families knew each other, and teachers knew the children's families and home environments. Now, because of busing, changes in school district boundaries, and increased mobility of families, teachers often find themselves cut off from these roots in the community. Students, too, may not know their neighbors or be familiar with the area around them. As many communities become more heterogeneous and include sharply divided islands of particular groups, school classrooms come to mirror these distinctions, and even students who live close together geographically may find that they come from totally different worlds. As teachers, we need both to learn more about the communities our students come from and also help our students learn more about each other's community.

The Neighborhood

Explore the concept of a neighborhood with your students. Does the area where your school is located have a name? Do all students live in the same neighborhood? Talk about the neighborhood. What are the most significant spots to students? (Church, school, park, ice cream store, etc.) Bring a city map and have the students mark where they live. What are the boundaries? You can show students that a word such as *neighborhood* is a *concept,* an idea in people's minds rather than a physical object, so that there may be more than one definition of the neighborhood.

Have students write a description of their neighborhood. How do they feel about it? What are some of the people and places in it? What sights, sounds, smells do they think of?

For another writing activity have students complete these sentences.

- My favorite place in the neighborhood is _____.
- I like it because _____.
- The most important thing that ever happened to me in the neighborhood was

  _____.
- When I think of my neighborhood, I think of _____.

Students' responses to these prompts can be collected into an illustrated book entitled *Thoughts about Our Neighborhood.*

Neighborhood People

Are all the people in your neighborhood your neighbors? What's a neighbor? Do students know their neighbors? Discuss what neighbors can do for you. Some students' neighbors may take care of them after school and others may organize a local baseball team. How do neighbors help each other?

Have students draw a picture of a neighbor who has done something special for them — helped them when they were sick, given them a present, etc. — and have them tell the class about this person. What makes this neighbor a special person for them?

Students may be interested in knowing that *neighbor* comes from the Old English words: nēah (near) gebūr (dweller).

A Neighborhood Map

Talk about maps with students. What are different kinds of maps? What goes into a map? What can maps be used for? In discussions about the neighborhood, students have talked about places and people of importance to them. Now each student can make a list of elements they might like to include on a map of the neighborhood.

Construct a class map on a large sheet of butcher paper. Depending on the level of the students, you may decide to represent only one or two main streets, an interpretation of a larger area (not to scale), or a standard grid map with scale and/or cardinal directions. Students will enjoy developing symbols to use on the map (explained in the *key*) and illustrating or landscaping the map as much as they choose. A more elaborate project would be to create a relief map or three-dimensional model from clay, plaster, or similar material. Such a project will give students a different perspective of the place where all of them live.

Observing Your Community Firsthand

Take students on a walking field trip to explore the community they live in. As you walk down commercial streets and residential streets, have the students notice who lives there, how the people live, and what they do for a living. Pay attention to the age range of the people you see, what occupations are represented, what people do when they are not working.

When you return to the class, discuss what the students saw. Did they see anything during the walk that they had not noticed before? What did they like or dislike about what they saw? Discuss the importance of public transportation. What kinds are available in your community? Do people live near the stores where they shop or far away? What kinds of community services do people depend on — garbage, telephone, television, and so on? What kinds of businesses exist in the community? What kinds of industries?

This discussion may lead to developing a list of problems and issues that are important in your community. Students are usually sufficiently aware of and involved in their community to develop a sophisticated list. Write student suggestions on the board, delaying discussion of individual items until everyone has had a chance to make these items. Discussion should include suggestions for how things might be improved in the community. Concentrate on obtaining specific proposals.

This activity can culminate in a letter-writing campaign. If the class chooses to write letters about the issues identified as most important, students can write to the newspaper to publicize the issue and propose remedies. They can also write to the people or groups considered to have some responsibility for clearing up the problem.

A Community Guidebook

What kinds of things do students know about their community? How would they describe it to visitors? What do they think visitors might want to know about it?

Talk about the different elements that make up the community, such as people, services, places, history, and customs. Who might arrive in the community and need information? Have any students recently moved into the area? What did they have to find out? Talk about different types of visitors (including new arrivals), their reasons for coming, and the kind of information they would require. For example, if a family with young children moved into the area, they would want to know about schools, playgrounds, inexpensive places to eat with kids, and so on.

Decide what to include in your guidebook by determining who could benefit most from it. If there are other guidebooks to your area, examine them to discover what they have and have not included.

Divide students into small groups. Each group can take responsibility for a section of the book. They must decide among themselves how best to present this information (a list, description, story, illustration, etc.). Each student should have the opportunity to contribute something. Include other work done by students related to the community, such as the maps suggested in a previous activity.

When the groups have finished, their efforts can be assembled into a book that everyone will be proud of. You can have it duplicated for the parents, or even consider having it reproduced professionally and distributed by a local group such as the Chamber of Commerce.

Community History

Each community has its own history, reflecting the contributions of the various groups that comprise it. The history of the development of the community may reflect a mini-history of the state, or it may represent idiosyncratic development. In either case, students can learn a lot about the forces that formed this country by studying the example of their own community.

What is history? Talk about the idea of history. More than just a list of past presidents, history deals with events and their consequences, change, and the influence of the past on the present. Ask students why we would want to study history. Have them brainstorm a list of reasons and objectives for studying local history. What do they want to find out? The students might pose some of the following questions:

- Who was here first?
- What happened to them?
- Why did they come?
- What traces have they left behind?
- What did this area look like then?
- How did people live?

Next, talk about where the students would go to find the information they are seeking. Have students suggest as many different sources as possible. They might mention the following:

- Visit the local library
- Interview people who have lived here a long time
- Read old newspapers
- Review city records (archives) — maybe old maps?

The results of student research can be compiled in a booklet that is organized according to the questions the students asked, with the answers they found. This information would also be interesting to the community, so you might look into having it reproduced on a larger scale.

A Local Language Survey

Do students know what languages are spoken in their area? Begin with local names. What languages have influenced local names? Ask families. What languages are spoken in the students' families? Do students know people who speak different languages?

Make a map or chart of the area on which to record the information students find. Have them research local history to see what the earliest languages were. Were there any Native American groups living nearby? What language did they speak and what happened to them? What do names of local places mean in these languages? Ask who the first settlers were and what languages they brought with them. Trace the language history down to the present time. Students should be able to discover what the major local language groups are and how long their speakers have been in the area.

Once the major languages are identified, this can become an important resource for further study. Plan lessons around examples from these languages. Bring people in who speak various languages so that students can hear what the languages sound like.

Sister Cities

Does your town have a sister city? If it does, find out what you can about the sister city — how it was chosen, what kinds of people live there, what the children like to do. Students can make up a research team to investigate topics of particular interest, such as food, hobbies, and clothing. If your town doesn't have a sister city, find out if you can informally adopt a city, school, or class.

Your students may be able to become pen pals with students of the same age in another country. Students in many countries are studying English and they would welcome a chance to practice by writing to others their own age.

Interviewing

Investigating your community's history can turn into a year-long project if students decide to find out more information by interviewing people about their past. As students define questions they would like to have answered, they can begin to create a list of people who might know the answers. Brainstorm a list of possible interviewees. Have students tell everyone they know about the project in order to identify more names of people to interview. Questions they might ask include:

- How long have you lived here?
- What was this town like when you first came?
- Where did you live when you were a child about my age?
- What was school like for you at that time?

Discuss what an interview is. What does the interviewer do? What is the interviewee supposed to do? Decide what questions you want to ask. Decide how you will record the information. (Tape recorder, notes on paper?) Prepare an interview schedule.

The most important aspect of this activity is the process that students go through, so the task should be carefully adapted to suit the level of the students. Students will come into contact with a different group of people (older people) and they will learn about people who are similar to and yet different from themselves. Children not only gain information related to social studies through this technique but they also use language abilities. Both oral and written skills are developed as they conduct the interview, report back to the class, and record the results for a class book.

An English teacher in an Appalachian community developed the study of oral history to such an extent that his students have published several collections of their writings, first published in 1972. Your students would be interested in reading some of the interviews. Edited by Eliot Wigginton, these attractive paperbound books can be found in most bookstores: *Foxfire 1, 2, 3, 4, 5, 6* (Doubleday Anchor Books; current volume is 9, 1986). This group also publishes a newsletter, *Foxfire,* Rabun Gap, GA 30568. Also see *There Are So Many Things I Wish I'd Asked My Father: An Authentic Oral History of Truckee, California,* edited by Candy Carter (available from Learning Opportunities, Box 2466, Truckee, CA 95734).

A Community Time Line

A time line can help students organize the information they have discovered about their community. Make a list of all the various dates, events, and historical periods that are important to your study of the community. Transfer this list, in chronological order, to a line drawn across several sheets of butcher paper. This can become a class mural as students add to the time line and update it. You can also have students draw or cut out illustrations for significant historical events.

Making a Personal Time Line

As students learn more about the concept of history and the history of their community, they can transfer this understanding to their personal history. Have students draw a time line, beginning with their birth. On it, they are to locate four or five dates or periods that are important to them personally, such as the birth of a brother or sister, a new pet, an illness, or moving to a new school. Talk about why these events were important. How did the students feel at the time? How would their life have been different if this event had not happened? Sometimes, knowing that other students have been through the same experience makes it easier to cope with painful memories or consequences.

Talk about the future. How do the students see themselves five years from now? Ten years? Have students write a description of themselves and their life, as they imagine it, five years in the future. Encourage students to be creative, since there is no "right" answer.

Personalizing History

When students compare their own time lines with that of their community, they can begin to see the connections between historical events and what has happened to them. What was happening in the community when they were born? Have them ask their parents, if appropriate, what they remember from that time. Students can also look up the front page of the local newspaper for their birthdate to see what people were thinking and talking about. Then they can report to the class on the significant events of the day that was most significant to them.

What has happened in the community and the world since the students were born? Using the time line they developed for their community and researching important inventions and world events, they can construct a list of the most significant happenings of the past ten years, more or less. (Opinions on what to include may vary among the students.) Now have students discuss and write about how these events affected them and their family. How has the world changed since they were born? How is it the same?

DISCOVERING DIFFERENT GROUPS IN THE UNITED STATES

This country is composed of many different racial, ethnic, an religious groups, from large, well-recognized groups like the Amish to the less well-known Hmong. Large or small, newcomers or longtime residents, all of these groups contribute to the diversity that distinguishes the United States. If you walk down the streets of any major city today, you will receive graphic evidence of the presence of different groups, in the sounds, signs, languages, faces, and objects that surround you.

But the picture of our country that students receive in school does not reflect this world when it emphasizes the presence and contributions only of specific groups. The children that the students read about in books often inhabit an idealized, mythical world of families with two parents and two children, a boy and a girl, who live in a nice house on a tree-shaded street. And the history that students learn is usually that of the white, English-speaking settlement of this continent. Students who come from other groups need the chance to learn that there are people in this country like themselves. In fact, all students need the opportunity to discover the rich variety of our population.

Write an "Autobiography"

As students find out more about the history of their community and their origins, they can personalize their study by researching and writing an autobiography of an imagined ancestor. Tell the class to choose a period and decide what their ancestors might have been doing then—arriving in America, pioneering the West, struggling in a city or on a farm. Students will need to read books, both fiction and nonfiction, to supply information on how people lived as well as the position or treatment of groups in that period. Their autobiographies can take the form of a day in their character's life, several journal entries, or a description of the influences on that person. They can also illustrate their account and read it to the class.

Foreign-Born Americans

Many people that we think of as Americans were actually born in another country. Ask students if they recognize any of the following names: John James Audubon, Alexander Graham Bell, Albert Einstein, or John Muir.

Discuss how many people from other countries became known as Americans. The class can maintain a list of names of foreign-born Americans that they discover as they read. Many early citizens of our country were, of course, born in other countries; for example, Thomas Paine. A source of more information is *The People's Almanac Presents the Book of Lists* compiled by David Wallechinsky et al. (Morrow, 1977).

Citizenship

Are all the students in your class citizens? Some may not be citizens or some may know others who are not citizens. Students may not know that you can live and work in this country without being a citizen, or that you can be born and live in another country yet still be a citizen of this country. People born in U.S. possessions such as American Samoa are not citizens but U.S. nationals. They may apply for citizenship after they come to the mainland U.S.

What does citizenship mean? Why would people want to become citizens of another country? Discuss with students the advantages, disadvantages, rights, and responsibilities of being a citizen. How does one become a citizen? What are the requirements? Has anyone in the class been to a swearing-in ceremony? What is it and why is it important? Should *everyone* have to pass a test to become a citizen? Invite an immigration lawyer, a representative from the Naturalization Office, or a new citizen to speak to the class about becoming a citizen.

Names on the Map

The names of places on a map are souvenirs of our past. They can tell us who first settled in an area and what they found there. Look at a map with your students. Where do the local place names come from? What language do they represent: English, Spanish, French, Sioux, Tagalog, or another language? What can we conclude from this? Find out where the names come from and what they mean. *Names on the Map,* by George Stewart, is a classic resource for this study.

This lesson can be used to show the diversity of cultures that have combined to make up this country and how the past continues to influence us today.

Tossed Salad vs. Melting Pot

America is a Tossed Salad!

These expressions are two *metaphors* used to describe our country. Write each metaphor on the board and ask students what each phrase makes them think of. Write their ideas under the headings. Talk about metaphors. What are they are why are they used? What are the implications of using the metaphor *tossed salad* rather than *melting pot*? Have students try to apply the terms to their class. Which one do they feel is more appropriate, or are both accurate?

Life in a Relocation Camp

It is important not to forget what Americans have done to other Americans of a different race, even in our recent history. Students can learn to appreciate what many Japanese American children of their own age went through in this country in the 1940s. Several books describe life in a relocation camp, where large groups of families were imprisoned for several years, and the effect that this period had on children and the Japanese American community.

Florence Means. *The Moved-Outers.* Houghton Mifflin, 1945.

Takashima. *A Child in a Prison Camp.* Morrow, 1971.

Jeanne Houston. *Farewell to Manzanar.* Houghton Mifflin, 1973.

Daniel Davis. *Behind Barbed Wire; the Imprisonment of Japanese Americans during World War II.* Dutton, 1982.

Yoshiko Uchida. *Journey to Topaz.* Scribner's, 1971.

Read passages from one of these books to the class. If you have time, read the whole book. Afterwards, discuss the students' reactions to the book. They can discuss how they would feel going to a camp, what the people guarding the camp thought about their prisoners, whether this could happen again today, or what the people thought about the United States when they were released from the camp.

Have students write a letter to a friend, as if they lived in one of the camps, describing their life in the camp, or write a diary entry, telling what they do everyday and how they feel.

Intergenerational Relations

A very different kind of grouping in our society is the elderly. An indication of our confusion over how to treat this group is the variety of labels used to identify the group. Ask students if they know anyone who is "older." Perhaps a grandparent or other older relative is living with their family. What do we call these people? Some of the labels that have been used include: senior citizen, aged, mature adult, retirees, third agers. Which would students rather be called when they are old?

Talk about the aging process. What are the advantages and disadvantages of getting old? What happens to old people in our society who can't take care of themselves? Have students discuss and write how they would like their life to be at ages sixty and seventy-five.

Today, when many students have limited contact with people much older than themselves, they can read books about relationships between young people and old people, such as the following:

Tomie De Paola. *Nana Upstairs and Nana Downstairs.* Putnam, 1973.

Sharon Mathis. *The Hundred Penny Box.* Viking, 1975.

Cynthia Rylant. *Miss Maggie.* Dutton, 1983.

Wendy Kesselman. *Emma.* Doubleday, 1980.

Charlotte Zolotow. *My Grandson Lew.* Harper & Row, 1974.

Deborah Gould. *Grandpa's Slide Show.* Lothrop, Lee & Shepard, 1987.

What Do You Think?

Prepare a poster like this to stimulate a discussion of prejudice:

> **ECIDUJERP**
> No matter how you look at it,
> it still spells PREJUDICE!

Exploring Regions and Cultures

Throughout our country there are pockets of people who share a unique background and culture. Challenge students to discover such groups as the following: Amish, Pennsylvania Dutch, Mennonites, Creoles, Hudderites, Mormons.

They will discover a variety of interesting ideas, living patterns, and contributions. For example, the Pennsylvania Dutch have developed an attractive and distinctive style of art. They share such folk songs as the following with us:

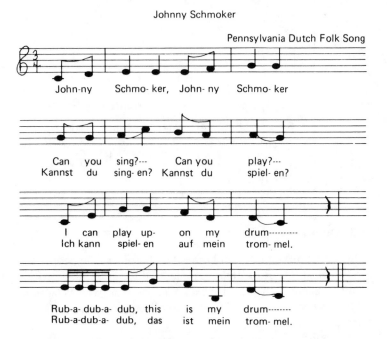

Johnny Schmoker

Pennsylvania Dutch Folk Song

John-ny   Schmo-ker, John-ny   Schmo-ker

Can   you   sing?---   Can you   play?---
Kannst   du   sing-en? Kannst   du   spiel-en?

I   can   play up-   on   my   drum----------
Ich kann   spiel-en   auf mein   trom-mel.

Rub-a-dub-a-dub, this   is   my   drum--------
Rub-a-dub-a-dub, das   ist   mein   trom-mel.

Find out how the Amish live by reading Merle Good's *Nicole Visits an Amish Farm* (Walker, 1983).

Special Centers

Feature specific groups around the room in centers at which students can work independently. Let children suggest groups that might reflect their own group membership; for example:

- Black Americans
- Teenagers in America
- Puerto Ricans in New York City
- The problems faced by people in Texas

Many of the ideas described in this book will be useful in developing such centers. Check the index for information about specific groups and refer to Chapter 8 for information about making centers and materials for individualized approaches.

Let students develop the centers with an aide as a resource person. You can suggest, for example, that they make a set of large task cards. Providing samples that they can copy will be helpful, for example:

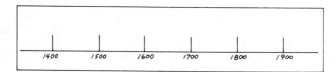

MAKING A TIME LINE

Collect information about significant events that happened in Puerto Rico. Make a time line on a long strip of paper like this:

1400	1500	1600	1700	1800	1900

Mark the events that happened above the date. Illustrate your time line in the space above the date.
Where can you find the information you need?

We Are All Americans

Focus attention not only on heroes and heroines, the people whose names are well-known, but also on ordinary people of different ethnic groups who make up this country. Prepare a display, for example, based on Walt Whitman's well-known poem, "I Hear America Singing," from the collection *Leaves of Grass*. Use the title of the poem as a caption.

Around the poem display pictures of Americans at work. Include members of different ethnic groups as well as people performing nonstereotyped jobs, such as a woman working on lines for the telephone company or a black father caring for his children.

Varied Religions

Because Christian holidays have become heavily commercialized, it becomes easy to overemphasize them in the classroom. Help your students recognize that there are many religions represented in the United States. Encourage students to become familiar with varied beliefs that may or may not be those of students in the classroom. The following books will help:

> Malka Drucker. *Shabbat: A Peaceful Island*. Holiday House, 1983.
>
> Kathleen Elgin. *The Mormons; The Church of Jesus Christ of Latter-Day Saints*. McKay, 1969.
>
> Kathleen Elgin. *The Quakers: The Religious Society of Friends*. McKay, 1968.
>
> Larry Kettelkamp. *Religions, East and West*. Morrow, 1972.
>
> Susan G. Purdy. *Jewish Holidays; Facts, Activities, and Crafts*. Lippincott, 1969.
>
> Elizabeth Seeger. *Eastern Religions*. Crowell, 1973.

Invite guests to the classroom to talk briefly about a specific religion—a rabbi, a priest, a protestant minister (a woman?).

Recognizing Contributions of Others

Focus on broad topics that make it possible to observe the contributions of people from many ethnic groups. Consider such subjects as the following:

- Art through the Ages
- Folklore and Mythology
- Foods of the World
- The Urban Environment

Within such studies students will learn that cultures have their distinctive qualities and contributions. Students will discover the universals of art as well as folklore and mythology. They will also discover such human needs as eating and the problems of living together.

City Life

Urban living is a broad topic that encompasses many subjects of interest to those who live in the city as well as those who live in suburban or rural settings. As the subject of city living is explored, an important element to consider is the multiethnic population. Explore books such as the following about people living in the city:

> Rachel Isadora. *City Seen from A to Z*. Greenwillow, 1983.

Martha Munzer and John Vogel, Jr. *New Towns: Building Cities from Scratch.* Knopf, 1974.

Robert A. Liston. *The Ugly Palaces: Housing in America.* Watts, 1974.

An excellent bibliography that might be helpful is *What Is a City? A Multimedia Guide on Urban Living* edited by Rose Moorachian and published by the Boston Public Library.

Poetry of the City

Share poems about city living as another way of exploring. A useful collection for younger children is *A Song in Stone: City Poems,* compiled by Lee Bennett Hopkins (Crowell, 1983). A collection for upper elementary and junior high level is *On City Streets,* selected by Nancy Larrick (Bantam, 1969).

Writing City Poems

Children can write city poems, too. Begin with the words: *A city is . . . .* Collectively or individually, children can add phrases like this to form an unrhymed poem:

A city is . . .
Horns honking—
Red lights,
Green Lights—
Traffic on the go!

A city is . . .
People walking—
Down the street,
Up the street—
People everywhere.

Sharing What You Have Learned

An activity such as the following is an effective way to finish a unit of study. Students can present their work to the class and explain what they did.

MAKE A COLLAGE

Make a collage about a group of people in the United States

Native Americans	Women
City Dwellers	Black Americans
Aged Men and Women	Children
Workers	Drivers

Clip words and pictures to picture this group. Glue everything on a large piece of cardboard at least 18″ × 24″ in size.

LIVING IN A GLOBAL VILLAGE

Viewed from outer space, most of the earth's surface is composed of water. The people who live on land obviously must band together to share the resources and survive. There are no lines that mark national or other political boundaries, and the weather patterns shift without regard for religion, language, and race. Yet on earth itself, the perspective is often different and for many people, their country is the center of their universe. But as the world changes rapidly and becomes "smaller," students need to be prepared to grow up in a global village, recognizing the presence and interdependence of others. As we adapt our teaching to these changing demands, we help students discover themselves as they learn more about others in other lands. Economics, history, and culture are not abstract concepts but immediate practical influences on how we and others behave now and in the future.

Ideas in Common

Proverbs make fascinating study, especially if you compare those that say much the same thing in different words. In the United States we often hear the saying: "Actions speak louder than words." The same idea is expressed in proverbs from other countries, such as:

- Talk does not cook rice. (China)
- It is one thing to cackle and another to lay an egg. (Ecuador)
- Fancy words don't butter cabbage. (Germany)

Challenge your students to write this saying in still different ways. They might suggest, for instance:

- Laudable behavior indicates true brain power.
- The big wind only blows down the wheat!

Topic for Thought

Discuss the accompanying Chinese proverb. Have students notice the progression from *right* to *peace*. Students can discuss the importance of peace and how it can be brought about.

This poetic presentation can also be used as a model for student writing. They can follow this pattern:

If there is _____,
There will be _____.

Two-line free verse poems can be produced like this:

If there is prejudice anywhere,
There will be unhappiness.

Repeating this pattern produces additional verses. The verses could be rhymed, thus:

If there is one friend in your life,
There will be singing.
If there is love in your life,
There will be joy-bells ringing.

If there is right in the soul,
There will be beauty in the person;
If there is beauty in the person,
There will be harmony in the home;
If there is harmony in the home,
There will be order in the nation;
If there is order in the nation,
There will be peace in the world.

Chinese Proverb

International Treasure Hunt

What kinds of products do we buy from other countries? Ask if students know where everything in their house comes from. Have them go home and make a list of all the things they can find that come from another country. (They will have to read labels, look at the bottoms of objects, or ask their family.) Give a prize to the student who has listed the greatest number of different countries.

You can also ask students to locate objects from a specific country you are studying; for example, Mexico. Or you can give older students the challenge of accumulating points for each product or country by a certain deadline.

Where Does It Come From?

Who invented the products we take for granted in our daily lives? Have students brainstorm a lengthy list of familiar objects, such as the telephone, television, car, bicycle, eyeglasses, electric light bulb, paper, and so on. Each student can choose a different object or process to research (by checking an encyclopedia or reading a book in the library). Where did these ideas come from? What person or culture first invented them? If we don't know the origin of something, why is that?

When students have finished their research, have them report back to the class.

Discuss the results. What is the most surprising information they found? Did they predict which items were most recent and which were ancient? Did they realize how many products and ideas come from other countries and cultures? The results can be assembled in the form of a multiple-choice quiz, showing the multicultural diversity of our daily lives.

World Travelers

One way to find out more about a country and its people is to plan an imaginary trip there. A trip can be a focus for many lessons as students write for travel brochures, consult airline fares and schedules, research weather and seasonal variations, locate major cities on the map, and learn new vocabulary.

First, students should prepare an itinerary, based on their interests and investigations. Then show a film, filmstrip, or slide show about the country. Students can write a journal of the trip, describing the sights they saw and their reaction, as well as including the information they learned in preparation.

A Look at Language

When studying another country, take the opportunity to introduce students to another language. Students can quickly learn a few words and phrases such as *please, thank you, hello,* and *good-bye.* Display samples of writing in the language, particularly if the writing system is unusual. Students will enjoy examining copies of familiar books written in the foreign language. You can locate dictionaries of most common languages in the public library. A good book for students is *Picnic: How Do You Say It in English, French, Spanish, Italian,* by Meredith Dunham (Lothrop, Lee, Shepard, 1987). Also see Chapter 6.

Living in Other Countries

One of the best ways for students to experience what it is like to live in different countries is to read books about children of their own age who have traveled to a different country or who are growing up in another country. Here are some books you can suggest.

Books about Childhood in Another Country

Egypt: Betsy Byars. *The 18th Emergency.* Viking, 1973.

England: Lucy Boston. *The Children of Green Knowe.* Harcourt Brace Jovanovich, 1955.

England: Mabel Alan. *A Dream of Hunger Moss.* Dodd, 1983.

Greece: William Mayne. *The Glass Ball.* Dutton, 1962.

Netherlands: Meindert DeJong. *The Wheel on the School.* Harper & Row, 1954.

Soviet Union: E.M. Almedingen. *The Crimson Oak.* Coward, 1983.

Spain: Maia Wojciechowska. *Shadow of a Bull.* Atheneum, 1964.

Books about American Children Living in Other Countries

China: Jean Fritz. *Homesick: My Own Story.* Putnam, 1982.

France: Carol Ryrie Brink. *Family Sabbatical.* Viking, 1956.

Italy: Leo Politi. *Little Leo.* Scribner's, 1951.

Lebanon: Belle D. Rugh. *Crystal Mountain.* Houghton Mifflin, 1955.

A Visitor

After reading a book about children in another country, students can pretend to be someone from that country visiting the United States for the first time. What do they think would be their first impressions? What would be strange? What would they like or dislike? What might they not understand? Students can discuss their ideas and then write a brief account of their "visit."

What Others Believe

Invite students to share with the class some of their religious beliefs, if any. Since stereotypes and prejudice are fed by ignorance, open discussion will aid in accepting and understanding different beliefs. Almost every Jewish child has seen a Christmas tree but how many non-Jewish children have seen a *dredl*? Mormon children are sometimes taunted by those outside their faith because of misconceptions about Mormonism.

An investigation of different religions can focus on the importance of symbols and the universal themes. For example, the cross takes different forms in different religions. What do the different shapes mean? What does the cross represent? Another common symbol is the star. What are some religions that use a star? What does the star mean?

A discussion of symbols should include examples that students would be familiar with from their daily lives. In talking about the power of an object to represent many

different objects, ideas, and feelings, students' suggestions may range from corporate insignias to road signs.

Making Sense out of Population Figures

How many people live in the world today? Have students guess and write their estimates on the board. Did anyone come close to 4.8 billion? (Source: "World Population Data Sheet," Population Reference Bureau, 1984.) Such a large number has virtually no meaning to most of us unless we can express it in familiar terms. Research some comparative figures. How many people live in your city? How many live in the state? What's the population of the United States?

Explore different strategies to represent the relative sizes of the population of the United States and the world. Students can make pie charts or block graphs. Another technique is to choose a small object such as a book, pencil, or apple to represent a fixed number (1,000, for example). How many books would it take to show the population of your city, state, country, the world? Demonstrations like this help students to understand and visualize large numbers and the relation between thousands, millions, and billions.

Studying Population: Demography

Ask students if they know what a demographer does. Can they figure it out on the basis of the roots *demo* and *graph*? (Think of other words that have these roots in them.) Reward the first student who uses the meanings of the roots to come up with a definition close to "one who measures population and its characteristics."

Challenge students to become *demographers* and find out how fast the population is growing. Has the rate of growth changed over time? Compare the growth rate in this century with the past century. What does this growth rate predict for the next ten years? Twenty years? Some areas are growing at different rates. How will the composition of the world change in the next ten years? Twenty years? What about age? How will the percentage of old and young people change over the next ten years? Why will this change? What effects might this have on all of us?

Dance — A Universal Language

Dance is something that is shared and understood around the world. Demonstrate the universality of dance and its themes by showing films of dancing performed by different cultures. Here are a few examples:

African Rhythms. 13 minutes, color. Associated Film, Inc., 1621 Dragon St., Dallas, TX 75207.

The Strollers. 6 minutes, color. The Moiseyev Dance Company in a Russian folk dance.

Dancer's World. 30 minutes. NET. Martha Graham discusses dancing as her students dance the emotions of hope, fear, joy, and love.

Different Rhythms for Movement

Encourage students to move to various rhythms by playing recordings of music from different countries around the world. Representative records available include:

Authentic Afro-Rhythms. LP 6060, Kimbo Educational, P.O. Box 246, Deal, NJ 07723. Rhythms from Africa, Cuba, Haiti, Brazil, Trinidad, Puerto Rico.

Authentic Indian Dances and Folklore. Kimbo Educational. Drumming and storytelling by Michigan Chippewa chiefs who narrate history of dances.

Authentic Music of the American Indians. 3 records. Everest. Chesterfield Music Shops, Inc., 12 Warren St., New York, NY 10007.

The Lark in the Morning: Songs and Dances from the Irish Countryside. Everest.

The REAL Flamenco. Everest.

Folk Music from around the World

Folk songs from other countries offer immediate enjoyment with their patterned verses and easy-to-learn choruses. You will find listings for recorded songs from Mexico, the British Isles, France, and many other countries in the catalogs of Caedmon and Folkways.

Learning from Others

Students will appreciate what other cultures have to offer when they learn to make something new. Students can practice craft techniques such as *origami* (from Japan) and *ojos de Dios* (from Latin America). UNICEF is an excellent source of ideas and information about children's games, crafts, and activities in other countries. Write: U.S. Committee for UNICEF, 331 E. 38th St., New York, NY 10016.

Human Needs

Looking at other cultures can help students learn more about themselves and their culture. After you have been studying a particular group of people, or reading tales from several cultures, ask students to list the most basic needs they think are common to all cultures. Focus on the fundamental human needs for love, food, and shelter. Relate these to students' lives. How are these provided for in their lives? How do different groups satisfy them?

Students can brainstorm examples of how different people respond to one need, such as *love.* Then they can write personal responses, completing the sentence "Love is . . ." and illustrate their ideas. As a class, students can prepare a collage for the bulletin board, showing how different needs are met in different cultures, based on their own illustrations or examples they have found.

BLACK AMERICANS:
OUR LARGEST MINORITY

A large, significant part of the history of this country is the story of Black Americans: how they came here and what they did. Yet this group is rarely acknowledged in historical or contemporary accounts, except for discussions of specific race-related issues such as slavery and civil rights. Even today with more Blacks seen and heard on the mass media, a truly integrated picture of this country is still not being presented. We need to continue to make a conscious effort to discover and recognize the presence and contribution of this major group to the identity of this country.

Famous Black Americans

Students need to hear about black men and women who have made contributions in areas other than sports and music. Challenge students to match these names with their contribution.

__C__	Matthew Henson	A. astronomer
__A__	Benjamin Banneker	B. first person killed in Boston Massacre
__D__	Charles Drew	(Rev. War)
__B__	Crispus Attucks	C. went to North Pole with Admiral Peary
__G__	Shirley Chisholm	D. invented blood transfusions
__E__	Phyllis Wheatley	E. poet in colonial America
__F__	Harriet Tubman	F. led slaves to freedom
		G. first female Black in Congress

Once students realize the number of Blacks who have been recognized for their accomplishments, they will want to discover more names and find out more information about these people. Start a chart on the bulletin board where students can write the name of an achiever or someone to admire, and the reason. Students will be motivated to seek out names of historical figures, as well as people they know and respect today. *Profiles of Black Americans,* by Richard Boning (Dexter and Westbrook, 1969), is an excellent source of more information. Also see listing in the Appendix.

Does Negro Mean Black?

Does it make any difference what a group is called? Most people must think so since they make such a point of it. What are some of the labels that Blacks have used or have had applied to them? Put a list on the board; for example:

Black Americans	Negroes
Afro-Americans	African Americans
Blacks	Colored

Can students put these labels in historical order from the oldest to the most recent? Discuss how they made their decisions. What are the relative positive and negative qualities of each label? What does each one focus on? Talk about each label and how it originated. Do students know that *negro* means the color *black* in Spanish? *Colored* is still used in South Africa and Great Britain to refer to non-whites, which includes people from India. *African* is used to connote pride in African origins, though Blacks have been in this country for so long that they bear small resemblance to native Africans.

Which label do students think is the most positive? Which would they prefer to use for themselves? Ask them to suggest alternative labels. Have students vote on their favorite. They can write a brief explanation of why they prefer the one they chose.

Children's Books by Black Authors

Include in your classroom reading collection a selection of books featuring Blacks. Books by black authors that portray Blacks in familiar human situations give the message that Blacks *can,* show an acceptance of Blacks as a group with a special culture and history, and portray Blacks in all their human diversity. The following authors have written many outstanding books:

Virginia Hamilton. *Willie Bea and the Time the Martians Landed.* Greenwillow, 1983.

Mildred D. Taylor. *Let the Circle Be Unbroken.* Dial, 1981.

John Steptoe. *Mufaro's Beautiful Daughters.* Lothrop, 1987.

Sticks and Stones

Does name-calling really hurt? Ask any victim. Children are especially vulnerable to unthinking taunts. As a teacher, you can help students recognize the harmful effect of name-calling. Invite students to produce a list of all the epithets they can think of, from *Fatty* to *Honky.* Be sure to include names you have heard them use, as well as racial or ethnic labels they may hear around them. Putting these names on the board in "print" defuses some of their power to hurt.

Now you can have a serious discussion of how the children would feel if someone said this to them and how name-calling really only reflects on the speaker. Talk about alternative ways to express anger.

You can use this method to lighten potential tensions in a heterogeneous classroom or when students begin to taunt a "different" student, spreading name-calling through ignorance. Use roleplaying to help students experience reality and to try out new ways of dealing with difficult situations.

Black English in Books

Many contemporary writers attempt to reproduce the sound of Black English (BE) in their books. Some just include black slang and others incorporate both vocabulary and grammatical features of BE. Unfortunately, no written version can accurately portray spoken BE, just as standard spoken English is very different from written English. However, these books have the advantage of sounding more familiar to BE speakers and are sometimes easier to read than standard English. They also are important for introducing other students to BE because the context makes the meaning of unfamiliar words and constructions clear.

Read passages from some of the following books to the class and discuss the language used. How do students feel? Does it sound realistic or familiar? Do they understand what the people are saying? Why would someone want to write like that?

Brenda Wilkinson. *Ludell.* Harper & Row, 1975.

Eloise Greenfield. *There She Come Bringing Me That Little Baby Girl.* Lippincott, 1974.

Virginia Hamilton. *Sweet Whispers, Brother Rush.* Philomel, 1982.

John Steptoe. *Train Ride.* Harper & Row, 1971.

John Shearer. *I Wish I Had an Afro.* Cowles, 1970.

See Chapter 6 for more information about the structure of Black English. Also note that some Blacks don't speak Black English and many Blacks can switch among several varieties of English.

A Book to Read Aloud

An excellent book for grades 3–8 is *Sound of Sunshine, Sound of Rain* by Florence P. Heide (Parents' Magazine Press, 1970). This book is outstanding in both content and the beautiful illustrations by Kenneth Longtemps. The story of a young black boy who is blind offers these possibilities for activities and discussion:

- Understanding of a handicapped person
- Some grasp of attitudes toward "color"
- Examples of imagery—similes and metaphors
- Development of plot and characterization
- The family interaction
- Sensory experiences
- Art ideas
- Different points of view
- Discussion of dreams
- Personal feelings

Poetry by Black Poets

How many students know the names of any black poets? Students may be surprised to learn that there are famous male and female black poets. Share with the class poems such as "Motto" by Langston Hughes and "We Real Cool" by Gwendolyn Brooks. Both of these poems make especially effective use of "street" language.

As you discuss the poems, ask students why the poets chose to use this kind of language. The poems don't read like conventional poetry — can we still call them poems? Are they written to be read silently or aloud? Using these poems as models, students will be motivated to write poems based on their experience, with familiar words and rhythms.

Have students look for other examples of this kind of poem or for more poetry by the same poets.

Images of Blacks in Advertising

The portrayal of Blacks and other ethnic groups in advertising has changed considerably over time as public consciousness and protests have increased. Also, as various groups developed more economic power, they were pictured in more positive ways. In any case, advertising has always been an excellent weathervane of public opinion.

In the 1960s, the picture of *Aunt Jemima* on pancake mix boxes enraged many radicals because of its demeaning associations. Since then, her picture has gone from the "fat, smiling servant" to an "average middle-class matron."

Students can study how a particular group is shown in advertising and what message is being communicated. Have students bring in ads that show pictures of Blacks, from package labels or magazines, for example. What information do these images convey? What kinds of Blacks are shown (age, color, etc.)? What are they wearing? What are they doing? Discuss whether or not students think this advertising promotes stereotypes or realistic images. If students feel strongly about what they find, encourage them to write a letter to the product manufacturer or the publisher, expressing their opinions.

After discussing how advertising influences people, students will want to compose advertising of their own. They can choose to illustrate the same product or each pick a favorite place, product, or service. Post these on the bulletin board as an excellent example of what students think would really appeal to people.

Slavery and the Underground Railroad

The period of slavery is only four generations away, yet its lessons are worth repeating. How could a group of people, mostly illiterate and supposedly stupid and uncivilized, manage to escape in great numbers into freedom? Students will want to research this period, especially the Underground Railroad. Why did they call it *underground*?

Put a map of the United States on the board. Which were the slave states and which the free states? Have students trace the paths by which slaves could escape to freedom (to the North, frequently later to Canada, and also to the Bahamas, since they were British, and therefore, free). How far would slaves have to travel and how long would it take? What motivated people to risk such a long, difficult journey into unknown territory?

Since they couldn't read maps or directions, one way people found their way North was to follow the North Star. Sing the song "Follow the Drinking Gourd," which commemorates the advice passed among slaves to watch for the Big Dipper and follow the direction it pointed.

Research the history of the Underground Railroad in your area, if possible. Are there any remains or memories of stations where slaves were directed and hidden? Helping slaves escape was illegal and especially dangerous in the South, yet all kinds of people (northerners, southerners, Indians, Quakers, Canadians, British, free Blacks, and other slaves) risked their own lives. Why would people do something for which they could be arrested or killed?

Read a biography of Harriet Tubman, who inspired respect in all who met her. Called the Moses of her people, she escaped to the North but returned countless times to lead others to freedom.

For more information, see:

Charles L. Blockson. "The Underground Railroad." In *National Geographic,* July 1984.

Students can read books set in the period of slavery to find out more about what it was like to live then. The following are some suggested titles:

James Lincoln Collier and Christopher Collier. *War Comes to Willy Freeman.* Delacorte, 1983.

Virginia Hamilton. *The Magical Adventures of Pretty Pearl.* Harper, 1983.

Belinda Hurmence. *A Girl Called Boy.* Houghton, 1982.

Anne Petry. *Tituba of Salem Village.* Cromwell, 1974.

Exploring Africa

Africa still holds a fascination due to its size, diversity, and long history. From Marcus Garvey to the establishment of Zimbabwe, Africa has exerted a powerful hold on the imaginations of American Blacks. Bring Africa into the classroom through stories, music, games, and pictures.

Put a map of Africa on the board. Can students name any of the countries? How big is it compared to the United States? To your state? What different languages are spoken on this continent? Why would some countries use English for their official language and others use French? These are languages they have to learn in school. Why don't they use the language they learn at home?

Talk about the diversity of Africa. What do the people look like? Display pictures to show the population: Arabs, South African whites, Asians (Indians), different black African tribes. Locate these groups on the map. A reference book that students can use is *African Countries and Cultures: A Concise Illustrated Dictionary* by Jane Hornburger and Alex Whitney (McKay, 1981).

Learn what life is like in the different countries by listening to music and playing games. *African Children's Games,* from Howard University Press (1978), presents six games from West Africa. Caedmon Records has collections of songs from different regions, such as *Songs of the Congo.*

Read stories about children in Africa. The first of several books about a black child in South Africa is Hugh Lewin's *Jafta* (Carolrhoda Books, 1983).

African Tales

All students will enjoy reading stories from various traditional African cultures. They will learn about the lives and values of the major African groups, from Ashanti to Zulu, and compare these cultures with their own.

Most short tales reflect common human problems and traits and are easily adapted to storytelling or creative dramatics. A typical story is *The Vingananee and the Tree Toad,* a Liberian tale retold by Verna Aardema (Warne, 1983).

Or you can read a story aloud and have students illustrate the characters and incidents. A good place to start is *The Crest and the Hide and Other African Stories* by Harold Courlander (Coward McCann, 1982). Not only does the famed collector include a variety of stories but he also offers important background on sources and related tales.

Students can also investigate a particular genre of folktale; for example, the trickster tales exemplified by West African stories about Anansi the spider.

What We Can Learn

After students have read a series of folktales from one culture or region, they will be ready to abstract concepts of human values and behavior from their study and apply them to a comparison of the other culture and their own. How did the people in stories behave? What kinds of problems did they face? Have students compare that to what they and their families would do. Would they have the same problems? What would they do instead? What can we learn from the problems and solutions in these stories that we could apply to our own lives? Students can write examples of similar problem stories, suggesting original solutions.

African Words

When Blacks were first brought to this country as slaves, they spoke many different languages. Because they could not understand each other, it was difficult to preserve their different native languages against the influence of English. It is not surprising, therefore, that few African words were borrowed into English. Even when a word appears to be originally African, it is difficult or impossible to pin down the source language.

Prepare a bulletin board to reflect the African contribution to English. List some of the following:

tote—to carry
jubilant, jubilee (from "juba," a dance)
gumbo
goober—peanut (from "guba")

voodoo
cooter—tortoise (from "kuta")
OK (origin unknown—possibly from yaw kay)
hip—with it
guy—man

Discovering Swahili

Students enjoy learning about another language. Offer them the challenge of learning Swahili, one of the major languages of Africa. Two books that present Swahili for students are:

Muriel Feelings. *Moja Means One*. Dial, 1971.

_____. *Jambo Means Hello*. Dial, 1974.

Have these books available for students to read. Prepare task cards for them to use with the books. Include some of varied difficulty, ranging from matching the words *one* through *ten* with the corresponding Swahili words, to writing a paragraph using as many Swahili words as possible.

A recording of Swahili is also available from Folkways Records: *Jambo and Other Call and Response Songs and Chants* (includes a guide).

REFLECTIONS

In this chapter we have tried to show the individual as the center of a number of concentric circles, growing larger until the circle includes all people. In addition, these circles intersect in different ways, because we all live in communities that include different groups of people and we live in a time of increasing mobility, so that the diversity of our world has become more apparent. Teaching that is based on multicultural principles will help students see that world around them and develop the appropriate strengths to live in this world.

APPLICATIONS

1. Students can identify with others of their own age. Begin to collect resources so that you can present a unit on childhood in other countries, for example. You can include books that describe growing up in a particular country, names of possible speakers who could talk to your class about going to school in other countries, and examples of children's toys or games. (UNICEF is a good source of simple childhood games from different countries.) Identify suitable sources of information in the library so that older students can do their own research on this topic. Finish your unit by considering how you want students to present what they have learned

from this study. Primary students could assemble a notebook of stories, letters, and pictures. Older grades might prepare a dramatization for other classes.

2. Read three to five folktales from a particular region or culture. What can they tell you about the people? Find out more about the history and culture of these people. What themes are repeated in the folktales? What basis do they have in the group's history? Develop a plan for teaching these tales to students. How are universal themes depicted? What cultural values are being promoted? Decide what you expect students to learn from studying these tales. Prepare a folktale for storytelling. *Fairy Tales, Fables, Legends, and Myths: Using Folk Literature in Your Classroom* by Bette Bosma (Teacher's College Press, 1987) is a source of ideas and stories.

3. Develop a booklet of community resources for teaching about a local group. Many excellent sources of multicultural information are available right in your own community. Sometimes an organization has produced a list of possible contacts for materials, resources, or speakers. Your public library may have this information already compiled. If not, begin developing a list of your own. The best place to start is the telephone directory. Look for national organizations that have branches in a big city close to you. For example, names to look for include National Conference of Christians and Jews. Look also under group names to see what services are offered. Try Chicano, American Indian, Mexican American, Native American, La Raza, Black, Afro-American, and so on.

   Another important resource is the local community college or university. Write or call them for information about possible ethnic studies departments or organizations for students of different ethnic backgrounds. Check the catalogs to see whether courses are taught in the history or culture of a particular group that might be of interest to your students. Sometimes the teachers of courses can be of help in locating more materials and information as well as perhaps providing contacts with other people in the community. They might also come to speak to the class.

Endnote

1. Woodrow Wilson, speech given in 1916.

Resources

F. Aboud. *Children and Prejudice*. Blackwell, 1988.

Arnold, Adoff, ed. *Black Out Loud: An Anthology of Modern Poems by Black Americans*. Macmillan, 1970.

Anti-Defamation League of B'nai B'rith. *U.S.A.: A Cultural Mosaic*.

Virginia Olsen Baron, ed. *Here I Am: An Anthology of Poems Written by Young People in Some of America's Minority Groups.* Dutton, 1969.

Nguyen Ngoc Bich, trans., with Burton Raffel and W. S. Merwin. *A Thousand Years of Vietnamese Poetry.* Knopf, 1975.

B. T. Bliatout et al. *Handbook for Teaching Hmong-Speaking Students.* Southeast Asia Community Resource Center, Folsom, CA, 1988.

Shirley Blumenthal. *Coming to America: Immigrants from Eastern Europe.* Delacorte, 1981.

J. M. First and J. W. Carrera. *New Voices: Immigrant Students in U.S. Public Schools.* National Coalition of Advocates for Students, Boston, MA, 1988.

W. J. Lonner and V. O. Tyler. *Cultural and Ethnic Factors in Learning and Motivation.* Western Washington University, 1988.

John Ogbu. "A Cultural Ecology of Competence among Inner-City Blacks." In M. B. Spencer et al., *Beginnings: The Social and Affective Development of Black Children.* Erlbaum, 1985.

G. J. Powell, ed. *The Psychosocial Development of Minority Group Children.* Brunner/Mazel, 1983.

Gladys Nadler Rips. *Coming to America: Immigrants from Southern Europe.* Delacorte, 1981.

Maxine Seller. *Immigrant Women.* Temple University Press, 1980.

Stephen Thernstrom, Ann Orlov, and Oscar Handlin, eds. *Harvard Encyclopedia of American Ethnic Groups.* Harvard University Press, 1980.

Eileen Tway, ed. *Reading Ladders for Human Relations.* American Council on Education, 1983.

Dean Wood. *Multicultural Canada.* The Ontario Institute for Studies in Education, 1978.

FRIENDSHIP FOREVER

6

Discovering Our Linguistic Diversity

View'd freely, the English language is the accretion and growth of every dialect, race, and range of time, and is both the free and compacted composition of all.[1]

Walt Whitman

Preview

After reading this chapter, you should be able to show students:

- That people speak differently depending on what groups they belong to and where they come from.
- There are many varieties of English.
- That many languages are spoken in the United States besides English.
- That language is an essential part of one's identity and culture.
- How to support the student who is learning English as a new language.

Language is all around us yet we are hardly aware of its impact on who we are and what we think. We use language to interpret what we know about the world and we judge others by the language that they speak. Language to teachers often means standards of correctness and grammatical sentence patterns. To politicians, advertisers, and many others, however, language means knowledge of shades of meaning and effective word choice for persuasive purposes. But for language scientists, or linguists, language is a system of oral communication according to conventions established by the speakers of that language.

Our language both creates and limits the world in which we live. Two people can look at something and see it very differently: an English speaker sees a field of "snow," whereas an Eskimo speaker must differentiate many types of snow by choosing words that identify it as hard snow, soft snow, new snow, and so on. A child says, "That's a car," but a mechanic sees a sedan, a roadster, or a convertible. English speakers have words for simple family relations such as aunt/uncle or grandfather/grandmother, but must use "roundabout" phrasing to identify "brother-in-law" and "first cousin once removed," making these relations appear more distant. In contrast, languages like Spanish can identify those relationships with a single word. When we write in English, we have to choose our vocabulary carefully because options such as *paternal* or *fatherly* and *annual* or *yearly*, reflecting our double linguistic heritage from French (Latin) and Germanic sources, carry different connotations. In all these ways, the diversity of language affects how we see our world.

ENGLISH IN ITS INFINITE VARIETY

We may claim that we all speak English, but we know that people who live in another part of our country speak with "an accent." And what about the people who live in England, some of whom we can hardly understand? What language do they speak? When a popular television show from England, "Eastenders," was aired in the United States, broadcasters had to supply a glossary, as the dialogue was virtually incomprehensible to American ears. Comedians use phrases such as *pahk the cah* for *park the car* and their audience immediately recognizes the stereotyped Bostonian. And we may wince when we hear someone say *ain't*, because we know that person has just exposed himself or herself as "uneducated." Few people today realize that the word *ain't* identified polished, well-educated speakers in Britain only seventy years ago.

When we work with students, we want to make sure that we help them recognize the varieties of English that make up their world. We can talk with students about *dialects*: different patterns of English usage based on where you come from (regional dialects) and what group you belong to (social dialects). In New York City, for example, you can hear many regional and social dialects. The "slurred" speech we associate with southerners is another example of a dialect. Differences between the English in Great Britain and the English in the United States are dialect differences, as well. In fact, we all speak a dialect.

We can also talk with students about another kind of language variety, called *register*. Register refers to the fact that every speaker uses the language differently depending on the speech situation. We use different language patterns when we speak "formally" versus "informally," or when we give directions to strangers rather than people we know well. Again, we can draw students' attention to these differences and show how they enrich our language.

Regional Vocabulary Differences

Many common objects have different names in different parts of the country. Early dialectologists (people who investigated regional differences in pronunciation and vocabulary) developed maps that showed the spread of words for particular objects. Conduct a miniature experiment in dialectology and see how many different regional terms you can find. Ask students:

> What do you say to stop a game?
> (time out, times, pax, time, fins)

> What do you call being absent from school?
> (play hookey, ditch, bag school, bolt, lay out, lie out, play truant, skip class, cut school)

> What do you call someone from the country?
> (hayseed, rube, hick, hoosier, yokel, hillbilly, yahoo, moss back, cracker, redneck, sodbuster)

> What do you call a thick sandwich?
> (dagwood, hoagie, submarine, sub, grinder, hero, poor boy)

Have students ask their parents the same questions. If people give different responses, find out where they come from. Discuss the regional patterns you find. Do students from the same area use the same terms? Why or why not? Depending on how many different regions the students represent, can you divide the United States into several main dialect areas?

Students might be interested in seeing dialect atlases that have been prepared. There are atlases for most areas of the United States but the first one ever published, *The Linguistic Atlas of New England* (Hans Kurath), includes many interesting maps. Use these as sources of information on more regional differences in vocabulary and pronunciation.

We All Speak Dialects

It is important for students to realize that we all speak different dialects. Even the most highly educated persons differ in the way they pronounce words. Have students try pronouncing the following words as they compare the varied ways of saying them:

greasy	here	car
bath	dog	get
aunt	because	idea

The wide variation in pronunciation is important to keep in mind and to draw to the attention of students as you work together in the classroom. It is particularly evident as the teacher pronounces spelling words. For words that present obvious difficulty, you might have a student or two pronounce the same word aloud.

Consider particularly the problem of the vowels in Mary, merry, and marry. Some students may pronounce these as three different words. Other students say them as two homonyms or even as three homonyms. Remember to allow for student differences in pronunciation when teaching spelling and reading rules.

Regional Dialects

Practice listening for regional variation with the record *Our Changing Language* (McGraw-Hill) by Evelyn Gott and Raven I. McDavid, Jr. (available from The National Council of Teachers of English, 1111 Kenyon Road, Urbana, IL 61801). On one side of this record there are recordings of high school students reading a story that contains many words that are pronounced differently. Each student is from a different city in the United States, and the speech variation is fascinating. Students who are from these geographic regions will identify their own speech characteristics as they listen.

To demonstrate the difference in speech in your own classroom, have a number of children read the same passage onto a tape. Then play the tape. Discuss what kinds of variations are noted. Which words are pronounced differently?

Have students compare their pronunciations of the following words:

right	bath	were	here
house	child	fire	log
fit	Mary	park	sorry

Stump the Teacher

Encourage student interest in dialect differences or regionalisms by having them collect special words or phrases that they hear around the community. How many can they find that you do not know? How many that other students do not know? Have them report their findings orally, with definitions, for the class, or develop a bulletin board to record information gathered about language in the area. As students discuss their words, ask them who might use which words. Suggest different groupings, such as young people, old people, people new to the community, or members of specific ethnic groups. Use this activity to develop the ideas of speech variation within a community and appropriate speech for different groups.

Strange Dialects

What would English look like if we spelled it the way we talked? For one thing, we would be able to indicate differences in the way people talk, such as dialect differences. Investigate this topic with students. A favorite game is to write definitions of words from a strange dialect. The unsuspecting reader has to say the words aloud in order to figure out the meaning of this foreign English. Challenge students to figure out the following examples.

Strine

- Tiger — "Tiger look at this."
- Retrine — "How to speak Strine without retrine."
- Air fridge — "The air fridge man in the street."
- Baked necks — "Baked necks or fright shops for breakfast."

(Hint: Strine means Australian English. Try saying the sentences several times aloud.)

American examples are also used. The following are supposed to be accurate representations of Texas talk. Can students understand these sentences?

Texas talk

- offen — "Now stan still so ah can shoot that apple offen yore hade."
- main — "That there is one main man."
- cheer — "Yawl come riot cheer this minute."

Now that students are familiar with these dialects, have them write similar versions of their own speech. They can develop dialogues or write definitions for incomprehensible words. The spelling is meant to be creative but it has to represent the pronunciation closely enough for another person to say it correctly. Students will become more aware of how, in rapid speech, we slide together words that must be separated in learning to spell and write properly.

British-American Differences

The English spoken in Britain is also made up of various dialects. It is interesting to point out differences between English spoken in the United States and that spoken in Great Britain. Although you may not wish to investigate the full range of British dialects, you can have students investigate variations in vocabulary. For example, mix these words up and challenge students to match the British word with the correct American interpretation.

Food

biscuit	(cookie)
jelly	(jello)
tinned meat	(canned meat)
pud	(dessert)
tea	(light meal, supper)

Transport

boot	(trunk of car)
lorry	(truck)
lift	(elevator)
underground, tube	(subway, metro)

Professions

chemist	(druggist, pharmacist)
dustman	(garbage collector)

Personal

vest	(undershirt)
knickers	(underpants)
jumper	(pullover sweater)
fringe	(bangs, hair)

In many cases, the British words are familiar but less common. However, some words have very different meanings in Britain and the United States.

Spelling across the Atlantic

Write several of the following familiar words on the board for students to read and pronounce. Wait for students to notice something strange about these words. Tell them that these represent British rather than American spellings. Can they identify the differences?

gaol	colour	programme	civilise
kerb	practise	grey	behaviour
tyres			

Discuss the use of spelling conventions with the students. Why do we insist that everyone spell the same way?

You can also point out that some words are spelled the same way in the two countries but pronounced differently. Examples are *schedule* (pronounced *sh*edule) and *clerk* (pronounced clark). What are some of the implications of these differences? (Learning to read or spell, writing poetry-rhymes, etc.)

British English in Books

Have students search for additional examples of British English. Reading books written by British authors will bring out more items. Suggest titles by these British authors to upper-grade students:

Lucy Boston
   The Children of Green Knowe
   A Stranger at Green Knowe

Joan Aiken
   The Wolves of Willoughby Chase
   Black Hearts in Battersea

Students could also investigate the language used in familiar books such as *Mother Goose*. Ask students what *curds and whey* and *pease porridge* mean. *The Annotated Mother Goose,* by Martin Gardner, is a useful source for the origin of many of these phrases.

Early Spelling

Dictionary Day, October 16, commemorates the birth of Noah Webster. Students may be surprised to learn that the spelling they have so much trouble with has been standardized only relatively recently. When Noah Webster was preparing the first American dictionary, he wanted to emphasize that American English was distinct from British English, and thus further the Revolutionary cause. He set a standard against which we could measure our spelling. Previously, well-educated people could spell words as they chose. Because of Webster, we write *civilize* and *theater*, not *civilise* and *theatre*, as they do in England.

Is there any reason to have everyone spell the same way? Discuss with students the advantages and disadvantages of standardized spelling. (Students might be comforted to know that many spelling demons are reminders of how words used to be pronounced; for example, *night* was once pronounced with a hard *g*.) Organize a debate on spelling reform: Resolved — the English language should be spelled the way it sounds.

Focus on Black English

Despite the controversy over how to introduce so-called Standard English to students who speak Black English, all students need access to the "language of wider communication," or Standard English. Enlist students' assistance in the project of determining when and where particular forms are appropriate. Have them listen to black characters on television. Compare the speech of different people. How does the same person talk in different situations? Why would people speak differently depending on to whom they were talking? What are some of the reasons that people adjust their speech? Even young children can understand the distinctions we label "formal–informal" or "intimate–distant."

Comparing the speech of different people will help students learn to hear distinctions that they do not make. Depending on student abilities and interest, the class can write descriptions of Black English (BE) and Standard English (SE), identifying areas of important differences and including aspects of pronunciation, vocabulary, word order, and speaking style. This study will help students learn to use SE well, enabling them to predict translation problems by approaching SE as a "foreign language." Teachers can also use the descriptions to reduce confusion in spelling, for example. Student problems in hearing and spelling correctly can be avoided by learning "silent" letters (as in *desk*, pronounced "des") and homonyms (*coal/cold*, pronounced alike).

Black English and Written English

In order to learn to read, students must learn the specialized variety of language used in books. However, Black English-speaking students find book language extremely different from the language they are familiar with. Help students work with the differences between spoken and written English. Write examples of common sentences found in books on the board. Have students suggest how they would say it in natural speech. Try to obtain versions in both BE and standard spoken English. Include some of the following to illustrate the differences between speaking and writing BE and SE.

	Written	*Spoken*	
		Standard English	*Black English*
	A book is on the desk.	There's a book on the desk.	It's a book on the desk.
	The man was hit on the head.	The guy got hit on the head.	The guy got hit upside the head.
	Nobody can come.	There isn't anyone who can come.	Ain't nobody can come.

Differences Between Black English and Standard English: Summary

In talking of black dialects, one must be careful to recognize that not all black Americans speak dialects that are labeled "Black English." Also, remember that these are variant dialects within the general term: Black English. However, these generalizations may be helpful if Black English is unfamiliar to you.

1. *It* will often be used for *there* (e.g., "It's a book on the table" instead of "There's a book on the table").
2. The verb will tend to be missing where a contraction is commonly used in standard English, especially in the present tense (e.g., "I here" and "We going").
3. More than a single negative form is acceptable in the Black English vernacular (e.g., "I don't take no stuff from nobody").
4. Two or more consonant sounds appearing at the end of words in standard English tend to be reduced in the Black English vernacular (e.g., *tes* for test and *des* for desk). The reduction of consonant clusters affects words that end in *s* (e.g., plurals, third person singular forms, and possessives like *its* and *father's*). The reduction also affects verbs in the past tense ending in *-ed*.
5. Words in which a medial or final *th* appears often change pronunciation in the Black English dialect (e.g., *wit* or *wif* for with and *muver* for mother).
6. There are words in which *r* and *l* appear in medial or final positions in standard English. These sounds are often absent in the Black English dialect.
7. Labels and concepts different from the dominant English dialect are generated from a variety of different experiences (e.g., the use of *bad* to mean good).*

In addition, a few more specific points might be helpful. Black English does not distinguish gender. The form *he* is used for "he, she, it." Black English has a verb form not found in Standard English. *Be* is used to mean the habitual aspect. It does not change for person or tense. Singular and plural are often not distinguished

*Source: *Framework in Reading for the Elementary and Secondary Schools in California.* California State Department of Education, 1973.

in nouns in Black English. Instead, the pronoun can follow the noun to indicate number (e.g., The boy he . . . , Those guys them . . .).

There are a number of books that discuss Black English—its structure, use, history, and differences from standard English. The following are recommended resources:

Robbins Burling. *English in Black and White.* Holt, Rinehart and Winston, 1973.

J. L. Dillard. *Black English: Its History and Usage.* Random House, 1972.

English Borrowings

English is a mixture of many languages. Although English is historically related to German (see the Language Tree on page 150), it has been heavily influenced by French and has borrowed words from many of the other languages it has been in contact with. Words that were borrowed a long time ago are now considered part of English. Words borrowed recently usually show their foreign origins. When students look up word origins in the dictionary, point out that any word that does not come from Old English must have been borrowed into English at some time.

List a number of borrowed words on the board for students. How many of the words do they know? Can they guess what language each word was borrowed from? Borrowed words include:

Language	Word
Malay	ketchup
Arabic	alcohol
German	kindergarten, sauerkraut
French	souvenir, menu, encore
Hindi	shampoo
Spanish	bonanza, mosquito
Dutch	cole slaw, sleigh
American Indian	squash, raccoon
Italian	macaroni, piano
Yiddish	kosher
Japanese	kimono
Scandinavian	smorgasbord

After you have discussed these words with the students, prepare a display showing the origins of the words. Use a map of the world pinned to the bulletin board with the words printed on cards placed near their country of origin. Or mount the Indo-European tree on the bulletin board and place the borrowed words on leaf shapes attached to the proper branches. Discuss how the display shows which languages have contributed most to the English language. Why are some languages represented more than others? Speculate on why these words might have been borrowed.

The best desk dictionary for researching English origins is *The American Heritage Dictionary of the English Language* (William Morris, ed. American

Heritage/Houghton, 1969), because it includes the Indo-European root from which a word derives.

When English Wasn't English

Many students may not realize how the English language has changed over time. Ask them to imagine they are time travelers, going back in time. How far could they go and still be able to understand people speaking English? Record their guesses — 100, 500, 1,000 years? Have them check out their predictions.

Bring in examples of books written at different periods, including Chaucer for Middle English, and *Beowulf* for Old English. The first is partially recognizable, but the second is utterly foreign. If possible, include records of these works being read in the original, so that students can hear what English sounded like in different periods.

Why We Speak English

Although this country was settled by people from many different countries who spoke such languages as Spanish, French, and German, English was the only language recognized as the national language. How did this happen? Discuss possible causes with the students and have them develop a list of hypotheses, such as:

- English speakers were the first settlers.
- England was the most powerful mother country.
- The settlers voted English the official language.

Students will be motivated to read and research in order to determine the accuracy of their predictions. Once they have established the facts (there was no vote), they can come up with a reasonable idea of what led to the acceptance of English.

Compare the development of the United States and Canada. How and why did Canada set up two official languages (French and English)? How many people speak Spanish in the United States? Should Spanish be the second official language of the United States? (Everyone would have to learn both languages.) Discuss the implications with students.

Slang

Although slang is not considered a usual part of the language arts curriculum, it is an essential part of the students' language. The language that students find familiar and comfortable is often labeled slang by teachers. However, this attitude not only reflects lack of respect for the children's language but misses the important role of slang in the transmission of culture. Read the following quotes to students and discuss.

> Slang is language that takes off its coat, spits on its hands, and goes to work.
> —*Carl Sandburg*

> All slang is metaphor, and all metaphor is poetry.
> —*G. K. Chesterton*

Rewriting Proverbs

Slang can be considered another level of language, appropriate for use in specific situations. It increases the choice of ways by which we can express an idea. Proverbs are traditionally expressed in archaic language, yet the ideas represented are universal. Have students suggest how they would translate simple proverbs into slang. Are there expressions in "street talk" that cover the same ideas as the proverbs? How many different ways can students think of to restate the following proverbs in familiar language?

Do unto others as you would have them do unto you.

A stitch in time saves nine.

Discuss the differences in what these expressions communicate, depending on whether they use slang or archaic language. Which would be appropriate when and why?

Students' Right to Their Own Language

The following is a statement prepared by the National Council of Teachers of English in response to the controversy over how to teach speakers of Black English. Read this to the students and discuss it. Do they agree with the position expressed? What do they think teachers should do?

We affirm the students' right to their own patterns and varieties of language—the dialects of their nurture or whatever dialects in which they find their own identity and style. Language scholars long ago denied that the myth of a standard American dialect has any validity. The claim that any one dialect is unacceptable amounts to an attempt of one social group to exert its dominance over another. Such a claim leads to false advice for speakers and writers, and immoral advice for humans. A nation proud of its diverse heritage and its cultural and racial variety will preserve its heritage of dialects. We affirm strongly that teachers must have the experiences and training that will enable them to respect diversity and uphold the right of students to their own language.[2]

WE CAN SPEAK OTHER LANGUAGES

English is not the only language spoken in this country. Many people speak other languages, usually in addition to English, because they were born in other countries, their parents were born elsewhere, or they grew up in communities where other languages were spoken. Languages spoken in particular regions often reflect the history of settlement of that region, and maintaining those languages is a demonstration of pride in regional traditions. Unfortunately, under the pressure of population changes, today many of these languages are spoken less frequently, and children are less likely to know the language of their parents. When we discuss language diversity with our students, we want to represent the presence of different languages in this country.

The United States, like so many countries, is composed of different groups speaking different languages. However, in countries such as Switzerland, the Soviet Union, and Canada, families can expect that their children will go to school to learn one language but be able to speak another language at home. In the United States, on the other hand, people often assume that knowledge of a language other than English will interfere with the development of proficiency in English and they fear that the existence of other languages will downgrade the role of English as the language of common communication. Based on the experience of other countries, neither of these fears appears to be accurate. Instead, knowledge of several languages is not only the international norm, but is seen as an asset in a world of increasing contact between nations. Moreover, English is in no danger of losing its position as a language of communication across groups, when more and more people in other countries find it useful. We can provide students with the best foundation for their future development when we include other languages as opportunities for learning and when we support the languages that they already know.

Linguistic Diversity in the Classroom

According to the 1980 census, over 14 million U.S. residents were born in other countries. This table shows the distribution for the twenty nations (out of 155). In addition to the foreign-born, more than 14 million U.S. residents come from a Hispanic background. (Compare this to 49 million Americans of German origin.) Not surprisingly, Spanish is the second most widely spoken language in the United States, with estimates of up to 11 million speakers, and still growing. This in-

Country	Total
1. Mexico	2,199,221
2. Germany	849,384
3. Canada	842,859
4. Italy	831,922
5. U.K.	669,149
6. Cuba	607,814
7. Philippines	501,440
8. Poland	418,128
9. U.S.S.R.	406,022
10. Korea	289,885
11. China	286,120
12. Vietnam	231,120
13. Japan	221,794
14. Portugal	211,614
15. Greece	210,998
16. India	206,087
17. Ireland	197,817
18. Jamaica	196,811
19. Dom. Rep	169,147
20. Yugoslavia	152,967

formation is of great importance to the classroom teacher. Students need to learn this aspect of the history, geography, and sociology of the United States.

Determine what languages are represented in your classroom. Ask students not only what languages they speak but what languages their ancestors spoke. Students can learn about the history of this country as they find out what languages their families spoke before coming here and when their family started speaking English. Make a list of the languages represented and show on a map where they are spoken. Students can better understand the concept of ethnic diversity when they see how many of their parents and grandparents (and their friends' parents and grandparents) came from another country and had to learn to speak English when they arrived. Students will also identify more with the problems of recent immigrants when they realize how recently their own families arrived. An interesting fact to share is: Two out of every five Americans are descended from an Ellis Island immigrant.

Compare the languages of your class with the data on the chart below, showing the distribution of speakers of other languages. Which states have populations speaking the languages found in your classroom? Why do New York and California have the most languages listed? Which states have no non-English-speaking populations listed? Why? Students will have to apply facts and concepts learned in social studies in order to answer these questions and to understand the implications of this list.

LANGUAGE LOCATION

Location	Language
Arizona	Spanish, Uto-Aztecan
California	German, Italian, Spanish, Polish, Yiddish, French, Russian, Hungarian, Swedish, Greek, Norwegian, Dutch, Japanese, Chinese, Serbo-Croatian, Portuguese, Danish, Arabic, Tagalog, Armenian, Turkish, Persian, Malay (Indonesian), Scandinavian, Basque, Mandarin, Gypsy (Romani)
Florida	Spanish
Hawaii	Japanese, Tagalog, Polynesian
Idaho	Basque
Illinois	German, Italian, Spanish, Polish, Yiddish, Russian, Swedish, Greek, Norwegian, Slovak, Dutch, Ukrainian, Lithuanian, Czech, Serbo-Croatian, Danish, Balto-Slavic
Maine	French, Amerindian
Massachusetts	Italian, Polish, Yiddish, French, Swedish, Greek, Lithuanian, Portuguese, Celtic, Armenian, Albanian, Breton
Michigan	German, Polish, French, Hungarian, Dutch, Finnish, Arabic, Balto-Slavic, Near E. Arabic dialects, Amerindian, Iraqi, Algonquin, Gypsy (Romani)
Minnesota	Swedish, Norwegian, Finnish
Montana	Algonquin
New Hampshire	French

(continued)

New Jersey	German, Italian, Polish, Yiddish, Russian, Hungarian, Slovak, Dutch, Ukrainian
New York	German, Italian, Spanish, Polish, Yiddish, French, Russian, Hungarian, Swedish, Greek, Norwegian, Slovak, Dutch, Ukrainian, Lithuanian, Czech, Chinese, Portuguese, Danish, Finnish, Arabic, Rumanian, Balto-Slavic, Celtic, Hebrew, Armenian, Near E. Arabic dialects, Turkish, Uralic, Albanian, Persian, Scandinavian, Amerindian, Dalmatian, Breton, Mandarin, Egyptian, Georgian, Gypsy (Romani), Athabascan
Ohio	German, Polish, Hungarian, Greek, Slovak, Czech, Serbo-Croatian, Slovenian
Pennsylvania	German, Italian, Polish, Yiddish, Russian, Hungarian, Greek, Slovak, Ukrainian, Lithuanian, Serbo-Croatian
Rhode Island	French, Portuguese
Texas	Spanish
Washington	Swedish, Norwegian, Scandinavian, Amerindian
Wisconsin	German

Adapted from: Theodore Andersson and Mildred Boyer. Bilingual Schooling in the United States. *U.S. Office of Education, 1970, pp. 26–27.*

Welcoming Vietnamese Students

The following chart shows the distribution of substantial numbers of Vietnamese throughout much of the United States. As recent immigrants, however, Vietnamese students have had to struggle against fear and ignorance as they try to fit into the classroom environment and begin the task of learning English. Help them become accepted by sharing information about their country with the class. A book such as *The Brocaded Slipper, and Other Vietnamese Tales* by Lynette Dyer Vuong (Addison-Wesley, 1982), with its familiar themes, will show students how much they have in common. Several books about children in Vietnam are listed on page 293. Also see the Appendix.

THE VIETNAMESE POPULATION IN THE UNITED STATES*

State	Number of Vietnamese	Percentage of the Vietnamese Population
California	89,587	34.2
Texas	29,112	11.1
Louisiana	10,877	4.2
Virginia	10,000	3.8

*Figures taken from 1980 Census of Population.

Washington	9,833	3.8
Pennsylvania	9,257	3.5
Florida	7,592	2.9
Illinois	7,025	2.7
New York	6,644	2.5
Minnesota	5,866	2.2
Oregon	5,564	2.1
Oklahoma	4,671	1.8
Michigan	4,208	1.6
Maryland	4,131	1.6
Colorado	4,026	1.5
Kansas	3,690	1.4
Ohio	3,509	1.3
Hawaii	3,459	1.3
Massachusetts	3,172	1.2
New Jersey	2,884	1.1
North Carolina	2,391	.9
Indiana	2,338	.9
Georgia	2,294	.9
Wisconsin	2,249	.9
Utah	2,108	.8
Arizona	1,989	.8
Connecticut	1,825	.7
Missouri	1,179	.5
Total:	261,714	.1% of U.S. population

Discussing the Value of Knowing More than One Language

Open discussions about languages in our country will aid students in recognizing the issues involved. Discuss the topics listed on the next page.

A FABLE

In a house there was a cat, always ready to run after a mouse, but with no luck at all.

One day, in the usual chase the mouse found its way into a little hole and the cat was left with no alternative than to wait hopefully outside.

A few moments later the mouse heard a dog barking and automatically came to the conclusion that if there was a dog in the house, the cat would have to go. So he came out only to fall in the cat's grasp.

"But where is the dog?"—asked the trembling mouse.

"There isn't any dog—it was only me imitating a barking dog," explained the happy cat, and after a pause added, "My dear fellow, if you don't speak at least two languages, you can't get anywhere nowadays."

Reprinted from BBC Modern English, Vol. 2, No. 10, p. 34, December 1976.

- List the advantages of knowing a second language. List the disadvantages (if any).
- How many different languages are spoken in your area? Do you know someone who speaks more than one language?
- What languages would you like to learn? Why?

The Language Tree

Prepare a bulletin board to provide information about the family of Indo-European languages, spoken by half the world's population, and the relationship of English to other languages. Construct a large tree out of construction paper, with eight branches representing the main groups:

- Albanian
- Armenian

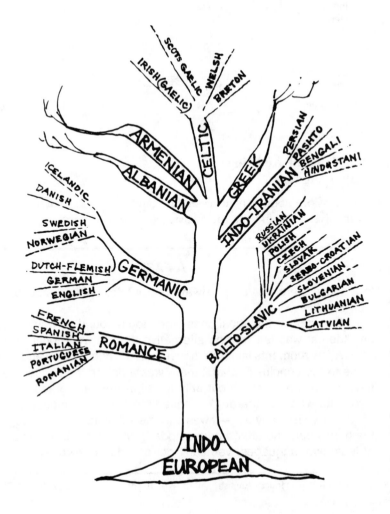

- BaltoSlavic: Russian, Polish, Serbo-Croatian, Czech, Ukrainian, Bulgarian, Lithuanian
- Celtic: Irish, Scots, Gaelic, Welsh, Breton, Cornish
- Greek
- Indo-Iranian: Hindi, Urdu, Bengali, Persian
- Romance: French, Italian, Spanish, Portuguese, Rumanian
- Germanic: German, English, Dutch, Danish, Norwegian, Swedish
- Tocharian ⎫
- Hittite   ⎬ extinct languages

Have students research what languages belong to each branch. Where does English fit in? Hittite and Tocharian died out a long time ago and are known today only through archaeological discoveries. Latin is no longer learned by anyone as a first language. Other languages have died out recently (such as Cornish) or are now dying out (Breton). Which are the most populous branches? In what countries are these languages spoken?

Exploring Different Languages

When the tree is constructed and the branches labeled with some of the major languages they include, have students add life to the tree by discovering words in these different languages. Students can look up words or use words they have found in books. Provide "leaves" cut out of construction paper on which to write words to place on the tree according to the "branch" they belong to.

Exercises such as looking up the word for *ten* in many languages will help demonstrate to students the relationship among these languages, as well as their similarities and differences. Here are some examples to begin with; check dictionaries and encyclopedias for more:

English	Ten	German	zehn
French	dix	Dutch	tien
Italian	dieci	Swedish	tio
Spanish	diez	Danish	ti
Portuguese	dez	Norwegian	ti
Rumanian	zece		

Other Language Families

Ask students to name languages that do not belong to the Indo-European language family. (Check names against the Indo-European family tree you constructed.) Names they may suggest include:

Language	Family
Chinese	Sino-Tibetan
Japanese	Japanese and Korean
Hebrew	Hamito-Semitic
Hungarian	Ural-Altaic

After the class has accumulated a list, have them look up the languages to find out which languages are related to each other. There are many language families besides the Indo European and some include languages with many speakers. Students may be surprised to learn that Chinese and Japanese are not related but belong to separate families. Many American Indian languages belong to distinctly different language families as well.

English in Other Languages

Just as English has borrowed many words for new things, so other languages have borrowed words from English for objects or ideas that came from English-speaking people. Familiar appearing or sounding words can be found in French, Japanese, Russian, Spanish, and many other languages. Ask students to guess what the following words are.

le pique-nique	(French, picnic)
le coquetel	(French, cocktail)
el ampayer	(Spanish, umpire)
los jonroneros	(Spanish, homerun hitters)
jiipu	(Japanese, jeeps)
gamu	(Japanese, chewing gum)
garu-furendo	(Japanese, girlfriend)
futbol	(Russian, football)
parken	(German, to park)
hitchhiken	(German, to hitchhike)

Comparing Languages

Challenge students to bring in examples of different languages. How many different languages can they find? Places to look include food labels and instruction booklets that accompany games or appliances. Can they understand anything in the different languages? Do any words look familiar? Are certain words repeated many times? Can they guess what some of the words mean? Which languages look most like English? Which are most different?

Languages in the World

Ask students if they know which language has the most speakers in the world. Write several guesses on the board. Have students research how many people speak each language. They can prepare a chart of the most widely spoken languages in the world. Figures can be obtained by counting the population of countries that speak a particular language, or you can use information on what languages people learn as a second language. Check figures in almanacs and encyclopedias. Because the population of China is large, more people grow up speaking Chinese than any other language. However, English is the most widely used second language.

Compare how many people speak English and how many speak Spanish. Which languages in the world would be the most useful to learn as second or third languages? Why?

Languages in the Classroom

Bring other languages into the classroom by giving students a chance to hear what different languages sound like. Students can listen to radio stations that broadcast in different languages. Folksongs are an easy way to introduce students to other languages. Learn a song in Spanish, such as "Cielito Lindo" or any song in a language that your students know. Talk about what the words mean and why they sound different. Use the languages that are represented in your classroom. Have students teach the rest of the class how to say *hello, good-bye, please,* and *thank you* in their language.

Esperanto

The following paragraph is written in Esperanto. Write it on the board and read it to the class. (It is pronounced approximately like Spanish—follow the rules given on page 161). See how much students can understand.

La inteligenta persono lernas la interlingvon Esperanto rapide kaj facile. Esperanto estas la moderna, kultura lingvo por la internacia mondo. Simpla, flekselbla, praktika solvo de la problemo de universala interkompreno, Esperanto meritas vian seriozan konsideron. Lernu la interlingvon Esperanto!

Esperanto is an artificial language invented to be used as an international language. It is easy to learn and easy to understand because it is completely regular. Spanish-speaking students will find Esperanto much easier to understand than will English-speaking students because it is based on the Romance languages.

Bring books about Esperanto to the class. Students can learn enough from several lessons to read the preceding paragraph. They will enjoy practicing the new language and using it in interesting ways. They can write to each other in Esperanto and perform simple translation exercises. In addition, they will learn more about how their own language is constructed by comparing it with Esperanto.

Discuss why Esperanto was created. Is there a need for an international language? Why doesn't everyone know English? What are the advantages and disadvantages of Esperanto? Esperanto is only one of a large number of artificial international languages. Ask students if they think any of these proposed languages will succeed. Have students investigate the history of Esperanto and other artificial languages (Interlingua, for example).

Greetings

We have other ways of communicating with people besides talking with them. When we greet someone, we not only say hello, hi, or how ya doin', but we also shake hands, kiss, or slap one another on the back. What we do depends on the particular situation—where we are, how well we know each other, and other social factors. Have students suggest some of the different ways we greet each other nonverbally and when each behavior is appropriate. Discuss ideas of appropriateness and how these might vary from individual to individual.

Other cultures have different conventions for greeting. Japanese people bow to each other and the depth of the bow indicates relative status. Eskimos rub noses. Can students think of other customs? People in some cultures hug each other more than others. Compile a list of American greetings. Ask students to write a description of various greetings as if they had to teach a foreigner how to greet people American style.

A good book for young children is *Face Talk, Hand Talk, Body Talk* by Sue Castle (Doubleday, 1977).

Learn Fingerspelling

Another kind of special language is a silent language, the language of hands. This kind of language is used by deaf people and takes the place of speech. Although ASL (American Sign Language or Ameslan) uses signs that generally correspond to English words, it also has signs for each letter (fingerspelling). Fingerspelling is sometimes called the manual alphabet. Anyone can quickly learn to fingerspell and the exercise helps practice English spelling. Students enjoy being able to signal each other secretly, across a noisy room, and without making a sound. Several books present fingerspelling for beginners. *Handtalk* by Remy Charlip, Mary Beth Ancona, and George Ancona (Parents Magazine Press, 1974) and *My First Book of Sign* by Pamela Baker (Gallaudet, 1986) include photographs of a person signing.

Sign Language

Discuss the differences between sign language and spoken language. What are the advantages of sign language? What are the advantages of spoken language? What language is best when you are eating? Under water? On the phone? Students may not believe that sign language is a "real" language. Present some of the following information about sign.

Facts about Sign Language

There are different sign languages used in different countries, just as there are spoken languages. People who use American Sign Language (ASL) cannot understand people who use British Sign Language.

ASL is not a word-for-word translation of English. Signed English is used for simultaneous translation and matches spoken English more closely.

Children who are deaf learn ASL as a first language, similar to the way hearing children learn a spoken language. Signers (people who use sign) can express themselves as well in sign as hearing people can in a spoken language.

Exploring Sign

Invite a hearing person who knows sign to speak to the class and demonstrate signing. (Try facilities for the deaf, teachers of sign language, and relatives of deaf people.) If students watch closely, they will be able to guess what some of the signs mean.

- Drink—fingers shaped around glass move to mouth
- See—two fingers move away from eyes
- Nose, Mouth—point to them on face

Find out what services are available for deaf people. Sometimes television news programs have simultaneous sign translations. Discuss with students why these services are necessary. Would printing the news on the screen as subtitles work?

Signed poetry can become a dance. The shape of the movements contributes to the poem in the same way as the shape affects a written poem. The National Theater of the Deaf combines sign language and movement for a striking, dramatic presentation. If these facilities for the deaf are in your area, try to arrange for a local group to give a performance totally in sign.

Codes

Learning a language is like learning a code. What kinds of codes do students know about? Is there a special handshake that some of them use? Would that be a code? What does it mean? What about clothing? Do some people wear their clothes a certain way in order to communicate something? How do people learn this information, this code? Is it like learning a foreign language?

Other kinds of codes include Morse code, semaphore (flag signaling), and the language of flowers (to send secret love messages). Some cultures have special codes, such as drum messages or smoke signals, or different ways to indicate whether a woman is married or unmarried, such as a certain hairstyle or a ring on a particular finger. Have students tell the class about some code they know and then write a description.

Alvin Schwartz's *The Cat's Elbow, and Other Secret Languages* (Farrar, 1982) describes special languages and codes from other countries.

Different Writing Systems

There are three basic types of writing systems. Alphabetic systems use symbols to represent individual sounds. Syllabaries have separate symbols for consonant-vowel pairs. Pictographic or ideographic systems represent entire words or ideas with a single symbol. Bring in examples of each type of writing (in print or handwritten) to show students how languages differ. Include some of the following:

- Alphabetic: *Cyrillic,* used for Russian and other Slavic languages, based on the Greek alphabet. *Hebrew,* an alphabet without written vowels, similar to *Arabic.*

- Syllabary: *Japanese,* despite adoption of some Chinese characters, still primarily uses *Kana,* syllable-based.
- Pictographic: *Chinese,* with large numbers of distinct characters, very difficult to memorize and write, is now being simplified and standardized by the Chinese government.

Discuss with students the implications of these different in writing systems. Consider, for example, how dictionaries would be organized. How would Hebrew students learn new words, written without the spoken vowels? The complex Chinese system is better for the Chinese than an alphabetic system. Speakers of different Chinese languages who cannot understand each other's spoken language can communicate through using the same writing system. How might these different writing systems make translation into English difficult? What would a typewriter look like in other writing systems?

Can students discover which alphabets are most widely used? (Roman, Cyrillic, and Arabic.) Compare these alphabetic systems. Each is used by more than one language. Why do different languages use different alphabets? Explore some of the reasons for the use and spread of an alphabet. (Religion, culture, colonization.) Why does English use the Roman alphabet, for example, and not the Arabic?

Where does the word *alphabet* come from? *Alpha* and *beta* are the first two letters of the Greek alphabet. Look at the Greek alphabet. Does it look anything like the alphabet we use? Where did our letters come from? Have students research the history of the English alphabet, from its origins in Greek and Phoenician letters, through Gothic, to its present form.

In an alphabetic writing system, each sound is represented by a symbol. Is this always true of English? What individual sounds in English are represented by pairs of letters? (Examples are *ch, sh, th,* etc.)

The Birth of Writing, by Robert Claiborne and the Editors of Time-Life Books, 1974, is an excellent resource for more information on the origin of writing and the importance of knowing how to write.

Language Differences and Similarities: Background

One of the tasks of linguistics is to describe the structure of various languages. On the basis of language structure and history, languages are classified together into families. Languages that superficially may seem very different are considered part of the same family; for example, English belongs to the family that includes German, French, Russian, Greek, and Sanskrit. Languages that belong to other families can be expected to appear even more different from English; for example, Japanese, Arabic, Hungarian, and Swahili. Examples of ways in which languages differ include the following:

1. Out of a limited number of possible sounds, no languages use precisely the same group of sounds. Many sounds do not occur in English and, therefore, sound strange to ears accustomed to English. However, no sounds are unusual or uncommon. All are found in the major languages of the world.

2. Some languages have a system for classifying nouns. Often this is based on gender. Objects are arbitrarily assigned to one of two groups called masculine and feminine (as in Spanish), or to one of three groups: masculine, feminine, and neuter (as in German and Russian). This use of gender is not equivalent to the division of humans into male and female. For example, in German, *madchen* (maiden) and *fraulein* (young woman) are both neuter. Different languages may assign the same object different genders. The word for table is *tisch* in German (masculine) and *mesa* in Spanish (feminine). In languages with gender, pronouns usually agree in gender with the nouns to which they refer. In addition, adjectives usually have different endings depending on the gender and number (singular or plural) of the noun modified. Note this example in French:

ils	préfèrent	les	tasses	blanches
they	*prefer*	*the*	*cups*	*white*
(3rd person, masculine, plural)	(3rd person, plural)	(plural)	(feminine, plural)	(feminine, plural)

In this sentence, the pronoun *ils* could refer to *les hommes* (men, masculine, plural) or to *les chats* (cats, masculine, plural) but not to *les femmes* (women, feminine, plural). Therefore, French speakers easily confuse the English he/she/it contrast and use he/she for inanimate objects. Examples of languages with a noun classification system not based on gender are the Bantu (African) languages. In these languages nouns are grouped into categories based primarily on the physical shape of the object; for example, long and thin, small and round.

3. The concept of *word* differs from language to language. The Japanese word *ikimasu,* for example, carries the potential meaning of these English words:

Japanese: ikimasu

English:
I
you
he
she
we
they
}
am
is
are
}
going

Japanese speakers decide who is going from the context of the conversation.

An example of the concept of *word* taken from the Yana Indian language in northern California* is even more complicated:

yābanaumawildjigummaha'nigi

yā = several people move
banauma = everybody
wil = across

*J.N. Hook, *The Story of American English* (New York: Harcourt Brace Jovanovich, 1972), p. 2.

dji = to the West
gumma = indeed
ha' = let us
nigi = we

Try reading these definitions as a "sentence."

Even with the parts of the long word defined, we still do not understand it, because we arrange our thoughts differently and do not repeat words as the Yanas did. An English sentence that conveys the same meaning as the Yana word might go like this:

Let us each move to the West.

4. Word order differs in various languages. In English, adjectives usually precede the noun described. Compare these phrases in English and Spanish:

English	*Spanish*
the blue book	el libro azul
	(the book blue)

5. Word order affects meaning in English, as is clear in these sentences:

The dog bit the man.
The man bit the dog.

In other languages special endings carry meaning so the words can be arranged in any order. For example, this Latin sentence says "Peter (subject ending *us*) sees Paul (object ending *um*)" no matter what the order.

Pet*rus* videt Paul*um*.
Paul*um* Pet*rus* videt.
Videt Paul*um* Pet*rus*.

Currently the emphasis in linguistics is away from the specification of language differences and toward the discovery of language universals. Through in-depth study of one language, linguists seek to describe structure that is common to all human languages and eventually to make claims about the nature of the human mind.

While languages differ in vocabulary for cultural and historical reasons, all languages have the same expressive potential. There is no such thing as a primitive language, just as there is no such thing as a primitive people. All human languages and all human cultures are rich and complex and capable of adapting to different circumstances. A language may not express some concepts that are considered important in our society, such as the linear notion of time, but it can develop the vocabulary to express any of these concepts if the speakers of the language consider it necessary. The use of formerly unwritten native African languages to conduct all the affairs of law, government, and education is an example of the flexibility of language. Another example is Hebrew, a dead language (not learned by anyone as a first language), which was revived for use as a national language in Israel. These languages have suddenly developed masses of new vocabulary as they expand to meet the demands placed on them. All languages possess the capacity to adapt to such new uses.

HISPANIC AMERICANS:
AN ETHNO-LINGUISTIC MINORITY

The most commonly spoken language in the United States, after English, is Spanish. In many classrooms, Spanish speakers are in a majority. But not all Americans who come from Spanish-speaking backgrounds speak Spanish themselves, and many who do speak Spanish also speak English. So the most appropriate label for this group may be "ethno-linguistic" minority, to reflect the fact that some people who identify with the culture do not speak the language, and vice versa. In addition, the label *Hispanic American* obscures the diversity of people who come from different countries and speak different varieties of Spanish. Today, people from communities with roots dating back to the settlement of California and the Southwest in the 1700s may feel they have little in common with the recent immigrants from El Salvador.

It is not surprising, then, that there is much confusion over how to determine who is a member of this minority (Spanish-sounding last name, lack of knowledge of English, or birth in a Spanish-speaking country are some of the criteria that have been suggested) or what label to use to identify people (Latino, Hispanic, and Chicano have been some of the options). The Hispanic students that teachers have in the classroom may have been in this country for a generation, immigrated from Mexico with many relatives still there, or arrived as war refugees with no option but permanent settlement in this country. These origins affect the extent to which the students have already learned English and also the family's desire to maintain Spanish as a language of the community.

We can serve all of our students best by exposing them to Spanish as a significant language in this country and a language of both historical and international importance. In addition, students who are able to contribute to the discussion through their own knowledge of this language will be able to take pride in this strength and this heritage.

Spanish on the Map

The importance of Spanish-speaking people in the history of this country can be easily seen in the names on the map. Project a copy of a U.S. map on the wall with the opaque projector so that all the students can see the names marked on the map. Have students find examples of Spanish place names. Talk about how you can tell whether a name is Spanish or not. If the first word is *San* or *Santa* the name is probably a Spanish saint name. What would these names be in English? (San Francisco/Saint Francis, San Antonio/Saint Anthony, for example.)

Look at different areas of the country separately. Students will notice that more Spanish names occur in certain areas. Which areas have more Spanish names and why?

As students search for Spanish names, they will notice other groups of foreign names. There are a number of French names in Louisiana, for example. Why? Ask students if they can think why the names used on the map might reflect the history of a region. Does the presence of Spanish names in an area necessarily mean that there are Spanish-speaking people living there?

Letter Names

What are the names of the letters of the alphabet? English-speaking children will be interested in learning how Spanish-speaking children say the alphabet. Have a child who speaks Spanish say these letters slowly for the group. This is more effective than reading or saying them yourself, for it makes the student aware that knowledge of Spanish can be important in school.

Spanish Letter Names

a	ä	n	ānā
b	bā	ñ	ānyā
c	sā	o	ō
ch	chā	p	pā
d	dā	q	kü
e	ā	r	ārā
f	āffā	rr	ārrā
g	hā	s	āsā
h	ächā	t	tā
i	ē	u	ü
j	hōtä	v	bā
k	kä	w	düblä bā
l	ālā	x	ākēs
ll	āyā	y	ē grē•agä (Greek i)
m	āmā	z	sätä

Comparing Alphabets

Show students how the Spanish alphabet is similar to yet different from the English alphabet. Write or print the letters on the board, circling the letters that are added, thus:

a	b	c	(ch)	d	e	f
g	h	i	j	k	l	(ll)
m	n	(ñ)	o	p	q	r
(rr)	s	t	u	v	w	x
y	z					

Explain that the letters *k* and *w* are used in the Spanish language only when words have been borrowed from other languages *(kilómetro* and *Washington).*

Comparing Phonemes and Graphemes

After examining the alphabet letters that are used in writing Spanish, show students the phonemes used in speaking Spanish, some of which are similar to English but none of which are exactly the same. Also show them corresponding graphemes for these phonemes. Here they will notice many differences between Spanish and English, as shown in this chart:

Consonants	Spanish	English
b	también	rib
	abrir	like v, but with lips almost touching
c	casa	case (before a, o, u)
	nación	cent (before e, i)
ch	chico	church
d	donde	down
	madre	the
f	familia	family
g	gente	like exaggerated h (before e, i)
	gordo	game
h	hacer	silent
j	jugar	like exaggerated h
k	kilómetro	kitchen
l	lástima	little
ll	llena	yellow } million } (regional variation)
m	mañana	morning
n	nada	nothing
n	niño	canyon
p	piña	supper
q	queso	key
r	pero	rich
	rico	trilled r
rr	perro	trilled r
s	sala	sad
t	trabajar	time
v	enviar	like b in también
	la vaca	like b in abrir
w	Wáshington	wash
x	examen	exam
	extranjero	sound
	México	hit
y	yo	yes
z	zapato	save
Vowels		
a	padre	father
e	es	they
i	nida	police
o	poco	poem
u	luna	spoon
	querer	silent after q

(continued)

Dipthongs	Spanish	English
ai, ay	traiga	n<u>i</u>ce
au	auto	m<u>ou</u>se
ei, ey	aceituna	tra<u>y</u>
eu	deuda	a<u>y</u> plus <u>oo</u>
ia, ya	hacia	<u>y</u>onder
ie, ye	nieve	<u>y</u>es
io, yo	dios	<u>y</u>olk
iu	ciudad	<u>y</u>ule
oi, oy	soy	bo<u>y</u>
ua	guante	<u>w</u>ander
ue	vuelve	<u>w</u>eight
y	y	e<u>v</u>en
ui, uy	muy	<u>w</u>e
uo	cuota	<u>w</u>oe

Spanish in the Classroom

As you work with Spanish in the classroom, whether or not you have Spanish-speaking students, you will need to have books on Spanish available for students. An easy-to-use, accessible book is: *How Do You Say It? In English, Spanish, and French* by Frank Martin (Platt and Munk, 1973). *Books in Spanish for Children and Young Adults: An Annotated Guide,* by Isabel Schon (Scarecrow Press, 1987), lists books you can use in the classroom.

Spanish Words We Know

Students may be surprised to see how many Spanish words they know. If Spanish is frequently used in the community, students should have no trouble recalling words seen on signs and heard in conversations. Have students list words they know as you write them on the board. Do they know what the words mean? Words they might suggest include:

    amigos   fiesta   siesta
    adiós   tortilla piñata

Do any stores in the community have signs in Spanish? Where do the children hear Spanish spoken? What does "Aquí se habla Español" mean? ("Spanish is spoken here.") Are there any Spanish place names or street names in the community?

Spanish Borrowings

English has borrowed extensively from Spanish, particularly in the Southwest. List examples of borrowings on the board. Do students know what these words mean? What kinds of words have been borrowed? Discuss why borrowings might take place. The following are examples of borrowings from Spanish:

arroyo	canyon	adobe	frijole
bronco	lasso	mustang	mesa
rodeo	chili	plaza	sierra
sombrero	avocado	stampede	tortilla
burro	vanilla		

Have students research Spanish borrowings. What do the original Spanish words look like? What happens to the words when they enter English?

Indian Borrowings

The Spanish spoken in Latin America is distinctively different from the Spanish of Spain because of the influence of the Native American languages. Many words borrowed into English from Spanish come originally from these languages. *Chocolate* was borrowed from Nahuatl, the Aztec language, into Mexican Spanish and then into English. As students research Spanish borrowings, have them notice examples of Native American words. The following are examples of words borrowed from Guaraní, a language spoken in Paraguay, into English: *tapioca, maracas, jaguar, jacaranda, tapir,* and *toucan.*

Spanish spoken in our country differs from the rest of Latin America because it has continued to borrow from the Native American languages and it has also been influenced by English.

Varieties of Spanish

The information on Spanish presented in this book is very general. There are many varieties of Spanish spoken in the United States, depending on where the speakers live, how long they have lived in this country, and where they came from originally. Spanish in the Southwest is different from Spanish in the Midwest (Chicago), the Northeast, and Florida. Even in New York City, there are important cultural and linguistic differences between persons from Puerto Rico, Cuba, Dominican Republic, Colombia, Ecuador, Peru, Mexico, Venezuela, Bolivia, and other South American communities.

The differences in the Spanish of Latin America are primarily vocabulary and pronunciation. Some vocabulary differences are due to influence from local Indian languages, others are due to independent development of Spanish.

The following are examples of different words used in Latin America for *boy:*

Mexico	chamaco	Panama	chico
Cuba	chico	Colombia	pelado
Guatemala	patojo	Argentina	pibe
El Salvador	cipote	Chile	cabro

Pronunciation also varies regionally. The following are some of the differences found:

- Syllable final *s* becomes *h* or disappears—*estos* is [éhtoh] or [éto]

- *ll* becomes same as *y* — *valla* and *vaya* are alike
- Syllable final *r* sounds like *l* — *puerta* is [pwelta], *comer* is [komel]

Introduce vocabulary specific to local Spanish-speaking groups by having a variety of children's books available. Many books, written about members of particular groups, take pride in presenting common Spanish words that are special to that group. The following are some suggestions. Include as many books on the locally represented groups as possible.

Puerto Ricans in New York

Cruz Martel. *Yagua Days*. Dial, 1976.

Ruth Sonneborn. *Friday Night Is Papa Night*. Viking, 1970.

Nicholasa Mohr. *El Bronx Remembered*. Harper & Row, 1975.

Southwest United States

Barbara Todd. *Juan Patricio*. Putnam, 1972.

Edna Chandler. *Indian Paintbrush*. Whitman, 1975.

California

Ernesto Galarza. *Barrio Boy*. University of Notre Dame, 1971.

The Color Wheel

A Spanish color wheel is helpful to show students the names for colors they know. Make a large poster to display on the wall like that on the top half of the next page.

This idea can be easily adapted for use with any language spoken by students in the class. With languages such as Tagalog and Navajo, it is often difficult to find printed materials for use with students. Prepare a variety of displays similar to the color wheel showing basic vocabulary. Include numbers, days of the week, and words used in the classroom.

Review Charts

Help students practice Spanish vocabulary they have learned or seen by preparing review charts. Construct a slip chart with common Spanish words written on the front. Students read the Spanish, say it aloud, give the English equivalent and check their response by pulling the tab that shows the English word below each Spanish example. These are especially useful for practicing limited sets of words such as numbers and days of the week. (See example on bottom of the next page.)

Charts can also be made with pictures of objects on the front. Students review by saying the name of the object in Spanish and then lifting the picture (which is attached at the top) to read the correct answer. Use these charts for independent student review or small group work. Both kinds of charts are useful for practicing English as a second language as well.

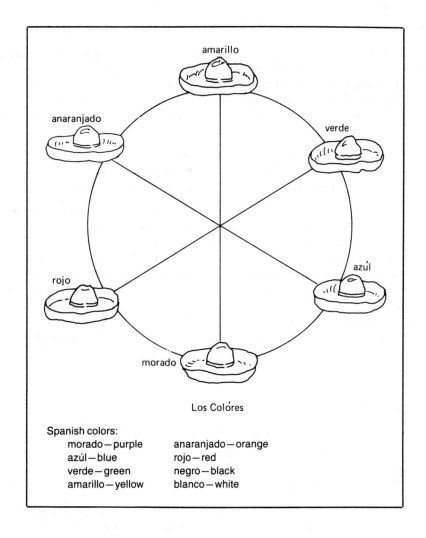

amarillo

anaranjado

verde

rojo

azúl

morado

Los Colóres

Spanish colors:

morado — purple	anaranjado — orange
azúl — blue	rojo — red
verde — green	negro — black
amarillo — yellow	blanco — white

la casa
house

el queso
cheese

la mesa
table

la puerta
door

la noche
night

el pan
bread

Idioms

Every language has a set of special expressions, called *idioms*, that are not meant to be taken literally. Idioms are especially difficult for people learning a new language because, even if they understand the words, they do not know what the phrase means. Have students collect idioms that they know or discover in Spanish. Post examples on the board with student drawings illustrating literal interpretation of the idioms. Begin with the following:

- hacer el papel—to play a part (literally, make a paper)
- tomar el pelo—to be kidding (literally, take the hair)
- me hace pedazos—thrills me (literally, makes me pieces)

As students look for Spanish idioms, they will become more aware of idioms in English. Encourage them to collect English idioms and illustrate them. These can be used for working with students learning English as a second language. Have students prepare a dictionary of English idioms. Include the idiom, a humorous illustration, its meaning, and an example using it in a sentence. Idioms that might be used are the following: all tied up, put your foot in it, raining cats and dogs, and to be broke.

Some interesting books for students to investigate include Jane Sarnoff and Reynold Ruffin's *Word, a Book about the Origins of Everyday Words and Phrases* (Scribner, 1981) and Marvin Terban's *Mad As a Wet Hen, and Other Funny Idioms* (Clarion, 1987).

Tongue-Twisters

The word for tongue-twister in Spanish is *trabalengua*. Challenge students to say the following example:

Tres tristes tigres trillaron trigo en un trigal.
(Three sad tigers thresh wheat in a wheat field.)

Collect examples of tongue-twisters from different languages. Share some interesting ones in English, too, for the benefit of all students. Spanish-speaking students might find the following examples helpful in developing the pronunciation of specific English sounds:

- Six silent snakes slither slowly southward.
- Eight gray geese graze gaily into Greece.
- The sun shines on shop signs.
- Thrice times three; twice times two.

An interesting source of varied tongue-twisters is *A Twister of Twists, A Tangler of Tongues* by Alvin Schwartz (Lippincott, 1972).

Spanish Folklore

An important aspect of studying Spanish language and culture is Spanish folklore. This folklore reflects Spanish, English, and Indian influences and is unique to the

Spanish-speaking culture as well as an important part of the American experience. Folklore includes stories (cuentos), sayings (dichos), songs, music, legends (leyendas), and drama. Special types of songs are corridos, mañanitas, and rancheras. Many legends center around La Bruja (the Witch) and La Curandera (the Healer).

Provide examples of different kinds of folklore and discuss the ritualized characteristics of each form. Encourage students to research more examples. Because all of the stories and songs are short, they are particularly suitable for presenting in front of the class. Several students can take turns telling stories that are spooky or humorous. You can also obtain records of traditional ballads and songs to play.

Suggested references and resources for exploring Chicano or Mexican American folklore include:

Richard Dorson. *Buying the Wind: Regional Folklore in the United States.* University of Chicago Press, 1964.

Gilberto Espinosa. *Heroes, Hexes and Haunted Halls.* Calvin Horn, 1972.

José Espinosa. *Spanish Folk-Tales from New Mexico.* Kraus Reprint Co., 1969.

Luís Valdez and Stan Steiner. *An Anthology of Mexican American Literature.* Knopf, 1972.

Aspects of Spanish that May Cause Problems for Children Learning English: Summary

Many Spanish-speaking children make consistent mistakes as they learn English because they apply their knowledge of Spanish rules. The following points will help you to understand these mistakes and also to explain to students how English is different from Spanish.

1. Strong influence of the Spanish *ch* on the English *sh* is a common problem. When *sh* is introduced, because of its proximity in sound, the student may appear to say *share* for *chair* and *shoes* for *choose*.
2. In Spanish, *b* and *v* are exactly alike phonetically; each has two sounds. The use of one sound or the other is governed by accompanying sounds as follows:
   a. Sound one is made by the buzzing of both lips (e.g., *Ella botó la caja; Ella votó ayer*). The letters *b* or *v* surrounded by vowel sounds must be buzzed.
   b. Sound two is *b* as in boy (e.g., *El bote se caja; El vaso se caja*). Both sound like the *b* in boy. When *b* or *v* begins an utterance or is not surrounded by vowel sounds it is pronounced as the *b* in boy.
3. Spanish uses one word for *it is (es)* and for *there are* and *there is (hay)*. Examples: *It is* a nice day *(Es un día agradable). There are* many children at school *(Hay muchos niños en la escuela). There is* a teacher in the classroom *(Hay un profesor en la clase).*
4. In Spanish, articles are placed in some positions where English does not require them: *Veo al doctor Brown* (I see *the* Dr. Brown); *Así es la vida* (That's *the* life).
5. In Spanish the adjective usually follows the noun and must agree with it in gender and number: *Yo tengo zapatos blancos* (I have shoes white).
6. There are five vowels in Spanish. The corresponding sounds in English are as

follows: *a* as in father; *e* as in step; *i* as in machine; *o* as in over; and *u* as in ooze. The short vowel sounds *a, i, o,* and *u* are not used in Spanish.

7. The adverb, not the direct object, usually comes right after the verb. Example: I immediately saw . . . *(Yo vi imediatamente . . .).*

8. The consonant sounds *v, b, d, t, g, h, j, l, r, w, v,* and *z* are not pronounced the same in Spanish as in English. Knowledge of the point of articulation for the production of these sounds is necessary.

9. Beginning and ending sounds.

   a. Spanish words never begin with consonant clusters, identified in italics as follows: *sp*eak, *st*ay, *sc*hool, *st*reet, *sp*ring, *sc*ratch, *sp*here, *sl*ow, *sm*all, *sn*ail, *sv*elte. Speakers of Spanish add an initial vowel sound *e* as, for example, in *e*speak, *e*street.

   b. Spanish words can end in any of the five vowels — a, e, i, o u — or the consonants listed as follows:

l	*papel*	
d	*verdad*	*cara*
r	*señor*	*come*
z	*zariz*	*casi*
j	*reloj*	*todo*
y	*estoy*	*tu*
n	*son*	
s	*casas*	

   Note: Speakers of Spanish have difficulty with ending sounds such as *m, p, k, c, b, d, f, g, j, l, t, v,* and *x* (voiced z). They also have difficulty in pronouncing the 371 consonant-cluster endings used in English.

10. Some factors of intonation such as pitch and stress that can cause problems in communication are the following:

    a. *Stress.* Spanish words are stressed as follows:

       1) Stress on the last syllable: *pa pél, vi vi rás, te le vi sión, ciu dád*
       2) Stress on the next to last syllable: *cá sa, ma dé ra, clá ro*
       3) Stress on the third to last syllable: *jó ve nes, áng e les, te lé fo no*
       4) Stress on the fourth to last syllable: *llé va te los, mánd a se lo, có me te los*
       Most Spanish words are stressed on the last syllable (Group A words) or next to last syllable (Group B words). In contrast, English words are usually stressed on the first or second syllable; e.g., *constant (constante), t*elephone *(teléfono).* In English, long words may have two or even three stresses. Spanish uses only one stress except for adverbs ending in *mente* (e.g., *fácilmente, rápidamente*).

    b. *Tone system.* English and Spanish have four tone levels. Spanish normally operates on the lower three levels except in cases of extreme anger or alarm. Then the fourth (upper) pitch is used. English usually operates on all four levels.

11. Spelling differences. Although many Latin derivatives are common to Spanish and English, there are some interferences between spelling systems. Teachers should help students with the transfer of cognate vocabulary. Spanish does *not* use the doubled consonants or combination of consonants; i.e., *bb, dd, ff, gg, mm, pp, ss, tt, zz, th, gh, ph, sh,* or *hn.**

*Source: *Framework in Reading for the Elementary and Secondary Schools in California.* California State Department of Education, 1973.

SUPPORTING SPEAKERS OF OTHER LANGUAGES AS ENGLISH LEARNERS

One of the ways in which today's classrooms are heterogeneous is in the number of students who come from different language backgrounds and are learning English in school. Some of these children have parents who are working in this country for a limited time and expect to return to their home country. These parents often view learning English as an asset for their child and they continue to take responsibility for maintaining another language in the home. Other children may have been born in this country but grew up in communities where English was not a dominant language. Perhaps their parents do not speak English. In this case, teachers may encounter communication barriers that make it difficult to find out important information about the students. Another group of students are refugees. They may have undergone great hardships to come to this country and the student's family may be separated, thus the position of parental responsibility is unclear. In some cases, these students have not gone to school before, although they are older, and learning about school expectations may be the primary language task before they can participate in a class.

All of these situations place different demands on the teacher, who is usually not trained as a language teaching specialist. Nonetheless, we need to offer the best teaching we can to all students who are encountering English as an unfamiliar language. We can help students develop the oral fluency that provides a base for further language learning. We can also structure activities that help students attend to the elements of the English language. Reading, writing, and many word games support the essential vocabulary development for students. Finally, we can make sure that all students feel included in the class because they know they make an important contribution.

Developing a Literacy Base

Students who come to school with little or no English-speaking proficiency need a solid foundation in basic areas to achieve literacy in either or both of their languages. In any program that starts with the student's first language and gradually introduces English in order to develop literacy skills, the following points are fundamental to an effective program.

1. *Read aloud to students.*   Students need to hear the special kind of language used in books. Have them respond by writing in the language they choose.
2. *Give students time to write everyday.*   Beginning writers need frequent practice to develop fluency. Invented spelling and grammatical mistakes are evidence that students are applying hypotheses about how each language works.
3. *Publish some student writing.*   This gives students an incentive to polish some of their pieces. As they revise and edit, they learn the conventions of written language. Use teacher-student writing conferences to focus attention on aspects of form and content.

4. *Provide many books and printed material, particularly in the language other than English.* Students can transfer their literacy skills from one language to another. The more they read, the more they will learn about language.

Choral Speaking

Many students learning English as a second language (ESL) respond well to choral activities because they are not singled out or embarrassed by their mistakes. The class can learn a short piece to recite together, or a group of students can prepare a passage to present to the class. "The Old Woman Who Swallowed a Fly" is a traditional choice. Different parts can be spoken by different groups or parts of the class. Poems and prose with a strong rhyme and rhythm are easier to learn and more fun to recite. ESL students will learn oral skills such as pronunciation and intonation by participating.

In the following example, divide the class in half and ask each group to alternate lines.

> If all the seas were one sea,
> What a *great* sea that would be!
> If all the trees were one tree,
> What a *great* tree that would be!
> And if all the axes were one ax,
> What a *great* ax that would be!
> And if all the men were one man,
> What a *great* man that would be!
> And if the *great* man took the *great* ax,
> And cut down the *great* tree,
> And let it fall into the *great* sea,
> What a splish-splash that would be!
> *(Old Nursery Rhyme)*

For more examples, see *Presenting Reader's Theater: Plays and Poems to Read Aloud* by Caroline Bauer (Wilson, 1987).

Visual Stimuli

Pictures can be used to start the students talking, thereby developing oral language skills. Show a large picture to the class. After students identify the elements in the picture, ask them to tell a story about it. They can talk about what happened before, what is happening now, and what might happen next.

Students who are reluctant to talk in front of the class may open up more in a small group. First, one student selects a picture and begins a story, then he or she passes it to the next student, who continues the story. A series of related pictures can help students learn to build a narrative.

Language Experience Stories

With this approach, even ESL students can write their own stories. Introduce students to the technique by composing a story as a group. After an experience shared by the class, begin writing about it on the board. As students make comments, write down the sentences they contribute. Prompt them to include more information if necessary. After the story is completed, read it back to the class so that they can see it is *their* story. Then have students copy the class story and read it themselves.

The same technique can be used for individuals. Students can dictate a story to the teacher or an aide, or write it themselves, in their own fashion, to read back later. ESL students can dictate stories to a tape recorder. After these stories are transcribed and typed, they can be read back to the students, showing the relation between the spoken and written language.

Reading through Dictation

Dictation helps develop student reading skills, particularly for the ESL student. Before reading a passage to the class, dictate a few lines for students to write. After each line, stop and discuss what students know about the story. Based on this information, what do they think will happen next? Continue this procedure for several lines and then have them read the rest of the story to find out what happened. This exercise promotes the ability to analyze and predict what could come next, which is an essential thinking skill for reading comprehension.

Tape-Assisted Reading

Tape record several stories from a class reading textbook or other literature book. (Enlist parents, aides, or older students to help you with this, providing a variety of voices.) ESL students can listen to the stories on cassette as they follow along in the book. (If you use multiple headsets, a group of students can listen and read at the same time.) They will enjoy listening to these stories over and over again and, in the process, they will begin to make the connection between sound and symbol.

The ESL Cloze

Adapt the cloze test, used for reading diagnosis, for ESL students as an extra review exercise, to check their understanding. In a cloze test, you delete words (or letters) from a text according to a predetermined formula. You can delete every fifth word; every noun, preposition, consonant, or vowel; or any item you want to check, but you must use a passage that is familiar to the ESL students (unlike its use with English speakers). The deletions force the students to use their knowledge of the regularities of English and make predictions about possible completions.

This type of exercise, where the student has to write in the missing word, is also useful as an ESL listening exercise. Students can listen to a taped passage several times, to fill in the blanks and check their answers.

"Pictionary"

"Pictionary" is a popular game with many students and adults. Adapt this game for classroom use, particularly for ESL students. One team draws a picture and the other team has to guess what the picture is. You can set a time limit appropriate to the level of your class. Students can use this game to practice new vocabulary they are learning as well as to challenge each other with more difficult words. You can also increase the difficulty by making them spell the word correctly.

Oral Practice

The following techniques are particularly useful for ESL students, but benefit all students by increasing oral fluency. Students need to listen carefully in order to produce the appropriate grammatical constructions.

Repetition:	Listen and repeat exactly as heard.
Teacher:	I see a dog.
Child:	I see a dog.
Analogy:	Repeat exactly with one change.
Teacher:	I am a man.
Anne:	I am a woman.
Fred:	I am a boy.
Sue:	I am a person.

Begin a PROGRESSIVE CONVERSATION so that all members of the group participate in this type of analogical replacement, thus:

Teacher:	I see a dog. What do you see, Jim?
Jim:	I see a cat. What do you see, Janet?
Janet:	I see a mouse. What do you see, Gerri?
Inflection:	Change the form of a word.
Teacher:	There is one girl.
Sue:	There are two girls.
Teacher:	There is one house.
Fred:	There are two houses.
Completion:	Finish the statement.
Teacher:	Susan is tall, but . . .
Joan:	Mary is taller.
Teacher:	John is big, but . . .
Carol:	Phil is bigger.
Expansion:	
Teacher:	Steve is happy.
Chuck:	Steve is happy because he finished his work.
Teacher:	Milly is happy.
Ann:	Milly is happy because she has a new dress.
Transformation:	Change a given sentence to negative or interrogative form.
Teacher:	Judy is here today.
Carol:	Judy is not here today.

Teacher:	Judy is here today.
Fred:	Is Judy here today?
Restoration:	Student makes sentences from a group of words.
Teacher:	picture, wall, hanging
Chuck:	The picture is hanging on the wall.
Phyllis:	Is the picture hanging on that wall?
Response:	Answer or make a rejoinder.
Teacher:	It is chilly in this room.
Mary:	It feels fine to me.
Jim:	I think you are right.
Joan:	Shall I close the door?*

Pattern Books

ESL students of any age can learn about English grammar by reading primary/ picture books that establish a syntactic pattern and then repeat it through many variations. For example, Wanda Gag's *Millions of Cats* provides excellent practice with number words and the plural ending. After the first couple of pages, students will have no trouble filling in the refrain: "Millions and millions of cats." *The Judge,* by Margot Zemach, focuses attention on the *-s* ending as it repeats verbs in the third person singular. And Marjorie Flack's *Ask Mr. Bear* is an excellent exercise for pronouns, especially the possessive adjective.

These books achieve their appeal through repetition, making them easy to memorize. Students learn the patterns quickly and practice important grammatical elements painlessly. Students will be motivated to "read" these books that they have memorized.

Rewriting for Grammar Practice

When ESL students need to focus on particular grammatical features in English such as the past tense or the third person singular *-s* ending, provide necessary practice by giving them a passage (perhaps in a story or a letter from their text) and having them rewrite it. You can have them change it from present tense to past tense and vice versa, or from *I* to *he*, or *she* to *they*, for example. More advanced students can practice changing active sentences into passive. *(They built the house* becomes *The house was built.)*

ESL Writing

When assigning writing exercises, keep in mind the special needs of the ESL student. If you're asking students to write about a circus, for example, check to be sure that they know what a circus is. Discuss the subject with the class beforehand. Has anyone

*From Iris Tiedt, *The Language Arts Handbook* (Englewood Cliffs, N.J.: Prentice-Hall, 1983).

been to a circus? What's it like? Present important vocabulary on the board. If some students have no experience with a circus, ask them if they're familiar with anything similar.

ESL students can also benefit from using prose models. Give them an example of the same kind of writing you expect from them and have them follow the model, putting in their own words.

Traveling Sentences

Exercises that allow more than one right answer are especially important because they give the ESL student more chances to succeed. Begin by placing a simple sentence on the board and then go around the room, inviting students to add to it. Have them write the sentence on the board as it is revised. You can restrict the additions to one word each time, or you can require that each contribution make a complete sentence.

I	*II*
Manolo flew	Manolo flew.
Manolo flew kites	Manolo flew kites.
Manolo flew blue kites	Manolo flew kites in the park.
Manolo flew blue kites in	

Remind students that they can add words anywhere in the sentence, even in front.

Class Log

All students can participate in recording class activities and other information on a daily basis. They can make weather observations, write about special events, and note birthdays and other news. Students can take turns being secretary, making entries in a class log or diary by copying information off the board or from weather instruments. This is useful to refer to later and it is interesting to show to visitors as a record of the class year.

October 3

It was 76 degrees outside and partly cloudy at 10 AM. Today a woman from the Police Department came to talk to us about bicycle safety. She gave us a list of rules and taught us how to lock up our bikes. We saw a filmstrip about life in the ocean. My favorite part was how the hermit crab lives in other shells.

Alliterative Sentences

This game stimulates students to make up sentences of words that begin with the same sound, thus reinforcing vocabulary development. Give students a name to start with, and see who can come up with the longest sentence.

Carmen:
Careful Carmen can't come.
Catty Carmen cut Conrad crushingly.

Students will also have to review the phoneme-grapheme relationship as they are forced to decide: Can I include *center*? What about *kangaroo*? Or *charming*?

Steven Kellogg's *Aster Aardvark's Alphabet Adventures* (Morrow, 1987) is an amusing alphabetical collection of alliterative sentences.

Scrambler

Play word games such as scrambled words to teach ESL students possible letter combinations in English and develop their vocabulary. If you write scrambled words on cards with the answer on the back, students will enjoy playing this game singly or in pairs. You can even have students develop their own cards.

A version for older students is to present a sentence out of order. Can they arrange the words to form a correct sentence? Be careful—sometimes there's more than one right answer. This exercise gives students practice in English word order patterns, groups of words that go together, and how the beginning of a sentence constrains the ending.

Students can also arrange mixed-up sentences to form a paragraph. They will enjoy creating examples to challenge their classmates. The skills involved in sorting out this mixed-up paragraph reinforce those required for successful reading and writing.

Students Can Help

Your English-speaking students can help you enormously to integrate the student with limited English skills into the class. Assign a "buddy" to each new student. This buddy can show the student where to go and what to do, as well as help explain what the teacher wants. Most significantly, the buddy, by speaking lots of English, provides important vocabulary and grammar input for the English language learner. And both participants in the pair-up receive rewards.

For more information, see Elizabeth Buchler and Dianne Meltesen's "ESL Buddies" in the September 1983 issue of *Instructor*.

Guide for New Students

Encourage ESL students to prepare a guide to the school. It could include information useful for other ESL students as well as any new students. Have students take pictures of classrooms, student activities, and other important elements of school life. They can prepare captions ranging from a few words to a longer description of what is expected of a student. If you work with one particular language group, you might consider having the guide translated and sent out to incoming families as a bilingual introduction to the U.S. school system.

Older students can extend this project by preparing a guide to the community. It might include information about important resources for non-English-speaking families.

Group Problem Solving

Students learn language most readily when they need to communicate with each other in order to work out problems in a group. Assign small groups of students such practical problems as reading bus schedules, working out arrangements for a class trip, or planning a class party. New vocabulary is easily learned in context and students can help others who can't find the right word. Each person has an opportunity to contribute and each contribution is valuable in group work.

ABC Books

Challenge students to prepare their own ABC books. Limit the words to a certain category (animals or plants, for example) in order to stimulate a hunt for new words. ESL students will particularly benefit from this approach to vocabulary learning as they seek out dictionaries. Have students prepare "real" books—writing one example for each letter per page, illustrating it, and stapling the pages together. Encourage students to pass their books around and share their unusual discoveries. They can choose their favorite word in each book.

Some examples of alphabet books that are also useful for vocabulary work are:

Kate Duke. *The Guinea Pig ABC*. Dutton, 1986.

Marty Neumeier and Byron Glaser. *Action Alphabet*. Greenwillow, 1985.

Anne Rockwell. *Albert B. Cub and Zebra: An Alphabet Storybook*. Crowell, 1977.

Categories

Another vocabulary game that helps ESL students is the familiar "Categories." Most often used as a unit review, it consists of a word (the topic) written down the left side of a sheet and several categories across the top. Students fill in words under each category that begin with the letters of the topic word. For example, after discussing the subject of "space" for several days, give students this challenging exercise:

	Heavenly Bodies	*Colors*	*People/Professions*
S	Saturn	silver	scientist
P	Pluto	purple	pilot
A	Asteroid	azure	astronaut
C	Ceres	cocoa	chemist
E	Earth	emerald	engineer

This game works best if there is more than one possible answer. If you want to make it more difficult, you can give points for each letter and reward students who have the longest entries.

Individualized Dictionaries

Have primary ESL students develop their own picture dictionaries. They can cut out or draw illustrations of all the new objects they encounter and copy the English word next to each one. Then students can refer to these dictionaries in class and even take them home for extra practice. Some older students may benefit from recording the pronunciation phonetically in their own language.

Intermediate and upper-grade students could construct a dictionary/notebook that focuses on signs and symbols. They could include examples such as the following:

Vocabulary Patterns

When you teach vocabulary, pay particular attention to teaching *morphemes*. (Morphemes are units of meaning that are put together to form words.) Demonstrate the power of morphemes by taking a familiar word such as *telephone* and exploring the meaning of each morpheme. *Tele* is a morpheme meaning *far*, and *phone* is another morpheme meaning *sound*. Ask students if they can list other words that contain one of these morphemes. Words they might know are *telegraph* and *phonograph*. They can look up more examples in the dictionary.

Based on the list, what do they think *graph* means? Did they guess it meant *write*? Once students learn that morphemes have meanings, independent of the words they are found in, and that they can be combined to form new words, students will be able to understand many more words.

Expanding Vocabulary

As students encounter new words, be sure to provide all the forms of the word (noun, verb, and adjective groups or the present, participle, and past forms for a verb). Draw students' attention to spelling and pronunciation changes, if any. This is particularly important for the ESL student, as it reinforces learning of regular patterns (ones that English speakers are already accustomed to) and exposes them to the common exceptions.

admire	(verb)
admirable	(adjective)
admiration	(noun)

(Note stress change in adjective form.)

creep	(present)
crept	(past)
crept	(participle)

Factors that Accelerate Language Learning: Summary

As you prepare your lessons, keep the following points in mind. Frequent application of these principles (based on extensive second language research) will maximize students' language learning potential.

1. *Need to know:* Design lessons based on students' immediate needs and interests.
2. *Context:* Try to teach words as they occur in sentences, and grammatical constructions where they occur naturally in conversations.
3. *Inductive presentation:* Give examples of a rule or generalization, then let students try to figure out the pattern.
4. *Manipulation:* Engage the physical aspect of learning by having students act out what they are learning.
5. *Relaxation:* Get students to talk (or write) without fear of making mistakes. They will absorb more and remember more.

REFLECTIONS

In school, students *learn* language, they learn *about* language, and they learn *through* language. As teachers, we need to recognize the central role that language plays in teaching and learning. For education that attempts to address multicultural issues of difference and diversity, language is the heart of the students' identity. We have the responsibility to bring language into the classroom in a way that acknowledges its importance in knowing who we are and what the world is about. We do this by reflecting on our own language, its history and variety, and by exploring other examples of languages and their uses.

APPLICATIONS

1. Investigate the children's literature available in the library and select several books that are based on patterns: refrains, repeated story lines, or questions and answers. Write lesson plans to show how you could use these books with students who need English as a second language support to help them develop oral fluency, to provide writing models, or to practice vocabulary.
2. Collect examples of writing in different languages. Try to find different scripts and different systems (pictographic, syllabary). Look for familiar children's books in different languages. Can you find *Winnie the Pooh* in French, Spanish, and Latin? Design a lesson plan to use these books to introduce children to different languages and their writing systems.
3. Look at different books that attempt to reproduce how people really talk (regional or social dialects, Black English). Are they accurate? What effect

are they trying to produce? How would you read these aloud to students? Compare and analyze treatment of the same dialect in several books and make recommendations for the teaching of these books and the dialect.

Endnotes

1. Walt Whitman. "Slang in America." *North American Review* (November 1885).
2. *Students' Right to Their Own Language*. NCTE, 1976.

Resources

Charlotte Brooks, ed. *Tapping Potential: English and Language Arts for the Black Learner.* NCTE, 1985.

California State Department of Education. Sacramento, California. *Basic Principles for the Education of Language Minority Students: An Overview.* 1983.

————. *Individual Learning Programs for Limited-English-Proficient Students.* 1984.

Courtney Cazden, Vera John, and Dell Hymes. *Functions of Language in the Classroom.* Teachers College Press, 1972.

Donna Christian. *Language Arts and Dialect Differences.* Center for Applied Linguistics, 1979.

Donna Christian and Walt Wolfram. *Exploring Dialects.* Center for Applied Linguistics, 1979.

Robert Claiborne. *Our Marvelous Native Tongue.* Random, 1983.

James Cummins. *Bilingualism and Minority Language Children.* Ontario Institute for Studies in Education, 1981.

Johanna DeStefano. *Language, Society, and Education: A Profile of Black English.* Charles A. Jones, 1973.

J. L. Dillard. *Black English: Its History and Usage.* Random House, 1972.

Alan Dundes, ed. *Mother Wit from the Laughing Barrel.* Prentice-Hall, 1973.

Charles Ferguson and Shirley Brice Heath, eds. *Language in the USA.* Cambridge, 1981.

Joshua Fishman and Gary Keller, eds. *Bilingual Education for Hispanic Students in the United States.* Teachers College Press, 1982.

J. N. Hook. *The Story of American English.* Harcourt, 1972.

Stephen Krashen and Tracy Terrell. *The Natural Approach: Language Acquisition in the Classroom.* Alemany, 1983.

Michael Linn and Maarit-Hannele Zuber, eds. *The Sound of English: A Bibliography of Language Recordings.* NCTE, 1984.

Robert McCrum, William Cran, and Robert MacNeil. *The Story of English.* Viking, 1986. (See also the PBS video series of the same title.)

Raymond Rodrigues and Robert White. *Mainstreaming the Non-English Speaking Student.* NCTE, 1983.

Geneva Smitherman. *Talking and Testifying: The Language of Black America.* Houghton, 1977.

Earl Stevick. *Teaching and Learning Language.* Cambridge University Press, 1982.

Orlando Taylor. *Cross-Cultural Communication: An Essential Dimension of Effective Education.* The American University, 1987.

Eleanor Thonis. *Literacy for America's Spanish Speaking Children.* IRA, 1976.

Walt Wolfram and Donna Christian. *Dialogue on Dialects.* Center for Applied Linguistics. 1979.

Walt Wolfram, Lance Potter, Nancy Yanofsky, and Roger Shuy. *Reading and Dialect Differences.* Center for Applied Linguistics, 1979.

P eople get better at using language when they use it to say things they really want to say to people they really want to say them to, in a context in which they can express themselves freely and honestly.

John Holt

7

Integrating Multicultural Education into Reading and Language Arts

As children and young people learn their language, they learn to think.[1]

James Squire

Preview

After reading this chapter, you should be able to:

- Introduce multicultural concepts through oral language experiences.
- Integrate multicultural concepts into literacy instruction.
- Select multicultural literature for individual and group study.
- Use questions to stimulate thinking about human concerns.
- Guide student response to multicultural literature through such strategies as the dialectical journal.
- Design lessons that incorporate sound theory and practice in language arts instruction with content from multicultural education.
- Organize a unit of study around a novel or theme.

Because we live in a multicultural world, multicultural education is an integral part of instruction in any area of study. Every teacher makes a choice, conscious or unconscious, about allowing multicultural education to exist only as the "hidden curriculum" that children absorb or to plan explicit learning experiences designed to enlighten or to combat misunderstanding. The language arts curriculum, including reading instruction, offers teachers excellent opportunities to present multicultural concepts. In this chapter we will focus on the following:

> The language arts curriculum
> Oral language foundations
> Writing as a way of expressing thinking
> Literature as a source of multicultural content

THE LANGUAGE ARTS/READING CURRICULUM

A comprehensive language arts program includes instruction that promotes development of basic language skills: listening, speaking, thinking, reading, and writing. In addition to these skills, however, language arts includes content about both language and literature.

A Curriculum Framework

We see the language arts curriculum as grounded in a strong oral facility with language, such as depicted in the schema on the following page.

Language arts instruction should integrate the development of skills and content so as to stimulate learning for real purposes. As students develop listening, speaking, and thinking skills, they can also learn information about the diverse population of the United States. Students can:

1. Discuss the problems of being poor
2. Listen to Martin Luther King, Jr.'s "I Have a Dream" speech
3. Argue about our treatment of the native American Indians
4. Read newspaper accounts of dissension in Israel
5. Tape letters to young people living in China

The possibilities are endless, and the topics generated lend stimulus to language and literacy instruction. Notice also that the suggested topics could well be presented in social studies classes, too, which suggests the integration of language arts and social studies instruction for a more powerful effect. We will continue this discussion in the next chapter.

Renewed concern about teaching writing is a second trend that we will address in this chapter. Perceiving writing as another way of expressing thinking makes it a natural step following listening and speaking activities. A strong oral language foundation prepares the student to write successfully. Multicultural concepts and controversies provide food for thought, something to communicate to the world in writing.

Evaluating
Development

Reading and
Responding to Literature

Reading/Thinking/Writing
for Varied Purposes

Extending Thinking Abilities

Strengthening Reading/Writing
Connections

Gaining Power through Reading/
Thinking/Writing

Discovering Basic Literacy Concepts

Developing a Strong Thinking/Language Foundation

From I. M. Tiedt, R. Gibbs, M. Howard, M. Timpson, and M. Y. Williams, *Reading/Thinking/Writing: A Holistic Language and Literacy Program for the K–8 Classroom.* Copyright © 1989 by Allyn and Bacon. Reprinted with permission.

Reading literature, an essential component of an outstanding language arts program, also plays a special part in teaching multicultural understandings. Good fiction enables the reader to "walk in another person's moccasins," to feel the humiliation or the joy experienced by a boy or girl of a different color. Well-written nonfiction provides background information about other countries and other cultures. Poetry gives students insight into the thinking of a writer who has a message to share about living. Multicultural literature provides vicarious experiences that lead students to recognize the commonalities they share with others.

Thus, English or language arts and reading classes offer an unusual opportunity to introduce multicultural concepts to students at any age. Through selection of topics for discussion or literature to read, you can encourage students to think about other people who live next door or perhaps across the ocean. For those who may not be familiar with the "cutting edge" of theory and practice in the language arts, we begin this chapter with a summary of what we know about teaching language and literacy skills. We will build on the ideas that were presented about teaching in Chapter 2.

What Research Tells Us

Studies of the language arts curriculum and instruction provide us with a knowledge base from which to begin planning a multiculturally based language arts program. The following basic assumptions will guide the development of multicultural lessons to integrate into the language arts curriculum:

1. A strong thinking-language base is necessary for success in reading and writing. Thinking and language permeate all learning.
2. Reading and writing cannot be taught in isolation. Integrating the language arts reinforces learning efficiently and effectively.
3. Beginning readers need to learn basic phonics information, but they can best learn and then reinforce this learning through reading and writing whole language. Decoding (unlocking meaning from words presented in the English code) and encoding (spelling/writing words according to the English code system) should be presented as complementary processes applied during meaningful reading and writing activities.
4. Students learn to read, write, and think by engaging frequently in composing and comprehending activities that emphasize quality of the learning experience as well as quantity or frequency of practice. These experiences can involve learning in any subject area (e.g., multicultural concepts).
5. Literature must be an integral part of instruction across the curriculum at all levels. It should be presented as something to be read and also as an example of good writing by a real person who is sharing his or her thinking.
6. Both reading and writing entail a transaction between author and audience as they work together to construct meaning. The work of both reader and writer are influenced by prior knowledge—what each brings to the task of making meaning. All learners come to school with a store of prior knowledge, which includes cultural backgrounds.
7. Reading, writing, and thinking abilities grow uniquely for each individual. Instructional strategies should be selected to promote individual progress. Evaluation must also be adapted to fit individual growth with appropriate expectations established for each learner.

Refer to the list of titles at the end of the chapter if you would like to know more about studies in this area. *Composing and Comprehending,* edited by Julie Jensen (NCTE, 1985), is an especially good overview. Another up-to-date summary of research in this field is *The Dynamics of Language: Research in Reading and English,* edited by James Squire (NCTE, 1987). See also the *Annual Summary of Investigation Relating to Reading* from the International Reading Association.

Summary

An integrated language arts curriculum is firmly rooted in oral language. Students progress developmentally, gaining independence as they experience success in making meaning first through observing, thinking, and listening. Emergent whole language approaches lead them naturally into reading ideas presented by others and expressing their own thinking through speaking and writing. In the following sections we will examine ways of working with oral language, writing, and reading literature.

ORAL LANGUAGE: FOUNDATION FOR LEARNING

As presented in the holistic model for language arts instruction, oral language — thinking, listening, and speaking — forms the foundation for all of learning. Learning begins aurally and orally, and oral language continues to be an important way of communicating in adult life.

Unlike Japanese educators who stress oral communication, however, instruction in our classrooms tends to move quickly toward an emphasis on written language.[2] It is interesting to conjecture on our hesitance to offer a strong oral language curriculum. Is it perhaps because studies that use the written language are more predictable and more easily controlled? Do teachers feel more comfortable with written exercises or reading assignments followed by workbook pages for which they know the answers? Is oral performance more difficult to evaluate?

Using Oral Language in the Classroom

Our contention is that we need to allocate more classroom time for learning with oral language than we do at present. In this section, we will explore ways of incorporating speaking and listening activities that promote multicultural thinking in language arts instruction. Focusing on multicultural concepts will, as noted previously, suggest the use of such approaches across the curriculum. This discussion will continue in Chapter 8.

Oral language is the foundation on which we base all language learning. Unless a child has a facility with a spoken language — Swahili, Tagalog, Spanish, English — he or she will not become a fluent reader or writer. Children who have difficulty with language, for example those who are learning English as a second language, need to spend more time working orally. Through oral language we develop an "ear for language" that enables us to construct grammatical sentences as we write and to interpret the meaning of sentences as we read.

Oral activities should be part of the daily learning experiences, for they assist children in continuing to learn more about the language they use. Prewriting and prereading motivation is usually oral. Sharing writing and responding to books offer further opportunities for bringing oral activities into the classroom. For instance, some of the following ideas will help students plan oral book reviews:

- Interview a character in the book. Two members of the class may share this review with one serving as the character to be interviewed.
- Give a first-person account of an event in the book read: Wilbur speaks, for example: "I tell you I was so lonesome I thought I'd die when suddenly I heard Charlotte's sweet voice. . . ."
- Tape a portion of the story after having practiced reading that part of the book aloud in order to achieve the best interpretation.
- Present an award to the author of a prize-winning book (either for illustrations or for story content) explaining why this book was selected for the award.
- Prepare pictures of important incidents in a book. Then tell the story briefly as the pictures are shown. (This could be a scroll theater presentation prepared by several students who have read the same book.)
- Prepare a commercial to sell a book to fellow students. This activity might involve several students and could be correlated with art.

Roleplaying

Roleplaying is a versatile oral activity that allows students to express their opinions in a realistic situation. They can literally stand in someone else's shoes as they speak for the role they have assumed. Ideas for roleplaying come from all areas of the curriculum, for instance:

- A group of parents discussing a city problem
- Children greeting a new student
- A family that has just come from Vietnam
- A Japanese American family that is to go to an intern camp
- Children in school in colonial America
- An American Indian tribe in 1700

Roleplaying may be performed by a group of three to five students as the others observe and take notes. After the performance, class discussion focuses on the strengths and weaknesses of the performance; for example, the language used and the appropriateness of the topics discussed. After this analysis, another group can perform with the same roles and situation.

At other times, the whole class can roleplay a situation, such as the American Indian tribe in 1700. Before beginning this activity, of course, students need to study to determine what the various roles would be. Group activities in specific areas of the room might focus on the campfire, the corral where horses are located, or a group of hunters in the woods. Simple costuming lends interest to this dramatic play.

Roleplaying can lead to formal debate as students discuss the pros and cons of an issue. After arguing informally in roleplay, students may be stimulated to search out more information to be presented in a panel discussion or debate. These oral activities lend interest to learning, and they provide a firm foundation for writing to express opinions. They also teach advanced thinking skills.

For more information about roleplaying, refer to *Role-Playing in the Curriculum,* second edition, by Fannie and George Shaftel (Prentice-Hall, 1982). This excellent book includes suggestions for beginning and advanced experiences in roleplaying for students of all ages. Many suggestions are specific to multicultural education.

Philosophical Discussions

We often allude to discussion as part of classroom instruction. However, studies show that what is called discussion often is teacher-dominated with the teacher asking questions to which students respond one by one. The percentage of student involvement revealing real thinking remains very low.[3]

Focusing on multicultural understanding offers an opportunity to deal with meaty concerns, matters of consequence. Introducing topics that are presented in fiction is a safe way for a less confident teacher to open up what we can identify as "philosophical discussions," the kind of talk informed adults engage in frequently. Depending on the content of a particular book, a worthwhile discussion might involve students in talking about "experiences all children have had, such as being embarrassed by not knowing an answer. They may have wanted to talk about these experiences, but not in a personal way. By discussing what happens to the characters in a novel, they can talk about things in the third person: somebody else is the one involved."[4]

Classroom climate is crucial to developing a successful oral program. Once a climate of trust is built up, discussions may lead to sharing experiences or problems that individuals have faced. As students gain skill in such discourse, they can meet in small groups so that the percentage of participation for each student will increase. For some students a small discussion group is less inhibiting than a large group. A few conclusions from each group can then be shared with the larger group. Such discussion may serve as a prewriting stimulus as each student expresses his or her thoughts in writing about the topic discussed.

Following is a lesson that illustrates the kind of discussion that can follow the reading of almost any novel.

Sample Lesson: The Need for Friendship

Level of Difficulty: Grades 4–7

Outcomes:

Students will:

1. Discuss the need for friends.
2. Identify problems that occur between friends.
3. Suggest solutions to problems that arise.

Description:

After listening to the teacher's reading *Always and Forever Friends,* students discuss Wendy's search for a friend. Through discussion they identify the need for friendship as a universal need that they share with all other human beings. In small groups they discuss problems that can arise between friends. They also discuss possible solutions to such problems.

Procedures:

Obtain a copy of *Always and Forever Friends* by C. S. Adler (Houghton Mifflin, 1988) or any similar book about friendship. Read the story aloud to the whole class, chapter by chapter, over a two-week period. Give students a chance to talk about the events depicted in each chapter following the reading. This lesson is designed to follow the completion of the whole book. It requires at least 2 periods.

Stimulus

Present the following quotation from the book on a transparency:

> "The way I look at it," Honor continued earnestly, "you don't wind yourself around a friend like a strangler vine, and you don't expect friendship to be always and forever."
> "But Honor, if it doesn't last, what good is it?"
> "I didn't say it *wouldn't* last. All I'm saying is, we shouldn't expect it to because life's sure to change us, you and me. In high school, we'll be different people, and boys will come in the picture—for you anyway. I don't know if I'll have time for them if I'm going to be a lawyer. And if boys don't do us in, then after high school we'll go our separate ways, and that'll make it hard."

Ask students to state Wendy's view of friendship. Then ask someone else to restate what Honor is saying.

Activity

Have students number off from 1 to 6 to form six cooperative learning groups. (Adjust these numbers to produce groups of four to six students.) Assign a Leader and a Recorder for each group. Give each group leader copies of the following sheet. (Include an extra copy for the Recorder.)

---

1. Could you live without having friends?

2. Why do people feel the need of friends?

3. What are problems that make finding friends difficult?

4. What problems can come up to break up a friendship?

5. What can we do to make a friendship last?

Directions:

Take a few minutes for each person to read the questions and to write at least one response to each question.

Then discuss each question in turn. Each person should read one answer to the first question. Talk about the answers that were shared and agree on one answer for the whole group. You may combine answers that were shared.

After the Recorder has written the group answer on the Group Answer Sheet, go to Question 2, and so on.

Followup

Working with the full class, have one person share the group response to each question in turn.

After ideas have been shared, have each student write a paragraph about the importance of friendship in his or her life.

Evaluation

Have students meet in the same groups to share their paragraphs. After the group listens to a student's paragraph, each student will identify one aspect of the writing they especially like. Then each student will make one suggestion for improving the writing of the paragraph.

Students will then rewrite their first drafts. The revised copies will be placed in a three-ringed notebook entitled Friendship Forever. After class members have had ample time to read it, place this class publication in the school library.

Summary

Oral language provides the foundation for all learning. From the time children acquire speech in the early years, they continue to use speaking and listening as the primary mode of communicating. Thinking is inextricably integrated with language learning. Effective teachers use oral language to support to the development of literacy skills at all levels and in all subject areas. Listening, thinking, and speaking will support multicultural learnings in the same way they do for all other learning.

WRITING "THINKING"

The most important development in working with written language in the classroom is the discovery that *what we read is writing — an expression of a person's thinking.* Whole language approaches based soundly in the child's oral language encourage children to begin scribble writing their original stories as best they can, literally becoming authors. Only then do they gradually discover how to read their own writing. Thus, literacy emerges in a natural fashion akin to the way children learn oral language.

What We Know about Teaching Writing

Through a process of evolution, we have changed our approaches to teaching students how to write. Even though there is some resistance and clinging to traditional approaches, elementary and secondary teachers have received support for methodologies that demonstrate concern for students' self-esteem and that reduce the paperload for composition instructors. Following is a summary of beliefs supported by current research compiled by K–12 teachers trained by the National Writing Project:

This We Believe. . .

1. Writing is a processs that involves thinking; it should not be defined as assignments or products.
2. Students need a prewriting warm-up, a stimulus that is often oral, before they begin to write. Oral language provides the foundation for both writing and reading.
3. Our first emphasis in a writing program should be on developing fluency. Students need to write daily and they need to experience a variety of forms and types of writing in order to write effectively.
4. Writers need to be aware of the audience for whom they are writing; this audience should not always be just the teacher.
5. Teachers should draw from a variety of theories and strategies for teaching writing.
6. An effective writing lesson includes (1) prewriting (talking, gathering ideas), (2) writing (organizing thinking, sharing, responding, editing, rewriting), and (3) post-writing (making the writing public).
7. Not every piece of writing goes through the full editing process; many will be short "finger exercises" designed to develop fluency and to break down writing apprehension.
8. A teacher should not expect to read or to grade every piece of writing that students do.
9. Teachers should write frequently with their students to model the writing process and to show value for writing as well as to share themselves.
10. Writing develops critical thinking skills and facilitates learning across the curriculum.
11. Evaluation of writing should be on-going and should emphasize more than just the correct use of conventions. Students should engage in self-evaluation, peer evaluation, and conferences with the teacher.
12. Writing is the most difficult of the language skills, so we should appreciate what students are able to achieve.[5]

Kinds of Writing Students Can Try

Students will enjoy trying varied kinds of writing rather than writing the same forms repeatedly. James Moffett provides an interesting way of connecting thinking and writing processes and the forms of writing we use.[6]

Thinking Up	*Thinking Over,*
(Imagination)	*Thinking Through*
Fiction	*(Cogitation)*
Plays	Column
Poetry	Editorial
	Review
Looking Back	Personal Essay
(Recollection)	Thesis Essay
Autobiography	
Memoir	*Looking Into*
	(Investigation)
Noting Down	Biography
(Notation)	Chronicle
Journal	Case
Diary	Profile
	Factural Article
	Reportage and Research

Here are eight forms of writing that young authors can use to express their ideas:

1. Report of Information
   The writer collects data from observation and research and chooses material that best presents a phenomenon or concept.
2. Eye Witness Account
   The writer tells about a person, group, or event that was objectively observed from the outside.
3. Autobiographical Incident
   Narration of a specific event in the writer's life and stating or implying the significance of the event.
4. Firsthand Biography Sketch
   Through incident and description the writer characterizes a person he or she knows well.
5. Story
   The writer shows conflict between characters or between a character and the environment including dialogue and description.
6. Analysis—Speculation about Effects
   The writer conjectures about what may result from a specific event, cause and effect.
7. Problem Solution
   The writer describes and analyzes a specific problem and then proposes and argues for a solution.
8. Evaluation
   The writer presents a judgment on the worth of an item—book, movie, artwork, consumer product—supported with reasons and evidence.

The types of writing specified reflect the intent of the author and ways of thinking rather than prescribed poetry or prose forms. For example, a report of information could be a resume or a book review. A story might take the form of a fable or an extended dialogue. Thus the emphasis is not so much on producing a specific form as it is on the expression of students' ideas for a specific purpose.[7] Following are ideas for engaging students in writing.

Clustering: A Prewriting Technique

Clustering is a brainstorming technique that can be used individually or in a large group. It can be used to probe into a topic that students are planning to write or talk about. It can also be used as a preassessment tool to determine what students know or do not know about a topic to be studied. Clustering serves well to help students organize their thinking before they begin to write a report.

A good way to introduce clustering to a class is to create collectively a large clustering of ideas on the chalkboard. If, for instance, you are beginning a study of the Northwest, you might lead students through the clustering process, grouping ideas as shown on page 195.

Students quickly learn to use clustering as a way of collecting their thoughts before writing. Encourage them to spend five minutes clustering before writing anything, even the answer to a test question.

You can use clustering as an individual or group activity to assess student knowledge or attitudes before beginning a unit of study. The students may be surprised to discover how little they know about Black History or Alaska, our forty-ninth state. After a study has been completed, a second clustering should provide an interesting comparison as students see graphically how much they have learned. The clustering activity in the module on Chinese Americans is an example of preassessing the class's collective knowledge before beginning a study (see page 245).

Writing a Report

The following lesson demonstrates just how to engage students in writing a report. In this case the report is the review of a book.

Sample Lesson: Introducing Students to the Book Review[8]

Type of Writing: Report of Information

Level of Difficulty: Grades 3–12 (Adjust material and expectations.)

Outcomes:

1. Read a book review.
2. Identify characteristic features of this form.
3. Write a book review that includes these features.

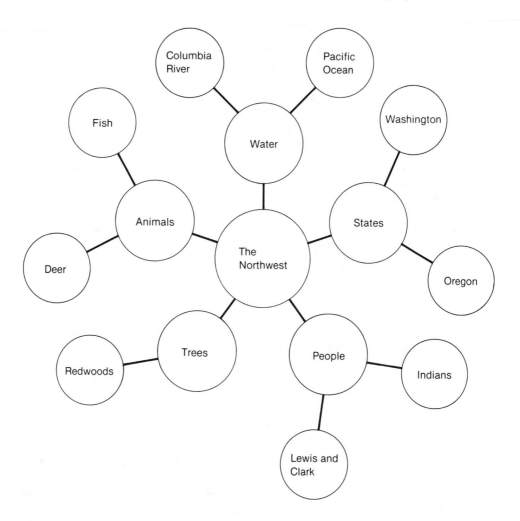

Procedures:

Locate the review of a book that you would like students to know or perhaps an author you would like to introduce. Duplicate a class set of copies of the review. (You can write one yourself following the model presented here.) This lesson requires at least 2 periods.

Book Review: *Where the Red Fern Grows*

Wilson Rawls was a country boy from the Ozarks. He spent much of his time roaming the hills with a blue tick hound, hunting and fishing, enjoying the out of doors. It was natural, then, for him to write a book about a boy who wanted hunting hounds, a boy who also roamed the hills and river bottoms of the Cherokee country so familiar to Rawls. He describes the setting, thus:

> Our home was in a beautiful valley far back in the rugged Ozarks. The country was new and sparsely settled. The land we lived on was Cherokee land, allotted to my mother because of the Cherokee blood that flowed in her veins.
>
> It lay in a strip from the foothills of the mountains to the banks of the Illinois River in northwestern Oklahoma.

Where the Red Fern Grows is a story of love for family, for animals, and for this country. It is also a story of adventure as Billy achieves his greatest dreams.

Ten-year-old Billy wanted a pair of coon dogs, but hounds cost more money than the family could possibly afford. Determined, Billy began saving his money, storing it in an old K. C. Baking Powder can. After almost two years, he had fifty dollars, enough to buy the two redbone coon hound pups that would change his entire existence.

Billy, Dan, and Little Ann spent their lives together from the time he brought them home. As he said:

> It was wonderful indeed how I could have heart-to-heart talks with my dogs and they always seemed to understand. Each question I asked was answered in their own doggish way.
>
> Although they couldn't talk in my terms, they had a language of their own that was easy to understand. Sometimes I would see the answer in their eyes, and again it would be in the friendly wagging of their tails. Other times I could hear the answer in a low whine or feel it in the soft caress of a warm flicking tongue. In some way, they would always answer. (page 68)

The high point of the book is Billy's winning the gold championship cup in the annual coon-hunting contest. With the cup came a large cash prize that answered his mother's prayers for a new house.

Billy continued to hunt with his dogs until one night they met the "devil cat of the Ozarks, the mountain lion." His brave little dogs tried to save Billy from the lion whose "yellow slitted eyes burned with hate." Although Billy finally killed the huge animal with an ax, the dogs were badly wounded. Old Dan died from his injuries, and Little Ann soon died, too, of heartbreak at losing her hunting companion. Billy sadly buried the two dogs in a beautiful spot on the hillside.

As the family was leaving the Ozarks the following spring, Billy ran to this grave for one last farewell. It was then that he saw the beautiful red fern that had sprung up above the graves of the little dogs. He remembered the old Indian legend that said "only an angel could plant the seeds of a red fern, and that they never died; where one grew, that spot was sacred." As they drove away, the family could see the red fern "in all its wild beauty, a waving red banner in a carpet of green."

Fast action, human interests, and believeable characters make this a book for readers of all ages. A master storyteller, Wilson Rawls has shared a piece of himself.

By Iris M. Tiedt

Stimulus (Prewriting)

Give students copies of the book review you have selected. Read the book review aloud slowly as students read their copies. (This is especially helpful for students who are less able readers and ESL students, and it helps keep the class together for purposes of the lesson.)

Then have students return to the beginning of the review and direct them to identify the kinds of information the author included in the review. Begin a chart, Features of a Book Review, as students list such characteristics as the following:

Features of a Book Review

1. Includes quotations from the book
2. Comments about the content presented by the author
3. Tells something about the author, biography
4. Expresses personal reaction to the book
5. Includes the title and author of the book

Direct the students to bring a book that they have already read to class the next day.

Activity (Writing)

See that each student has a book to review. Display the Features of a Book Review list that the class compiled. Go through the features one by one with the class as students take notes based on the books they are reviewing.

Tell students to complete the first draft of the new book review they have begun as homework.

Followup (Postwriting)

On the next day students should have the first drafts of their book reviews and copies of the book to be reviewed. Have students work in cooperative learning groups of three to five students. Each student is to read his or her book review aloud as the others listen to see if all features on the list have been included. After listening to a review, each member of the group should answer the following two questions for that writer:

1. What one aspect of this review was especially well written?
2. What one recommendation would help improve the writing?

Each student should mark the writing that was commended with a big star. The writer should also take notes on the suggestions for improvement to aid revision.

Students should complete a revision of this first draft as homework that night. They should bring both the first draft and the revision to class.

The next day revised versions of the book reviews can again be shared in the same editing groups. Each writer should point out exactly what changes were made from the first draft. Any further changes should be made, as needed.

Evaluation

Before completing the final draft of the book reviews, students should work as a class to determine just how these reviews will be evaluated. They might consider these types of evaluation:

- Pass or Fail (based on what is being taught)

  10 points   The completed book review contains all of the features listed.
   0 points   The completed book review does not contain all of the features listed.

- A Simple Rubric or Standard (some recognition for excellence)

  10   Uses excellent detailed description
       Shows clear personal involvement
       Includes important biographical information
       Speaks clearly to the audience
       Includes all features listed, very well-presented
   5   Presents all features adequately
       Needs further revision
   2   Presents most features, very weak writing
       Needs extensive revision

Students who are involved in determining evaluation measures for their own work are assuming responsibility for their work. They also have clear ideas of what they need to do to get the top score, and they can help each other so that potentially everyone in each group can get the top score. Thus the teacher moves out of the authoritarian role of Grade Giver.

Students can also implement the scoring, reading each paper to see which scores it deserves. Students learn much about writing by reading each other's work. They are also engaged in thinking as they evaluate each other's writing.

When book reviews are fully revised, they can be published instantly in a three-ringed notebook that bears the title: Books We Recommend. Have someone decorate the cover. This collection, containing something by everyone in the class, should be available in the classroom for reading. Later, it can be shared with others by placing the collection in the library.

Summary

Learning to write is an outcome that is an essential part of the curriculum at all levels and in all subject areas. In an effective writing program, students will:

Write frequently.
Learn to write by writing.
Learn to write by reading.
Talk about the writing process.
Write for varied purposes.
Write to different audiences.
See writing as a way of expressing "thinking."
Edit their own writing and that of others.
Revise some writing selections to be made public.
Be involved in evaluating their own progress.
Confer with their instructor periodically.[9]

Students in a multicultural education program will write about topics related to that area of study.

LITERATURE-BASED LANGUAGE ARTS INSTRUCTION

A second influential trend in literacy instruction is the strong move toward bringing literature into the mainstream in reading programs at the elementary school level. Tradebooks (library books, as opposed to textbooks) are appearing in the publishers' series, and the books are being used directly as texts. We believe firmly that children should learn to read from real literature and that teachers' dependence on the basal reading series is turning students away from reading. Lessons focusing on multicultural literature offer students and teachers a wonderful way to share meaningful experiences. Most literature lessons also offer an opportuntity to make connections with oral language and writing.

Responding to Literature

We can develop language skills at the same time we present language and literature concepts. Here are just a few suggestions for each skill:

Listening:

Retell a folktale that the teacher has read aloud.
Act out an Indian coyote tale after hearing it at the Listening Center.

Speaking:

Discuss the problems that Karana faced in *Island of the Blue Dolphins* by Scott O'Dell.
Prepare to tell a "flannel board story" to children in another room.

Reading:

Select a poem to read aloud as part of a class presentation for Black History Month.
Read a book about someone your age who lives in another country.

Writing:

Keep a process journal as you read a book by a Black American author.
Use mapping to outline the story of the life of a famous American Woman.

Thinking:

How is your life like that of Peter in *The Snowy Day?*
What questions would you want to ask Katherine Paterson after reading her book *Bridge to Terabithia?*

Teaching Literature Concepts

The study of literature is a broad area that offers a wealth of material from which to choose. Literature concepts can be presented on a story chart.

A STORY CHART		
Who?	characters	dialogue
When?	setting	mood
Where?		
What?	plot	theme
Why?		problem
How?	conclusion	solution

Such concepts can be identified after reading James Houston's fine Canadian Eskimo trilogy—*Frozen Fire, Black Diamonds,* and *Ice Sword*—as well as other multicultural selections. The choices we make determine information that students will learn. Literature we choose to share in the classroom should always be by the very best authors, for example:

Primary Grades

The Snowy Day (Ezra Jack Keats)

Arrow to the Sun (Gerald McDermott)

The Hundred Penny Box (Sharon Bell Mathis)

Elementary Grades

M. C. Higgins the Great (Virginia Hamilton)

Roll of Thunder, Hear My Cry (Mildred Taylor)

Dragonwings (Laurence Yep)

Advanced Students

Phillip Hall Likes Me, I Reckon Maybe (Bette Green)

Road from Home (David Kherdian)

Many other books are listed in the appendix. Ways of bringing multicultural literature into the classroom are also presented in Chapter 8.

Bibliotherapy

Universal Feelings Children and Adolescents Share.   Sharing a good book can be a way of stimulating discussions about needs that students have in common. Read books aloud for this purpose; for example, *North Town* by Lorenz Graham for grades four and up, or *Stevie* by John Steptoe for primary grades. These two books happen to be about black characters, but children will identify with them as human beings who are experiencing emotions familiar to them.

Other good books that reveal universal needs and feelings include:

Primary Grades

Jan Brett. *Fritz and the Beautiful Horses.* Houghton, 1981. A gentle pony is excluded from the in-group.

Susan Jeschke. *Perfect the Pig.* Holt, 1980. The runt of the litter wishes for wings.

Patricia Lakin. *Don't Touch My Room.* Little, Brown, 1985. Adjusting to a new baby.

Norma Simon. *What Can I Do?* Whitman, 1969. A little Puerto Rican girl is looking for something to contribute.

Books for Older Students

Alice Bach. *The Meat in the Sandwich.* Harper & Row, 1975. Ten-year-old Mike creates a fantasy world to make his life more interesting.

Paula Fox. *Lily and the Lost Boy.* Orchard, 1987. Growing up.

Ruth Meyers and Beryle Banfield. *Embers: Stories for a Changing World.* Feminist Press, 1983. Collection of fiction, biography, and poetry about children struggling to overcome prejudice.

Laura Nathanson. *The Trouble with Wednesdays.* Bantam, 1987. Sexual abuse.

Emily Neville. *Its's Like This, Cat.* Harper & Row, 1963. Adolescent Dave Mitchell learns to get along with his father.

Cynthia Voigt. *Homecoming.* Atheneum, 1981. Growing up.

Linda Woolverton. *Running Before the Wind.* Houghton, 1987. Incest.

Universal Problems Young People Face. Children today need to be able to talk about varied problems that were not so freely discussed ten years ago. Death and divorce are two topics that we can talk about in the classroom as an aid to students who are faced with these events in their lives. Books can often serve to provide a realistic perspective as well as to open up controversial topics for students and teachers who may find it difficult to introduce such topics. Many fine books written for young people handle these subjects sensitively.

Divorce or Single-Parent Families. The following books are suggested:

Primary Grades

Anne N. Baldwin. *Jenny's Revenge.* Four Winds, 1974.

Joan Lexau. *Me Day.* Dial, 1971.

Paul Zindel. *I Love My Mother.* Harper & Row, 1975.

Books for Older Students

Charlote Anker. *Last Night I Saw Andromeda.* Walck, 1975.

Rose Blue. *A Month of Sundays.* Watts, 1972.

Sue Bridges. *Permanent Connections.* Harper, 1987

Barthe de Clements. *No Place for Me.* Viking, 1987.

Constance Greene. *I Know You, Al.* Viking, 1975.

Florence P. Heide. *When the Sad One Comes to Stay.* Lippincott, 1975.

Patricia MacLachlan. *Sarah, Plain and Tall.* Harper, 1985.

Mary Mahoney. *The Hurry-Up Summer.* Putnam, 1987.

Colby Rodowsky. *Fitchett's Folly.* Farrar, 1987.

Death and Relationship with Aged People.   The following books are suggested:

Primary Grades

Jennifer Bartoli. *Nonna.* Harvey House, 1975.

John Burningham. *Grandpa.* Crown, 1985.

Tomie de Paola. *Nana Upstairs and Nana Downstairs.* Putnam, 1973.

Wendy Kesselman. *Emma.* Doubleday, 1980.

Miska Miles. *Annie and the Old One.* Little, Brown, 1971.

Helen Oxenburg. *Grandma and Grandpa.* Dial, 1984.

Charlotte. Zolotow. *My Grandson Lew.* Harper & Row, 1974.

Books for Older Students

Katherine Bacon. *Shadow and Light.* Macmillan, 1987.

Vera and Bill Cleaver. *Where the Lilies Bloom.* Lippincott, 1969.

Lucille Clifton. *Good Times.* Random House, 1969.

Penelope Jones. *Holding Together.* Bradbury, 1983.

Alfred Slote. *Hang Tough, Paul Mather.* Lippincott, 1973.

Doris B. Smith. *A Taste of Blackberries.* Crowell, 1973.

Toby Talbot. *Away Is So Far.* Four Winds, 1974.

Phyllis Wood. *Then I'll Be Home Free.* Dodd, 1986.

An excellent resource to help you find more books like these is Sharon Dreyer's *Bookfinder,* 2 volumes (American Guidance, 1981). Another resource is *Your Reading: A Booklist for Junior High and Middle School Students,* edited by James and Hazel Davis (NCTE, 1988), which is categorized by subjects.

Reader's Theater

Reader's theater involves students in reading various kinds of literature related to a theme, a unit of study in the social studies. You might, for example, divide the class in groups of five or six for planning reader's theater presentations. All may focus on a presentation for Black History Month or each group might plan a presentation on one ethnic group in your school community. Several weeks are required for planning, searching for material, and giving the presentations to an audience. The work will follow these steps:*

Step 1: Planning.   Talk with students about the idea of a reader's theater presentation. Explain that the presentation is read, not acted out. The presenters sit on stools or chairs and read their assigned parts. Choose a theme for the presentation and discuss the kinds of materials that might be used, for example:

- Poetry
- Exerpts from novels
- Short stories (fables, myths, etc.)
- Sayings, proverbs, quotations
- Factual statements
- Lyrics from songs

Step 2: Searching for Material.   Plan a visit to the library as the groups search for material related to the selected theme. If you notify the librarian ahead of time, she or he will be able to locate appropriate sources for the class use. The material does not have to be written in play form for this kind of presentation, as you will see in the next step.

Step 3: Preparing the Script.   Duplicate copies of folktales or poems that students plan to use. These copies can then be marked and revised as the group deems appropriate. In narrative, roles are identified; for example, Anansi, the Spider. There may be three or four roles to read plus one or more narrators who read the descriptive passages. Students can supply dialogue to add interest and to develop a character. Sometimes passages will be deleted.

Step 4: Rehearsing.   One student should be the director to signal the group when to stand and to sit. This person listens during rehearsals to see that students read clearly and effectively, makes suggestions for timing, and so on.

Poetry and nonfiction can be divided in various sections or verses. One or more persons may read to provide variety.

Step 5: The Presentation.   Select an audience for whom to perform the finished production. The audience may be the rest of the class, another class that is studying the same topic, or the whole school in an assembly. A reader's theater presentation can be given to the Parent Teachers' Association meeting to show parents what students are studying.

A study of Japanese Americans and contemporary Japan might culminate with a reader's theater presentation based on student reading and research. Readings could be selected from such books as:

*Iris M. Tiedt, *The Language Arts Handbook,* © 1983, pp. 392–385. Adapted by permission of Prentice Hall, Inc. Englewood Cliffs, New Jersey.

Sumiko Yagawa (translated by Katherine Paterson). *The Crane Wife.* Marrow, 1981.

Toshi Maruki. *Hiroshima No Pika.* Lothrop, 1982.

Nancy Luenn. *The Dragon Kite.* Harcourt, 1982.

Collections of Japanese folktales by Yoshiko Uchida include:

The Dancing Kettle and Other Japanese Folktales
The Magic Listening Cap
More Folktales from Japan
The Sea of Gold and Other Tales from Japan

To enhance a presentation for their audience, students could add songs or dances. Pictures could be displayed with original student haiku. A filmstrip or film would add to a very impressive sharing time for both adults and children, which might be planned for May 5th, Children's Day in Japan. (See the Multicultural Calendar for other suggestions.)

Reading and Writing Poetry

Poetry is especially suitable for enhancing a social studies lesson. Your own enthusiasm will be contagious as students listen to you read (or recite) a favorite poem related to the current study. Explore collections of poetry to find poems to fit your needs, for example:

- Henry W. Longfellow, "Paul Revere's Ride." (early American history)
- Robert Frost, "The Road Not Taken. (decision making)
- Robert Service. "The Cremation of Sam McGee." (Alaska)

A wonderful collection of poems about people in history is *The Book of Americans* by Rosemary and Stephen Vincent Benet. *Bronzeville Boys and Girls* is a collection by Pulitzer Prizewinner Gwendolyn Brooks. Sample the work of a black poet, Langston Hughes; the composer of outstanding free verse, Carl Sandburg; and the well-polished haiku written by Japanese poets of the thirteenth century. To teach poetry effectively you must first know and enjoy poetry yourself.

Writing poetry is another way of involving students with expressing their ideas about social studies topics. Begin with unrhymed forms such as the cinquain (sank'en), a five-line poem like this:

Line 1: One word (which may be the title)
Line 2: Two words (describing the title)
Line 3: Three words (an action)
Line 4: Four words (a feeling)
Line 5: One word (referring to the title)

Indian,
Native American,
Gliding through forests,

Praising Great Spirit above,
Free.
　　— Iris Tiedt

Use the work of Walt Whitman and Carl Sandburg to stimulate the writing of free verse. Students might study the life of one person before writing a poem to celebrate the contribution he or she made.

Have students write haiku as part of a study of Japan. Here are two examples of haiku translated from the original Japanese:

First cold showers fall.
Even little money wants
A wee coat of straw
　　— *Bashō*

All sky disappears
The earth's land has gone away;
Still the snowflakes fall.
　　— *Hashin*

In popular use today many poets have taken liberties with this versatile verse form. American haiku have been written about a wide variety of topics, and lines have not always remained the prescribed length. Translator and poet Harry Behn comments, "Any translation into English should be, so I believe, what the author might have done if English had been his language." These rules that have grown out of Zen should be followed as much as possible in "the same packaging," but writing haiku is not a game. "It is not easy to be simple."[10]

An excellent source of information for the teacher who wants to know more about haiku is *An Introduction to Haiku* by Harold Anderson (Doubleday). Children are most successful with this brief verse form if emphasis is rightly placed on the thoughts they are expressing rather than on the confining form. The beauty of haiku for children is that they do succeed in producing charming examples which compare well with those created by adult writers. The following examples corroborate this point.[11]

The sun shines brightly.
With its glowing flames shooting
It goes down at night.
　　— *Ricky*

The old cypress tree,
So beautiful by the rocks,
Has been there for years.
　　— *Marjorie*

After first thinking about an idea they wish to express, the students are encouraged to write it on paper. They can then examine their own written thought to determine how it can be divided into three parts. Experimentation with word arrangement, imagery, changing the order of the lines, and choice of words used should be encouraged as the poem is developed. The deceptively simple form requires more delicate handling than does free verse. Here are ideas for working with haiku in the classroom:

- One way of introducing a class to haiku is through the reading of a number of examples such as those in *Cricket Songs* by Harry Behn. After reading a number of these short poems, provide each student with a duplicate sheet (or write on the board), containing several examples of haiku. Let them discover the haiku pattern, the subject treated, and other characteristics by rereading the poems, thus:

Count the number of syllables in each line. How many syllables does each line contain?
1 _____ 2_____ 3_____
Is this true of each poem?_____
What season of the year is indicated in each haiku?

_____

- Japanese poetry makes us think of cherry blossoms or other spring blossoms. Use a twig of any flowering fruit tree to prepare an attractive display to motivate the writing of haiku. The flowers may be combined with pictures mounted on a bulletin board or music may be played to assist the development of a mood for haiku.
- Type haiku written by a class on a duplicating master using two long columns so that the folded sheets will produce two long, slim pages. Cut the duplicated sheets to form pages of an attractive booklet, and make a decorative cover.

- Motifs for booklet covers should be appropriate to the poetry. Students can experiment with brush stroking to simulate Japanese writing or the reeds, bamboo, flowers, and so on, associated with their art.
- The word HAIKU can be printed using letters that have an oriental appearance.
- Two films on haiku well worth investigating are:

In a Spring Garden. Pictures by Ezra Jack Keats. Weston Woods Studios, 6 min., color, n.d. (See the book on which this film is based, too: *In a Spring Garden* by Richard Lewis.)

The Day Is Two Feet Long. Weston Woods Studies, 9 min., color, 1968.

- A most rewarding art experience which correlates well with the writing of haiku is the blowing of ink with a straw. Washable black ink is applied in a swath near the bottom of an unlined file card (or any nonabsorbent paper). The wet ink is then blown with a straw to direct the ink in the desired direction. Blowing across the ink causes it to branch attractively. When the ink is dry, tiny dabs of bright tempera may be applied with a toothpick to add spring blossoms to the bare branch. The student then writes the haiku on the card below the flowering branch, and the card is used for display or as a gift for parents.

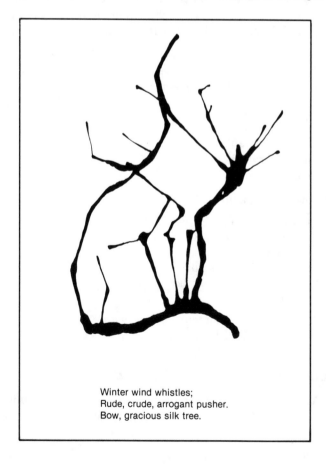

Winter wind whistles;
Rude, crude, arrogant pusher.
Bow, gracious silk tree.

Folded slightly overlapping . . .
. . . tied with ribbon

- For an authentic presentation of haiku use rice paper (or thin onion skin or tissue paper) mounted inside colored paper. The poem is written (a felt pen will write on thin paper) together with an oriental motif — reeds, moon over water, flowering branch — and the author's name. The cover is folded so that the front flaps overlap slightly as in the sketch. A ribbon is then tied around the folder, which is ready for presentation as a gift, as shown.

Tanka are five-lined Japanese poems which contain a haiku (the first three lines). Like the haiku, they are unrhymed and follow a well-defined syllabic pattern with a total of 31 syllables for the entire poem:

Line 1: 5 syllables
Line 2: 7 syllables
Line 3: 5 syllables
Line 4: 7 syllables
Line 5: 7 syllables

Following is an example of tanka:

Silver raindrops fall:
A puddle of water stands.
  Ocean before me,
All the world is reflected.
Look hard and you see black mud.
    — Irene Tabata

A beautiful book on tanka is *The Season of Time,* edited by Virginia O'Baron and published by Dial Press.

Focus on Language: The Cloze Technique

The Cloze technique forces students to make clozure by filling in missing words in sentences. To prepare materials for this purpose you can omit all adjectives or all verbs if you want to focus on the use of vivid language. In the example presented here, every fifth word is omitted, which focuses attention on grammatical constructions and comprehension. The selection is from the beginning of *The Slave Dancer* by Paula Fox.

There was nothing to ___1___ to the slave Tituba ___2___ this morning in November ___3___ be unlike other mornings ___4___ had known in Bridgetown. ___5___ sun was out. The ___6___ of Barbados lay like ___7___ jewel sparkling in the ___8___. Its yellow-white coral ___9___ coast line blazed in ___10___ brilliant light. Tituba could ___11___ part of the shore ___12___ from the windows of ___13___ Endicott's kitchen because the ___14___ sat on the edge ___15___ Carlisle Bay, just where ___16___ made an wide inward ___17___.

The slave John, Tituba's ___18___, had been fishing and ___19___ was showing her the ___20___ snappers he had caught. ___21___ had carried them into ___22___ in a big ___23___ woven basket. The basket ___24___ a deep dark brown, ___25___ as dark as his ___26___, and the fish as ___27___ took them out of ___28___ basket were silvery by ___29___. He had covered the ___30___ with leaves to keep ___31___ cool.

"Good eating," John ___32___, holding one of the ___33___ fish up for Tituba's ___34___. He was a tall, ___35___ built man with broad ___36___. He wore only a ___37___ of white cotton trousers ___38___ up to the knee. ___39___ was barefooted. He leaned ___40___ the basket and then ___41___ up with a fluid, ___42___ movement that made the ___43___ on his back ripple ___44___ the dark brown skin. ___45___ smiled, and his face ___46___ had looked dark and ___47___ in repose was lightened ___48___ brightened by the smile.

After students fill in all of the blanks, discuss the words they chose for each blank. Any answer that sounds right (is grammatical) is acceptable. Lead students to observe that almost everyone will have the same answer for space #5 while a variety of equally good ideas will fit space #20. Be sure to have several copies of this book on hand when you use the exercise because students will be motivated to read the book following this exposure to the beginning paragraphs.

Literature Promotes Awareness of the Conventions

La Dictée: A Dictation Method[12]

Following the method of teaching French students to write described by Rollo Brown in *How the French Boy Learns to Write* is an effective way of teaching writing by using literature selections. The procedures are simple and easily carried out by any teacher.

1. Select a good book that students can enjoy at the level you teach. Then choose one paragraph from the first chapter that contains sentences and vocabulary that you think your students should be able to write.
2. Introduce the book and author to your students. Read the first chapter aloud so that students know what the story is about and how the selected paragraph fits into the story.

3. Explain that you have selected a paragraph that you plan to dictate to them. Read the paragraph aloud as students listen. Then ask questions about the paragraph to help students understand the full meaning of words, images, and references.

4. Tell the class that you are going to dictate the paragraph sentence by sentence. You will first read a sentence, and they will listen. Then they will begin writing. You will repeat the sentence once more, but no more than two times. Follow this procedure, giving students ample time to write before beginning the next sentence.

5. After students have written all sentences in this manner, read each sentence again as you help them correct their writing. You may choose to have several students write each sentence on the board before you discuss the necessary punctuation, capitalization, and spelling. Discuss any unusual features. Students will study these sentences in order to write them more correctly when you dictate them again the following day.

6. On the next day, repeat the same dictation passage. This time have students pass their papers to the person on the right as they correct each other's sentences.

7. You may have a third dictation. This can be conducted by a student who wrote the sentences correctly. You may wish to collect the third writing in order to assess the kinds of errors students are making.

The advantages of la dictée as a method of teaching writing are several:

- It provides structure for student writing, adaptable to any grade level.
- Writing can be selected to introduce or reinforce any aspect of writing the teacher desires.
- Good literature is introduced which may stimulate students to read the book.
- Students are seeing the connection between reading and writing.

Sample Lesson: La Dictée Based on *Farewell to Manzanar* (Jean Watsuki Houston and James Houston)

Level of Difficulty: Grades 5–12 (Adapted by selecting different literature.)

Outcomes:

Students will:

1. Learn multicultural concepts.
2. Learn writing conventions.

Procedures:

Obtain copies of *Farewell to Manzanar* by Jeanne Watsuki Houston and James Houston. You can use this lesson over a two-week period. Tell the students something about Jeanne Watsuki Houston and her experiences:

This book was written by a Japanese woman who was born just before World War II. Her family, up until the war, had been middle class. Her father owned his own fishing boat and carried on many of the Japanese traditions while integrating into the American culture. Jeanne had been raised primarily around Caucasians—in fact she had fears of Chinese children.

With the onset of the war, her family was "moved" to a camp in Southern California in the desert. This story is about that move, the life they were forced to live, and the changing effects upon her life. Even after the war, Jeanne suffered the effects of the camp and its strain on her family.

Stimulus:

Read the selected dictation passage aloud to the students:

> Mama took out another dinner plate and hurled it at the floor, then another and another, never moving, never opening her mouth, just quivering and glaring at the retreating dealer, with tears streaming down her cheeks. He finally turned and scuttled out the door, heading for the next house. When he was gone she stood there smashing cups and bowls and platters until the whole set lay in scattered blue and white fragments across the wooden floor.

Tell the students that this paragraph comes after the family has been told that they have to evacuate their home. Since their new home is much smaller and for an undetermined duration, the family is forced to sell some of their precious items. The dealer has told her that all she can get for her heirloom china is $15.00, maybe $17.50 at the most. The value of the china is over $200.00. Mother's reaction, surprising as it was, was to throw the china on the ground in disgust.

Discuss the paragraph, emphasizing the emotions involved. Talk about the reaction of Mother, the dealer, and any witness, such as Jeanne.

Activity

Proceed to dictate the paragraph, one sentence at a time as students write each sentence. You may have to divide some of the sentences at the natural breaks of the phrases.

Repeat the sentence only two times so students will listen carefully. Challenge them to do their best, but make it clear that what they write will not be graded.

Followup

Have several students write each sentence on the board. Discuss any errors and have students correct his or her own copy. Make conventions clear to the students.

After students have a chance to correct their papers, have them work in pairs to see if they have correctly copied the paragraph.

Evaluation

Students study the dictation as homework. The dictation is then repeated. Correct a few papers until you find several that are written without errors. Appoint these students as Experts who note any errors on the remaining papers.

Students who made errors may take the dictation again, given by one of the Experts (or recorded on tape).

Additional Lessons:

After this introductory lesson, build additional lessons as suggested here.

Activity 2:

Talk again about the paragraph. Discuss the emotions. Brainstorm various emotions with your students (anger, love, sadness, happiness, loneliness).

Develop lists (the writing activity for the students) for two or three emotions of the type of things people do to display, for example, anger (slam door, hit fist, stick out tongue, shout, curse) or love (hold hands, kiss, help, buy gifts, bake cookies). Share these lists with a partner.

Have students circle, underline, or star those things on their list that they thought were especially good.

Activity 3:

Have students write in their journals about a time when they were angry. Point out that some of the things on their list might be (should have been) things that they did that could be included in the paragraph(s).

Activity 4:

Have the students look at their copy of the paragraph. Elicit from them the strong verbs that were used. Discuss how these words create pictures.

Give the students a copy (or write on the board) this paragraph from page 101:

> Again, Papa did not answer. They both knew what it would be. This time his long pause slipped into pure silence. Without the answer he could continue dabbling with the dream. Mama's eyes squinted shut. His fingers worked below her shoulder blades. He had found the knot, the tension node, and he homed in on it with a practiced knuckle. Mama rolled her head from side to side, pulling at the tendons in her neck, groaning loudly now, hissing with the painful pleasure of his cure.

Have the students underline the strong verbs.

Have the students start a list of strong verbs. (We recommend that you make a chart that can be displayed from words that they offer.) Have students write sentences using some of their strong verbs.

Summary

Literature offers an outstanding way of promoting multicultural understandings. Selected novels present people of different cultures experiencing emotions and solving the problems they face. Student readers can respond to the ideas presented by each author as they gradually develop empathetic feelings for people and their needs through vicarious sharing.

REFLECTIONS

The language arts comprises a broad range of content and skills that can become part of any multicultural education program. Wise selections from language and literature will teach multicultural concepts and enhance the language arts classes. In summary, a teacher can strive to teach students how to:

1. Use language that is free of racist and sexist terms or labels.
2. Recognize careless use of language and stereotyped perceptions of people that can hurt human beings and limit their potential.
3. Talk about people as individual human beings who have varied characteristics not limited by sex, race, class, or ethnic background.

You can lead students gradually to greater awareness without being preachy or hostile. Every teacher can, for example:

1. Model appropriate behavior and usage of language.
2. Initiate discussion of questionable practices or language to promote awareness.
3. Plan lessons designed to break down stereotyped thinking.
4. Select nonstereotyped text materials.

The overall aim of the language arts curriculum is *communication.* In order to send messages, children speak and write. In order to receive them, they read and listen. In addition, we recognize the overriding language function: thinking, which is a part of any language activity. Our goal is to assist students in moving from the acquisition of language through listening and speaking to working effectively with written language and, above all, to learn to think.

Multicultural experiences presented in the language arts classroom will utilize all of these skills and content. As we present multicultural lessons in other subject areas, we will continue to use the same language skills and content.

APPLICATIONS

1. Begin developing a unit of study related to one group in the United States; for example, Jews. Brainstorm the topics or names of Jewish people you can research — Israel, synagogue, Golda Meir. Use the index of this book, encyclopedias, and the library subject cards to suggest avenues of investigation. Locate a copy of the *Children's Catalog* in the reference room of the library to see what kinds of books are listed. Outline the kinds of activities you could engage children in as they learn more about the contributions Jews have made to the world.

2. Begin reading books that you can recommend to students or read aloud to a class. *The Children's Catalog,* the children's librarian, and other teachers can suggest titles. You might start with these outstanding authors:

Cynthia Rylant	Florence Heide
Virginia Hamilton	Ezra Jack Keats
Langston Hughes (poetry)	Jane Yolen
Scott O'Dell	Virginia Haviland (folktales)
Laurence Yep	Doris B. Smith

3. Plan three lessons that begin with a book as the stimulus and involve students in writing. Follow the lesson plan described on page 33–36.

4. 1984 was the year of the rat! (Check the Chinese calendar on page 254.) When you think of the rat, the images are usually very negative. Plan a lesson that introduces students to books that present the rat from different perspectives, for example:

> Wayne Anderson. *Ratsmagic.* Pantheon, 1976.
>
> Robert Browing. *The Pied Piper of Hamelin.* Warne, 1888, illustrated by Kate Greenaway. Lothrop, 1977, illustrated by Tony Ross.
>
> James Cressey. *Fourteen Rats and a Rat-Catcher.* Prentice-Hall, 1976.
>
> Julia Cunningham. *Dear Rat.* Houghton, 1961.
>
> Beatrice De Regniers. *The Boy, The Rat, and The Butterfly.* Atheneum, 1971.
>
> Kenneth Graham. *The Wind in the Willows.* Scribner's, 1922, 1953, 1961. Aeriel Books (Holt), 1981.
>
> Thatcher Hurd. *Mystery on the Docks.* Harper, 1983.
>
> Joseph Jacobs. *The Pied Piper and Other Fairy Tales of Joseph Jacobs.* Macmillan, 1963.
>
> Dorothy Ann Lovell. *Rufus the Seafaring Rat.* Faber & Faber, 1968.
>
> Miska Miles. *Wharf Rat.* Little Brown, 1972.
>
> Edna Miller. *Pebbles, A Pack Rat.* Prentice-Hall, 1976.
>
> Robert O'Brien. *Mrs. Frisby and the Rats of NIMH.* Atheneum, 1972.
>
> Dave Ross and Donnie Kinzel. *Rat Race and other Rodent Jokes.* Morrow, 1983.
>
> Barbara Schiller. *The White Rat's Tale.* Holt, Rinehart & Winston, 1967.
>
> Gloria Skurzynski. *What Happened in Hamelin.* Four Winds, 1979.
>
> Barbara Steiner. *The Biography of a Kangaroo Rat.* Putanm, 1977.
>
> James Stevenson. *Wilfred the Rat.* Greenwillow, 1977.
>
> Dorothy Van Woerkom. *The Rat, The Ox, and The Zodiac.* Crown, 1976.
>
> E. B. White. *Charlotte's Web.* Harper, 1952.
>
> Brian Wildsmith. *The Lion and the Rat.* Oxford, 1963.
>
> Kaethe Zemach. *The Beautiful Rat.* Four Winds, 1979.

Endnotes

1. James Squire. "The Ten Great Ideas in the Teaching of English during the Past Half Century." Speech given at the CCCTE Conference, September 1982.

2. "Japanese Education." Cincinnati *Enquirer,* May 16, 1989.

3. James Marshall. "Classroom Discourse and Literary Response," in *Literature in the Classroom: Readers, Texts, and Contexts* edited by Ben F. Nelms. National Council of Teachers of English, 1988, p. 45.

4. Mathew Lipman. "Some Thoughts on the Foundations of Reflective Education," in *Teaching Thinking Skills: Theory and Practice* edited by Joan B. Baron and Robert J. Sternberg. Freeman, 1987, pp. 151–161.

5. South Bay Writing Project. "This We Believe." Training Institute, 1986.

6. James Moffett. "Thinking and Writing Connections." Address to Thinking Workshop, San Jose State University, June 15, 1985.

7. California State Department of Education. *Training Materials for Writing Consultants.* Training Institute, March 1987.

8. Iris McClellan Tiedt. *Writing: From Topic to Evaluation.* Allyn and Bacon, 1989, pp. 102–07.

9. Ibid., p. 40.

10. Harry Behn. *Chrysalis: Concerning Children and Poetry.* Harcourt, 1938, p. 39.

11. Fourth-grade children at the Van Meter School, Los Gatos, California.

12. Iris M. Tiedt. "La Dictée: A Dictation Method." *ERIC,* July 1982.

Resources

James Britton. *Language and Learning.* Penguin, 1970. A classic work on child langauge acquisition and language development as part of the learning process.

California State Department of Education. *English Language Arts Framework,* The Department, 1987.

Jane Davidson, ed. *Counterpoint and Beyond: A Response to Becoming a Nation of Readers.* NCTE, 1988.

Kenneth Goodman. *What's Whole about Whole Language?* Heineman, 1986. A short summary of emergent reading theory and applications.

Julie Jensen, ed. *Composing and Comprehending.* National Council of Teachers of English, 1984. Studies of the connections between writing and reading.

James Moffett and Betty Jean Wagner. *A Student-Centered K–13 Language Arts and Reading Curriculum.* Houghton, 1983. A good overview of language arts instruction across the levels.

Ben Nelms, ed. *Literature in the Classroom: Readers, Texts, and Contexts.* National Council of Teachers of English, 1988. Clarification of the central place of literature in the English language arts curriculum.

Frank Smith. *Reading without Nonsense.* Teachers College Press, 1978. A succinct explanation of the reading process.

James R. Squire, ed. *The Dynamics of Language Learning: Research in Reading and English.* National Conference on Research in English, 1987. An excellent overview of current thinking in language and literacy instruction.

Iris M. Tiedt. *The Language Arts Handbook.* Prentice-Hall, 1983. A summary of topics included within the language arts; numerous applications and resources.

Iris M. Tiedt et al. *Teaching Thinking in K–12 Classrooms: Activities, Information, and Resources.* Allyn and Bacon, 1989. A comprehensive explanation of the many aspects of thinking instruction with numerous sample lessons.

Iris McClellan Tiedt. *Teaching Writing: From Topic to Evaluation.* Allyn and Bacon, 1989. An up-to-date summary of theory and practice for K–12 levels; speaks to the practicing teacher.

Iris McClellan Tiedt et al. *Reading/Thinking/Writing.* Allyn and Bacon, 1989. An integrated holistic program for K–8 classrooms.

Constance Weaver. *Reading Process and Practice from Socio-linguistics to Whole Language.* Heineman, 1988.

8

Multicultural Education Across the Curriculum

Unlike many other peoples, Americans are not bound together by a common religion or a common ethnicity. Our binding heritage is a democratic vision of liberty, equality, and justice.[1]

Kenneth T. Jackson

Preview

After reading this chapter, you should be able to:

- Define the need for integrating multicultural education across the curriculum at all levels of learning.
- Identify outcomes that reflect multicultural goals and those in a specific subject, both affective and cognitive.
- Describe methods for integrating multicultural concepts into instruction in varied subject areas.
- Select multicultural literature to support instruction in specific subject areas.
- Plan lessons that integrate multicultural and subject-specific objectives.

Photo on opposite page courtesy of NASA.

A basic assumption in this book is that multicultural education should not be presented in a single class apart from other instruction. As stated in Chapters 1 and 2, we believe that multicultural concepts should permeate all teaching. For example, a first-grade teacher will choose to read Ezra Jack Keats' *The Snowy Day*, a story about a young black child. Following the reading, the class will cut out snowflakes and write a collaborative story about Peter's adventures in the snow and his attempt to save a snowball in his pocket.

A high school history teacher may develop a unit of study around the shared reading of *The Good Earth* by Pearl Buck. Students will read other novels by the same author. They will study the geography and history of China—a vast country that is just opening up to us. They will collect clippings from the newspaper and record current linkages between China and the United States. Connecting literature and contemporary events with history instruction gives the study a reality that is missing from many history textbooks.

Notice that the examples above are necessarily also related to language arts, which are discussed in the preceding chapter, as well as to the other content area instruction we address in this chapter. At this time we intend to focus more directly on ways of bringing multicultural concepts into subject-specific instruction at elementary, middle school, and high school levels. This chapter is divided into two major parts with subdivisions, as follows:

> Multicultural Concepts for All Subject Areas
> > Art
> > Music
> > Physical Education
> > Mathematics
> > Science
> > Social Studies
> Selected Teaching Strategies Across the Curriculum
> > The Venn Diagram
> > The I-Search Paper
> > Organizing a Learning Center
> > Creating a Unit of Study

MULTICULTURAL CONCEPTS FOR ALL SUBJECT AREAS

In this section we will brainstorm ideas that you can apply at any level of instruction. Ideas presented under each subject heading are only suggestions of what you may develop. As you begin brainstorming, collect your ideas in a special notebook labeled, for example, Teaching Multicultural Concepts in Art. Scan through all the ideas presented throughout this chapter; an idea presented under science may relate to another subject, or an idea under physical education may trigger an adaptation you could use.

As you plan for instruction in any subject area, consider how students can learn multicultural concepts in the context of your subject-specific lessons. The following questions may lead you to discover pertinent ideas:

Who creates what in my field?
Who has contributed to development in this field?
What is happening in my field today?
Are there specific stereotypes or biases in this field?
What are the universals in this field?
How does this field fit into the global village?
What is the future of this field?
How does this field fit into the global village?
What is the future of this field?

In addition to your notebook, begin a file (a large cardboard box) of materials that will help you promote multicultural education in your classroom. Include the following:

Pictures of men and women
Quotations by scholars or practitioners
Clippings from the newspaper about current events
Publications—books, articles, art, records
List of films
Realia

Don't expect multicultural education to be your primary emphasis in teaching. As you explore, however, you will find that multicultural concepts fit naturally into your plans. You can sometimes select literature by or about persons from different cultures, and you can point out the contributions of a great variety of people to the development of this field. Thus, you will be teaching multicultural concepts, both explicitly and implicitly.

Art

Art reveals historical development. Share information with students about the role art has played in human development over the years—the pictographs of the cave dwellers, the art of the Native Americans, painting developed through the years in Europe, American folk art, and so on. Point out the contributions of artists from diverse cultures.

Arrange a fieldtrip to a local museum to view a special exhibit of Egyptian art or an exhibit from China. Share a slide presentation on the history of art or a specialized kind of art such as Appalachian basket weaving or quilt making.

The arts are an integral part of a humanities approach to instruction. Work with a language arts, music, and history teacher to plan a humanities core program that integrates music, art, history, and literature. This approach works very well in junior high or middle school core plans, as well as in the self-contained elementary school classroom.

Children's books offer a special art form in their illustrations. Outstanding illustrators whose work you will enjoy sharing include:

Mitsumasa Anno. *Anno's U.S.A.* Japanese artist; many books.

Ezra Jack Keats. *In a Spring Garden.* Collection of haiku.

Maurice Sendak. ***Outside Over There.*** Jewish author-illustrator; this book won the Caldecott award in 1987.

Also look for Paul Goble's books about American Indians (e.g., *The Friendly Wolf*), which are beautifully illustrated. A Caldecott honor book, *Mufaro's Beautiful Daughters,* is an African tale illustrated by black author, John Steptoe.

Art enhances instruction in other fields. Particularly in the elementary school, art activities can readily be tied into units of study in science or history. Encourage students to enhance information they have learned in other subject areas through such media as:

Papier maché figures

Masks as art or for performance

Dioramas to depict exploration, great discoveries, scenes from literature, animal habitats

Murals picturing Westward Expansion, scenes from a biography

Covers for books and reports — gadget printing, finger painting, crayon resist

Books to Explore

Literature can support understanding of art and artists. Explore the school and public library to ascertain what kinds of books are available. Search for nonfiction, fiction, and poetry. Biographies of artists are available in children's literature as well as that for adults. Look for some of the following titles:

Fiction

Elizabeth B. De Trevino. *I, Juan de Pareja.* Farrar, 1966. A slave in the household of Velasquez.

Zibby Oneal. *In Summer Light.* Viking, 1985. Girl wants to be a painter.

Autobiography and Biography

Natalie Bober. *Breaking Tradition: The Story of Louis Nevelson.* Atheneum, 1984. Sculpture.

Nathaniel Harris. *Leonardo and the Renaissance.* Bookwright, 1987. Painting and sculpture.

Milton Meltzer. *Dorothea Lange: Life through the Camera.* Viking, 1985. Photography.

Judith St. George. *The Mount Rushmore Story.* Putnam, 1985. Carving.

Philip Sendak. *In Grandpa's House.* Harper, 1985. Illustrated by Maurice Sendak, son of the author of this autobiography.

Beverly Sherman. *Georgia O'Keeffe: The "Wideness and Wonder" of Her World.* Atheneum, 1986. Painting.

Sample Lesson: Beautiful Writing

Level of Difficulty: Grades 3–12

Outcomes:

Students will:

1. Learn an interesting art form.
2. Select quotations from diverse cultures.
3. Create an attractive display.

Procedures:

Collect examples of quotations presented in calligraphy. (See pages 1, 44, 68, and 104 in this book.) Bring in books of quotations that students can use as resources.

Stimulus

Show students examples of quotations presented in calligraphy. Explain the history of calligraphy.

Teach students the rudiments of italic calligraphy which is not unlike manuscript or Danelian handwriting which they may have used in primary grades.

Activity

Have students select and print a quotation or saying they like from a specific culture.

Followup

Have each student frame the quotation. Framing can be done by mounting the quotation on a sheet of 9″ × 12″ red construction paper, or you may prefer to frame the quotations in simple black wooden frames that can be made or purchased.

Evaluation

Students should display their work in the classroom or in the library or another more public place where other students can view their art and the wise words depicted. No grades should be assigned for this project. Give credit or no credit for completing the task.

Music

Music is a part of every culture. Get assistance as you teach students some of the folk dancing representative of different countries. Students should experience a variety of music, either live or recorded—the blues, blue grass, the classical—by members of many cultures. Introduce them to the fine musicians who have contributed to the world's musical heritage such as Rachmaninoff, Mozart, Sibelius, Benny Goodman, Mahalia Jackson, Pete Seeger, and others.

Music should be an integral dimension of units of study that focus on any group or country. Students should be made aware of music as a universal language that all can share. They can create their own music to express their ideas and emotions.

Books to Explore

Fiction

Bruce Brooks. *Midnight Hour Encores.* Harper, 1986. Cellist.

Gillian Cross. *Chartbreaker.* Holiday, 1987. Rock band.

Karen Dean. *Stay on Your Toes, Maggie Adams!* Avon, 1986. Ballet.

Karen Dean. *A Time to Dance.* Scholastic, 1985. Ballet.

Marisa Gioffre. *Starstruck.* Scholastic, 1985.

Rumer Godden. *Thursday's Children.* Viking, 1984. Ballet.

Suzanne Newton. *I Will Call It Georgie's Blues.* Viking, 1983. Jazz piano.

Jean Ure. *The Most Important Thing.* Morrow, 1985. Ballet.

Autobiography and Biography

Alan Blackwood. *Beethoven.* Bookwright, 1987.

Pete Fornatale. *The Story of Rock 'n' Roll.* Morrow, 1987.

Robert Love. *Elvis Presley.* Watts, 1986.

Susan Saunders. *Dolly Parton: Country Goin' to Town.* Viking, 1985.

Catherine Scheader. *Contributions of Women: Music.* Dillon, 1985. Beverly Sills and four other women.

Nonfiction

John Langstaff, ed. *What a Morning! The Christmas Story in Black Spirituals.* McElderry, 1987. Singing plus piano accompaniment.

Nicki Weiss. *If You're Happy and You Know It.* Greenwillow, 1987. Picture book includes 18 songs to sing together.

Physical Education and Health

Today there is much interest in health and fitness. Around the world, eyes watch the performance of the Olympic contestants who represent their countries proudly. All share the emotion as the national anthem is played for the Gold Medal winner. Physical performance, the power and the grace, is another universal language we all understand.

We can help students become aware of the diverse cultures these athletes represent. Just listening or displaying pictures of the top performers such as gymnasts, tennis players, long distance runners, and skiers will demonstrate clearly the diversity of these athletes' family backgrounds. Students can discuss the fact that cultural origins do not dictate the success of an individual athlete nor do they keep anyone from performing well.

Books to Explore

Fiction

Matt Christopher. *Red-Hot Hightops.* Little, 1987. Basketball.

Jeffrey Kelly. *The Baseball Club.* Houghton, 1987. Baseball.

R. R. Knudson. *Rinehart Shouts*. Farrar, 1987. Racing shell.

Doris B. Smith. *Karate Dancer*. Putnam, 1987. Karate.

Cynthia Voigt. *The Runner*. Atheneum, 1985. Running.

Autobiography and Biography

Maury Allen. *Jackie Robinson: A Life Remembered*. Watts, 1987.

R. R. Knudson. *Babe Didrikson Athlete of the Century*. Viking, 1985.

Herma Silverstein. *Mary Lou Retton and the New Gymnasts*. Watts, 1985.

Nonfiction

Dave Anderson. *The Story of Football*. Morrow, 1985.

Charles Cooms. *All-Terrain Bicycling*. Holt, 1987.

————. *Let's Rodeo*. Holt, 1986.

Edward F. Dolan. *Drugs in Sports*. Watts, 1986.

Joseph Murphy. *Adventure beyond the Clouds: How We Climbed China's Highest Mountain — and Survived!* Dillon, 1986.

Margaret Ryan. *Figure Skating*. Watts, 1987.

Suggested Activities

Collage.   Have students create a collage focusing on one sport. They can collect pictures, clippings, and any materials related to the topic. When completed, students present their collages to the class explaining the contributions of diverse cultures to this sport.

Teaching Games.   Assign a research project on games typical of different cultures. Each student writes a short report, including diagrams and other illustrations. Each person teaches a game to the group.

Reports on Diseases or Disabilities.   Have students research information about specific diseases or disabilities. Each should include an interview and a telephone investigation in their research. Completed reports are presented to the group and then included in a publication that can be placed in the library.

Mathematics

The use of numbers and mathematical concepts represent yet another universal language that we share around the globe. Students can study variations in applied mathematics around the world, for example:

Monetary systems — compared worth of coins
The abacus and its use
Metric system compared to U.S. weights and measures
The evolution of measurements over time
Standard weights and measures

Computer use around the world
Math anxiety for women—why; possible solutions
Calendars (see page 318)
Purchase of stocks; economic systems

Help students make connections between mathematics and other subjects or areas of interest. For example, how does math relate to art and music? What are the many relationships between math and the sciences? How are mathematics concepts displayed in nature, for example, Fibracci numbers?

Books to Explore

Counting Books for Children

James Haskins. *Count Your Way through the Arab World.* Carolrhoda, 1987. Numbers related to concepts of geography and culture.

Nonfiction

Laura Greene. *Careers in the Computer Industry.* Watts, 1983.

Nigel Hawks. *Computers: How They Work.* Watts, 1983.

Christoher Lampton. *Computer Languages.* Watts, 1983.

Jack R. White. *How Computers Really Work.* Dodd, 1986.

Suggested Activities

Comparing Currency.   Use the Task Card on the opposite page. The names of the coins or bills are given as well as their worth compared to the U.S. dollar based on May 1985 figures. On the other side of the card, students are directed to work with this informative chart. They are directed, for example, to check the newspaper to see whether the comparative values have changed (figures are posted daily in the business section). This kind of activity encourages reading, involves students in mathematics activities, and provides information about life in other countries. It is a worthwhile activity that provides valuable learning experience.

A Mathematical Dictionary.   Have students prepare a dictionary of terms appropriate to their level of mathematical understanding. Include etymology of terms. Students will be surprised to discover the origins of words in math, for example, *algebra, algorithm,* or *googol.*

Women in Mathematics.   Students can focus a special unit of study on the achievements of women in mathematics. Invite female mathematicians to visit your classroom. Discuss math anxiety and how or why these women were able to overcome it.

Science

Literature selections frequently provide science backgrounds, for science appears in both fiction and nonfiction. Science fiction has long fascinated students, especially

MONEY FROM OTHER COUNTRIES

Country	Currency	Worth in dollars*
Argentina	peso	.0020
Australia	dollar	.6805
Austria	schilling	.0461
Belgium	franc	.0160
Britain	pound	1.264
Canada	dollar	.7287
Chile	peso	.0066
Colombia	peso	.0076
Denmark	krone	.0896
Ecuador	sucre	.0104
France	franc	.1061
Holland	guilder	.2865
Hong Kong	dollar	.1282
Israel	pound	.00102
Italy	lira	.000508
Japan	yen	.003979
Mexico	peso	.00393
Norway	krone	.1124
Peru	sol	.00011
Portugal	escudo	.0057
South Africa	rand	.502
Spain	peseta	.00574
Sweden	krone	.1116
Switzerland	franc	.3860
Uruguay	peso	.0110
Venezuela	bolivar	.0791
W. Germany	deutschmark	.3237

*May 1985.

MONEY AROUND THE WORLD

Have you ever heard of a guilder?

In which country would you find this coin? (Look at the chart on the other side of this card.)

How much is a guilder worth compared to our dollar?

Do other countries use dollars besides the United States?

Which countries use dollars?

Are these "dollars" worth the same amount?

Which "dollar" is worth the most?

Every day this list of currencies appears in the newspaper. See if you can find it in the financial or business section. Compare the values for each coin to see how it has changed since this list was published in May 1985.

Why might values of coins or bills go up or down?

See if you can find information about what determines the value of a piece of currency.

Pretend you are traveling to several different countries. As you enter each country, you exchange $10.00 for the currency of that country.

How many pesos would you get in Mexico?

How many francs would you get in France?

How many pounds would you get in Great Britain?

How many rands would you get in South Africa?

Find pictures of some of these coins. Perhaps someone you know has money from different countries.

227

when they read older fiction (by Jules Vernes, for example) and note that much has come to pass in the present. Conversely, they may see science fiction published in the twentieth century and into the twenty-first century as predicting the future. You can encourage them to read such writers as Isaac Asimov, a biochemist who writes scientific texts as well as fiction, Arthur C. Clarke, Ray Bradbury, and many other authors who are writing good science fiction today.

Naturalist Jean Craighead George authors titles for the middle grades that portray the interaction of humans and animals. Her Newbury award-winning *Julie of the Wolves* tells us of the habits of wolves, serving to break down the stereotyped thinking of the wolf as ferocious, mean animal. She tells of a crow's imprinting on a human in *Talking Crow* and the plight of whales in *Water Sky*. *Shark Beneath the Reef* focuses on sharks, depicting Mexican fishermen in Baja, California and a young boy's decision point.

Science is also related to humanities approaches. Following is a commentary published in a "A Naturalist's Perspective" which comments on the history of the Midwest and uses a selection from literature to help describe the imagined scene.

Two hundred years ago, Southwestern Ohio was at the "edge of civilization," home and hunting land for Miami and Shawnee, a mystic land of wealth and opportunity to land-hungry settlers to the east and south, and the new U. S. Government's answer to its revolutionary war debts. By 1788, Kentucky was already home to 70,000 settlers, but almost none ventured north of the Ohio River, primarily because the Miami, Shawnee, Wyandot, and Delaware were determined that they would not be pushed farther west by endless streams of white settlers. Southwestern Ohio was then a forested wilderness.

Oh, what I would give to be able to travel back in a time machine to see that land of endless trees! Conrad Richter in his historical novel *The Trees* takes us back:

They rounded a high ridge. A devil's racecourse cleared the area of limbs below. Here was something Worth had not told them about. . . .
Then she saw that what they looked down on was a dark, illimitable expanse of wilderness. It was a sea of solid treetops broken only by some gash where deep beneath the foliage an unknown stream made its way. As far as the eye could reach, this lonely forest sea rolled on and on till its faint blue billows broke against an incredibly distant horizon (Richter, 1978).

When the Ohio country was first settled, 25 million acres of 10,000-year-old hardwood forest covered 95% of the state. It had a continuous forest canopy of trees 50–100 feet tall, and up to 14 feet in diameter! Sycamores large enough to stable horses within their hollow centers grew beside the stream! In the bottoms grew cottonwood, black willow, green ash, pin oak, box elder, silver maple, American elm, honey locust, and river birch. On the uplands climax forests of American beech, sugar maple, oaks, and hickories could be found. Where the Indians had burned away the timber to clear land, open, young forests of eastern red cedar, wild cherry, red maple, sassafras, ash, redbud, and sumac stretched toward the sunlight. Through these dark and massive forests, enormous bands of squirrels migrated, as did passenger pigeons, bison, wolves, deer, and more.[2]

Books to Explore

Fiction

James Lincoln Collier. *When the Stars Begin to Fall.* Delacorte, 1986. Pollution.

Midas Dekkers. *Arctic Adventure.* Orchard, 1987. Whales.

Jean G. Howard. *Bound by the Sea: A Summer Diary.* Tidal Press, 1986. Science diary.

Gary Paulsen. *Hatchet.* Bradbury, 1987. Wilderness survival.

Autobiography and Biography

Nathan Aaseng. *More with Less: The Future World of Buckminster Fuller.* Lerner, 1986.

Edwina Conner. *Marie Curie.* Bookwright, 1987.

Nonfiction

Gilda Berger. *Crack: The New Drug Epidemic!* Watts, 1987.

Robert Cattoche. *Computers for the Disabled.* Watts, 1986.

Anne Ehrlich and Paul Ehrlich. *Earth.* Watts, 1987.

Dorothy Francis. *Computer Crime.* Dutton, 1987.

Kathlyn Gay. *The Greenhouse Effect.* Watts, 1986.

Jonathan Harris. *Drugged Athletes: The Crisis in American Sports.* Four Winds, 1987.

Noel Simon. *Vanishing Habitats.* Gloucester, 1987.

Social Studies

Concern about cultural literacy has focused heavily on student knowledge of geography and history. Integrating such studies with multicultural education may lend impetus to lively studies that will correct this deficiency. Recognizing that social studies is a broadly inclusive term, we choose to focus on geography and history as those aspects of social studies that are more commonly taught within the K–12 curriculum.

Geography

The study of geography provides a sense of place, where we are in relation to others and how we fit into the huge global village. As such, its content is related to every other study in the curriculum. Familiarity with maps and mapping can begin with the earliest years as children develop a sense of the layout of a classroom, the setting for a story, the school building, and the local community. Using a globe clarifies their understandings about the location of the United States and its immediate neighbors as well as the relative distances between the United States and the areas from which our ancestors came.

Suggested Activities

Discussion Topics.   Children can study and discuss such topics as: Why do we use the term *global village* today? Why has the creation of a new country — Israel — been difficult? Middle-grade students might read the novel, *The Boy from Over There* by Tamar Bergman (translation from the Hebrew by Hillel Halkin, Houghton Mifflin, 1988).

Assessing Class Knowledge.   After discussing the general definition of geography (the study of the earth's surface, climate, continents, countries, peoples, industries, and products), have the class divide into small groups with each group assessing their knowledge about one of these subdivisions of the topic. Have each group present its knowledge to the class, using maps and charts. Other members of the group can add to the knowledge. Cooperatively, the class can compose a compendium of What We Know about Geography. This knowledge can be referred to during multicultural studies with each group assuming an Expert role.

Mapping the Origins of the Members of the Class.   Create a large outline map of the world by enlarging a map from a text with the opaque projector. Have students interview their parents to ascertain general information about where grandparents and earlier ancestors came from. Each student can then locate these places outlining the trail of their individual origins on the map with colored pens. Each student can then tell his or her story and show the trail on the map.

History

The hope of history instruction is that "civic education can help us to see that not all problems have solutions, to live with tentative answers, to accept compromise, to embrace responsibilities as well as rights — to understand that democracy is a way of living, not a settled destination."[3] History lessons can lead even young students to appreciate how difficult it is to preserve our way of life and that we cannot take democracy for granted. Students of all ages can begin to answer the following questions:

1. What conditions — geographic, military, economic, social, technological — have nurtured democratic society, and what happens when conditions change?
2. What ideas, values, and educational forces have promoted freedom and justice for us in the past, and can we take these for granted now?
3. What have Americans in each generation actually done to extend democracy, and what needs doing still?[4]

Timely topics in this field can be debated. More advanced students need to be involved in thinking about the pro and con positions about real concerns as they learn to be active, informed citizens living in a global village. Contemporary history, for example, suggests the following topics related to learning to get along with the diverse people in the world:

1. Democracy's solutions for war-related problems at home and abroad and the strains on democracy produced by them.
2. The Cold War response to the threat of Soviet power.
3. The tragedy of Vietnam.
4. The rise of the "imperial presidency."
5. The dramatic advances made by women and minorities in civil rights and in political and economic life.
6. The emergence of new economic and environmental problems that affect democratic society in the technological age.[5]

Books to Explore

Throughout the extensive list of books in the Appendix are books that increase students' understanding of geography and history, contemporary and ancient. Historical novels, folklore, nonfiction, biography, poetry—all forms of literature add to each student's cultural literacy. Representative newer titles include:

Fiction

Paula Fox. *The Moonlight Man.* Bradbury, 1986. Nova Scotia.

Rudolf Frank. *No Hero for the Kaiser.* Lothrop, 1986. Germany, 1914.

Ellen Howard. *When Daylight Comes.* Atheneum. 1985. Virgin Islands.

Liza Murrow. *West against the Wind.* Holiday, 1987. California Gold Rush.

Scott O'Dell. *The Serpent Never Sleeps.* Houghton, 1987. Jamestown.

Yoko Kawashima Watkins. *So Far from the Bamboo Grove.* Lothrop, 1986. Korea; autobiographical.

Autobiography and Biography

Linda Atkinson. *In Kindling Flame: The Story of Hannah Senesh, 1921–1944.* Lothrop, 1985. Hungary.

Ida Cowen and Irene Gunther. *A Spy for Freedom: The Story of Sarah Aronsohn.* Dutton, 1984. Palestine.

Dorothy Hoobler and Thomas Hoobler. *Nelson and Winnie Mandela.* Watts, 1987. South Africa.

Edith Nesbit. *Long Ago When I Was Young.* Dial, 1987. Autobiography of author of *Five Children and It.*

Nonfiction

David M. Brownstone. *The Jewish-American Heritage.* Facts on File, 1988. Part of series: America's Ethnic Heritage.

Renata Von Tscharner and Ronald Fleming. *New Providence: A Changing Cityscape.* Harcourt, 1987.

Summary

Multicultural education belongs in every classroom. Teachers who are aware of the importance of teaching multiculturally will find it easy to bring in the contributions of people from diverse cultures to any field of study. Literature—fiction, nonfiction, poetry, autobiography and biography—contributes to students' understanding of people from varied cultures. Emphasis can be placed on the universality of such studies as art and music, which speak alike to people who cannot communicate verbally. In the same way, science and mathematics are "spoken" around the world. The studies of geography and history provide a foundation for young people's recognition of the earth as a global village.

SELECTED TEACHING STRATEGIES ACROSS THE CURRICULUM

Teachers need to step down from the podium, to decrease the use of lecture methods in favor of teaching strategies that permit students of all ages to become involved with the subject of study. We need to select methods that engage students in thinking, in making choices and decisions, and in solving problems. Multicultural teaching should guide students to make connections, to personalize learning in a way that will lead to greater human understanding.

In this section we describe just a few methods that will enhance your teaching:

The Venn Diagram
The I-Search Paper
Organizing a Learning Center
Creating a Unit of Study

The Venn Diagram

Developed by John Venn in the nineteenth century, the Venn diagram is used in mathematics to compare two sets. This diagram can be used to compare two concepts or two books in a very effective social studies lesson.

After each student has read a novel about young people living in different lands, ask each one to complete a Venn diagram that compares his or her life with that of the book character, thus:

Title and author of the book: *Seven Daughters and Seven Sons* by Barbara Cohen (Atheneum, 1982).

Brief description: This book is based on an Iraqi folktale that demonstrates the worth of daughters. Buran disguises herself as a man to help her family, and all kinds of adventures follow. It's really an exciting story.

In sections 1 and 2 unique characteristics are listed for each person. In section 3, the student lists adjectives that describe both, showing how they are alike. After completing the Venn diagram, each student writes a five-paragraph essay following this pattern:

Paragraph 1: Introduction
Paragraph 2: Description of herself or himself
Paragraph 3: Description of the book character

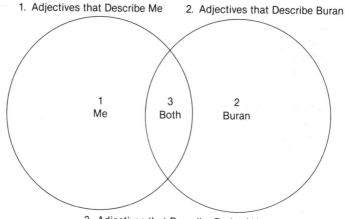

3. Adjectives that Describe Both of Us

> Paragraph 4: Summary of how the two are alike
> Paragraph 5: Summary paragraph

This exercise may lead students to observe that people are more alike than different, particularly when we consider personal characteristics and problems we have.

Once students know how to use this diagram, you can use it to guide comparisons of more complex topics; for example, two ethnic groups, two religions, or two forms of government.

The I-Search Paper

The I-Search paper begins with the identification of something a student really wants to know. It ends with a formal presentation of what the student discovered through independent research. Because the topic is student-selected, the project has genuine purpose. The I-Search paper is recommended for most students rather than the traditional research paper. The students are guided through these four developmental stages:

Stage 1: Identifiction of a Problem to Study. Students should make a list of three to five questions they have or things they would like to know; for example:

> I would like to know
> what Benjamin Franklin was really like
> how a slave family lived
> how the underground railroad worked

> I would like to know
> what our town was like a hundred years ago
> how my grandfather lived when he was my age
> the story of my great-aunt who died before I was born

By writing several ideas, students will be able to select one that they would really like to work on. After choosing the question for investigation, students should write a paragraph outlining the problem to be researched and reasons for selecting that particular topic. This piece of writing, called the Statement of the Problem, will be the first part of the report compiled at the end of the study.

Stage 2: Conducting the Study.   Talk with the students about the resources available to them as they search for information. Plan a visit to the school or public library to show them reference tools they may not know; for example:

- Atlases
- Almanacs
- *Reader's Guide to Periodical Literature*
- Card catalog

Ask the librarian to help plan for this visit so students will be able to use their time to advantage.

List on the the board all the other ways of gathering information that students can name; for instance:

- Telephoning; yellow pages
- Writing letters
- Interviewing people

Plan class instruction to assist students in using these techniques effectively. Discuss the interview process and interview a person in the classroom before students work individually. Prepare an interview schedule consisting of the questions to be asked with space for recording the answers. Letter writing and notetaking lessons will also assist students in gathering information.

As students begin their search, they should keep a log containing dated entries describing the process they are experiencing. This process journal will also include their notes from reading or interviewing. The log will become part of the final report, The Procedures.

Stage 3: Reporting the Findings.   After the data have been compiled, students should reread their notes. They can plan a presentation of the information they have gathered. This presentation will be written in paragraphs, but it may also include pictures, graphs, or other ways of sharing the information in an interesting way. Students may compile their work in an attractive booklet with a specially designed cover. The findings comprise the main portion of the final report.

Stage 4: The Summary.   The last part of the report is the summary which notes the significance of the study. The students might state their plans for using the information or doing additional research. Their personal feelings about the study can be included.

After students complete their research and the final reports, discuss ways of sharing the results. Students should have a chance to tell others in the class about their studies. They may also share them with another class and certainly with their parents.

After having students try the I-Search paper, you will observe distinct advantages of this type of research. When students begin with a problem that interests them, they are less likely to copy pages directly from the encyclopedia. The final report is the product of more thought and represents the student's own work. Since the focus is on the process an much as the result, the reports do not need to be extremely long. The satisfaction comes from finding out just what each one wanted to know, a process that students can transfer to other learning experiences.

Organizing a Learning Center

A learning center is a portion of the classroom, large or small, devoted to the study of a specific topic or set of skills. For example, you might have a language center, a United Nations center, a center for the study of Native Americans, or a center for the study of prejudice. Here are collected books, pictures, and other items related to the center focus. Here, too, are placed teaching materials and equipment to aid students working in the center as they engage in varied learning experiences.

How to Develop a Center

Plan with your students. First, decide what kind of center is needed. This depends, of course, on the focus of study in your classroom. Give the center a name that can

be printed on a large sign to place above the space allocated for this learning center. You may have several centers operating at any one time.

Use your ingenuity in creating a suitable place to focus activities. A reading table can be used to collect materials together. You may have students construct a kind of cubicle, as shown on the preceding page.

The bottom and sides of a large carton form the back of this center which is placed on a table; varied shapes and sizes of tables are appropriate. This particular center focuses on Americans from Scandinavia. Feature any kinds of information pertinent to the study.

A corner of the room is easily transformed into a center focusing on Alaska. In this case you might include a map of Alaska, the number of people living in Alaska, and other information.

Invite students to participate in collecting all kinds of pertinent information and materials that might be useful—clothing, postal cards, magazine articles. Brainstrom possible activities, people to contact, and places to visit as you develop the study together. Provide paper, pencils, and other materials that may be needed as students engage in work at the center. Depending on the type of study being developed, you might consider the following materials and equipment for the center:

- Tape or cassette recorders
- Typewriter
- Stapler

A Cozy Corner

- Scissors
- Rulers
- Various papers
    lined and unlined
    drawing paper
    colored construction paper
    cardboards
    posterboard
    corrugated cardboard for construction

In addition to pictures and information displayed to make the center attractive and inviting, there will be a variety of activities. Planned activities should range from easy to more difficult as well as involve using varied skills—listening, speaking, reading, and writing. Included, too, can be activities that draw from different subject areas and those that stimulate student creativity in music and art. In the following sections of this chapter we will explain how to produce two useful kinds of teaching materials for the learning center—the task card and the learning module.

How to Use the Learning Center

After you and your students have created one or more learning centers, you need to talk about using them. Discuss how many students can work at each center at any one time. The number of seats provided is a good way to indicate how many can work at a center. As a seat is vacated, someone else may come to the center. Students may need to sign up for a particular center.

A good way to begin work at learning centers is to post a schedule so each student has a specific assignment for the day. You can prepare the schedule for a week, two weeks, or a month, depending on how long the study will take and how many centers are available. Working in the library could be one center activity that would accommodate a number of students. Your schedule might look like this for ten days.

Name	M	T	W	TH	F	M	T	W	TH	F
Felipe	1	1	2	2	L	3	3	4	4	L
James	1	1	2	2	L	3	3	4	4	L
Julia	1	1	2	2	L	3	3	4	4	L
Sandra	2	2	L	3	3	4	4	L	1	1
Hope	2	2	L	3	3	4	4	L	1	1
Harold	2	2	L	3	3	4	4	L	1	1
Marisa	3	3	4	4	L	1	1	2	2	L

Enlarging specific centers to provide more activities and seating space will permit additional students to participate. Sometimes, activities can be completed at the student's desk. Adding other learning centers also expands the capacity.

Keeping track of materials at each center is another important part of planning. Here are several tips that may help you.

1. Package all the parts of a game in one large envelope. Label the envelope in big print, thus:

2. Color code everything that belongs at one center. If the center on France is blue, then mark games, task cards, modules, etc., with a blue felt pen. Students soon learn to replace task cards or games at the appropriate center.

3. Hang activities in envelopes or plastic bags on the wall where they are visible. Pegboard is ideal for this purpose, but you can improvise with cork bulletin boards, or strips of wood in which hooks can be placed. If you have a specially marked hook for each item, you can quickly tell when something is missing at the end of the day.

Whenever there are problems regarding classroom operations, have a class meeting to thrash out the problems and possible solutions. If students decide on the solution, their decision is more likely to carry weight, and they will enforce it, not you!

The teacher role in working with learning centers is to help students organize their work toward a goal and specific objectives. The teacher facilitates and guides the learning experiences and serves as a resource, a person to be consulted when help is needed. The teacher guides the students in assessing their own growth and what they have learned as well as checking their own work. Avoid playing the undesirable role of corrector or grader. Instead, use your talents and expertise to respond to student needs, to plan strategies for stimulating further learning, and to explore new resources and materials that come your way.

Developing Task Cards

The task card is one of the most useful and versatile forms of presenting learning activities. Especially appropriate for the learning center and individualized instruction described in the preceding section, task cards can also be used in conjunction with whole class presentations.

Developing sets of cards is well worth the time invested, for the cards can be used repeatedly and in various ways, as we will point out. In this section we will suggest ways of working with task cards under the following topics:

How to Make Task Cards
Cards for a Specific Learning Center: Americans with French Origins

How to Make Task Cards.   Task cards are sometimes called job cards or activity cards. They come in various sizes, from small ones about 3″ × 5″ to large ones about 8½″ × 11″. The size you choose depends on the age of the students who will use the cards (young children can handle large cards more easily) and on your instructional purpose.

Making Small Cards.   Small cards are an excellent idea for *idea files* to which students refer individually. For example, a set of cards might be designed for a file called *Choice*. The ideas on these cards would stimulate creativity as well as develop understandings about different people of the world. In addition, you might use small cards for sets focusing on:

- *Acting Out*   On each card a problem situation is described that calls for role-playing. Activities could be for small groups.
- *Books to Read*   Each card lists the title and author of a book as well as a short synopsis of the story. Students use this file as they are searching for a book to read about Mexico, living in New York City, or any other topic you want to include.

Have students themselves develop these sets of cards. If you prepare just a few cards to show the kinds of ideas that can be included, the students will soon generate a useful set. Each person can prepare a card, for example, about the book he or she has read. This activity serves a dual purpose—the students have a purpose for reading and they create a set of cards about books other students will find interesting.

Preparing *acting out situations* gives students a purpose for writing a short paragraph. Then the students use the set of cards for further educational experience.

Sets of cards can be made easily with purchased, unlined file cards. Either 3″ × 5″ cards or 4″ × 6″ cards are good for this purpose.

Making Large Cards.   Large cards are usually constructed of sturdy poster board so they are stiff and durable. These cards are used to present an activity that one or more students will undertake at different times. Directions must be clear if students are to work independently in an individualized approach.

On page 227 is a task card for upper-grade students that focuses on the money used in various countries. When material is prepared for your use like this, you can simply copy the material presented. The information about currencies can be typed. If available, use a primary typewriter to facilitate reading. Directions can also be typed. If they are short, however, printing with felt pen is effective. Throughout this book you will find informative material and activities that can be presented in similar fashion on task cards.

Make these cards more durable by covering them with clear contact paper. They can also be laminated if you have access to a laminating machine. This kind of coating makes it possible to have students write on a card with a grease pencil which can later be wiped off.

Cards for a Specific Learning Center:
Focusing on French Origins

French Canadians and Americans with French backgrounds will be interested in a learning center that focuses attention on the French language and France as the country

country of origin. Such a study should also be of interest to students who know nothing about France, the French language, or French Canada (Québec).

Create a Center.   Varieties of learning centers are shown in this chapter and elsewhere in this book. The preceding page shows only one possibility. It can be quickly set up and put into use. Use a reading table, the bigger the better. Create a display like the one shown that focuses on whatever aspect of this study you wish to emphasize; for example, Traveling in Québec, Flying to France! or Parlez-Vous Français? For an attractive display consider using a map of the area, pictures, postcards, and/or items from the newspaper. Students can add to the display as the study progresses.

Making Cards for the Center.   Develop a variety of learning experiences that will lead students to discover facts about France. Make cards that direct students to discover facts about France or to draw their own map of France, as shown on these examples:

FACTS ABOUT FRANCE

1. List as many things as you can that you already know about France.
2. List any words you know that we have borrowed from the French language.
3. Use the encyclopedia to find the answers to these questions:
   How big is France?
   Which other countries touch its borders?
   What products is France known for producing?
   (Add more questions to guide student research.)

Display a map of France on the bulletin board to aid students in drawing their own maps as directed on this card. Divide the map in fourths to assist them.

TRAVELING THROUGH FRANCE

As you prepare to take a trip to France, draw your own map. Use a large sheet of paper.

Step 1: Draw light pencil lines to divide your paper in fourths. This will help you make the map the right size. Then draw the outline of France; notice the harbors and seaports.

Step 2: Locate the larger cities and rivers. Try to place them accurately. The pencil lines will help you.

Step 3: Print in the names of the countries and bodies of water that touch France on all sides. Locate the mountains.

Now choose one of the cities on your map to investigate. Find out as much as possible about it. You may be able to find a book that takes place there. Be ready to tell something about your city. We will record each person's talk on a cassette.

Create a set of small cards that will help students learn French-English vocabulary. Begin with basic vocabulary such as numbers, objects around the room, expressions students can use, for example:

	Numbers	
1	un	*uhn*
2	deux	*duh*
3	trois	*twah*
4	quatre	*kat truh*
5	cinq	*sank*
6	six	*sees*
7	sept	*set*
8	huit	*weet*
9	neuf	*nuhf*
10	dix	*dees*

Colors		
red	rouge	*roozh*
yellow	jaune	*zhone*
blue	bleu	*bloo*
green	vert	*vair*
white	blanc	*blahnk*
black	noir	*nwahr*

Family		
mother	mère	*mehr*
father	père	*pehr*
sister	soeur	*suhr*
brother	frère	*frair*

Expressions		
hello	bonjour	*bohn zhoor*
good-by	au revoir	*oh ruh vwahr*
thank you	merci	*mair see*
please	s'il vous plait	*seel voo pleh*

Any standard high school French book will provide an ample vocabulary to introduce to your students. Note that the suggested pronunciations above are only approximate, as many French sounds cannot be directly translated into English. We suggest that you find a French teacher or perhaps a parent who can pronounce the words on a tape for you and your students if you do not know French yourself.

Students can use these cards in numerous ways. They will enjoy just using them as flash cards to test each other. For this purpose prepare the cards with the French word or words on one side and the translation in English on the other, as shown here:

To encourage students to use these vocabulary cards, construct a gameboard. To give the gameboard a French motif, glue pictures from travel brochures around the board. Spaces are colored with alternate colors such as blue and white. Cover the board with clear contact paper or have it laminated. Use a die to determine the number of moves a student is to make. If the student lands on blue, he or she draws a card from the French pile (French words are on top, and the student must supply the English). If the player lands on a white space, he or she draws from the English pile (English words are up, and the player must supply the French word.) Students

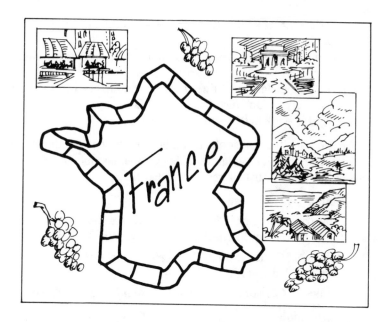

who are unable to answer correctly move back three spaces. Before they move, however, they read the correct answer, and the card is placed at the bottom of the pile.

Focus a learning center on the Canadian province of Québec which touches our states of Maine, New Hampshire, Vermont, and New York (see page 240). The largest of the provinces, its capital is Québec City. Québec is especially interesting because of its French origins; 80 percent of its population is French-Canadian. You might develop task cards that involve students in the following activities:

- Draw a map of Québec. Identify its cities and waterways.
- Reproduce Québec's flag on paper or cloth.
- Write letters to obtain information about places of interest such as: Montréal, the Gaspé Peninsula, The Citadel in Québec City, the St. Lawrence River.

(Address: Canadian Government Travel Bureau Ottawa, Ontario, Canada KIA OH6).

• Make a poster featuring facts about Québec — the provincial tree, the flower, coat of arms, flag, and so on.
• Develop a class time line showing the history of Québec beginning with its discovery by Jacques Cartier in 1534.
• Read a book set in some part of Québec.

Have a number of books available for student use during this study. In addition to the appropriate volumes of encyclopedias, include both nonfiction and fiction. Following is a list of recommended titles:

Fiction

C. Marius Barbeau. *The Golden Phoenix and Other French-Canadian Fairy Tales.* Retold by Michael Hornyansky. Walck, 1958.

Natalie S. Carlson. *The Talking Cat and Other Stories of French Canada.* Harper & Row, 1952.

Natalie S. Carlson. *Jean-Claude's Island.* Harper & Row, 1963.

Nonfiction

Morris G. Bishop. *Champlain: The Life of Fortitude.* McClelland, 1963.

Hazel Boswell. *French Canada: Pictures and Stories of Old Québec.* Atheneum, 1967.

Thomas B. Costain. *The White and the Gold: The French Regime in Canada.* Doubleday, 1954.

Anne F. Rockwell, ed. *Savez-Vous Planter les Choux? and Other French Songs.* World, 1969.

Joseph Schull. *Battle for the Rock: The Story of Wolfe and Montcalm.* Macmillan, 1960; St. Martin's, 1960.

J. Fred Swayze. *Frontenac and the Iroquois: The Fighting Governor of New France.* Macmillan, 1959.

Ronald Syme. *Champlain of the St. Lawrence.* Morrow, 1952.

William Toye. *Cartier Discovers the St. Lawrence.* Oxford, 1970; Walck, 1970.

This study of French-speaking Americans or those who have French backgrounds could also include a New Orleans or Louisiana learning center. Another center might focus on French in our language — the many English words borrowed from French (*ballet, adroit*), place names that are French, or French expressions that we use (R.S.V.P.). This approach to teaching is truly interdisciplinary as students study concepts from the various social studies, mathematics, and literature and develop such skills as reading, writing, painting, and singing.

Notice, too, that you can develop similar learning centers that focus on any group, its locations within the United States, and the country or countries of origin:

Swedish Americans—Minnesota, Sweden; Irish Americans—New York City, Ireland; Italian Americans—San Francisco, Italy; Spanish-speaking Americans—California, Texas, Southwest USA, Florida, Spain, Mexico, Puerto Rico, Cuba.

Simply follow the steps described in developing a center focusing on Americans who have French backgrounds. Use some of the same activities. Interspersed throughout the chapters of this book you will find additional suggestions for different groups. Check the index as well as the special listing of activities and information related to specific groups.

Creating a Unit of Study

The most effective way of teaching multicultural studies is through an integrated study that involves students in thinking, reading, writing, speaking, and listening for a purpose. The theme or subject to be studied varies according to your curriculum. The unit developed here focuses on China and Chinese Americans.

Introducing the Study

Begin with a preassessment exercise. Have each student cluster around the word *China*. Each writes all the words he or she associates with China. Save this preassessment activity for examination later after the students learn more about the land and people. Comparison should show growth and perhaps changed viewpoints.

Clusters will look something like this:

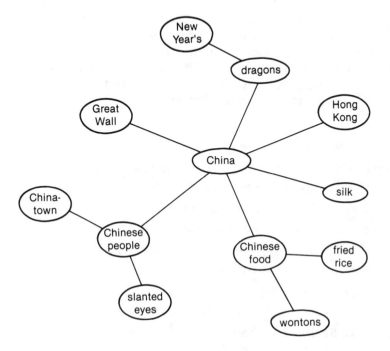

Collect the clustering exercises to use again after this study is completed.

Saturate your classroom with books, pictures, and other items of interest related to China. Use these materials as a basis for discussion designed to get students involved in the topic to be explored.

You might begin your study by reading a folktale from China; for example, *Tikki Tikki Tembo,* the story of a little boy who had such a long name that he almost drowned because his little brother has so much trouble repeating the name. This book is also recommended because it is illustrated beautifully by Blair Lent. A film and filmstrip of the story are available from Weston Woods (Weston, Connecticut).

Retold by Arlene Mosel, this story is a good example of a *pourquoi* tale, a story that explains why something has happened: Why the Chinese have such short names. After hearing this story, students of all ages can write original pourquoi (the French word for *why*) tales to explain, for example:

- Why our clock has 12 numbers.
- Why the cherry has a pit.
- Why corn has a tassel on top.
- Why we have stoplights on city streets.

After students have written their pourquoi tales, have them collected in a book entiled: *Pourquoi?,¿Porque? Why?* Place the book on the reading table where everyone can read it.

Collecting Resources

Explore your school library as well as the local public library to see what kinds of resources are available. To accommodate a wide range of reading abilities, include both easy and more difficult fiction. Also bring in the C volumes of several encyclopedias because they also vary in reading difficulty. You can find other nonfiction written for young people. Here is a selection of titles to look for. Ask the assistance of your librarian in discovering other resources.

Fiction

Easy Books

Eve Bunting. *The Happy Funeral.* Hayser.

Marjorie Flack. *The Story of Ping.* Viking.

Thomas Handforth. *Mei Li.* Doubleday.

Eleanor Lattimore. *Peachblossom.* Harcourt.

Yen Liang. *Happy New Year.* Lippincott.

Kurt Wiese. *Fish in the Air.* Viking.

Short Stories and Myths

Arthur Chrisman. *Shen of the Sea.* Dutton.

Alice Ritchie. *The Treasure of Li-Po.* Harcourt.

Catherine Sadler (retold by). *Treasure Mountain: Folktales from Southern China*. Atheneum.

Laurence Yep. *Dragon of the Lost Sea*. Harper.

Books for Older Students

Meindert De Jong. *The House of Sixty Fathers*. Harper.

Adrienne Jones. *Ride the Far Wind*. Little, Brown.

Jeanne Lee. *Legends of the Milky Way*. Holt.

Jean Merrill. *The Superlative Horse*. Scott, Foresman.

Katherine Paterson. *Rebels of the Heavenly Kingdom*. Lodestar.

Carolyn Treffinger. *Li Lun, Lad of Courage*. Abingdon.

Nonfiction

Hal Buell. *The World of Red China*. Dodd.

John Caldwell. *Let's Vist China Today*. Day.

Cornelia Spencer. *The Land and People of China*. Lippincott.

Cornelia Spencer. *The Yangtze, China's River Highway*. Garrard.

Betty Lee Sung. *The Chinese in America*. Macmillan.

An excellent resource for teachers is *Studying China in Elementary and Secondary Schools* by Leonard S. Kenworthy (Teachers College Press. 1975).

Creating a Center of Focus

Create a learning center something like the one shown here which will serve as the center of focus for the study of China and Chinese Americans. Have students help develop the Center for the Study of China.

You can feature any pertinent information to add interest to the center. Here we have presented facts designed to pique student curiosity, such as the fact that 600 million people speak Chinese or that China is the third largest country in the world. The gameboard, Challenging the Dragon, can be presented as part of the module or as a separate activity with the directions displayed where students can read them easily. Place the modules, varied supplies, and numerous resources such as books at this work center.

Preparing a Module for Students

We find it helpful to prepare learning modules that guide students through the study, stressing activities that are stimulating and informative.

A learning module, as defined here, is a booklet, usually 8½ × 11, that focuses on a single topic. Rather short, about five to twenty pages, the module is designed to teach two to three objectives that are part of an overall goal. Both goal and objectives are stated clearly. The module begins with a simple pretest and concludes with a posttest or culminating activity that aids student self-evaluation. The learning module is self-contained and speaks directly to the student. A teacher's guide is usually included with suggestions for use and such teaching aids as test answers, additional enrichment activities, and recommended resources. Read through the sample module that follows so that you have a clearer picture of how a module can be used.

The U.S. Bicentennial, 1976, was the year of the dragon, as was 1988; the dragon will come again in the year 2000. 1990 is the year of the horse. The title of the module could be modified according to the symbol for the year in which you plan to present this unit of study to provide a more contemporary flavor. The dragon, however, is still a useful motif for the gameboard.

Copy the module directly on duplicating masters so that you can produce a number of booklets at one time. Enlarge drawings by projecting them with an opaque projector. Prepare a simple construction paper cover that bears the title and perhaps the head of the dragon. Or the cover might be decorated with a Chinese ideograph.

DISCOVERING CHINA

Discovery*

---

*Derived from symbols dated 1523–1028 B.C. during the Shang dynasty in China, now the People's Republic of China.

THE YEAR OF THE DRAGON—2000

A Study of China and Chinese Americans (Student Module)

The Cover of the Module

Module Activity 1: Gifts from China

Look at the chart on the next page. You will discover that we have received many gifts from China.

China's civilization developed long before that of the United States. Our country is an infant compared to such countries that trace their history to the years before Christ (B.C.)

Since China existed so many years before we did, naturally many things we take for granted today came originally from China. Can you name three things that we use today that were gifts from China?

1. _____
2. _____
3. _____

CHINA'S GIFTS TO THE WEST

CHINA*		THE WEST*
Silk, about 1300		
Folding umbrella (?)	−300 B.C.−	
Lodestone, 240	−200 B.C.−	
Shadow figures (?)	−100 B.C.−	
	Birth of Christ	
Lacquer		
Paper, 105	−A.D. 100−	Peach and apricot
	−200−	
Tea, 264-273	−300−	
Word for porcelain first used		
Sedan chair	−400−	
	−500−	
Kite, 549	−600−	Silk, 552-554
Playing cards	−700−	
Dominoes		
Gunpowder (?)	−800−	
Porcelain described, 851		
First printed book, 868	−900−	
	−1000−	
Movable type, 1041-1049		Orange
Compass		
Zinc in coins, 1094-1098	−1100−	
		Paper, 1150
Explosives, 1161	−1200−	Compass, 1190
	−1300−	1330
		Gunpowder and cannon, Playing cards, 1377
	−1400	
		Block printing, 1423
		Gutenberg's Bible, 1456
	−1500	

*Dates in the "China" column indicate approximate date of origin: in "The West" column they indicate approximate date of receiving item described. From Derk Bode, *China's Gift to the West*, American Council on Education, Washington, DC, 1978.

	CHINA		THE WEST
Chaulmoogra oil and ephe- drine described, 1552–78			Zinc described Kite. 1589
		—1600—	Sedan chair, tea, folding umbrella, 1688
		—1700—	Wallpaper manufactured, Porcelain, 1709 Lacquer produced, 1730
The use of the following also originated in China in early times, but cannot be accurately dated: peach, orange, apricot, lemon, pomelo, Chrysanthemum, tea rose, camellia, azalea, China aster, gingko, "German silver," wallpaper, goldfish.		—1800—	Zinc in industrial production, 1740 "German silver" production Chrysanthemum, tea rose, camellia, azalea, China aster, grapefruit
		—1900—	Shadow figures Gingko, tung oil, soy bean, ephedrine, chaulmoogra oil

Module Activity 2: Your Own Book about China

Begin a book about China. You can put everything you do in this study in your book. Choose a title for the book. Select a piece of colored construction paper to use as the cover. Use a brush and black tempera paint to create a Chinese ideograph (a symbol used for a word or idea) to decorate the cover. You may find some ideas in your encyclopedia or other books about China. Follow the directions given in Module Activity 3. Make a page for the table of contents. You can add titles to this page gradually as you make new pages for your book. Make a page now about Gifts We Received from China. You can make a chart like the preceding one or you can simply list the things we received from China. You can add pages of your own to this book, too. Perhaps you would like to include a picture from a magazine or a newspaper clipping. If you like to draw, you may include some of your own illustrations.

Module Activity 3: Chinese Brush Painting

Combine art with reading and the study of the Chinese culture. Try your hand at the beautiful figures used in classic Chinese writing. Use white art paper (9″ × 12″), a brush, and black tempera to create the words shown here. To explore further, find *You Can Write Chinese* by Kurt Wiese in your library.

man   **beautiful**   **country**

Module Activity 4: Exploring China

Find an article about China in an encyclopedia. Read this article to see what you can find out about:

- The people of China
- The land—its boundaries, size
    comparison with the United States
    mountains and rivers
- China's government
- The languages of China

Study the map of China. Make an outline of this country. First divide your paper in fourths with light pencil lines. This helps you draw the map in proper proportion. The lines can be erased later.

Locate provinces, major cities, and rivers. Print the names of countries that border China. Identify the bodies of water that touch China.

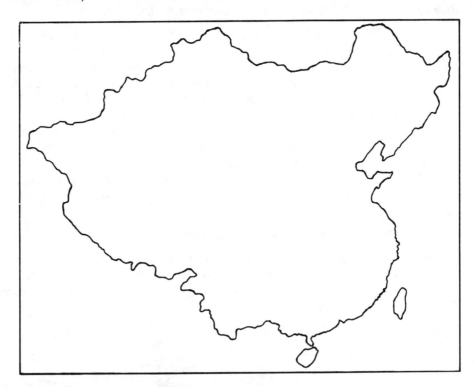

Module Activity 5: The Puzzling Pagoda— A Chinese Crossword Puzzle

After reading about China and drawing a map of this country, you should be able to complete the crossword puzzle. If you can't think of an answer, refer again to the encyclopedia.

PUZZLING PAGODA

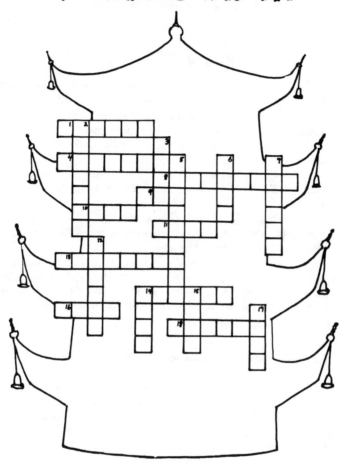

Definitions (For answers see page 265.)

Across

1. The capital of China
4. People's _____ of China
8. Chinese philosopher and scholar
9. Jewel
10. Luxurious cloth
11. Basic Chinese coin
13. Largest city in China
14. Useful cloth produced
16. Leader: _____ En-lai
18. Unique building

Down

2. Tallest mountain
3. Common cereal
5. Kind of government
6. Fishing boat
7. Country larger than China
12. Large woody plant
14. Common fish eaten
15. Prized lumber
17. Precious stone

Module Activity 6: Chinese Folktales

Every country has its share of stories, tales that have been passed down through the years. Here is an interesting fable that comes to us from China.

The Mussel and the Bird

Once upon a time there was a Mussel who lived in the cliffs along the edge of the ocean. After a long winter, sunshine at last reached the rocks, and the Mussel drowsily opened its shell to the warmth. A Bird dropped suddenly from the sky swooping down on the Mussel to snatch a meal from the shell. The Mussell quickly snapped shut, closing tightly on the Bird's beak. The Mussell squeezed the Bird's beak, but no matter how hard the Mussel squeezed the Bird wouldn't leave.

Finally the Bird spoke to the Mussel: "Mussel, if you don't open your shell soon, not in one day, not in two days, but in three days surely you will die." The Mussel made no reply.

Eventually the Mussel spoke to the Bird: "Bird, if you don't take your beak out of my shell, not in one day, not in two days, but in three days surely you will die." The Bird would not heed the Mussel.

Then along came a child on her way to play in the ocean. The Bird saw the child, but still it would not remove its beak. The Mussel also saw the child, but still it would not open its shell. The child spotted the Bird and the Mussel locked together, picked them up, and carried them away for the family stew pot.

—Retold by Pamela Tiedt

Can you think of a moral for this story?

Moral: _____

_____

_____

Find another folktale from China. Read it together with a friend. Plan how you can act the story out for others in the class. Invite other people to join you if you need their help.

Module Activity 7:
The Chinese Calendar

The Chinese Calendar is much different from the one we usually refer to. It is based on ancient traditions. An animal symbol is identified for each year, and persons born in that year are supposedly ruled by this symbolic animal and have characteristics associated with the animal. Twelve symbols are repeated continuously so that 1988 was the year of the Dragon, and the year of the Dragon will come again in the year 2000.

Examine this chart showing the symbols for the twentieth century. What is your symbol? Do you think the characteristics listed fit you?

IN WHICH YEAR WERE YOU BORN?

Ox (1913, 1925, 1937, 1949, 1961, 1973, 1985, 1997) You have a calm patient nature. Friends turn to you because you are that rarest of creatures—a good listener. Love bewilders you so many people wrongly consider you cold.

Tiger (1902, 1914, 1926, 1938, 1950, 1962, 1974, 1986, 1998) You are a person of great extremes. A sympathetic and considerate friend. A powerful and dangerous enemy. In your career you are both a deep thinker and a careful planner.

Hare (1903, 1915, 1927, 1939, 1951, 1963, 1975, 1987, 1999) You are blessed with extraordinary good fortune and will inevitably provide financial success. This luck of yours not only extends to your business interests, but also to games of chance.

Dragon (1904, 1916, 1928, 1940, 1952, 1964, 1976, 1988, 2000) Your reputation as a fire-eater is based on your outward show of stubbornness, bluster and short temper. But underneath you are really gentle, sensitive, and soft-hearted.

Serpent (1905, 1917, 1929, 1941, 1953, 1965, 1977, 1989, 2001) You Snake people have more than your share of the world's gifts, including basic wisdom. You are likely to be handsome, well formed men and graceful, beautiful women.

Horse (1906, 1918, 1930, 1942, 1954, 1966, 1978, 1990, 2002) Your cheerful disposition and flattering ways make you a popular favorite. Great mental agility will keep you in the upper income.

Ram (1907, 1919, 1931, 1943, 1955, 1967, 1979, 1991) You are a sensitive, refined, aesthetic type with considerable talent in all the arts. Indeed success or failure will depend upon whether you can shepherd your ability and energy into a single field.

Monkey (1908, 1920, 1932, 1944, 1956, 1968, 1980, 1992) In today's parlance you are a swinger. And because of your flair for decision making and sure-footed feel for finance, you are certain to climb to the top.

Rooster (1909, 1921, 1933, 1945, 1957, 1969, 1981, 1993) You either score heavily or lay a large egg. Although outspoken and not shy in groups, you are basically a loner who doesn't trust most people. Yet you are capable of attracting close and loyal friends.

Dog (1910, 1922, 1934, 1946, 1958, 1970, 1982, 1994) You are loyal and honest with a deep sense of duty and justice. You can always be trusted to guard the secrets of others.

Boar (1911, 1923, 1935, 1947, 1959, 1971, 1983, 1995) The quiet inner strength of your character is outwardly reflected by courtesy and breeding. Your driving ambition will lead you to success.

Rat (1912, 1924, 1936, 1948, 1960, 1972, 1984, 1996) You have been blessed with great personal charm, a taste for the better things in life, and considerable self control which restrains your quick temper.

Module Activity 8: Chinese Celebrations

Through the years many Chinese have immigrated to the United States, especially to the West coast. San Francisco and Los Angeles have large sections called Chinatown where you can eat Chinese food and visit Chinese shops.

Many Chinese Americans still celebrate the traditional holidays and festivals of China. There is nothing so festive and exciting as a Chinese New Year's parade with the flamboyant dragon leading the way down the streets of Chinatown. Chinese New Year falls on a variable date depending on the moon. It is celebrated as each person's birthday with fireworks, gongs and cymbals, and of course, wonderful delicacies.

Other traditional Chinese holidays include:

Spring Festival   Honors the planting season.

The Dragon Boat Festival   Sometimes called the Double Fifth, this holiday falls on the fifth day of the fifth month of the Chinese calendar. On this day dragon-shaped boats race, and inhabitants of Chinatown eat *jung,* three-cornered rice dumplings, in the local teahouses.

Ch'ung Yang Festival This summer holiday, celebrated with kite flying, originated with a legend. The story goes that a fortune teller foretold disaster for a certain farmer on the ninth day of the ninth month, so he took his family to a high windy hill. Upon returning home, they found that, indeed, their animals had all perished.

Festival of the Moon This harvest festival is celebrated privately at night. This romantic celebration is the women's festival. They prepare large moon cakes made of flour and brown sugar to resemble the moon and its palaces.

Double Ten Festival On the tenth day of the tenth month, the dragon appears again to celebrate the Chinese Revolution and the fall of the Manchu Empire in the early twentieth century.

Ching Ming Festival Also called the Festival of the Tombs, it falls on the 106th day after the winter solstice. At this time the Chinese go to private cemeteries to honor the dead.

Winter Festival A family celebration, this holiday usually occurs in December shortly before Christmas.

See if you can find out more about Chinese celebrations. Try one of these means of gathering information:

- Interview someone whose family originated in China. Find out if they celebrate these holidays, and if so, how the celebration is carried out.
- Read about Chinese holidays in a book in your library.
- Go to Chinatown to observe a celebration.
- Write to a tourist agency or the Embassy of China to request information.

Write a short report of your findings.

Module Activity 9: Chinese Come to America

People of Chinese origins have made major contributions to the development of the United States. Many are doctors, college professors, and business executives. As immigrants, however, their life was difficult.

Read this list of events that are significant in the history of Chinese Americans from the first immigration to the present.

1785 First record of Chinese in the United States. Three Chinese seamen from the ship *Pallas* were left stranded in Baltimore.

1815 First record of a Chinese in California. Ah Nam, a cook for Governor de Sola, was baptised as a Christian on October 27, 1815. (California was not yet a part of the United States.)

1849 In the year of the Gold Rush, Chinese in San Francisco recorded as 54; in 1850 there were 787 men and 2 women. First anti-Chinese riot at Chinese camp, Tuolumne County, California

1850 First laundry business begun in San Francisco by a Chinese person.

1852   First Chinese opera performed in San Francisco. First Chinese theater built in San Francisco. Columbia Resolution expelled Chinese from gold mines in Tuolumne County; followed by a similar action in other counties.

1854   First Chinese newspaper in America, *Gold Hill News.*

1869   Completion of Transcontinental Railway. Chinese labor used by Central Pacific. Chinatown established in Deadwood, South Dakota, with discovery of gold. Chinese followed development of the mining industry as well as agriculture, and fishing; resentment by whites.

1871   Chinese massacre in Los Angeles.

1877   Special Report by Joint Committee of Congress investigated the "Chinese Question." Labor agitation; anti-Chinese movement.

1879   California Constitution contained anti-Chinese legislation prohibiting employment of Chinese by corporations and government agencies.

1882   Chinese Exclusion Act passed by U.S. Congress; ten-year ban on immigration. Anti-Chinese riots.

1892   Geary Act extended exclusion for another ten years; required aliens to register.

1893   Anti-Chinese riots grew numerous; Fresno, California; Napa, California; Redlands, Tulare, Visalia, Ukiah, California.

1894   Vacaville, California, riot; Chinese driven to cities where they formed Chinese ghettos, called Chinatowns.

1902   Exclusion laws extended indefinitely.

1907   Vancouver, British Columbia, riot.

1943   Repeal of Chinese Exclusion Act: Chinese aliens in U.S. may become citizens. Chinese immigration quota set at 105 per year.

1965   Quota system repealed. Permits up to 20,000 Chinese to enter United States each year.

Work with others in your class to prepare a time-line on a long strip of paper that looks something like this:

```
1780  1800  1820  1840  1860  1880  1900  1920  1940  1960  1980
```

Add illustrations and other information related to the history of Chinese immigration into the United States.

Module Activity 10: Challenging the Dragon—Making a Game

Directions to the Student.   Here is a fiery dragon whose breath can destroy you or bring you fortune. Which will it be? (See pages 258–259.)

This dragon guards a Treasure Chest that you can reach only by performing the many tasks required by the fearsome beast.

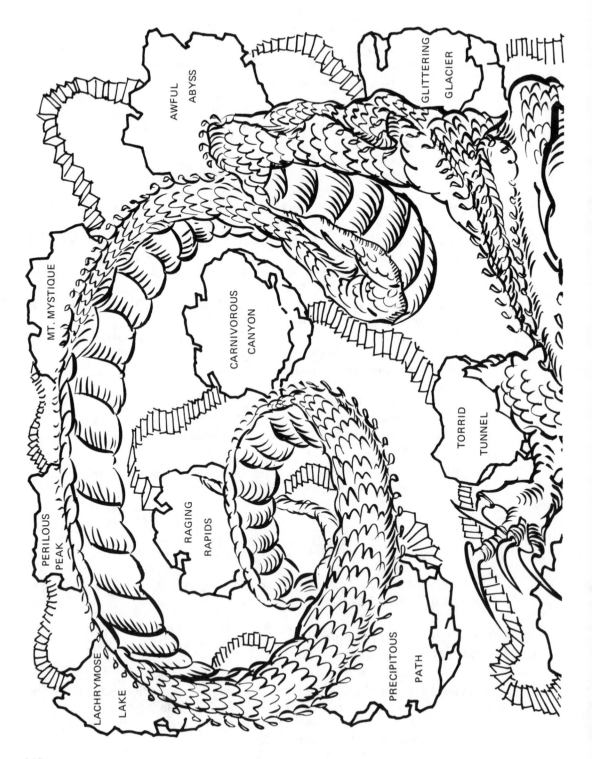

GLITTERING GLACIER

AWFUL ABYSS

MT. MYSTIQUE

CARNIVOROUS CANYON

TORRID TUNNEL

PERILOUS PEAK

RAGING RAPIDS

LACHRYMOSE LAKE

PRECIPITOUS PATH

At each step roll the dragon's Curious Cube to see how many tasks you must perform. To learn what the tasks will be, draw forth a Cardinal Card for each task. If you perform the required tasks, the dragon will permit you to move to the next perilous step. If you fail even one of the tasks, you must slide back to the previous step.

You have only a limited time to perform each task. As you complete each task, place the Cardinal Card under the great pile of Arduous Tasks. That task may be assigned to another unlucky challenger who dares to challenge the dragon.

Making the Curious Cube.   Copy the pattern shown here to make the cube that will tell how many of the Arduous Tasks you must perform. After cutting the cube pattern from heavy red paper, print the numbers indicated with a felt pen. Then fold the pattern on each line, folding in the same direction each time. Form the six-sided figure and tuck the flaps in after applying glue on each.

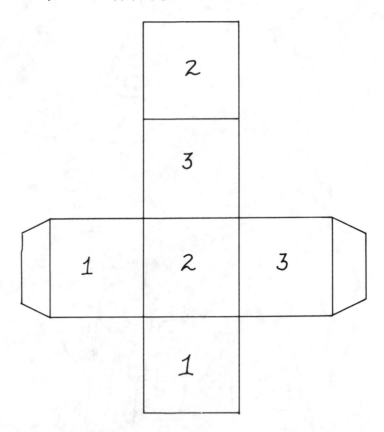

Preparing the Arduous Task Cards.   Cut the cards apart. Mount each one on red (cardinal) construction paper that is 3″ × 4″ so the color frames the card.

Playing the Game Alone.   This is a good game to play individually as you challenge the dragon alone. You may need a person to serve as Timer and Checker to see if your answers are acceptable. Use any means to discover the correct answer within the time limit, for instance, a dictionary.

Playing the Game with a Friend.   You may wish to play this game with a friend or two. In this case do not wait for each person to finish the tasks assigned. If one player finishes a task in a short time, he or she can move to the next step, throw the Curious Cube, draw the Cardinal Cards and work on the tasks assigned. In this way, each person moves ahead individually depending on the number of tasks received each time and how quickly they are completed. You will want to hurry, of course, if you are to reach the Treasure before someone else gets it away from the Dragon!

1. About how many people live in China?	6. Name the tallest mountain in China.

2. Name the 3 largest countries in the world.	7. Identify the following:
	  a. pagoda
	  b. junk
	  c. carp.

3. What kind of cloth was a gift from China?	8. Where did Chinese immigrants first settle?
4. What city is the capital of China?	9. Which of these names is likely to be Chinese? Martin Chang Yomura
5. Which city is the largest in China?	10. Name two countries that border China.

Module Activity 11: Exploring Your Community

What do you know about Chinese Americans in your own community? Begin a survey by turning to your local telephone book. Check the following:

- The number of persons listed under several common Chinese names such as Wong, Chang, or Yee. What other names might you try?
- Look under the word *Chinese* to see how many listings begin with that word; for example, Chinese Alliance Church.
- In the Yellow Pages, look under *Restaurants*. How many Chinese restaurants are listed?

- Look under the entry, *Physicians and Surgeons, M.D.,* in the Yellow Pages. How many doctors have Chinese names?

Write a summary of your findings. Then write a paragraph explaining your conclusions about the Chinese in your community.

Do your findings surprise you? How can you find out more about Chinese Americans in your community?

Module Activity 12: A Writing Lesson

Sample Lesson: La Dictée, A Dictation Method[6]

Level of Difficulty: Grades 1–12 (Adapt materials selected.)

Outcomes:

Students will:

1. Listen to sentences read aloud.
2. Write each sentence dictated.
3. Discuss spelling and mechanical errors.

Procedures:

Select a paragraph from a good book that students have already heard or one that you would like to introduce. Choose a paragraph that includes interesting sentence structures, varied uses of punctuation and capitalization, and new vocabulary. (Choose a less complex paragraph for the first experience with la dictée.) In this lesson we will use a paragraph from *Dragonwings* by Laurence Yep (Harper), a story of the Chinese in California during the early twentieth century.

Stimulus

Introduce the book and author to your class, for example:

> *Dragonwings* was written by a California author, Lawrence Yep, who was inspired by the account of a Chinese immigrant who built a flying machine in 1909. This is how the story begins:
> "Ever since I can remember, I had wanted to know about the Land of the Golden Mountain, but my mother had never wanted to talk about it."

Invite students to conjecture about what the Land of the Golden Mountain is. Tell them that the main character, Moon Shadow, lives in China with his mother and grandmother, but his father, Windrider, lives in San Francisco's Chinatown.

Then share the interesting paragraph you have selected for the la dictée exercise, for example:

> Mother had talked quite a bit about him and so had Grandmother; but that too was not the same. They were speaking about a young man who had lived in the Middle Kingdom, not a man who had endured the hardships and loneliness of living in the demon land. I knew he made kites; but as marvelous as his kites were, he and I could not spend the

rest of our lives flying kites. I was afraid of the Golden Mountain, and yet my father, who lives there, wanted me to join him. I only knew that there was a certain rightness in life—the feeling you got when you did something the way you knew you should. I owed it to Father to obey him in everything—even if it meant going to such a fearful place as the Golden Mountain. And really, how really frightening could it be if Hand Clap wanted to go back? I turned to Mother and Grandmother. "I want to go," I said.

Talk about the passage the students have heard. Ask them such questions as:

1. Who is talking?
2. What characters are mentioned in this paragraph?
3. Who is Hand Clap?
4. What is this fearful place, The Golden Mountain? Where is it? How did it get that name?
5. Why was Moon Shadow afraid? Why did he decide to go?

Activity

Tell the students that you are going to dictate this paragraph to them, sentence by sentence. You will read each sentence only twice: The first time they are to listen without writing; the second time will be after they have begun writing. Challenge them to write each sentence as well as they can without help.

Followup

After you have completed the dictation exercise, have students correct any errors together. Ask two students to write the first sentence on the chalkboard. Ask if any changes need to be made in spelling, punctuation, or capitalization. Tell students to correct any mistakes they made on their own papers.

Students should study this passage in preparation for writing the same passage again on the next day.

Evaluation

Have students compare the results of the two dictations. Have each one write several sentences summarizing what they learned from doing this exercise.

Have them staple the three papers together to place in their writing portfolios. Schedule la dictée lessons once a week for a period of time. After four weeks have each student examine his or her packet of dictation exercises to analyze how this learning experience is working, perhaps noting what he or she might do to improve performance on this task.

Related Learning Activities

Extend student learning by providing instruction related to the literature you have introduced, as described in these examples.

1. *Repetition of the same dictation.* Dictate the same passage to students a month later to see if they have retained the knowledge. Students who have

repeated difficulty can work together in pairs, dictating one sentence at a time to each other. This is a good exercise for ESL students.

2. *Exploring sentence patterns.* Choose a sentence from the passage to serve as a model for students. Show them how to identify the structural features of the sentence that form a pattern, thus:

_____ had _____ and so had _____; but that _____.

Students can generate sentences that follow this pattern like this one:

John had lied and so had Mildred; but that didn't make any difference now.

3. *Responding to literature through writing.* This passage suggests a number of topics that seventh-grade students might identify, for example:

How would you feel if you were Moon Shadow? Would you have made the same decision?

Write the dialogue that you think might have taken place between Moon Shadow and his father, Windrider, when they met in San Francisco.

Module Activity 13: What Do You Know Now?

Write three things that you know about China or Chinese Americans now that you did not know before you began this study:

1. _____
2. _____
3. _____

Examine the answers you gave to the questions on the first page of this module. Would you change any of them now?

Choose one of the following activities to complete your work on this study:

- Write a poem or story about a person from China.
- Act out a story set in China that you have read. (You may work with several students on this task.)
- Plan a reader's theater presentation of a folktale from China. (Work with several students.)
- Make a diorama of a scene from China.
- Make a table-size relief map of China. (Work with another student.)

Module Activity 14: Sharing Information

Your class may want to share your information about China and Chinese Americans with other classes or the whole school. How can you do this?

Notes to the Teacher

Preparing the Gameboard

If you choose to prepare the gameboard yourself as a stimulating extra activity for this study, begin by enlarging the drawing with an opaque projector. Have students help you as much as possible because involvement pays off. Examine this part of the module again before reading the following directions so you will understand the instructions.

Duplicate or copy the directions to the student on page 257. Mount these directions on a heavy piece of colored cardboard. Cover the directions with a sheet of clear contact paper to protect the sheet as it is used repeatedly. Pressing the direction board (covered with a sheet of clean paper) with a warm iron will make the protective sheet adhere well.

Have a student construct the curious cube as instructed (page 260). Have several other students finish the cardinal cards (see page 261). You will need to prepare additional cards similar to the examples given if a number of students wish to play at once.

Answers:

1. 600 million
2. Russia
   Canada
   China
3. silk
4. Peking
5. Shanghai
6. Mt. Everest
7. a. special kind of building
   b. Chinese boat
   c. kind of fish

8. California
9. Chang
10. Russia
    North Korea
    North Vietnam
    Laos
    Burma
    India
    Bhutan
    Sikkim
    Nepal
    Pakistan
    Afghanistan
    Mongolia

Answers for the Pagoda Puzzle (page 253)*

Across	Down
1. Peking	2. Everest
4. Republic	3. Rice
8. Confucius	5. Communist
9. Gem	6. Junk
10. Silk	7. Russia
11. Yuan	12. Bamboo
13. Shanghai	14. Carp
14. Cotton	15. Teak
16. Chou	17. Jade
18. Pagoda	

*Sources for the Pagoda Puzzle were *China,* edited by Thomas W. Chinn, and *California, A Syllabus.* The Chinese Historical Society of America, 17 Adler Place, San Francisco, CA 94133.

Additional Activities

As students are working on the study of China, you might wish to interject additional interesting activities that can involve the whole group or may be designed for small group interaction. Here are a few suggestions:

- Invite a parent who was born in China to visit your class to tell about China as they remember it, childhood experiences, coming to the United States, what his or her life here is like. Students then write these stories together.
- Prepare a simple Chinese meal of rice and a combination of vegetables—celery, onions, green peppers, canned water chestnuts, soy sauce. See: *Eating and Cooking Around the World; Fingers before Forks* by Erich Berry (Day).
- Read a version of "Cinderella" that comes from China. See: *Favorite Children's Stories from China and Tibet* by Lotta C. Hume (Tuttle).
- Write a Chinese play or produce one that is available in the library. See: *7 Plays and How to Produce Them* by Moyne R. Smith (Walck).
- Learn how Chinese New Year is celebrated. See: *Holidays Around the World* by Joseph Gaer (Little, Brown).
- Explore Chinese poetry. See: *Chinese Mother Goose Rhymes* edited by Robert Wyndham (World); *The Moment of Wonder* edited by Richard Lewis (Dial).
- Read stories aloud that are set in China, for the well-told story adds much to our understanding of another culture. You might choose, for example, *Seven Magic Orders: An Original Chinese Folktale*, beautifully illustrated by Y. T. Mui (Lippincott).

Chinese Children in Your Classroom

Presenting a study related to the country of origin for students in your class gives them a good feeling of belonging. They can often contribute special information and personal experiences. Their parents may be willing to share in the study, too. The students will learn as they participate in the study. Students who may have arrived recently from China or Hong Kong will be very much interested in finding out about Chinese Americans in the community and in the United States.

As you work with Chinese-speaking children, it is helpful to be somewhat aware of the problems they may experience as they learn English.

ASPECTS OF THE CHINESE LANGUAGE THAT MAY CAUSE PROBLEMS FOR CHINESE STUDENTS LEARNING ENGLISH

1. The verb has only one form. Unlike the English verb, the Chinese verb is not conjugated to indicate tense. Tenses are indicated by the use of auxiliaries placed before or after the stable verb form.
2. Nouns are not inflected to indicate plural forms. Plurality is indicated by the use of auxiliaries in the form of specific or general number indicators placed before a noun (e.g., three book, many boy).
3. The Chinese article *a* is very specific and complex. It refers to the noun that it modifies and varies according to that noun. It is used as a unit of measure rather than as a general article (e.g., a book, a building, a string, a coat, a horse, a pencil).

4. Word order may not be manipulated to change meaning as is done in English. In Chinese the word *is*, for example, may not be repositioned to convert a statement into a question (e.g., "She is a nurse" may not be repositioned to "Is she a nurse?").
5. Spoken Cantonese and spoken Mandarin have an identical spoken sound to represent the pronoun he and she; but the written forms for these and three other singular pronouns in the third person are very distinct when genders are indicated basically by word-radical forms: She (feminine); he (masculine); it (inanimate object); it (animate object); and He (deity).
6. In a Chinese dictionary, words are not arranged in alphabetical order. Instead, they are listed by the number of strokes each character has.
7. There is a tendency for Chinese speakers to drop, glottalize, or add a vowel sound to English endings in the consonants *t, d, s, l, p, b, k, f, g, r,* and *v.*
8. A tone system is used in Chinese as a device for distinguishing word meanings. Words having the same pronunciation may have four different meanings. These meanings are, in turn, represented by four written forms.
9. There is a distinction between *n* and *l* in spoken Chinese; but some speakers, especially the Cantonese, use the letters interchangeably. The difference in pronunciation is particularly distinct in Mandarin.

SOURCE: *Framework in Reading for the Elementary and Secondary Schools of California.* California State Department of Education.

Summary

Multicultural education, taught across the total curriculum, should lead students:

> to develop a sense of "shared humanity"; to understand themselves and "otherness," by learning how they resemble and how they differ from other people, over time and space; to question stereotypes of others, and of themselves; to discern the difference between fact and conjecture; to grasp the complexity of historical cause; to distrust the simple answer and the dismissive explanation; to respect particularity and avoid false analogy; to recognize the abuse of historical "lessons," and to weigh the possible consequences of such abuse; to consider that ignorance of the past may make us prisoners of it; to realize that not all problems have solutions; to be prepared for the irrational, the accidental, in human affairs; and to grasp the power of ideas and character in history.[7]

REFLECTIONS

Multicultural education fits well into the total curriculum. Teachers need to confer as a faculty to determine just how they can best promote the understanding of diversity in any particular school. If each teacher agrees to present multicultural literature or to use a lesson that teaches a multicultural concept at least once a month, student empathy will gradually grow, reinforced by instruction in all classrooms. Teachers in self-contained classrooms can readily plan integrated units of study that incorporate multicultural studies in all area of the curriculum.

APPLICATIONS

Begin exploring on your own. Consider the ways you can use the resources listed in this chapter. Try several of these ideas.

1. Chose one state to study in detail. Think chiefly about the people who now live in that part of our country. Find out their backgrounds and how they came to settle there. As you focus on the people, you will discover how they make their living, the cities and towns in which they live, and the issues that concern them. Use the library as a resource, but also watch the daily newspaper and talk with people who have lived in that state.

    Begin a file of books that you or young students might read to learn more about the state. If you choose Hawaii, for example, you might list:

   > Marcia Brown. *Backbone of the King: The Story of Paka and His Son Ku.* Scribner, 1966. Middle-grade students will enjoy this story written by an outstanding author.

   > Eleanor Nordyke. *The Peope of Hawaii.* The University of Hawaii Press, 1981. This book tells you about the multiethnic population on the islands.

   > Ruth Tabrah. *Hawaii: A Bicentennial History.* Norton, 1980. Written for the bicentennial, here is a good overview of Hawaiian history up to the present.

   > Vivian Thompson. *Hawaiian Myths of Earth, Sea, and Sky.* Holiday, 1966. Students can act out the tales of the Hawaiian gods as a way of learning more about the people of Hawaii.

    If each person in your class develops a collection of resource material about one state, you can duplicate them for sharing so that everyone will have a rich packet to use in the classroom.

2. Outline a study of religious groups in the United States. How might you guide students to learn more about the various beliefs? Include a list of the many groups in the United States, and begin listing books that could be used with a study of comparative religions, for example:

   > Eileen Weiman. *Which Way Courage.* Atheneum, 1981. A story about the Amish.

   > *Ann the Word; The Life of Mother Ann Lee, Founder of the Shakers.* Little, 1976. Information about the Shakers, founded in 1776 by a woman of greath faith.

    Also refer to the list of materials about Jews in America on pages 385–388 and Edward Rice's *American Saints and Seers: American-Born Religions and the Genius Behind Them* (Four Winds, 1982).

3. Plan a letter-writing unit of study in which each student writes for free or inexpensive materials that are made available by different companies and

organizations. Here is a list that you can add to as you read magazines and newspapers. After students receive the materials that were requested, they can share them orally.

> Agency for Instructional TV. Box A, 1111 V. 17th St. Bloomington, IN 47401. "Trade Offs."
>
> Cooperative Extension Service. Box U-35, The University of Connecticut, Storrs, CT 06268. *Mexican Foods and Traditions.*
>
> Delmonte Teaching Aids. Box 4007, Clinton, IA 52732. *The Big Four Daily Countdown (Basic Foods). Consuma Diariamente Los Cuatro Alimentos Básicos.*
>
> Frito-Lay Tower. Dallas, TX 75235. *Tasty Recipes from from Frito-Lay, Inc.*
>
> National Dairy Council. Chicago, IL 60606, *Una Guía Par Comer Bien* — Chart.
>
> Procter & Gamble. Box 599, Cincinnati, OH 45201. "Consumer."
>
> Texas Education Agency. 201 East 11th St., Austin, TX 78701. *El Corrido de Gregorio Cortez.* (Send blank tape, cassette size.)
>
> World Research, Inc. 11722 Sorrento Valley Rd., San Diego, CA 92121. "The Inflation File."

4. Begin a file of source addresses. Include those that you discover after reading this book. After writing to each source for any available materials for multicultural education, record what you received on the address card. Begin with these addresses:

> AFL-CIO
> Dept. of Education
> 815 16th Street, NW
> Washington, D.C. 20006
>
> Bay Area Global Education Project (BAGEP)
> c/o World Affairs Council of Northern California
> World Affairs Center
> 213 Sutter St., Suite 200
> San Francisco, CA 94108
>
> Center for Public Education in International Affairs
> School of International Relations
> University of Southern California
> Los Angeles, CA 90089-0043
>
> Overseas Development Council
> 1717 Massachusetts Ave., N.W.
> Washington, D.C. 20036
>
> Population Reference Bureau
> 1337 Connecticut Ave., N.W.
> Washington, D.C. 20036

5. Design a module for use in teaching a specific unit of study. Plan an integrated study that will last for three to four weeks. Draw from the entire text of *Multicultural Teaching* for ideas that fit your topic. Modules can be produced for any subject area. You must first decide, of course, on what you want to teach. Modules can focus on groups of people, geographic areas, or broad concepts related to multilingual/multicultural studies. Examples of good topics for presentation in modular form are the following:

- Prejudice in America
- Native Americans Today
- Americans from Puerto Rico
- Breaking Down Stereotypes
- The People in New York City

Endnotes

1. Kenneth Jackson. Chair, Bradley Commission on History in Schools. *Building a History Curriculum: Guidelines for Teaching History in Schools.* The Educational Excellence Network, 1988, p. 15.
2. "A Naturalist's Perspective." *Nature Center News* (September 1988): 4.
3. Paul Gagnon. "Why Study History?" *The Atlantic Monthly* (November 1988): 43.
4. Ibid., p. 45.
5. Ibid., p. 64.
6. Iris McClellan Tiedt. *Writing: From Topic to Evaluation.* Allyn and Bacon, 1989, pp. 145–148.

Resources

Carolyn Field and J. S. Weiss. *Selected Children's Books of Fiction and Fantasy.* Library Professional Books, 1987.

Paul Gagnon. "Why Study History?" *The Atlantic Monthly* (November 1988): 43–66.

Kenneth Jackson. *Building a History Curriculum: Guidelines for Teaching History in Schools.* Bradley Commission on History in Schools, 1988.

James Moffett. *Active Voice: A Writing Program across the Curriculum.* Boynton/Cook, 1981.

Joy F. Moss. *Focus Units in Literature: A Handbook for Elementary School Teachers.* National Council of Teachers of English, 1984

Iris M. Tiedt et al. *Teaching Thinking in K–12 Classrooms.* Allyn and Bacon, 1989.

The world is my country. All mankind are my brethren. Thomas Paine... We dare not just look back to great yesterdays. We must look forward to great tomorrows. Adlai E. Stevenson... Beware, as long as you live, of judging people by appearances. La Fontaine... If you have built castles in the air, your work need not be lost. Now put foundations under them. Osa Johnson... Until you have become really in actual fact, a brother to everyone, brotherhood will not come to pass. Fyodor Dostoyevsky... You must look into people as well as at them. Lord Chesterfield... True friendship is a plant of slow growth. George Washington... Coming together is a beginning; keeping together is progress; working together is success. Henry Ford... He has a right to criticize who has a heart to help. Abraham Lincoln... Democracy is based upon the conviction that there are extraordinary possibilities in ordinary people. Henry Emerson Fosdick!... While democracy must have its organization and controls, its vital breath is individual liberty. Charles Evans Hughes. Whoever seeks to set one race against another seeks to enslave all races. Franklin D. Roosevelt... Nothing happens unless first a dream. Carl Sandburg... No man is an Island, entire of itself. John Donne... Breathes there the man with soul so dead, who never to himself hath said, "This is my own, my native land." Sir Walter Scott... Ask not what your country can do for you; ask what you can do for your country.. John F. Kennedy... No man is good enough to govern another man without that others consent. Abraham Lincoln... Gently scan your brother man. Robert Burns...

9

Multicultural Teaching Around the Year

O brave new world,
that has such people in't.
William Shakespeare, *The Temptest*

Preview

After reading this chapter, you should be able to:

- Incorporate multicultural perspectives into all aspects of your teaching.
- Show students how many different groups have contributed to the history and identity of this country.
- Build student knowledge about different groups and how they have been treated in this country.
- Stimulate student interest in and appreciation for the value of different perspectives.
- Encourage students' pride in their own heritage.

To develop multicultural understandings in your students involves more than presenting a unit on Black Americans in February (for Black History month) or a unit on Mexican Americans in May (for Cinco de Mayo). Multicultural understandings can develop only when students are constantly involved in exploring and discussing the differences and similarities among people and the way that the presence of many cultures in this country affects the students' own identity.

This chapter is organized around a monthly calendar, beginning with the school year and including the summer months, so that you can incorporate information and discussions that build these multicultural understandings into your teaching plans as you move through the school year. The notes on each day and the suggested activities are intended to serve as a base upon which your class can build their own Multicultural Calendar, personalizing it as appropriate with student birthdays and local holidays and festivals.

PREPARING THE CALENDAR

Challenge students to decide on the most effective way to prepare the calendar for the class. Have them brainstorm to develop ideas and alternatives for displaying the months. Students can work in teams to construct a display. While some students mount a frame for the month, others can be researching and collecting quotes, pictures, and other items to supply background information. The materials collected for each month can be assembled in a class notebook for students to consult throughout the year as they work on other projects.

The Multicultural Calendar should always be the result of the effort and interests of the whole class. Although you may want to keep the materials developed from year to year, each class will need to create their own version, reflecting their own perspectives and making their own discoveries.

Displaying the Calendar

You can reproduce the calendar directly on a large bulletin board. Divide the display space into squares or rectangles using thick, colored yarn or strips of colored construction paper as shown here:

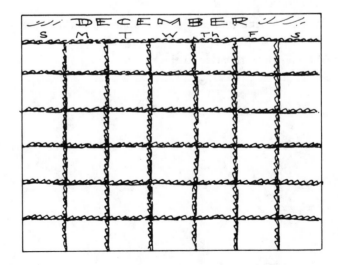

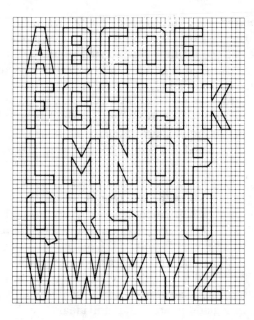

Make the spaces as large as possible. (Challenge several students to solve this measurement problem!) Cut large block letters for the days of the week and the names of the months. Cut a set of numbers from 1 to 31. Both letters and numbers can be made easily if you use graph paper as shown above. To enlarge these letters, simply use graph paper with bigger blocks or double the number of blocks for each pattern. Cut a few samples to check the size against the display space after it is organized. Although the same numbers and many of the letters can be used for each month, you might want to use different colors for variety.

Developing the Calendar

Students can type or print the names and dates on slips of colored construction paper or unlined file cards to mount in the appropriate block for each month. Be sure that they check the current calendar so that the number 1 is placed under the correct day of the week; the rest of the dates will then fall in place accordingly. Add events that occur locally or dates of personal interest to your students. If the blocks for each day are big enough, you can include pictures and quotations wherever possible.

Quotations are of special interest for the multicultural calendar. Find as many as possible for people whose names appear for that month. Begin with the quotations presented throughout this book. Additional sources of quotations include:

Joseph Robert Conlin. *The Morrow Book of Quotations in American History.* Morrow, 1984.

Gorton Carruth and Eugene Ehrlich. *The Harper Book of American Quotations.* Harper, 1988.

The Oxford Dictionary of Quotations, 3rd ed. Oxford University Press, 1979.

Your public library will be able to supply numerous books of quotations. Advanced readers will enjoy poring over these books which they probably have not yet explored.

Pictures add a special dimension to the calendar. Although they are not always easily found, you can gradually build up a collection. Let other teachers know that you are searching for multiethnic pictures for this purpose. Include pictures of people as well as places and events. Keep your eyes open as you look at the daily newspaper or magazines; it is surprising how many suitable pictures you will find. If you have a large bulletin board on which to display the calendar, you might place a ring of pictures around the calendar. Challenge students to identify the people and events pictured.

Encourage students to add to the calendar. As they read, they can take notes on information to include in the calendar. They can even do research in particular areas for this purpose as they search the newspapers, their textbooks, library reference books, and fiction. Newspapers are an especially good source of articles on contemporary and historical events to add to the bulletin board. Students can become investigators as each one takes responsibility for exploring a specific topic.

Students can also decorate the bulletin board by adding appropriate designs, symbols, or illustrations. Snowflakes for the winter months, leaves for the fall, and flowers for the spring add interest and individuality to the calendar. Other popular seasonal motifs include pumpkins, kites, butterflies, and shamrocks.

Strategies for Using the Calendar

In the next section of this chapter we present specific ideas about individual people and events as they appear on each calendar. Here we are providing suggestions for teaching that may extend over a period of time not limited to one day or month. Sometimes a more extensive study is triggered by a single event or even a series of dates on the calendar. The following are examples of units that cross subject areas as well as periods of time and require students to use affective and cognitive abilities.

- Childhood in Other Countries
- Ethnic Groups in Our Community
- Native Americans Yesterday and Today
- Religions of the World
- Holidays and Celebrations
- Women in Sports
- What We Do for Fun
- Puerto Rico: The Fifty-first State?

Almost any topic that you study in the elementary and junior high school classroom will lend itself to a multicultural approach. As you plan, therefore, consider the ways you can bring out the kinds of understandings that will promote better human relations in our country. Point to the contributions of various groups—ethnic, religious, young and old, male and female—as a strength of our society. Described here are representative strategies that will add stimulus to your curriculum.

Who Am I?

Challenge students to identify the month's mystery guest. Give them a picture or a quote and a few hints to get them started, as well as a variety of reference books to make the task more stimulating. As students discover the mystery guest's identity, they can record the results of their research on a Fact Sheet on the bulletin board for all the students to see. The first student to guess correctly gets to choose the candidate for next month's challenge. As a variation, students can each select an individual to research and report on to the class.

Great Interviews

Students can play the roles of Barbara Walters or David Frost as they interview anyone they choose, past or present. Two or more students will need to develop this activity together as they plan the best questions and appropriate responses. Students can also have several people being interviewed, perhaps from different times. They should, however, try to play these roles as realistically as possible.

Conversations

Imagine a conversation between Presidents Lincoln and Bush. Imagine a conversation among Abigail Adams, Eleanor Roosevelt, Harriet Beecher Stowe, Shirley Chisholm, and Yvonne Braithwaite Burke. Students could have fun selecting the groups of people to engage in a conversation as well as participating in the conversations. Tape the conversations for later evaluation.

In the Words of . . .

Students could pretend to be someone from the past who has suddenly entered your community. For example, how might George Washington react to many of the problems of today? What would he think of New York City? How would he react to being introduced to Sandra Day O'Connor or Shirley Chisholm? Students could then write a diary for the person from the past, which would include an account of such personal reactions. Naturally, students should be allowed to select the topics or situations that interest them.

Letters

Encourage students to write letters to pen pals who live in different countries. They can write letters to the editor of the local newspaper when there is an issue on which they have an opinion. They can also write letters to people from whom they would like information — congressmen or women, authors of articles or books, leaders of groups or movements, and so on.

Book of Lists

Students can focus on individual interests when they assemble their own lists of interesting facts. The results can be collected in a class "Book of Lists" so that students have a chance to show off their research and share the interesting information they have found. The lists can be organized around geographical, chronological, ethnic, or occupational groupings. Possible topics include: Native American Heroes and Heroines, Spanish Place Names in Our State, Personalities in Our Community, and The Most Important Events in the History of Black Americans.

Collage

Have each student choose one person or group represented on the multicultural calendar about which to develop a collage. They might choose César Chávez and his activities, black women in the United States, author Alex Haley, or Japanese Americans. Pictures, words, maps, poetry, small objects—almost anything can be included in this composite picture.

Illustrated Lecture

Upper-grade students can prepare a formal lecture to present to the class. Students select a subject from the calendar to research. They prepare the lecture, including appropriate illustrations to make their presentation more effective; for example, pertinent newspaper clippings mounted on a poster, a time line displayed on the bulletin board, transparencies showing statistics, or a list of words that might be new to their listeners. If these lectures are presented over a period of months, the selection of topics will be larger and the class will not get tired of hearing "lectures." Emphasis should be placed on making the presentation informative and stimulating.

It Happened in November

A special bulletin board display can be prepared, featuring facts, events, and personalities associated with a month. Over a period of a week, students can collect newspaper articles, books, pictures, quotations, and other current and historical materials. The variety of materials used results in an eye-catching display that will motivate students to explore further. Discuss what influence the past events have had on the present. What influence might the current events have on the future?

THE MONTHLY CALENDAR

In this section you will find ideas for celebrating multicultural understandings every day of the year. The names and events recorded on these pages will help students see the influence of history on the present, as they find out more about human beings leading real lives. In addition, they will build a better understanding of where they come from and who they are as they discover the diversity of people who have contributed to our world today. The activities presented in this section provide opportunities for students to ask and answer questions, to discuss fundamental issues such as race and identity, and to begin to develop the skills and information essential to live in a complex world.

The calendar includes:

- Birthdays of historical and contemporary Americans from major ethnic groups
- Important dates in the history of different groups
- People from other countries who have influenced Americans
- Special days commemorating specific groups
- Religious and cultural holidays and festivals

Following each month is a short list of suggested activities for incorporating the calendar information into your everyday teaching.

The calendar listings were chosen to introduce students to the history and contributions of various groups. Unfortunately, Black, Asian, and Native American heroes have often gone unrecorded and unsung. Thus, this calendar can provide only a sampling, a place to start. Most individuals are listed under their birthdate. However, for many Native Americans, or Blacks born in slavery, the birthdate is unknown. Other important events are difficult to record on this calendar because they follow a different measure of time such as the Chinese lunar calendar. Information on these calendars will be found on pages 254–255.

To facilitate presentation, we have not prepared the calendar for one specific year. You will need to make slight adaptations to correct the dates accordingly. For each month, too, there are certain special weeks or holidays that occur on variable dates. July and August are included so that you can present this information during the rest of the school year.

We begin with September and the opening of the school year.

September Activities

16   Prepare the class for Mexican Independence Day by featuring Mexico in the classroom. Use all available materials to create an atmosphere of Mexico. Travel posters, clothes, and objects from Mexico will contribute a festive appearance. Display books about Mexico. Older students can write reports on different aspects of Mexico to put around the room. Use a map of Mexico as a focus for featuring facts about Mexico. Have students research information to construct a time line of significant events in Mexican history. Why is Mexican Independence Day important? What are other dates that are celebrated in Mexico? Make task cards such as the one shown on page 281 for individualized approaches.

SEPTEMBER

1	2	3	4	5	6	7
	Liliuokalani, 1838–1917, last sovereign of Hawaii	Prudence Crandall, 1803–?, first to admit Negro girls to her school	Richard Wright, 1908–1960 Henry Hudson discovered Manhattan, 1609	Harriet E. Wilson published first novel by American Black		
8 International Literacy Day	**9** Sarah Douglass, 1806–1882, Black teacher and abolitionist Mao Zedong died, 1976	**10** Alice Davis, 1852–1935, Seminole tribal leader	**11**	**12** Henry Hudson named Hudson River, 1609	**13** Maria Baldwin, 1856–1922, Black educator and civic leader	**14**
15 Porfirio Diaz, President of Mexico, 1830–1915 National Hispanic Week begins	**16** Mexican Independence day, 1810 Mayflower Day (Pilgrims left England 1620)	**17** Citizenship Day Constitution Day Steuben Day Constitution Week begins	**18** Quebec surrendered to English, 1759	**19** Lajos Kossuth, Hungarian patriot, 1802–1915	**20**	**21**
22 First French republic established, 1792 Martha Corey hung for a witch, Salem, 1692	**23**	**24** Francis Watkins Harper, 1825–1911, Black author and reformer	**25** Balboa discovered Pacific Ocean, 1513 Columbus began second trip to America, 1493	**26**	**27** American Indian Day	**28** Confucius birthday (National holiday, Taiwan)
29	**30**					

I am a red man. If the Great Spirit had desired me to be a white man he would have made me so in the first place. He put in your heart certain wishes and plans, in my heart he put other and different desires. Each man is good in his sight. It is not necessary for eagles to be crows.
— *Sitting Bull*

280

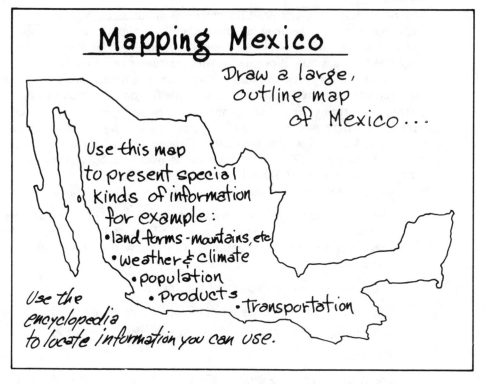

Sample Task Card

17   The importance of citizenship is recognized on the anniversary of the signing of the Constitution (1787). Do students know what it means to be a citizen of a country? Ask them what a citizen can do that a noncitizen cannot. Discover how someone becomes a citizen. If possible, arrange for the class to visit the government offices that handle immigration and naturalization. Find out what countries the people are from who want to become citizens. Read portions of the Constitution; for example, "The Bill of Rights." Discuss how the Constitution came to be written. Read the second paragraph of the Declaration of Independence:

> We hold these truths to be self-evident,
> That all men are created equal,
> That they are endowed by their Creator with certain inalienable rights,
> That among these are life, liberty, and the pursuit of happiness —
> That to secure these rights, governments are instituted among men, deriving their just powers from the consent of the governed. . . .

The Declaration talks about *men*. Ask students who they think the term refers to. Does it include women, poor people, and nonwhite Americans? Who did the writers of the Declaration mean to include? (Property-owning men, free, white, and of specific age.)

27   American Indian Day is a good time to focus attention on Native Americans. Ask students how many tribes they can name. Check your library for books about various Indian tribes. Look for books by Paul Goble, such as *Her Seven Brothers* (Bradbury, 1988), beautifully illustrated stories that cross grade levels.

In celebrating American Indian Day, take time to combat stereotyped images that students may have picked up about Indians from television or other sources. Instead of featuring generalized symbols such as the tepee or war bonnet, concentrate on showing how the tribes differ in clothing, housing, food, and other aspects of life. Read the well-written biography, *Woman Chief,* the story of a Crow chief, by Rose Sobol (Dial, 1976). Have students discover what tribe(s) once lived in your area. How did they live? What happened to them?

An excellent source of authentic tales for retelling or dramatization is:

The Indian Reading Series: Stories and Legends of the Northwest. The Pacific Northwest Indian Reading and Language Development Program, Northwest Regional Educational Laboratory, 300 Southwest Sixth Avenue, Portland, Oregon 97204.

Good books to use with primary students are:

Tomie de Paola. *The Legend of the Indian Paintbrush.* Putnam's, 1988.

William Toye. *How Summer Came to Canada.* Oxford, 1988.

A resource for olders students is:

Simon Ortiz. *The People Shall Continue.* Children's Book Press, 1987.

October Activities

2   The Pan American Conference marks the recognition that the countries of the Americas have shared needs and should support each other. Display a map of North, Central, and South America, showing the names of the countries and their capitals. Illustrate it with the flags of the different countries. Discuss what these countries have in common. They were all colonized by Europeans, for example, although descendants of the original inhabitants still live in all the countries. Ask students what languages are spoken in these countries (English and French in Canada; Spanish in Central America and most South American countries; Portuguese in Brazil). Do these countries share problems? The countries depend on each other for imports and exports. Research information to add to the map. What does the United States import from these countries? What does it export to them?

12   Columbus Day celebrates the landing of Columbus at San Salvador in 1492. Locate San Salvador on the map. Trace Columbus's journey from Spain to the New World. Where did he go after San Salvador? Why did he call the people he met "Indians"? People usually refer to Columbus as the discoverer of

OCTOBER

1	2	3	4	5	6	7
	Mohandas K. Gandhi, 1869–1948 First Pan American Conference—Washington, 1889		Tecumseh (Shawnee) died, 1813			Imanu Amiri Baraka (LeRoi Jones), 1934– Marian Anderson, first Black to sing at Metropolitan Opera, 1954
8	9	10	11	12	13	14
	Leif Erikson Day Mary Shadd Cary, 1823–1893, Black teacher, journalist, lawyer	Shawnees defeated in Battle of Point Pleasant (WV), 1774, ends Lord Dunmore's War Chinese Revolution began, 1911	Eleanor Roosevelt, 1884–1962 Pulaski Memorial Day	Columbus lands at San Salvador, 1492 Dia de la Raza (Latin America)		Eamon de Valera, Irish president, 1882–1975 William Penn, 1644–1718
15	16	17	18	19	20	21
3rd Week, Black Poetry Week World Poetry Day	Sarah Winnemucca died, 1891, Paiute Indian leader Fannie Lou Hamer Alaska Day Festival	Albert Einstein came to U.S., 1933	First Chinese opera performed in U.S.—San Francisco, 1852 Canada PM, Pierre Trudeau, 1919–			UN founded in San Francisco, 1945 Alfred Nobel, 1833–1896
22	23	24	25	26	27	28
4th Week, United Nations Week	Hungarian Freedom Day, 1956	United Nations Day		Mahalia Jackson, 1911–1972	Ah Nam, first Chinese in California, baptized, 1815	
29	30	31				
		Black Hawk died, 1838, Sauk Indian leader Roberta Lawson, 1878–1940, Delaware civic leader National UNICEF Day				

There is a sufficiency in the world for man's need but not for man's greed.
—*Mohandas Gandhi*

America. Is that true? After all, the Indians were there first. Research how the first people to arrive "discovered"America. It is possible that Scandinavian explorers landed in America before Columbus (Leif Erickson Day, October 9). If Columbus was not the first, why was his discovery particularly important?

14   Explore the history of Ireland and the Irish Americans in this country. To find out more about the country of Eamon de Valera, examine a map of Ireland, showing the political division into Northern Ireland and the Republic of Ireland (Eire). Ireland has a long history of war. What do students know about the basis of the present conflict in Ireland? Through books, newspapers, and magazines, research the issues involved. Talk about the similarities and differences with other wars over religion.

Ask students whether any of them are part Irish. When did their ancestors come over from Ireland and why? What kinds of attitudes did the Irish encounter in this country? Have students ask their parents about stereotypes of the Irish immigrants. Compare those attitudes to today's. Is there still prejudice against Irish-Americans? Look at the Kennedy presidential campaign for examples of people's attitudes.

18,27   Less than forty years elapsed between the first baptism of a Chinese in California (before California was part of the United States) and the performance of a Chinese opera. Have students read accounts of the Chinese immigration to this country in order to see how this rapid change occurred. How did the discovery of gold and the building of the railroad affect Chinese immigration?

Elicit from students statements about special characteristics of the early Chinese immigrants. Some examples might be:

- They were primarily single, young men.
- They maintained close ties with their family back in China.
- They saved their money and sent it home.

Discuss the consequences of these facts. Include some of the following:

- Families in San Francisco's Chinatown now occupy single rooms that were built as dormitories for the original bachelor immigrants.
- Many Chinese who live in all-Chinese ghettos (Chinatowns) do not speak English.

21,24   The organization of countries called the United Nations was founded in San Francisco, at the end of World War II, and succeeded the League of Nations. Have students discover what countries signed the UN Charter. How many countries belong to the United Nations now? Can they find these countries on a world map? (You will need an up-to-date map, especially of Africa.) Where are most of the new countries located? Why? Are there any countries that do not belong to the UN? Write to this address for further information about the UN and its activities: United Nations Information Center, Suite 209, 2101 L Street NW, Washington, D.C. 20037.

NOVEMBER

1	2	3	4	5	6	7
Sholem Asch, 1880–1957	Haile Selassie crowned Emperor of Ethiopia, 1930 Father Junipero Serra, Spanish explorer, 1713–1784			Shirley Chisholm, first black woman elected to House of Representatives (NY), 1968 Guy Fawkes Day (Canada)		William Harrison defeated the Shawnee Prophet at Tippecanoe (IN), 1811 Marie Curie, 1867–1934
8	9	10	11	12	13	14
Edward Brooke, first black U.S. senator in 85 years, elected (MA), 1966	W. C. Handy, 1873–1958 Benjamin Banneker, 1731–1806	Martin Luther, 1483–1546	Remembrance Day (Canada)	Dr. Sun Yat-sen, 1866–1925		Freedom for Philippines, 1935 Jawaharlal Nehru, 1889–1964
15	16	17	18	19	20	21
	Chinua Achebe, 1930– Brother and Sister Day (India, Nepal)	Opening of Suez Canal, 1869	First Thanksgiving, Pilgrims and Massasoit, chief of Wampanoags, 1777	Indira Gandhi, 1917–1984	Atahualpa, Inca of Peru, filled room with gold for Pizarro, 1532	
22	23	24	25	26	27	28
			St. Catherine's Day (Canada)	Sojourner Truth died, 1883		
29	30					
	Shirley Chisholm, 1924–					

To understand is hard. Once one understands, action is easy.

—Sun Yat-sen

November Activities

2   Father Junípero Serra is famous as the builder of the California missions. He is an important part of California history from the period before it became a state. Have students investigate the history of Father Serra and the California missions. Prepare a display with a map of California, showing the locations of the missions, pictures of the buildings, and the route of El Camino Real (The King's Highway) that connected them. The missions were part of the Spanish effort to Christianize the local groups of Indians. Missions were built in other parts of the Southwest as well.

There is a movement to have Father Serra declared a saint. At this point, he is officially "Beata," or venerated, one step away from being a saint. Yet many Native American groups oppose this blessing of Father Serra's activities. Can students predict why they might object? To answer this question, have them investigate what happened to the Indian groups in California as a result of Father Serra's missions.

5   I have been discriminated against far more because I am a female than because I am black.
    — *Shirley Chisholm*

Here is a provocative quote for students to discuss. Why would her statement be true? Shirley Chisholm was the first black woman elected to the House of Representatives. Was it harder for her to get elected than for a black man? Read portions from her autobiography, *Unbossed and Unbought* (Houghton Mifflin, 1970) showing her struggles to overcome race and sex prejudice.

Shirley Chisholm was elected in 1968. Now there are more Blacks, men and women, in the House of Representatives. Do students think that race prejudice still affects whether people are elected to Congress? If not, why are there not *more* Blacks in Congress (or women and members of other ethnic minorities)?

12   Discuss Sun Yat-sen, leader of the fight for China's independence. The quote on page 285 reflects the emphasis on *understanding* common to Asian philosophers, as opposed to the Western obsession with *action*. Ask students to describe what this quote means to them. What would they like to understand about themselves, other people, the world? Are there times when we act without understanding or thinking?

20   The Incas were one of the major Indian civilizations encountered by the first Spanish explorers of the New World. Have students investigate the Incas and their culture. The Spaniards were amazed at the achievements of the Incas. How were the Incas more advanced than the Spaniards? How did the Spanish treat the Incas and what happened to them? Have students make a model of the mysterious Inca city, Macchu Picchu.

26   In 1851, Sojourner Truth said:

The man over there says women need to be helped into carriages and lifted over ditches, and to have the best place everywhere. Nobody ever helps me into carriages or over puddles or gives me the best place . . . ain't I a woman? Look at my arm! I have ploughed

DECEMBER

1	2	3	4	5	6	7
Rosa Parks arrested, 1955	Monroe Doctrine, 1823 Pan American Health Day	Myrtilla Miner opened first Colored Girls School, Washington, D.C., 1851		Phyllis Wheatley died, 1784, Black poet	Feast of St. Nicholas Columbus discovers Haiti, 1492	Bombing of Pearl Harbor by Japanese, 1941
8	**9**	**10**	**11**	**12**	**13**	**14**
2nd Week, Human Rights Week Diego Rivera, 1886–1957		U.S. acquired Cuba, Guam, Puerto Rico, Philippines, 1898 Human Rights Day, Universal Declaration of Human Rights ratified, 1948	Aleksandr Solzhenitsyn, 1918– UNICEF established, 1946		Yehudi Menuhin makes N.Y. debut, 1927	
15	**16**	**17**	**18**	**19**	**20**	**21**
Bill of Rights day, Bill of Rights ratified, 1791 Sitting Bull killed, 1890		Maria Stewart died, 1879, Black teacher and lecturer	Ratification of 13th Amendment ended slavery, 1865	Bernice Pauahi Bishop, 1831–1884, Hawaiian leader	Cherokees forced off their land in Georgia because of gold strike, 1835 Sacajawea died, 1812, Shoshoni interpreter	Maria Cadilla de Martinez, 1886–, early Puerto Rican feminist Pilgrims landed at Plymouth (MA), 1620
22	**23**	**24**	**25**	**26**	**27**	**28**
Teresa Carreño, 1853–1917, Venezuelan-American concert pianist	First Chinese theater built, San Francisco, 1852 Madame C.J. Walker, 1867–1919, Black businesswoman	Feast of Sacrifice— Moslem Holy Day	Christmas Day	Mao Zedong, 1893–1976		
29	**30**	**31**				
	Pocahontas rescued Captain John Smith, 1607 Gadsden Purchase signed with Mexico, 1853	Ellis Island, New York Harbor, became immigrant receiving station				

Congress shall make no law respecting an establishment of religion, . . . or abridging the freedom of speech, or of the press . . . .
Amendment 1, U.S. Bill of Rights

and planted and gathered into barns and no man could head me—ain't I a woman? I could work as much and eat as much as a man—when I could get it—and bear the lash as well! And ain't I a woman? I have born 13 children and seen most of 'em sold into slavery, and when I cried out with my mother's grief, none but Jesus heard me . . . and ain't I a woman?

Who was Sojourner Truth? Investigate her life with the class. Here is a strong black woman, whose name we remember from a period when Blacks were mostly anonymous. Ask students why we do not know her birthdate, when we know the birthdates of the white women she worked with. Look up information on the life of women and of Blacks at that time. Why did Sojourner Truth fight for the women's movement and women's right to vote? What might she say about today's women's movement? A biography for young students is *Sojourner Truth, Fearless Crusader* by Helen Stone Peterson.

December Activities

10   Human Rights Day celebrates the Proclamation of the Universal Declaration of Human Rights by the United Nations (1948). This day provides an opportunity for students to discuss what Human Rights are. Ask each one to complete this sentence: Every human being has the right to. . . .

15   Related to Human Rights is the Bill of Rights, the first ten amendments to the U.S. Constitution. A group of students can present the Bill of Rights as part of a special program. They can prepare it as a reader's theater presentation.

Send for free teaching materials about the Bill of Rights from Standard Oil of California, 225 Bush Street, San Francisco, CA 94120, or *Boys Life Magazine*, New Brunswick, NJ 08903.

UNITED STATES BILL OF RIGHTS

Amendment 1
Congress shall make no law respecting an establishment of religion, or prohibiting the free exercise thereof; or abridging the freedom of speech, or of the press; or the right of the people peaceably to assemble, and to petition the government for a redress of grievances.

Amendment 2
A well-regulated militia being necessary to the security of a free State, the right of the people to keep and bear arms shall not be infringed.

Amendment 3
No soldier shall, in time of peace, be quartered in any house without the consent of the owner; nor in time of war but in a manner to be prescribed by law.

Amendment 4
The right of the people to be secure in their persons, houses, papers and effects, against unreasonable searches and seizures, shall not be violated, and no warrants shall issue but upon probable cause, supported by oath or affirmation, and particularly described the place to be searched, and the persons or things to be seized.

Amendment 5
No person shall be held to answer for a capital or otherwise infamous crime, unless on a presentment or indictment of a grand jury, except in cases arising in the land or naval forces, or in the militia, when in actual service in time of war or public danger; nor shall any person be subject for the same offense to be twice put in jeopardy of life or limb; nor shall be compelled in any criminal case to be witness against himself, nor be deprived of life, liberty, or property, without due process of law; nor shall private property be taken for public use, without just compensation.

Amendment 6
In all criminal prosecutions the accused shall enjoy the right to a speedy and public trial, by an impartial jury of the State and district wherein the crime shall have been committed, which district shall have been previously ascertained by law, and to be informed of the nature and cause of the accusation; to be confronted with the witnesses against him; to have compulsory process for obtaining witnesses in his favor, and to have the assistance of counsel for his defense.

Amendment 7
In suits at common law, where the value in controversy shall exceed twenty dollars, the right of trial by jury shall be preserved, and no fact tried by a jury shall be otherwise reexamined in any court of the United States than according to the rules of the common law.

Amendment 8
Excessive bail shall not be required, nor excessive fines imposed, nor cruel and unusual punishments inflicted.

Amendment 9
The enumeration in the Constitution of certain rights shall not be construed to deny or disparage others retained by the people.

Amendment 10
The powers not delegated to the United States by the Constitution, nor prohibited by it to the States, are reserved to the States respectively, or to the people.

---

18   13th Amendment: Neither slavery nor involuntary servitude, except as a punishment for crime whereof the party shall have been duly convicted, shall exist within the United States, or any place subject to their jurisdiction.

The ratification of the Thirteenth Amendment meant the official end of slavery. Begin reading a book such as *The Slave Dancer,* by Paula Fox (Bradbury, 1973), which won the Newbery Award in 1974, an excellent historical novel for grades 5-9.

> Mr. Lincoln had told our race we were free, but mentally we were still enslaved.
> —*Mary McLeod Bethune*

Discuss this quote. What does *mentally enslaved* mean? Is it possible to change people's thinking by passing a law? What factors made it difficult to change? (education, jobs)

25   Provide new perspectives of Christmas as you consider how this Christian holiday is celebrated in different countries. What is the origin of different practices such as the piñata, the Christmas tree, or the Yule log?

Point out, too, that many words associated with Christmas come from other languages, for example:

- *Noel,* French, from Latin *natalis*
- *Carol,* Greek, from *choros* (dance) and *arelos* (flute)

Merry Christmas around the World

Joyeux Noel — France, Belgium, Switzerland
Kala Hrystoughena — Greece
Glaedelig Jul — Norway
Froeliche Weihnachten — Germany, Austria
Stretan Bozic — Yugoslavia
Buon Natale — Italy
Feliz Navidad — Spain, Mexico
God Jul — Sweden
Merry Christenmass — Scotland
Um Feliz Natal — Portugal
Nodlaig Mhaith Dhuit — Ireland
Boldog Karacsony Unnep — Hungary
Wesolych Swiat — Poland
Kung ho shen tan — Chinese
Vrolyk Kerstmis — Holland
S Rozhdestvom Christovom — Russia
Happy Christmas — England

- *Crèche,* French, word for *crib*
- *Angel,* Greek, *angellos,* means messenger
- *Poinsettia,* red flower native to Mexico, brought to U.S. by Joel Poinsett, minister to Mexico
- *Yule,* Norse, *jol,* a feast
- *Xmas,* Greet letter *chi* (x) stands for Christ

A good book for children is Tomie de Paola's *An Early American Christmas* (Holiday, 1987).

January Activities

The name of this month comes from the Roman god Janus, who had two faces and looked back into the past and forward into the future. Janus guarded doorways and had special charge over the beginnings of undertakings. It is very appropriate, therefore, to take time at the beginning of the year to consider where we have been and where we are going. Talk with the class about the history of this country. Have them list ways in which the country has changed: inventions, attitudes,

1	2	3	4	5	6	7
Emancipation Proclamation, 1863 Commonwealth of Australia established, 1901	Emma, 1836–1885, Queen of Hawaii	Alaska admitted to Union, 1959 (49th state)	Louis Braille, 1809–1852 Selena Sloan Butler, 1872, founded first black PTA in country	George Washington Carver Day, 1864–1943 Sissieretta Jones, 1869–1933, Black singer	Celebration of King's Day—Pueblo Dances Lucy Laney, school for Negro children, 1886	Harlem Globetrotters played first game (Illinois), 1927
8	**9**	**10**	**11**	**12**	**13**	**14**
World Literacy Day	Joan Baez, 1941–	League of Nations founded, 1920, Geneva Prince Souvanna Phouma died (Laotian P.M.)	Eugenio de Hostos, 1839–1903, Puerto Rican patriot	Adah Thoms, 1863–1943, Black nursing leader	Charlotte Ray, 1850–1911, first Black woman lawyer First Black Cabinet member Robert Weaver becomes Secretary of HUD, 1966	Carlos Romulo, Philippine leader, 1901– Albert Schweitzer, 1875–1965
15	**16**	**17**	**18**	**19**	**20**	**21**
Martin Luther King, Jr., 1929–1968, Black minister and civil rights leader Human Relations Day						Fanny Jackson-Coppin died, 1913, Black educator Eliza Snow (Smith), 1804–1887, "Mother of Mormonism"
22	**23**	**24**	**25**	**26**	**27**	**28**
Sam Cooke, 1932–1964	24th Amendment barred poll tax in federal elections, 1964 Amanda Smith, 1837–1915, Black evangelist	Eva del Vakis Bowles, 1875–1943, Black youth group leader	Florence Mills, 1895–1927, Black singer and dancer	Republic of India established, 1950	Vietnam War ended, 1973	Louis Brandeis, first appointment of American Jew for U.S. Supreme Court, 1916
29	**30**	**31**				
	Mohandas Gandhi (India) killed, 1948	Jackie Robinson, 1919–1972				

It may be true that the law cannot make a man love me, but it can keep him from lynching me, and I think that's pretty important. . . .

—*Martin Luther King, Jr.*

and people. Then ask them to face forward and think about what might change in the future. What would they like to see happen? Will people be any different? Use the excitement of speculating about the future to show the importance of finding the roots of the future in the past.

1   Australia has a special fascination since it is "down under." Have students discover as much as possible about this island continent in a class search that begins in the library. Teach them a song from Australia such as "Waltzing Matilda." Discuss the words and phrases presented in this song. Would you call this English? Why might people speak English differently in different countries?

Waltzing Matilda

Once a jolly swagman camped by a billabong
Under the shade of a coolibah tree,
And he sang as he watched and waited till his billy boiled,
"You'll come a-waltzing Matilda with me!"

Chorus:
Waltzing Matilda, Waltzing Matilda,
You'll come a-waltzing Matilda with me!
And he sang as he watched and waited until his billy boiled,
"You'll come a-waltzing Matilda with me!"

Down came a jumbuck to drink at the billabong,
Up jumped the swagman and grabbed him with glee,
And he sang as he stowed that jumbuck in his tucker bag,
(Chorus)

Up rode the squatter, mounted on his thorough-bred,
Down came the troopers, one, two, three,
"Where's that jolly jumbuck you've got in your tucker bag?"
(Chorus)

Up jumped the swagman, sprang into the billabong,
"You'll never catch me alive," said he,
And his ghost may be heard as you pass by that billabong.
(Chorus)

10   Discuss the difference between the League of Nations and the United Nations. How did the United States get involved in each? Find out what the United Nations does. Students can write to the different groups (WHO, UNESCO, UNICEF) for information on their work and material to use in multicultural studies.

- World Health Organization, Avenue Appia, 1211 Geneva 27, Switzerland
- UNESCO, 9 Place de Fontenoy, 75007 Paris, France
- UNICEF, 866 United Nations Plaza, New York City, NY 10017

15   Discuss with students the quote on page 291 by Martin Luther King, Jr. What do they think was the context of this statement? Martin Luther King was a leader in the civil rights movement. What point of view was he arguing for and what was he arguing against? What does civil rights mean?

Ask students what they would do if they wanted to change someone's behavior or opinion. What methods work best and when? Do any laws protect them from other people? What about classroom rules – do they protect anyone? Discuss problems the students might have with a bully or a liar. Have them write possible strategies to resolve the conflict.

Martin Luther King is remembered for his "I have a dream" speech. Locate the text of this speech and read it to the class or have students prepare it for group presentation.

27   The Vietnam War is a powerful and painful memory for most adults today, but what do students know about it? Talk with the students about their impressions of Vietnam and the role of the United States in that country. What have they heard other people saying and what are their opinions? Students may find it hard to remember or imagine the emotions aroused by the U.S. involvement in Vietnam. Use old news magazines such as *Time* and *Newsweek,* and read selected portions about the war to the class. History books are now being written that refer to the war and its conclusion. As an exercise in living history, have students write a short description of the Vietnam War as they think it should appear in their history books. What would they like to know about the war? What part of the U.S. involvement is most difficult to understand? Possible sources for students to use in preparing this report include: (1) interviews with adults of different views, (2) newspapers and magazines for facts and editorials, (3) recent history books that mention Vietnam, and (4) talks with Vietnamese living in the area.

What is Vietnam like? Explore the following books:

Nguyen Ngoc Bich (translated by) with Burton Raffel and W. S. Merwin. *A Thousand Years of Vietnamese Poetry.* Knopf, 1975.

David D. Cooke. *Vietnam; The Country, the People.* Norton, 1968.

Betty Jean Lifton and Thomas Fox. *Children of Vietnam.* Atheneum, 1972.

Huynh Quang Nhuong. *The Land I Lost: Adventures of a Boy in Vietnam.* Harper, 1982.

Jon Nielsen with Kay Nielsen. *Artist in South Vietnam.* Messner, 1969.

30   Although Gandhi lived in another country, students should know something about his life and his ideas because he influenced so many people in the United States. Feature several quotations from Gandhi:

> *Ahimsa* ("harmlessness" or nonviolence) means the largest love. It is the supreme law. By it alone can mankind be saved. He who believes in nonviolence believes in a living God.

> All humanity is one undivided and indivisible family, and each one of us is responsible for the misdeeds of all the others. I cannot detach myself from the wickedest soul.

> All amassing of wealth or hoarding of wealth above and beyond one's legitimate needs is theft. There would be no occasion for theft and no thieves if there were wise regulations of wealth, and social justice.

> My nationalism is intense internationalism. I am sick of the strife between nations or religions.

Discuss his ideas. Gandhi is credited with forcing the British to give India its independence. How have his methods of nonviolence (demonstrations) and passive resistance (sit-ins and hunger strikes) been translated to this country? How effective have they been?

Gandhi and his ideas were very powerful, yet he led a simple life. Students can read a biography such as *Mohandas Gandhi* by Glenn Alan Cheney (Watts, 1983).

Read selections from an excellent book written for adults in which people who knew Gandhi describe his life: *Mahatma Gandhi and His Apostles* by Ved Mehta (Viking, 1977).

February Activities

February is Black History Month so you can look forward to a lot of programs, articles, speeches, and discussions about the history and current status of Black Americans. Formerly Black History Week, this celebration is sponsored by the Association for the Study of Negro Life and History, founded by historian Carter G. Woodson. The week was first observed in 1926 and it included the birthdays of Abraham Lincoln (12) and Frederick Douglass (14). However, the whole month is rich in the birthdays of exceptional Black Americans. Request from the association a publication list of materials to be used at this time: 1538 Ninth St., NW, Washington, D.C. 20001.

Use an activity such as "Celebrating Black Americans" found on page 296. Feature books about the achievements of Black Americans such as:

Arna Bontemps. *Frederick Douglass: Slave-Fighter-Freeman.* Knopf, 1959.

Virginia Hamilton. *W.E.B. DuBois; a Biography.* Crowell, 1972.

James Haskins. *From Lew Alcindor to Kareem Abdul Jabbar.* Lothrop, 1972.

Robert Hayden. *Eight Black American Inventors.* Addison-Wesley, 1972.

_____. *Seven Black American Scientists.* Addison-Wesley, 1972.

Patricia McKissack and Frederick McKissack. *Frederick Douglass.* Children's, 1987.

FEBRUARY

1	2	3	4	5	6	7
Langston Hughes, 1902–1967 National Freedom Day Louis S. St. Laurent, French-Canadian P.M. of Canada, 1882–1973 Treaty of Guadalupe Hidalgo, 1848	Candlemas Day		Philippine Rebellion against U.S. began, 1899	Constitution Day (Mexico)	Senate ratified treaty ending Spanish-American War, 1899	Mardi Gras
8	**9**	**10** Leontyne Price, 1927– End of French and Indian War, 1763	**11**	**12** Chinese Republic, 1912 Fannie Williams, 1855–1944, Black lecturer and civic leader Thaddeus Kosciusko, Polish patriot, 1746–1817 Abraham Lincoln, 1809–1865	**13**	**14** Frederick Douglass, 1817–1895 Valentine's Day
15 Galileo Galilei, 1564–1642 Week of Feb. 19, Brotherhood Week Susan B. Anthony, 1820–1906	**16**	**17** Marian Anderson, 1902– Chaim Potok, 1929–	**18** Toni Morrison, 1931–	**19** Nicolaus Copernicus, 1473–1543	**20** Birthday of the Prophet (Mohammed)	**21** Malcolm X Day, 1925–1965 Barbara Jordan 1931–
22 Gertrude Bonnin, 1876–1938, Sioux author and reformer Ishmael Reed, 1938–	**23** W.E.B. DuBois, 1868–1963	**24**	**25** First Negro in Congress, Hiram Revels (Miss), 1870 José de San Martin (the great liberator), 1778–1850	**26**	**27**	**28**
29 Emmeline Wells, 1828–1921, Mormon leader and feminist Mother Ann Lee, 1736–1784, Founder of the Shakers	**30**					

If a race has no history, if it has no worthwhile tradition, it becomes a negligible factor in the thoughts of the world and it stands in danger of being exterminated.

—*Carter G. Woodson*

Celebrating Black Americans

Fill in the last names of famous Black Americans to solve this puzzle. The First name is given as a clue.

Puzzle	Clue
_ _ _ _N_ _ _ _	Duke _____
_ _ _ _ _E	Ralph _____
_ _ _ _ _ _ _G_ _ _	Booker T. _____
_ _ _ _R_ _ _	Marian _____
_ _O_ _ _ _	Carter G. _____
_ _ _H_ _ _	Mary McLeod _____
_ _I_ _	Bessie _____
_ _ _ _ _ _S_ _ _	Dizzy _____
_ _ _T_ _ _	Sidney _____
_ _ _ _ _O_ _	Shirley _____
_ _R_ _	Lena _____
_ _Y_	Willie _____
_ _ _ _W_ _	James A. _____
_ _ _ _E_	Nat _____
_ _ _ _E_	Langston _____
K _ _ _	Martin Luther_____ , Jr.

1) Find out why each person is famous.
2) List 5 other Black Americans who are known in their fields.

SOURCE: *Reading Ideas*, February 1977.

A special activity for this week would be to learn James Weldon Johnson's song "Lift Every Voice and Sing," also known as the Negro National Anthem. Students will be interested in learning more about the man who wrote this song. Offer them the biography, *James Weldon Johnson* by Harold Felton (Dodd, 1971), which includes the song.

Answers to Celebrating Black Americans: Ellington, Bunche, Washington, Anderson, Woodson, Bethune, Smith, Gillespie, Poitier, Chisholm, Horne, Mays, Baldwin, Turner, Hughes, King.

1   Feature the poetry of Langston Hughes. An attractive collection is *Don't You Turn Back* compiled by Lee Bennet Hopkins (Knopf, 1969). Langston Hughes's poetry lends itself to graphic presentation. Have students create posters featuring a selection from a poem. Encourage them to use calligraphy and art on the poster in order to celebrate the poem. Begin reading his biography on this date; for example: *Langston Hughes, Poet of His People* by Elizabeth Myers (Garrard, 1970). Play the recording *Langston Hughes Reads and Talks about His Poems* for students (Spoken Arts).

4   Display a world map. Point out the location of the Philippines. (Note the spelling of this name.) Have students make a replica of the Philippine flag and discuss the history of this group of islands. Why did the United States get involved with the Philippines? Is the United States still involved? When and why did groups of Filipinos come to this country? What languages do people speak in the Philippines?

5   Celebrate Mexico's Constitution Day. Create a learning center on Mexico. (Let students contribute ideas.) Explore your library for nonfiction and fiction about Mexico as well as stories about Mexican Americans or Chicanos. For example:

> Frank Bonham. *Viva Chicano.* Dutton, 1970.
>
> Joe Molnar. *Graciela: A Mexican-American Child Tells Her Story.* Watts, 1972.

Develop task cards that focus on Mexico for reading in the content areas.

12   Have students prepare a bulletin board display about Abraham Lincoln, a president who has become a folk hero. He symbolizes the poor boy who rose to leadeship, the person who freed the slaves. Feature quotations by Lincoln around his picture, for instance:

> The ballot is stronger than the bullet.
>
> Any people anywhere, being inclined and having the power, have the right to rise up and shake off the existing government, and form a new one that suits them better. This is the most valuable, a most sacred right — a right which we hope and believe is to liberate the world.
>
> A house divided against itself cannot stand. I believe this government cannot endure, permanently half *slave* and half *free.*
>
> As I would not be a *slave,* so I would not be a *master.* This expresses my idea of democracy. Whatever differs from this, to the extent of the difference, is no democracy.

Have students prepare "The Gettysburg Address" for choric speaking. Plan a short program using this address, quotations, and poetry about Lincoln. One or two students might tell a story about Abe.

22   ***Brotherhood Week.***   Celebrated during the week that includes George Washington's birthday (22), this week was initiated by Father McNenamin of Denver, Colorado, in 1929. It is sponsored by the National Conference of Christians and Jews, 43 W.

57th St., New York, NY 10019. Feature books about promoters of peace and understanding such as Martin Luther King, Jr., or Ralph Bunche.

Explore different ways to present quotations in your classroom. Students might use quotations related to the topic of brotherhood to form a heart (see page 272). Other topics will suggest appropriate forms, such as the silhouette of Washington or Lincoln made of quotations related to freedom or patriotism, or a corncopia formed from quotations related to thankfulness.

Quotes for Brotherhood Week

We have committed the Golden Rule to memory; let us now commit it to life.
   —Edwin Markham

No man is an Island, entire of itself.
   —John Donne

Whoever seeks to set one race against another seeks to enslave all races.
   —Franklin D. Roosevelt

If our brothers are oppressed, then we are oppressed. If they hunger, we hunger. If their freedom is taken away, our freedom is not secure.
   —Stephen Vincent Benet

The world is my country;
All mankind are my brethren.
   —Thomas Paine

No one can make you feel inferior without your consent.
   —Eleanor Roosevelt

March Activities

8   Celebrate the achievements of American women. Here is an opportunity to point out the achievements of women of all races and creeds. Make a point of including lesser known persons. An excellent resource is *Notable American Women* by Edward T. James, ed. (Belknap Press, 1974), 3 volumes.

Discuss the role of women today. What kinds of work do women do? Talk about women the students know. Who do they admire? Bring in women who have unusual jobs to talk to students. Older students can write letters to the local newspaper, describing women they admire and explaining why.

9   Our country is named after Amerigo Vespucci. Some people thought it should have been named after Christopher Columbus. Do students know that *Columbia* is sometimes used to refer to this country? ("Columbia, the Gem of the Ocean"). What other countries does *America* refer to? North, Central, and South America are all called the *Americas*. People living in South America rightly resent the use of *America* to refer to the United States alone. Who is an American?

MARCH

1	2	3	4	5	6	7
Ralph Ellison, 1914— Black author Peace Corps est., 1961 St. David's Day (Wales)	Texas declares independence from Mexico, 1836	Doll Festival (Japanese)	Knute Rockne, 1888–1931		Fall of the Alamo, 1836	Tomás Masaryk (Czech patriot), 1850–1937
8 Week of March 8, National Women's History Week International Women's Day	**9** Amerigo Vespucci, 1451–1512, Italian navigator	**10** Harriet Tubman's death, 1913 Hallie Q. Brown, 1850–1949, Black teacher and women's leader	**11**	**12** Gabriele d'Annunzio, 1863–1938	**13** Birthday of the Prophet (holy day commemorating birth of Mohammed)	**14** Albert Einstein, 1879–1955
15	**16**	**17** St. Patrick's Day	**18** Hawaii's Statehood, 1959	**19** St. Joseph's Day (Italy)	**20** Harriet Beecher Stowe's *Uncle Tom's Cabin* published, 1852	**21** Benito Juárez, Mexican leader, 1806–1872
22 Emancipation Day (Puerto Rico)	**23**	**24**	**25** Seward's Day (Alaska)	**26** Kuhio Day (Hawaii)	**27** Marconi sends first international wireless message, 1899	**28**
29	**30** 15th Amendment Right to Vote passed, 1870 U.S. purchased Alaska from Russia, 1867	**31** Elizabeth Greenfield died, 1876, Black singer First treaty U.S. —Japan, 1854 U.S. took possession of Virgin Islands from Denmark, 1917 Octavio Paz, 1914–				

All novels are about certain minorities: the individual is a minority.
—*Ralph Ellison*

The name of a country is important. Ask students if they can suggest reasons why this country is called "The United States of America." What other names might have been proposed at different times? (Columbia, New India) Invite students to propose a new name for this country and justify their choice.

10   Harriet Tubman led an active and dangerous life. Read about her exploits and have students choose several crucial events to dramatize. They can prepare a play by writing dialogue and narration and using a few props. This play can be presented for other classes to watch. A good biography of Harriet Tubman was written by Ann Petry (Crowell, 1955).

13   Encourage students to research information about different religions. Have students clip articles about countries where Mohammedanism or the Moslem religion (Islam) is part of the culture—Saudi Arabia, Iran, Egypt. Discuss the importance of these countries today. What are some of the similarities and differences between the Arab culture and ours? Some Arabs are Christian believers, not Moslem. Are there any Muslims in this country? Who are the Black Muslims and what do they believe?

17   Although highly commercialized, St. Patrick's Day offers a good opportunity to recognize Irish Americans and the many Irish customs that we are familiar with. What Irish folk beliefs can students name? The leprechaun is the most familiar although the meaning of this figure has changed. One did not trifle with real leprechauns! Other symbols common around this time include the shamrock. Students can look up the origins and real versions of these symbols and beliefs and report their finding to the class.
Read aloud Irish folktales from such collections as the following:

Padraic Colum. *The King of Ireland's Son.* McGraw-Hill, 1966.

Eileen O'Favlain (retold by). *Irish Sagas and Folktales.* Walck, 1954.

Virigina Haviland (retold by). *Favorite Fairy Tales Told in Ireland.* Little, Brown, 1961.

Have students prepare stories for dramatization, assigning parts and rewriting the dialogue.

22   Have students research the history of Puerto Rico's relationship to the United States and the significance of this Emancipation Day. Read stories aloud. A story for younger children about Puerto Ricans in the United States is *Friday Night Is Papa Night* by Ruth Sonneborn (Viking, 1970). A book for older students is *Magdalena* by Louisa Shotwell (Viking, 1971).

Exploring Puerto Rico.   Puerto Rico is an island that is divided into many municipalities. See how many of their names you can find hidden in the puzzle that follows. Words go vertically or horizontally in either direction or they can be diagonal. Use an encyclopedia to help you. Of the 78 municipalities, 47 are included in the puzzle. Which ones are not included?*

*SOURCE: *Reading Ideas,* January, 1977.

```
S A N S E B A S T I A N J L A J A S B
A A D J U N T A S R A L L I D U A G A
N R B A R C E L O N E T A B F A D G R
T E A A B L W S J C G I J L H N U U R
A C Y C N V E G A A L T A A K A L A R
I I A I M A N P Y Y R A G Z D D O R N
S B M N Z Y G V U E T N U O S I D A Q
A O O A F B R Y Y C A A R D A A B U
B F N U O A C O A M O M S O N Z R O I
E G J G C J H P L N P R B C M R O S T
L T V G U A Y A M A D Y U Z C I D R A
Y B D F B R C T A R G E E J U N C O S
T M O C A D J I N A P O N C E C A L E
O C U A Y O N L I N R T A S B O M D C
A D I R O L F L L J F H S C G N U L A
A R B E L U C A O I S A B E L A Y O G
L A R E S P T S R T H A T I L L O I U
T V I L L A L B A O R B G B H M S Z A
A Z O D A U T U C P S O S A N I L A S
```

The puzzle features the municipalities into which the island of Puerto Rico is divided. Display a map of the island as students discover the following names:

Adjuntas	Ceiba	Isabela	Ponce
Aguada	Cidra	Jayuya	Ricón
Aguadilla	Coamo	Juana Diaz	Sabana Grande
Aguas Buenas	Corozal	Juncos	Salinas
Arecibo	Culebra	Lares	San Sebastián
Barceloneta	Dorado	Loiza	Santa Isabel
Barranquitas	Fajardo	Manati	Toa Alta
Bayamón	Florida	Moca	Vega Alta
Caguas	Guánica	Naranjito	Villalba
Camuy	Guayama	Orocovis	Yabucoa
Carolina	Gurabo	Patillas	Yauco
Cayey	Hatillo		

Looking at the calendar for this month you will notice a number of dates related to the U.S. acquisition of territory. Some of the areas acquired later became states (Texas, Alaska, Hawaii) and other areas have not (Puerto Rico and Virgin Islands). Discuss with students how and when territories have become states. (How did your area become a state?) Some had been part of other countries first—which ones? Many people who speak different languages and are from different backgrounds became part of this country when territories became states. Students can research who was living in each of these areas before the United States acquired them. What happened to these people? Did they become citizens? The language spoken in these areas reflects their history. For example, because the Virgin Islands were once owned by Denmark, the language has been influenced by Danish. Why have some areas become states and not others? Have students look up information on other U.S. possessions and territories (Samoa, for example).

APRIL

1	2	3	4	5	6	7
Spring Corn Dances (Pueblos)	Ponce de Leon landed in Florida, 1513; International Children's Book Day		Martin Luther King, Jr., killed, 1968	Booker T. Washington, 1856–1915; Pocahontas married John Rolfe, 1614	Peary and Henson reached North Pole, 1909; Joseph Smith founded Mormon Church, 1830; Alexander Herzen, 1812–	
8	**9**	**10**	**11**	**12**	**13**	**14**
First synagogue in America founded in NYC, 1730; Buddha's birthday (Japan)	Civil War ended, Treaty of Appomattox, 1865	Joseph Pulitzer, 1847–1911; Dolores Huerta 1940–		Civil War began 1861, Ft. Sumter; Yuri Gargarin, cosmonaut, became first person to orbit earth, 1961	Lucy Laney, 1854–1933, Black educator	Pan American Day; Abraham Lincoln assassinated, 1865
15	**16**	**17**	**18**	**19**	**20**	**21**
Bessie Smith, 1894–1937, Black blues singer	Mary Eliza Mahoney, 1845–1926, first Black nurse	World Health Day		Revolutionary War began, 1775		Spanish-American War began, 1898
22	**23**	**24**	**25**	**26**	**27**	**28**
Earth Day			Ella Fitzgerald, 1918–; UN founded, 1945	Gertrude (Ma) Rainey, 1886–1939, Black blues singer; Syngman Rhee, 1875–1965	Coretta Scott King, 1927–	
29	**30**					
Emperor's birthday (Japanese); Duke Ellington, 1899–1974	Louisiana Territory purchased, 1803; Loyalists and Negroes attacked Shrewsbury N.J., 1780					

The wisest among my race understand that the agitation of questions of social equality is the extremest folly, and that progress in the enjoyment of all the privileges that will come to us must be the result of severe and constant struggle rather than of artificial forcing.

—Booker T. Washington

April Activities

4   Refer to January 15 for more information about Martin Luther King, Jr.

9,12   Someone once said that the Civil War is the longest war in history. It began in 1861 and is still going on today. Discuss this with students. Do they agree? What does it mean to say the war is still going on? What kind of "war" is it? Are people being killed?

> You can't hold a man down without staying down with him.
> —*Booker T. Washington*

Discuss this quote with students. Who is he referring to? Who is being held down? How can oppressing someone hurt the oppressor?

29   April 29 marks the Emperor of Japan's birthday. This is a major holiday in Japan as is Constitution Day on May 3. Japan's national anthem is "Kimigayo" ("The Reign of Our Emperor"). At one time the emperor was considered a god, but the constitution of 1946 begins with these words: "The Emperor shall be the symbol of the State and of the unity of the people, deriving his position from the will of the people with whom resides sovereign power." The Emperor of Japan is a ceremonial position which is inherited, but the position carries no governmental powers.

This is a good time to explore writing Japanese haiku poetry. Introduce them to examples from the old masters found in such collections as *Cricket Songs* by Harry Behn (Harcourt Brace Jovanovich, 1964). Students can then experiment with this seventeen-syllable verse form: Line 1: five syllables, Line 2: seven syllables, Line 3: five syllables.

> Rain dripping slowly
> Soaks thirsty trees and bushes.
> Spring blossoms open.

Black Blues.   Three important blues singers were born this month—Ma Rainey, one of the first blues performers; Bessie Smith, a major influence on all subsequent blues singers; and Ella Fitzgerald, a contemporary singer whose repertoire includes the blues. The blues is an important part of American history, particularly of Black American history.

Ask students what the term *the blues* means to them. Discuss the following quote:

> The whites just *startin'* to get the blues
> —*John Lee Hooker*

He's not just talking about blues music. What does he mean?

Bring records of the blues to school to play for students. Try to get early recordings by singers such as Bessie Smith and Billie Holiday as well as current singers like Ray Charles and Aretha Franklin. What are some recurring themes in these songs? Why are most of the blues singers Black?

After students have talked about what makes blues different, suggest some books about blues people for them to read.

Hettie Jones. *Big Star Fallin' Mama; Five Women in Black Music.* Viking, 1974. Includes Ma Rainey, Bessie Smith, Mahalia Jackson, Billie Holiday, and Aretha Franklin.

Sharon Bell Mathis. *Ray Charles.* Crowell, 1973.

Elizabth Rider Montgomery. *William C. Handy: Father of the Blues.* Garrard, 1968.

Older students might enjoy writing their own blues lyrics, while younger students could complete the sentence, "I'm blue when. . . ."

May Activities

3   Golda Meir taught school in Milwaukee, Wisconsin, before going to live in Palestine. She later became Prime Minister of Israel, the first woman in the world to hold such a position. Read a biography, *The Golda Meir Story* by Margaret Davidson (Scribners, 1981), to learn more about this unusual woman, the American immigrant experience, and the founding of the state of Israel.

5   Today, Japanese children fly carp kites. Students can make their own gaily decorated fish to hang like streamers. Each student can draw a model, or you can provide one for everyone to trace onto construction paper. (See model on page 306.) They should have two fish shapes, one right side and one reversed. After the children color and cut out the fish, they glue the two pieces together around the edges (except for the mouth) and gently stuff with tissue paper for a three-dimensional effect. These fish can be hung around the room with thread tied to the back, or attached to a stick (fishing pole) by the mouth.

If you have Japanese-speaking children in the class, this is a good opportunity to have them teach the class how to count in Japanese.

ichi—one
ni—two
san—three
shi—four
go—five
roku—six
shichi—seven
hachi—eight
ku—nine
ju—ten

One, two, three,
(echo)
Listen to me,
(echo)
I can count to ten,

MAY

1	2	3	4	5	6	7
Loyalty Day Law Day Agrippa Hull, free black, began 6 years of army service, 1777	Early May: Asian/ Pacific American Heritage Week	Golda Meir, 1898–1978	Holocaust Remembrance Week	Chidren's Festival (Japanese) Gwendolyn Brooks won Pulitzer Prize for Poetry, 1950 Cinco de Mayo	Chinese Exclusion Act passed, 1882 Rudolph Valentino, 1895–1926	Rabindranath Tagore, 1861–1941
8	**9**	**10**	**11**	**12**	**13**	**14**
Chinese expelled from mines, Tuolemme County (CA), 1852 V-E Day, 1945		Chinese labor helped complete Transcontinental Railroad, Utah, 1869	Joan of Arc Day (France)		Joe Louis, 1914–1972 Congress declared war on Mexico, 1846	State of Israel proclaimed, 1948 Jamestown established, 1607
15	**16**	**17**	**18**	**19**	**20**	**21**
		Supreme Court declared racial segregation in schools unconstitutional, 1954	Hispanic Society of America founded, 1904	Malcolm X, 1925–1965 I Am an American Day Lorraine Hansberry, 1930–1965		
22	**23**	**24**	**25**	**26**	**27**	**28**
		Ynes Mexia, 1870–1938, Mexican-American botanical explorer	African Freedom Day	Susette LaFlesche Tibbles died, 1903, Omaha Indian rights advocate	Victoria Matthews, 1861–1907, Black author and social worker Buddha's birthday (China)	
29	**30**					
John F. Kennedy, 1917–1963	Hernando de Soto landed in Florida, 1539 Countee Cullen, 1903–1946 Joan of Arc burned, 1431					

What other countries have taken three hundred years or more to achieve, a once dependent territory must try to accomplish in a generation if it is to survive.

— *Kwame Nkrumah (Ghana)*

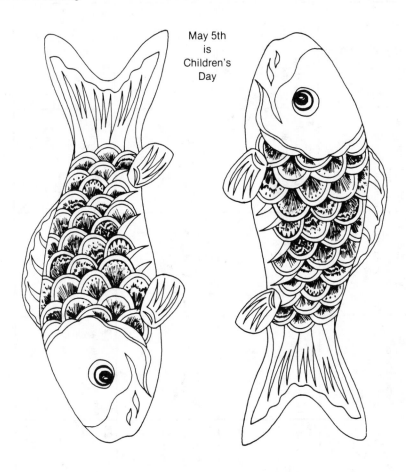

May 5th
is
Children's
Day

(echo)
In Japanese.
(echo)

Ichi, ni, san, shi, go,
(echo)
I can count to five,
(echo)
Let's try four more.
(echo)

Roku, shichi, hachi, ku,
(echo)
I can count to nine,
(echo)
Let's try one more,
(echo)
(together) JU!

Count Your Way Through Japan by Jim Haskins (Carolrhoda, 1987) is a good book for students, with numbers in Japanese accompanied by pictures of the country.

5 Cinco de Mayo marks the victory of Mexican forces over the French at Puebla, Mexico, on May 5, 1862. It is celebrated today in Mexican American communities in the United States as the occasion for a fiesta, with a parade, dancing, and other activities. You can hold a fiesta in your room. It won't be a fiesta without music, dancing, and food. Bring records of Mexican popular music, folksongs, or Mexican Indian music. The music will make anyone want to move and dance. Let the students prepare party food such as tortillas, guacamole, or buñelos. Students can decorate the room appropriately by using poster paint or felt pens to create murals that evoke Mexico and Mexican American life. Possible subjects include food, sports, clothing, arts and crafts, and historical figures.

6,8,10 Here are several important dates in the history of the Chinese in the United States. This month would be a good time to feature the learning module presented in Chapter 8, pages 248–267. An amusing but significant comment is attributed to the Chinese American philosopher and writer, Lin Yutang: "I have a hankering to go back to the Orient and discard my necktie. Neckties strangle clear thinking." Discuss with students the influence clothing can have on people. Show students pictures of children's clothing from the past, when little boys had to wear long dresses and girls couldn't wear pants. What effect might this have had on the children's activities? Show pictures of clothing from different periods and other countries. What do people wear in China? Do students feel different when they wear different clothes or dress up? Have students design and draw the kind of clothes they would like to wear.

14 Forgiveness is the key to action and freedom.
     —*Hannah Arendt*

The motto should not be: Forgive one another; rather, Understand one another.
     —*Emma Goldman*

Israel was established in 1948 when few countries would admit the large numbers of Jewish refugees. From what were they fleeing? Read some books with older students about children's responses to the Holocaust.

Linda Atkinson. *In Kindling Flame.* Lothrop, 1984.

Miriam Chaikin. *A Nightmare in History.* Clarion, 1987.

Anne Frank. *The Diary of a Young Girl.* Doubleday, 1952.

Johanna Reis. *The Journey Back.* Crowell, 1976.

_____. *The Upstairs Room.* Crowell, 1972.

Aranka Siegal. *Upon the Head of a Goat: A Childhood in Hungary 1939–1944.* Farrar, Straus, and Giroux, 1981.

Talk about feelings of helplessness that students have had. In this case, who was the enemy? Is it more difficult when the enemy is faceless? Does it help if you learn to forgive or understand your enemy?

25   African Freedom Day offers an opportunity to discuss the origins of Afro-Americans. Explore such books as:

Primary

Marc Bernheim and Evelyn Bernheim. *In Africa*. Atheneum, 1973.

Muriel Feelings. *Jambo Means Hello; Swahili Alphabet Book*. Dial, 1974.

Upper Grades

Ashley Bryan. *Lion and the Ostrich Chicks, and Other African Tales*. Atheneum, 1986.

John Chiasson. *African Journey*. Bradbury, 1987.

A. Okion Ojigbo. *Young and Black in Africa*. Random House, 1971.

Students can investigate early African civilizations. Too many books picture Africa as a land of barbaric people who were captured and taken to the civilized world. Show students that Africa was not "dark and uncivilized" before the Europeans arrived. Pictures of people from different African countries will teach that not all Africans look alike.

Even the youngest students can learn a few words of Swahili, a widely-spoken African language. Refer to:

Jambo and Other Call-and-Response Songs and Chants. Folkways Records, 1974.

June Activities

7   Gwendolyn Brooks received the Nobel Prize for poetry. She also wrote poetry for young people; for example, *Bronzeville Boys and Girls* (Harper & Row, 1956)). Read some of these city poems about black children which will appeal to all students. Encourage students to write their own poems about familiar places and events. These can be collected into a class booklet, titled, and distributed to all students. Students will enjoy listening to *Gwendolyn Brooks Reading Her Poetry* (Caedmon).

11   Discover Hawaii, the fiftieth state, with your students. One of the attractions of the fiftieth state is its multicultural, multilingual heritage. Investigate the history of Hawaii. How and when did it become a state? People from many different countries are represented in Hawaii. What are some of them? Are there native Hawaiians?

Ask students to find examples of unusual words used in Hawaii; for example, words for different foods. Here are a few words used commonly in Hawaii:

ae	(eye)	yes
aloha	(ah *loh* hah)	greetings
hale	(*hah* lay)	house
haole	(*how* lay)	foreigner (white person)
hula	(*hoo* lah)	dance

JUNE

Sunday	Monday	Tuesday	Wednesday	Thursday	Friday	Saturday
1 Brigham Young, 1801–1877; First Week, National Flag Week	**2**	**3** DeSoto claimed Florida for Spain, 1539; Roland Hayes, 1887–1977	**4**	**5** English colonists massacre Pequot village in Pequot War, 1637; Kaahumanu died, 1832, Hawaiian ruler; Socrates born c. 470 B.C.	**6** Evacuation of Japanese-Americans into concentration camps completed, 1942; Sarah Remond, 1826–1887, Black lecturer and physician	**7** Gwendolyn Brooks, 1917–, Black poet; Paul Gauguin, 1848–1903; Mohammed died, 632 AD; Nikki Giovanni, 1943–
8	**9**	**10**	**11** Kamehameha Day (Hawaii); Addie W. Hunton, 1875–1943, Black youth group leader	**12** Philippine Independence Day	**13**	**14** Hawaii organized as territory, 1900; Harriet Beecher Stowe, 1811–1896
15	**16** Flight of Valentina Tereshkova (first woman in space), 1963	**17** Susan LaFlesche Picotte, 1865–1915, Omaha physician; James Weldon Johnson, 1871–1938	**18** War of 1812 declared against Great Britain, 1812	**19** Statue of Liberty arrived in New York Harbor, 1885	**20** Start of French Revolution, 1789; Announced purchase of Alaska from Russia, 1867	**21**
22 Slavery abolished in Great Britain, 1772	**23** U.S. entered Korean War, 1950; William Penn signed treaty with Indians, 1683	**24** San Juan Day (Puerto Rico)	**25** Crazy Horse (Sioux) defeated Custer—Battle of the Little Bighorn, 1876	**26** Pearl S. Buck, 1892–1973; UN Charter signed, 1945	**27** Paul Dunbar, 1872–1906, Black writer; Joseph Smith, Mormon prophet, killed, 1844; Helen Keller, 1880–1968	**28** World War I began, 1914; Peace Treaty signed, 1919
29 First African church in the U.S. (Philadelphia), 1794; Azalia Hackley, 1867–1922, Black singer; Jose Rizal, 1861–1896	**30**					

. . . We could never learn to be brave and patient, if there were only joy in the world.
—Helen Keller

kamaaiana	(*kah* mah *ai* nah)	oldtimer
kane	(*kah* neh)	man
kaukah	(*kow* kow)	food
keiki	(*kay* kee)	child
lani	(*lah* nee)	sky
lei	(lay)	wreath
luau	(loo ah oo)	feast
mahalo	(mah *hah* loh)	thanks
malihini	(*may* lee *hee* nee)	newcomer
mauna	(*mou* nah)	mountain
moana	(moh *ah* nah)	ocean
nani	(*nan* nee)	beautiful
ohana	(oh *hah* nah)	family
pehea oe	(pay *hay* ah *oy*)	How are you?
wahine	(wha *hee* nay)	woman

Students can assemble a dictionary of Hawaiian words or expressions and their meaning.

20   Investigate Alaska, the forty-ninth state. Only half a million people (525,000 in 1987) inhabit this huge territory. Who are they? Read about Alaska in such books as *Julie of the Wolves* by Jean George (Harper & Row, 1972), the story of an Eskimo girl.

Alaska's flag was designed by Benny Benson, a thirteen-year-old schoolboy. The flag is deep blue with seven gold stars, which represent the gold found in Alaska, forming the Big Dipper. The eighth star is, of course, the North Star, which symbolizes Alaska's northern location close to the North Pole.

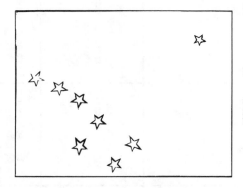

Alaska's song is "Alaska's Flag," which describes the flag and what it stands for. Sing or speak the words by Marie Drake:

Eight stars of gold on a field of blue —
Alaska's flag. May it mean to you
The blue of the sea, the evening sky,
The mountain lakes, and the flow'rs nearby;

The gold of the early sourdough's dreams,
The precious gold of the hills and streams;
The brilliant stars in the northern sky,
The "Bear"—the "Dipper"— and, shining high,
The great North Star with its steady light,
Over land and sea a beacon bright.
Alaska's flag—to Alaskans dear,
The simple flag of a last frontier.

27   Read the poem by Paul Laurence Dunbar that begins "We wear the mask that grins and lies." Use this selection to stimulate a discussion about feelings—how we express them and why we hide them. Ask students if people always show what they feel on their face. Why or why not? Have they every seen their parents pretend to be happy when they're sad inside? How do we show our feelings? With our eyes? Mouth?

After discussing expressions, have the students make papier-mache masks that illustrate a particular feeling (through eyes, mouth, color). They can write a story about a time when they wanted to show their true feelings or hide them. Then they can use the masks to tell the story.

July Activities

1,3   Recognize Canada on Dominion Day. Display its symbol, the maple leaf, with pictures of Canada from travel folders. (See pages 240–241 for ideas specific to Québec.) Can students name some famous Canadians? Display a map of Canada. Look at the names of the provinces. What do they indicate about the ethnic influences on Canada and where the early settlers came from? How is the history of Canada different from that of the United States? How is it similar?

Read aloud some poems from the prize-winning collection by Mary Alice Downie and Barbara Robertson, comp., *The New Wind Has Wings: Poems from Canada* (Oxford/Merrimack, 1985).

4   Independence Day for the United States can be recognized in many ways. Prepare a program that includes songs such as "America," "The Star-Spangled Banner," "American the Beautiful," and "Columbia, the Gem of the Ocean." Students can read some of the great poetic prose written by the patriots who drew up the Constitution as well as such eloquent words as those of Lincoln in "The Gettysburg Address":

Four score and seven years ago our fathers brought forth on this continent, a new nation, conceived in liberty, and dedicated to the proposition that all men are created equal.

Now we are engaged in a great civil war, testing whether that nation, or any nation so conceived and so dedicated, can long endure. We are met on a great battlefield of that war. We have come to dedicate a portion of that field, as a final resting place for those who gave their lives that the nation might live. It is altogether fitting and proper that we should do this.

But, in a larger sense, we can not dedicate—we can not consecrate—we can not hallow—this ground. The brave men, living and dead, who struggled here, have consecrated it, far above our poor power to add or detract. The world will little note, nor

JULY

1	2	3	4	5	6	7
Dominion Day (Canada)	Thurgood Marshall, 1908–	Champlain founded Quebec, 1608	Edmonia Lewis, 1845–?, Black-Cherokee sculptor; Lucy Slowe, 1885–1937, Black teacher and administrator; Giuseppe Garibaldi, 1807–1882			
8	**9**	**10**	**11**	**12**	**13**	**14**
		Mary McLeod Bethune, 1875–1955			Wole Soyinka, 1934–	Bastille Day (France), 1789
15	**16**	**17**	**18**	**19**	**20**	**21**
Maggie Walker, 1867–1934, Black insurance and banking executive; Chiu Chin died, 1875–1907	Ida Barnett-Wells, 1862–1931, Black journalist and civic leader; Mary Baker Eddy, 1821–1910, Founder, Christian Science	Spain transferred Florida to U.S., 1821; S. Y. Agnon, 1888–1970	Miguel Hidalgo, 1753–1811, Father of Mexican independence; Yevgeny Yevtushenko, 1933–	Alice Dunbar Nelson, 1875–1935, Black author, teacher		
22	**23**	**24**	**25**	**26**	**27**	**28**
		Simon Bolívar, 1783–1830; Mormons settled Salt Lake City, 1847	Puerto Rico became a Commonwealth, 1952		Korean War ended, 1953	
29	**30**	**31**				
		Sarah Garnet, 1831–1911, Black educator and civic worker				

The drums of Africa still beat in my heart. They will not let me rest while there is a single Negro boy or girl without a chance to prove his worth.
—*Mary McLeod Bethune*

long remember, what we say here, but it can never forget what they did here. It is for us the living, rather, to be dedicated here to the unfinished work which they who fought here have thus far so nobly advanced. It is rather for us to be here dedicated to the great task remaining before us — that from these honored dead we take increased devotion to that cause for which they gave the last full measure of devotion — that we here highly resolve that these dead shall not have died in vain — that this nation, under God, shall have a new birth of freedom — and that government of the people, by the people, and for the people, shall not perish from the earth.

Younger students can talk about words associated with the 4th of July, such as the following:

democracy   liberty
independence   fraternity
equality

What do these words mean? Where do they come from? Analyze the words by looking at the morphemes (prefixes, suffixes, and roots). Show how knowing the meaning of the morphemes can help you predict the meaning of unfamiliar words.

10   Who was Mary McLeod Bethune? The featured quote by her suggests her concern with education. Challenge students to find out about her life and achievements. Students can read *Mary McLeod Bethune* by Patricia McKisssack (Children's Press, 1985) or write to The Bethune Museum Archives, 1318 Vermont Ave. NW, Washington, D.C. 20006, for further information.

Talk about the words *segregation* and *desegregation*. Do students know what these words mean? At one time (during slavery) it was illegal to teach Blacks to read and write. Why would people be afraid to have Blacks learning? Discuss the consequences of segregated schools. What are some of the solutions?

August Activities

2   The fear I heard in my father's voice . . . when he realized that I really *believed* I could do anything a white boy could do, and had every intention of proving it, was not at all like the fear I heard when one of us was ill or had fallen down the stairs or strayed too far from the house. It was another fear, a fear that the child, in challenging the white world's assumptions, was putting himself in the path of destruction.
     — *James Baldwin*

James Baldwin grew up in Harlem (New York) and became a writer, but he had to leave this country in order to develop his writing abilities. He settled in Paris, as had other Black American exiles. What do the quotes indicate about Baldwin's opinion of the position of Blacks in American society? Why would someone like Baldwin leave the United States? What does "going into exile" mean?

7   I was offered the ambassadorship of Liberia once, when the post was earmarked for a Negro. I told them I wouldn't take a Jim Crow job.
     — *Ralph Bunche*

AUGUST

1	2	3	4	5	6	7
James Baldwin, 1924–1987		Columbus started first voyage, 1492	Anne Frank captured, 1944		U.S. bombed Hiroshima, Japan, 1945	Ralph Bunche, 1904–1971
8 U.S. bombed Nagasaki, Japan, 1945 Roberto Clemente, 1934–1973	**9** Janie Porter Barrett, 1865–1948, Black social welfare leader	**10**	**11** Alex Haley, 1921–	**12** U.S. annexed Hawaii	**13** Spanish conquered Aztecs, 1521	**14** Japan surrendered, World War II, 1945
15	**16**	**17** Charlotte Forten (Grimke), 1837–1914, Black teacher and author; V. S. Naipaul, 1932–	**18**	**19** Mammy Pleasant, 1814–1904, Black California pioneer	**20** Bernardo O'Higgins, Chilean patriot, 1778	**21**
22	**23**	**24** Lucy Moten died, 1933, Black educator	**25**	**26** Women's Equality Day	**27** Rose McClendon, 1884–1936, Black actress	**28**
29	**30**	**31** Josephine Ruffin, 1842–1924, Black leader				

The wonder is not that so many Negro boys and girls are ruined but that so many survive.
—*James Baldwin*

Discuss this comment with students. Ralph Bunche was a famous black diplomat. Ask students whether they know what a "Jim Crow" job is. Can they guess? Why would the ambassador to Liberia be expected to be Black? What would it feel like to go to Africa, after being treated as an inferior in this country, and find people like yourself in positions of power?

Collect and display pictures of Africans in different jobs and positions of responsibility. Show students what the world looks like when people aren't denied opportunities because of their skin color.

12   Who were the Aztecs and why did the Spanish conquer them? Pose such questions to the students and have them search for the answers. The Aztec civilization is particularly interesting because it was so advanced, and yet we know very little about it because the Spanish destroyed most of the records. Investigate the Spanish treatment of the Aztecs and compare it to the way the English settlers treated the Indian groups they met.

Have students research the Aztec calendar. The Aztecs were excellent astronomers and developed a calendar that was more accurate than the one the Spaniards used, yet they had not discovered the wheel. Prepare a display featuring the accomplishments of the Aztecs. Obtain pictures of the pyramids and Aztec cities. Show the Aztec circular calendar.

Students who are fascinated by pyramids might work cooperatively to make a sand table model of a pyramid. This can stimulate extensive research on the Aztecs and make this ancient civilization come alive for all students.

Variable Dates

Listed here are holidays or events that fall on different dates each year. Add them to the appropriate months.

United States Holidays or Special Days.   Note that many holidays are being celebrated on a Monday or Friday to provide a holiday weekend.

Mother's Day	2nd Sunday in May
Armed Forces Day	3rd Saturday in May
Memorial Day	last Monday in May
Father's Day	3rd Sunday in June
Labor Day	1st Monday in September
Election Day	1st Tuesday after 1st Monday in November
Veteran's Day	4th Monday in October
Thanksgiving Day	4th Thursday in November

Jewish Feasts and Festivals.   Because the Jewish calendar (described in the next section) is different from the school calendar used in this country, the dates of Jewish holidays vary each year. The following chart gives the names and dates for the holidays by year and shows the corresponding Jewish calendar year under Rosh Hashanah, when the new year begins. Note that each holiday actually begins at sunset on the preceding day.

Year	Purim (Feast of Lots)	Passover (Festival of Freedom)	Shevuos (Feast of Weeks)	Rosh Hashanah (New Year)	Yom Kippur (Day of Atonement)	Succos (Feast of Tabernacles)	Hanukkah (Feast of Dedication)
1990	Mar. 11	Apr. 10–17	May 30–31	Sept. 20–21	Sept. 29	Oct. 4–10	Dec. 12–19
1991	Feb. 28	Mar. 30–Apr. 6	May 19–20	Sept. 9–10	Sept. 18	Sept. 23–29	Dec. 2–9
1992	Mar. 19	Apr. 18–25	June 7–8	Sept. 28–29	Oct. 7	Oct. 12–18	Dec. 20–27

CULTURES AND TIME

The calendar itself is an object of interest in the multicultural classroom. Although students may assume that the calendar and the way people count time has always been the same, you can introduce the idea of cultural diversity in time measurement as you work with the Multicultural Calendar. In addition, the calendar has changed over time, due to political as well as scientific considerations. And once students begin to look at the calendar as an object of study, they will be interested to learn the origins of the names of the months and the days of the week, for example. Students will enjoy discovering the amazing diversity of contemporary and historical methods of telling time.

Marking Time: Background

As we begin an exploration of calendars, we might first discuss ideas about marking time in general. For example, students may be surprised to find that not every culture has the same concept of day that we do. We accept the concepts of day, hour, minute, and second as well as week, month, and year with little question. Let us examine a few ideas that you might discuss as examples of varied ways of considering time within different cultures.

What is a day? Our idea of day is a 24-hour period that includes both light and darkness. Is it not strange that we count a day from the middle of a night to the middle of the next night? In some cultures there is no word that means just that. Many ancient cultures recognized a single event such as dawn, the rising of the sun, and spoke of so many dawns or suns. Other cultures used the night and spoke of "sleeps." Gradually the light period was broken up with terms related to the sun: daybreak, sunrise, noon, afternoon, twilight, and sunset. The crowing of cocks, the yoking of oxen, and the siesta are other examples of ways of marking the time of day. For some peoples day begins with dawn, but, for example, in Israel it begins in the evening. Dividing the day into hours is a modern concept brought about by industrialization.

Beginning the day at midnight and having two sets of times designated one to twelve are arbitrary decisions that are not always followed. Many students will have heard of 24-hour clocks which are used in many countries and in some cases (such as military organizations) in the United States. They might not know, however, that astronomers begin their day with twelve noon in order to use the same date for observations made at night.

Our determination of months and weeks is also an arbitrary decision. Months roughly correspond to the cycle of the moon, which is 29½ days. Early societies noted the phases of the moon and used them as measures of time from new moon to full moon. The moon is still the basis for some calendars, as we will discuss in the next section. Today, we use a calendar that divides the year into months of 28–31 days to fit the solar year so the phases of the moon occur at different times of the various months.

The seven-day week is another interesting phenomenon that began when people who were trading needed some regular arrangement. The week, as the interval between trading or market days, has varied from four to ten days. It is thought that the selection of seven days as the "magical" number does, indeed, have something to do with the significance of the number *seven*. This hypothesis is supported by our use of the names of gods and goddesses to name the days of the week, thus:

Latin Name	*French Name*	*Saxon Name*	*English Name*
Dies Solis	Dimanche	Sun's day	Sunday
Dies Lunae	Lundi	Moon's day	Monday
Dies Martis	Mardi	Tiw's Day	Tuesday
Dies Mercurii	Mercredi	Woden's day	Wednesday
Dies Jovis	Jeudi	Thor's day	Thursday
Dies Veneris	Vendredi	Frigg's day	Friday
Dies Saturni	Samedi	Seterne's day	Saturday

The Saxon names which reflect Norse mythology are carried into our English names. In the French and Latin names, which are related, you can find Mars, Mercury, Venus, and Jupiter (Jove).

Although we now take for granted the knowledge of astronomy on which we base our year, this concept of year is a relatively new idea. Gradually, ancient peoples found a need for longer designations of time than market days or lunar months. This need was chiefly to count the ages of people and to compare these ages. Some of the following measures were used:

- Family generations
- Momentous events — plague, famine, war
- Reign of monarchs or chiefs
- Cycle of seasons
    monsoons
    wet and dry periods (rains)
    summer and winter (summers, snows)
    agricultural changes
    animal migration

Folklore provides a wealth of information related to these concepts of time. Encourage students to search out such ideas. They might begin with expressions or beliefs related to time; for example, Friday is a bad day, and Friday the thirteenth is the worst of all days! *Blue Monday and Friday the Thirteenth* by Lila Perl (Clarion, 1986) explores the origins of many beliefs.

Students might pursue the study of cultural beliefs and superstitions in such books as *Cross Your Fingers, Spit in Your Hat* by Alvin Schwartz (Lippincott, 1974).

How Calendars Developed

Encourage students to investigate the history of calendars. They can learn, for example, the origins of the word which goes back to the Latin *calendarium,* which means *account book.* Calendars are associated, therefore, with the payment of debts, marking times when payments were due. A calendar, as generally used, is a system for recording the passage of time. Congress, for example, has a calendar or schedule of events.

Before we had formal ways of measuring time, humans marked time by observing the rising and setting of the sun, the different phases of the moon, and the passage of the seasons. The first calendars, created by the Babylonians, were based on moons (months), the periods of time when the moon completed its full cycle of phases. Twelve moons make a 354-day year. When it was observed that every four years the year needed an adjustment to make the calendar fit the seaons, the Babylonians added another moon or month. This calendar was adapted by the Egyptians, Semites, and Greeks.

The Egyptians modified this calendar by basing their calculations on the regular rising of the Nile River, which occurred each year just after Sirius, the Dog Star, appeared. They developed a calendar that more nearly matched the solar year, using 365 days, which was still a little off from the 365¼ days we now consider accurate. Considering that they created this system more than 4000 years B.C., however, they were amazingly exact. They worked with 12 months of 30 days each and simply added 5 days at the end of the year.

The Roman calendar, introduced by Romulus around 700 B.C., was derived from that used in Greece. The Romans had ten months: Martius, Aprilis, Maius, Junius, Quintilis, Sextilis, September, October, November, and December. The names of the last six months correspond to the Latin number names — five, six, seven, eight, nine, and ten. One king, who wanted to collect more taxes, added two more months, Januarius and Februarius. Needless to say, the calendar soon became very confused and did not correspond with the solar year.

Then came the Julian Calendar which Julius Caesar created in 46 B.C. to correct the inaccuracy of the Roman Calendar. He divided the year into 12 months of 30 and 31 days except for February which he gave 28 days plus one every fourth year, so his year was a few minutes longer than the solar year. He changed the beginning of the year to January 1st instead of March 1st and changed the month of Sextilis to August, after Emperor Augustus. The month Quintilis was changed to Julius in honor of Caesar. Thus, we have the origins of our names for the twelve months. The Julian Calendar was used for more than 1500 years. The Gregorian Calendar was created to correct the error in the Julian Calendar which had become ten days off in 1580. The Gregorian Calendar was gradually adopted until it has become standard throughout much of the world.

Students might like to investigate further efforts to reform the calendar. The thirteen-month calendar would contain thirteen months of equal length. The perpetual calendar is another fascinating topic to explore.

The Christian Calendar

The calendar that Christians use is the Gregorian Calendar, which was developed by Pope Gregory around 1580. Students may know the old verse that helps them remember the number of days in each month according to this calendar:

Thirty days has September,
April, June, and November.
All the rest have thirty-one
Except February alone
Which has twenty-eight
Until Leap Year gives it one day more.

This Christian Calendar is based on the year Jesus Christ was born. Dates before his birth are marked as B.C. (before Christ). Dates after his birth are marked as A.D. (*anno Domini* — in the year of our Lord). Non-Christians sometimes use the markings B.C.E. (before the Christian era) and C.E. (Christian era). On this Christian calendar there are certain fixed dates, such as Christmas. Movable feast days include Easter and Thanksgiving.

Christian Holidays

	Ash Wednesday	Easter Sunday
1990	February 28	April 15
1991	February 13	March 31
1992	March 4	April 19
1993	February 24	April 11
1994	February 16	April 3
1995	March 1	April 16
1996	February 21	April 7

Easter falls on the first Sunday following the arbitrary Paschal Full Moon, which does not necessarily coincide with a real or astronomical full moon. The Paschal Full Moon is calculated by adding 1 to the remainder obtained by dividing the year by 19 and applying the following:

1 — April 14	6 — April 18	11 — March 25	16 — March 30
2 — April 3	7 — April 8	12 — April 13	17 — April 17
3 — March 23	8 — March 28	13 — April 2	18 — April 7
4 — April 11	9 — April 16	14 — March 22	19 — March 27
5 — March 31	10 — April 5	15 — April 10	

Thus, for the year 2000 the key is 6 or April 18. Since April 18th in the year 2000 is a Tuesday, Easter Sunday is April 23rd. *Caution*—If the Paschal Full Moon falls on a Sunday, Easter is the following Sunday. The earliest Easter can fall is March 23rd and the latest is April 25th.

Lent begins on Ash Wednesday which comes 40 days before Easter, excluding Sundays.

The Hebrew Calendar

Another calendar that is still widely used today is the Hebrew, or Jewish, Calendar, based on the Creation, which preceded the birth of Christ by 3760 years and 3 months. The Hebrew year begins in September rather than January. From the fall of 1991 to the fall of 1992, therefore, the Hebrew year will be 5752.

Based on the moon, the Hebrew year usually contains 12 months. Periodically, an extra month is inserted to adjust this calendar, as shown here:

Months in the Hebrew Calendar	Important Dates
Tishri	1–2 Rosh Hashanah (New Year)
Heshvan	10 Yom Kippur (Day of Atonement)
Kislev	25 Hanukkah (Feast of Dedication)
Tebet	2 or 3 Hanukkah ends
Shebat	
Adar	14–15 Purim (Feast of Lots)
(Veadar)	
Nisan	15–22 Pesach (Passover)
Iyar	5 Israel Independence Day
Sivan	6–7 Shabuoth (Pentecost)
Tammuz	
Ab	
Elul	

Encyclopedia Britannica puts out a series of three filmstrips called *Jewish Holidays* (1984) covering Rosh Hashanah, Yom Kippur, Hanukkah, and Passover.

The Islamic Calendar

Also based on the moon, the Islamic or Muslim Calendar dates from Mohammed's flight from Mecca, called the Hegira, which took place in A.D. 622. The year has only 354 days so that its New Year moves with respect to the seasons. It makes a full cycle every 32½ years. The names of the Islamic months are:

Muharram	Rabi II	Rajab	Shawwal
Safar	Jumada I	Shaban	Zulkadah
Rabi I	Jumada II	Ramadan	Zulhijjah

Clarify terminology for students who may be confused as they read news reports from the Near East. The word *Moslem* comes from an Arabic word *muslim* which means "one who submits" (to Allah or God). Arabic is the language spoken by the majority of Moslems, and Islam is the chief religion. An estimated 23 percent of the world's population is Moslem, and there are between 1.5 million to 6 million Moslems in the United States.

Other Calendars of the World

Students who are interested in calendars can research other systems that have been developed. The Chinese Calendar, consisting of a 12-year cycle based on Jupiter's positions in relationship to the constellations, is discussed on page 254. Other calendars that students can investigate include Hindu, Assyrian, Greek, and Maya.

REFLECTIONS

We have used the days of the months to present information and activities that support teaching for multicultural understandings. These dates are provided to encourage the incorporation of information about diversity throughout the curriculum and the school year. The activities also represent the contributions of different groups in order to counteract the tendency to recognize specific groups only at limited times of the year. The calendar, however, serves only as a base for your class to develop and personalize its own version, as the students become involved in the exploration of diversity.

APPLICATIONS

1. The celebration of Thanksgiving is an excellent base for a theme unit on interdependence, religious freedom, cultural conflict, or gifts from other countries. You will want to consider different perspectives: immigrants who are grateful for a chance to build a new life, the original inhabitants who didn't ask for these neighbors and found themselves pushed out of their homes, or today's individuals who can give thanks for what they have today.

   Plan your unit by collecting materials and writing lessons. You will want to include writing, art, and discussion activities that build understandings across the curriculum. You can develop a bibliography of Thanksgiving-related materials such as books and quotes to use with students. Here are some books with which to begin:

   > Margaret Baldwin. *Thanksgiving*. Watts, 1983.
   >
   > Barbara Cohen. *Molly's Pilgrim*. Lothrop, 1983.
   >
   > Gail Gibbons. *Thanksgiving Day*. Holiday House, 1983.
   >
   > Lucille Penner. *The Thanksgiving Book*. Hastings, 1986.

2. Focus on birthdays. Find out how to say "Happy Birthday" in 100 languages. How do people celebrate birthdays in different cultures? Make a list of ways

to create a multiethnic atmosphere (food, music, decorations) in the classroom and to make the children feel special.

3. Choose a group (ethnic, religious, or regional) to be responsible for and research names, dates, events, and other kinds of information to include in a multicultural calendar. Try to find special holidays celebrated by this group, names of significant individuals, and important contributions by the group.

    Where would you look for this information? What kind of information is most difficult to find? Why?

    Prepare lessons to present this information to students.

Resources

June Behrens. *Hanukkah: Festivals and Holidays.* Children's Press. 1983.

Miriam Chaikin. *Make Noise, Make Merry: The Story and Meaning of Purim.* Clarion, 1983.

Irving Howe. *World of Our Fathers.* Harcourt, 1976.

Leon Litwack and August Meier, eds. *Black Leaders of the Nineteenth Century.* University of Illinois Press, 1988.

Myra Cohn Livingston. *Celebrations.* Holiday House, 1985.

Milton Meltzer. *The Black Americans: A History in Their Own Words, 1619–1983.* Crowell, 1985.

Thomas Sowell. *Ethnic America: A History.* Basic Books, 1981.

A journey of A
thousand miles
Begins
with one step.

LAO-TZE

10

Reflecting on Multicultural Education

Education enables individuals to come into full possession of all their powers.[1]

John Dewey

Preview

After reading this chapter, you should be able to:

- Identify the assumptions underlying multicultural education as presented in this text.
- Explain desired outcomes for student learning.
- Identify the obstacles that may impede successful multicultural education programs.
- Discuss progressive thinking and promising practices that support effective multicultural education.

In this book we have presented a philosophy of teaching that is grounded in humanity and a sincere desire to make the world a better place in which to live. We believe that education offers the only route to the empathy for others that will lead to cooperative planning and harmonious living on our planet. It is our belief that multicultural education is subsumed in the meaning of democracy as we aim to carry it out in the United States. We hope to educate teachers who will bear this message.

To carry out this goal, we designed each chapter to present ideas and applications for classroom instruction that integrate multicultural concepts into every subject of study. We recommended lessons that engage students in such learning activities as identifying human values portrayed in literature, questioning the assumptions of those who write history, and recognizing the contributions of a myriad of men and women to the development of this complex country. We endeavored to share content and instructional strategies that we think will lead students to understand themselves and others — the ultimate aim of multicultural teaching.

As Dewey notes above, education can empower, but teachers are the enabling agents who can make it happen. We want to talk with you, therefore, about making all of education explicitly multicultural. In this chapter, we want to reflect with you on the beliefs that we have tried to share in this book, restating what we believe about teaching. We would also like to recognize obstacles that may impede multicultural teaching and to identify ways that education for understanding might realistically come about. Concluding on a positive note, we will identify progressive thinking and promising practices that are already in effect, with the hope that you will find support for your endeavors to implement multicultural education in your classrooms.

A REVIEW OF THE AUTHORS' BELIEFS

In Chapter 1 we introduced the ideas that we wanted to present in this book. Then, chapter by chapter, we developed the theory and practices that we hope teachers can carry out in classrooms across the country.

Multicultural teaching is a broad topic that cannot be taught in one single course. Therefore, we present multicultural education as a spiraling complex of concepts and understandings that evolves across years of schooling. It threads its way through all instruction.

The Underlying Assumptions

Underlying assumptions suggest something hidden from view — beliefs that we really don't want you to perceive. Since this is far from our intent, we want to restate our beliefs so that there is no doubt of our message.

1. In the United States we live in a multicultural society. All of living, including schooling, is therefore multicultural.
2. Educated thinking in the United States has changed from the expressed goal of making everyone alike (the melting pot metaphor) to recognizing and appreciating diversity in our society (the tossed salad metaphor). Educators play a role in disseminating this knowledge and its implications.

3. Multicultural education is too complex and pervasive a topic to be encompassed in a single course. *All* of education must reflect multicultural awareness. Multicultural education begins with self-esteem for each person.

4. If education is recognized as being multicultural, then we should not pretend or even aim at creating teaching materials that are bias-free. Instead, we can guide students to recognize the biases from which everyone operates.

5. We need to clarify our definitions of such terms as *cultural, ethnicity,* and *race;* and we need to be sensitive to the use of labels for groups of people within our population, speaking out against poor usage whenever necessary.

6. Every child grows up within a given culture that is shaped over the years by external influences such as education and personal interactions with other people. Education can guide students to become more aware of and appreciative of their individual cultures. All children enter school with a store of prior knowledge that is closely aligned with their individual cultures.

7. Education can guide all students to become more aware of and appreciative of the many cultures that people brought to what is now the United States. Because of our history, we cannot identify *an* "American" culture; rather, we should speak proudly of our diverse national population—a characteristic that clearly makes our country unique.

8. Teachers need to be aware of their own cultural backgrounds and biases. Open dialogue with students will acknowledge these cultural influences as common to all.

9. Approaching education multiculturally is exciting because it is real and involves students directly in their learning. At the same time, it may also be more difficult for teachers because it can become controversial and personal.

10. Multicultural education deals with values and attitudes. We can guide students to be aware of their own thinking and that of others (metacognition). As teachers, we do not aim at imposing our values on students; rather, we guide them to make choices based on expressed reasoning, problem solving, and decision making. Changes in values and attitudes—the development of empathy—take time, so that assessing such changes is not possible within short periods of time.

Multicultural education is a broad body of knowledge. It is a subject that students need to discover. Rather than lecturing about multicultural concepts, the effective teacher will plan lessons that guide students to discover universal needs and human understandings—to generate empathy. The study of our multiculture engages students in listening, speaking, thinking, writing, and reading. It also engages them in the study of language and literature and other subject areas such as psychology, sociology, political science, geography, and history. It is enmeshed in the total curriculum.

We are continuously reshaping our thinking based on new information that becomes available and experiences that provide new perspectives. At the end of each chapter we listed up-to-date sources that you may find helpful. It is important that you, too, continue to learn as you work with students in your classroom. Form your opinions based on your experiences and test them against those of others you encounter. Teachers who have open minds will generate learners who are open to acquiring new ways of thinking.

Education based on these ten assumptions will affect curriculum development, the selection of learning materials, the instructional strategies used to deliver the curriculum. These assumptions will also be reflected in the outcomes we specify for student learning in the next section.

Desired Outcomes for Every Student

Today we know that effective education is based on outcomes assessment. Just what are we trying to achieve with students during the time they spend in our classrooms? Multicultural education should lead to the achievement of specific outcomes for children and young people in our schools. The outcomes we specify for multicultural teaching are often interpersonal; they are both cognitive and affective objectives. If our multicultural curriculum is effectively taught, students will:

1. Identify a strong sense of their own self-esteem. Express the need and right of all other persons to similar feelings of self-esteem.
2. Describe their own individual cultures, recognizing the influences that have shaped their thinking and behavior.
3. Identify racial, ethnic, and religious groups that are represented in our pluralistic society (e.g., Afro-Americans, persons from Italian backgrounds, or Jews). Discuss the history of immigration to the United States after its discovery and the changing thinking about immigrants that evolved over the years.
4. List identity groups that each person belongs to based on age, sex, or physical condition. List special interest groups that each person belongs to by choice (e.g., lawyers, feminists, swimmers, or Republicans).
5. Identify universal needs and concerns common to people of all cultures (e.g., love, family, and health). Compare interesting cultural variations (e.g., food preparation, naming practices, or dance).
6. Read and discuss literature by and about members of diverse cultures. Share folklore from different cultures, noting the common subjects and motifs that occur in folk literature.
7. Discuss special gender-related concerns (e.g., job discrimination based on sex, sexual abuse, or the socialization of children).
8. Discuss age-related concerns (e.g., rights of children, problems of the adolescent, or caring for the elderly).
9. Discuss the needs of persons with disabilities (e.g., mainstreaming in school, parking facilities, or facilitative equipment).
10. Identify examples of stereotyped thinking and prejudice in real life and in literature. Discuss the negative effects of such thinking.
11. Inquire multiculturally as they engage in broad studies related to any field (e.g., science, history, or health). Demonstrate knowledge of such related

topics as slavery, the United Nations, the history of the English language, or desegregation.

12. Participate in community and school affairs as informed, empathetic young citizens who know and care about other people and recognize the enriching effect of having many cultures represented in our population.

Such outcomes can be assessed through student performance in speaking or writing as well as observed in their body language or behavior. Students should discuss a list of expected outcomes for any study they undertake before the work begins. The twelve outcomes listed above can be adapted for inclusion in the outcomes for a unit of study in any subject area.

OBSTACLES THAT MAY PREVENT SUCCESS

We need to continue working on multicultural outcomes for education at all levels. As stated previously, such outcomes should be an integral part of learning specific to any subject area. If all teachers emphasized such understandings in their classrooms, we could make a giant step toward achieving the full empathy that leads to world peace.

Clearly, there are obstacles that impede our progress in this direction. It is well to acknowledge the presence of these hurdles in order to overcome them.

Limited Knowledge about Multicultural Education

Prior to 1978, the entry *multicultural education* was not even listed in the *Education Index,* which indicates that few articles in pedagogical journals were being written about this topic. An entry for *Mexican Americans* first appeared in the 1963–1964 volume. At that time multiethnic topics were referred to as *Intergroup education.* All references to Blacks were entered under *Negroes* until 1978. References to Asian Americans were listed under *Orientals* until 1980. Only within the past few years do we find a number of books and articles appearing about multicultural education. (The first edition of this text, *Multicultural Teaching,* appeared in 1979.)

These findings make it clear that teacher education has not emphasized teaching about cultural diversity; thus, few of the teachers in classrooms today have been educated to teach multicultural concepts. They have not been taught to teach multiculturally. The public still frequently uses the melting pot metaphor with well-meaning but negative effects, and such terms as *culture* are frequently misused in college textbooks.

Standards listed in 1987 by the National Council for Accreditation of Teacher Education (NCATE) include multicultural education so that teacher education programs are now examined to see that multicultural concepts are present in class syllabi. The expected "multicultural perspective" is defined as:

. . . a recognition of (1) the social, political, and economic realities that individuals experience in culturally diverse and complex human encounters and (2) the importance of culture, race, sex and gender, ethnicity, religion, socioeconomic status, and exceptionalities in the education process.[2]

Teachers at all levels need to know accurate definitions and acceptable concepts that can be shared with students at all levels of instruction. They need to know literature that will inform such instruction. They also need to accept the responsibility of teaching to enhance empathy in all classrooms.

Stereotyped Thinking and Prejudice

All of us grow up within a culture surrounded by beliefs and behaviors that we accept without question. As young children, we usually associate with persons from the same culture, and we may tend to think our way of thinking and behaving is the "right" way to think or behave. Thus, stereotyped thinking begins, and we become prejudiced against those who think or behave differently.

Education, however, informs us. As we encounter people from broader circles, we learn that thinking and behavior differ. Gradually, we learn to accept diverse thinking as a normal state of affairs. Mobility, television, the newspaper, literature — all serve to broaden our perspectives. If minds are open to new ideas, stereotyped thinking will be revised as students learn to accept difference and to realize that difference does not connote "deficient" or "wrong."

Yet we continue to hear crude ethnic jokes or references in the speech of supposedly educated people. Children's rhymes and stories often contain stereotyped thinking that children may or may not understand. Women and the elderly are often discriminated against. Education still has work to do.

The Prescribed Curriculum

Those who influence curriculum development are not always well informed. For example, former Education Secretary, William Bennett, a highly literate man schooled in the classics, published a list of literature for K–8 classrooms in his report entitled *James Madison Elementary School: A Curriculum for American Students.*[3] Only a few titles that could be identified as "multicultural" in content are included, for example:

K–3

Behind the Back of the Mountain: Black Folktales from Southern Africa (Verna Aardema)
The Snowy Day (Ezra Jack Keats)
Anansi the Spider: A Tale from the Ashanti (retold by Gerald McDermott)
Crow Boy (Taro Yashima)

4–6

Sounder (William H. Armstrong)
Crickets and Bullfrogs and Whispers of Thunder: Poems and Pictures (Harry Behn)
Julie of the Wolves (Jean Craighead George)
Folk Tales (Virginia Hamilton)
Bridge to Terabithia (Katherine Paterson)
A Day of Pleasure: Stories of a Boy Growing up in Warsaw (Isaac B. Singer)

7–8

I Know Why the Caged Bird Sings (Maya Angelou)
Diary of a Young Girl (Anne Frank)
Spin a Soft Black Song (Nikki Giovanni)
A Raisin in the Sun (Lorraine Hansberry)
Legend Days (Jamake Highwater)
Story of My Life (Helen Keller)
To Kill a Mockingbird (Harper Lee)
Island of the Blue Dolphins (Scott O'Dell)
The Chosen (Chaim Potok)
Roll of Thunder, Hear My Cry (Mildred Taylor)
Journey Home (Yoshiko Uchida)
Up from Slavery (Booker T. Washington)
Dragonwings (Laurence Yep)

Of a total of 200 books listed by title, only 6 percent can be identified as multicultural. One title, *Sylvester and the Magic Pebble,* by William Steig, contains stereotypes of (1) a totally stereotyped female housekeeper/wife/mother and (2) police portrayed by this author-illustrator as pigs. (Such a book could only be recommended as a basis for a lesson on how stereotyped thinking permeates our society.) At best, this list of publications reveals a lack of information, if not concern. It is clear that "multicultural representation" was not one of the criteria for the selection of these books.

We must select instructional materials that include a greater percentage of quality literature by and about members of different ethnic groups as well as the many identity groups that have special needs and concerns. We must also find time in the already burgeoning curriculum for multicultural education. Multicultural concepts belong in every classroom and should, therefore, be written into the objectives of every lesson. From self-esteem to immigration to the contributions of members of every race, religion, and gender to the history of the United States—lessons must reinforce the worth of every person who makes up our diverse population.

The curriculum is prescribed in many ways, for example:

Textbooks selected
Commercial tests used by school districts
State Departments of Education—Course of Study

Specialty organizations—NCTE, NMA, NAEYC, IRA
Critics, researchers, authors

You may wish to explore this topic in the following resources:

William Bennett. *James Madison High School* and *James Madison Elementary School.* U.S. Government, 1988.

E. D. Hirsch. *Cultural Literacy.* Houghton Mifflin, 1988.

Mary Ellen Van Camp, ed. *Testing.* Support for the Learning and Teaching of English, NCTE, December 1988.

Fear of Handling Controversy

Teachers and textbook publishers have a tendency to avoid topics that invite controversy in the classroom. Teachers feel uncomfortable with the expression of real emotion—fear, anger, or conflict. Publishers deliberately excise multicultural issues from reprinted materials. An example of the latter is noted in reprinting *Sound of Sunshine; Sound of Rain* by Florence Heide. The climax of this outstanding short novel, a racial confrontation that provides insight into the development of a major character, is deleted from both the reprint in a basal reader and the filmed version of this well-written book.[4] Without this realistic scene, the quality of the author's work is diminished because the character development remains one-dimensional; and the students have missed an effective multicultural learning experience about humanity.

Dealing with real topics in the classroom adds vitality and stimulates student involvement in learning. Children who are confronting racism and dealing with the pain of conflict in their own lives benefit from classroom discussions that acknowledge the reality of what they face. Reading and discussion, for example, may suggest ways that others have found to deal with problems students encounter. Teachers need to seek ways of engaging students with multicultural topics even if these subjects may be controversial. Such literature as that cited above can help you present controversial issues and human feelings through a kind of simulation that is not threatening. Authors who include sensitive topics in well-written novels, dramas, or essays have created useful texts from which students can learn multicultural concepts. All educators share the responsibility for knowing and making skillful use of instructional options beyond the less inspiring textbook to support multicultural education.

Summary

We need to recognize obstacles that impede the inclusion of multicultural education in K–12 classrooms, for example, teacher preparation, the crowded curriculum, and fear of dealing with controversial issues in instructional materials. Once we acknowledge the existence of these problems, we can address them and find solutions. Multicultural education can be a reality.

PROGRESSIVE THINKING AND
PROMISING PRACTICES

Multicultural education is a relatively new curriculum consideration. First listed as an entry in *Education Index* in the 1977–1978 volume, the number of articles gradually increased during the following decade. Today we see visible efforts to deal with issues related to multicultural education. However, a difference of opinion remains. We need to support progressive thinking and to recognize exemplary practices that can be replicated across the country.

Self-Esteem — The Bottom Line

Humanistic educators wrote of self-image and self-concept in the 1960s, and affective education became a goal for many teachers.[5] Benjamin Bloom recognized both cognitive and affective domains in writing objectives for education.[6] Concern for the student as the center of the curriculum was expressed by such theoreticians as James Moffett in the first edition of *The Student-Centered Curriculum.*[7]

Currently there is renewed interest in the student's role in the learning process. We talk of student self-esteem as the foundation for learning; we recognize that all students need a sense of worth — an "I can" attitude — if they are to strive to achieve. We are concerned about the classroom climate as we try to build an attitude of trust between student and teacher. We try to let students know that making mistakes is an essential part of real learning, so they will dare to take risks as they brainstorm and solve problems together. We need citizens who have genuine self-esteem, for they are the people who can reach out confidently to others with empathy and caring. Self-esteem undergirds the effort to save "at-risk" students — a topic of national concern that we discuss later in this section.

You may wish to explore this topic in the following resources:

Jack Canfield and Harold Wells. *100 Ways to Enhance Self-concepts in the Classroom.* Prentice-Hall, 1976.

C. Combs. *Humanistic Education.* Allyn and Bacon, 1974.

Matthew McKay and Patrick Fanning. *Self-Esteem.* St. Martin's, 1987.

Eileen Tway, ed. *Reading Ladders for Human Relations,* 6th ed. National Council of Teachers of English, 1981.

Writing "Thinking"

Many educators recognize the need for instruction in K–12 classrooms (as well as preschool and adult levels) that encourages students to think. Whereas some educators focus only on "critical thinking" that they associate with the scientific method, others also recognize the importance of stimulating creative and reflective thinking.

Focus on the writing process, as advocated by National Writing Project consultant-teachers across the country for the past decade, is closely tied to the development of thinking skills. Thinking leads to writing as one way of expressing ideas, and the process of writing these ideas extends thinking. Thus the writing of "thinking" is a generative process that engages students in dealing with real issues and concerns. Students who have self-esteem express their ideas confidently, and their successful writing supports the growth of self-esteem, which is another interlocking learning process that should be in any classroom.

You may wish to explore this topic in the following resources:

Julie Jensen, ed. *Composing and Comprehending.* ERIC Clearinghouse on Reading and Communications Skills, 1984.

Judith Langer and Arthur Applebee. *How Writing Shapes Thinking: A Study of Teaching and Learning.* National Council of Teachers of English, Research Report No. 22, 1987.

Carol Olson. *Thinking/Writing: Fostering Critical Thinking Skills through Writing.* University of California at Irvine, 1984.

James Squire, ed. *The Dynamics of Language Learning.* National Conference on Research in English, 1987.

Iris M. Tiedt. *Writing: From Topic to Evaluation.* Allyn and Bacon, 1989.

Iris M. Tiedt et al. *Teaching Thinking in K–12 Classrooms.* Allyn and Bacon, 1989.

Humanization of the Curriculum

A developing trend is the use of literature or tradebooks to support instruction in all subject areas. The use of library books instead of the usual textbook humanizes the curriculum and lends a vitality to learning that has not heretofore been present. Studies point out that the usual history textbook, for example, presents a sterile summary of events compared to a well-written tradebook.[8] Furthermore, literature (including nonfiction, narrative prose, and poetry) is used to set historical events in a rich context that may more effectively engage student interest in learning. Students who read Scott O'Dell's novel, *Sarah Bishop,* for example, will have an affective knowledge of the War for Independence that is not produced by the sterile prose of most history textbooks for young adults.

Use of literature presumes that we will dismiss the necessity to "cover a textbook" in favor of guiding students to choose selections that provide different perspectives of the same period of history or the geography of a country. This approach also presupposes a different way of teaching—employing discovery methods that lead students to question and to think as they analyze, evaluate, and reflect. This approach presupposes, too, a confident teacher who can facilitate student learning and who does not need to lean on textbooks that provide questions at the end of each chapter and an answer key to ease the task of grading. We need a way of teaching that leads students to construct their own meaning based on knowledge gathered from varied sources. Literature study offers such a way that also engages students in a humanistic experience that may lead to the empathy we are attempting to achieve through multicultural education.

You may wish to explore this topic in the following resources:

California State Department of Education. *Handbook for an Effective Literature Program, K–12.* The Department, 1987.

James Moffett and Betty Jane Wagner. *A Student-centered K–13 Language Arts and Reading Curriculum.* Houghton Mifflin, 1983.

Ben F. Nelms, ed. *Literature in the Classroom: Readers, Texts, and Contexts.* National Council of Teachers of English, Forum Series, 1988.

Iris M. Tiedt. *Learning with Literature.* Macmillan, 1990.

Educating Teachers for Empowerment

True empowerment of the teacher comes from within. It is not something that an external task force can fund or that a legislator can enforce. We do, however, have a responsibility to nurture this sense of empowerment which is akin to self-esteem and self-confidence. The teacher who has this sense of power is best able to teach multiculturally, addressing controversy with equanimity and sharing leadership with young learners in the classroom.

Teacher education that empowers its novice teachers provides them with basic knowledge in the foundations, liberal studies, and pedagogy (including multicultural education). These teachers have confidence in their knowledge base, but above all, they know how to apply this knowledge in the classroom. The teacher who possesses a sense of empowerment is best able to nurture that same feeling in the students with whom he or she works. The self-confident, informed teacher does not fear issues that involve human emotion and controversy.

You may wish to explore this topic in the following resources:

Shirley Grundy. *Curriculum: Product or Praxis.* Falmer, 1988.

Susan Loucks-Horsley. *Continuing to Learn: A Guidebook for Teacher Development.* Regional Laboratory for Educational Improvement of the Northeast and Islands, 1987.

Gene I. Maeroff. *The Empowerment of Teachers.* Teachers College Press, 1988.

Lauren Resnick. *Education and Learning to Think.* Academic Press, 1987.

R. R. Schmeck, ed. *Learning Styles and Learning Strategies.* Putnam, 1988.

J. Segal et al., eds. *Thinking and Learning Skills: Relating Instruction to Research.* Erlbaum, 1985.

Schools as Centers of Inquiry

Gradually, teachers are recognizing that direct teacher-dominated instruction is not as effective as discovery methods that engage students in inquiry. We need to consider the goals of education in terms of student learning, the expected outcomes that we identify. The testing of student achievement should then reflect what we really mean to teach. The evaluation of teacher performance should in turn reflect our expectations for student learning.

In direct instruction the teacher typically lectures, perhaps addressing questions to individual students one by one; only a small percentage of students are actively involved at any one time and there is little student interaction. This is the quiet, orderly classroom; learning follows predictable lines and is easily evaluated. In this type of teaching, the teacher generates the questions, and the kind of question asked has one correct answer which, of course, the teacher knows. This has been the traditional mode of instruction for many years.

When inquiry approaches are used, however, the students generate questions to which they need to know the answers. There is self-motivation as each one works 100 percent of the class time on a self-selected problem or project. Metacognitive approaches guide students to awareness of the thinking processes in which they are engaged. They talk and write to express thinking and test it against the thinking of other students in pairs or small groups. They accept ownership for the learning that is going on because they selected a topic in which they have an interest. Far from abdicating their role, teachers plan extensively to set up discovery learning situations; often they plan directly with students. They facilitate and support the learning process and serve as resource persons.

Evaluation of progress is part of the inquiry—a process shared by teacher and student. In this kind of classroom students have an opportunity to learn more than is presented in a single textbook, and they naturally develop self-esteem. Thus, what they learn is both cognitive and affective, but it may not always be easily measured by tests used by school districts. Because such approaches are more sensitive to individual student needs, they fit with the outcomes we have identified for multicultural education. They also show promise in supporting the "at-risk" student, an identified group that needs special attention in our schools.

You may wish to explore this topic in the following resources:

Kenneth Goodman et al. *Report Card on Basal Readers.* National Council of Teachers of English, 1988.

Robert J. Marzano et al., eds. *Dimensions of Thinking: A Framework for Curriculum and Instruction.* Association for Supervision and Curriculum Development, 1988.

James Moffett and Betty Jean Wagner. *The Student-Centered Curriculum.* Houghton Mifflin, 1986.

Scott G. Paris. *Reading and Thinking Strategies.* Heath, 1987.

Iris M. Tiedt et al. *Teaching Thinking in K–12 Classrooms.* Allyn and Bacon, 1989.

Reflecting—A Vital Aspect of Learning

The active learner observes what is happening in the world and asks questions as a way of learning. From birth, the child is processing information. The child's acquisition of language is an example of the discovery process in action as the newborn human gradually abstracts the complexities of a grammar system from the language heard in the environment. Making hypotheses and constructing theories about how the language works, the growing child tests these hypotheses by communicating. Never afraid of making errors, the child talks, talks, and talks, trying out what he or she has learned.

Only in recent years are we recognizing the need to extrapolate what we know about the child's acquisition of speech to the acquisition of literacy abilities and other content. While recognizing the limitations of this way of learning more complex content and skills, we need to recognize that learner-generated questioning and the making of hypotheses is a natural and essential aspect of all learning.

In the discussion in the preceding section, we noted the difference between traditional direct teaching methods and inquiry or discovery methods. Questioning is used in both methods; the difference lies in who generates the questions. It has been said that if we taught children how to speak the way we teach them to read, they would never learn to speak. We are turning, at last, to student-centered approaches to teaching (learning) reading. We need to use these same methods in other subject instruction. Students are more likely to internalize multicultural education concepts if they are generating the questions and constructing the meaning. We cannot impose empathy on students; this kind of learning must come from within.

You may wish to explore this topic in the following resources:

Beau F. Jones et al., eds. *Strategies for Teaching and Learning: Cognitive Instruction in the Content Areas.* Association of Supervision and Curriculum Development, 1987.

Iris M. Tiedt et al. *Reading/Thinking/Writing: A Holistic Language and Literacy Program for the K–8 Classroom.* Allyn and Bacon, 1989.

Iris M. Tiedt et al. *Teaching Thinking in K–12 Classrooms.* Allyn and Bacon, 1989.

S. R. Yussen, and M. C. Smioth, eds. *Reading across the Life Span.* Springer-Verlag, 1990.

Early Childhood Education

We have long known that attitudes and values are firmly rooted in what is learned during the early years. What is not learned at this time, furthermore, constitutes a great loss that may never be overcome. Children who do not have the learning opportunities that we sometimes assume every child has during these early years enter kindergarten and first grade with a handicap that we now recognize and can work to correct.

Early childhood instruction for children in poverty-level homes (intervention education) may alleviate any discrepancy in the experiential base children bring to school. Such projects as Headstart and similar childcare programs being generated today strive to build up an experiential and knowledge base before children enter the formal school system. Thus, children are better prepared to interact with other children and to undertake more formal learning successfully from the beginning. At the same time that we are preparing children to enter school, we are also rethinking the concept of "readiness" as we emphasize the individualization of instruction and the need to adjust instruction to the needs of the individual learner. Thus, self-esteem can remain intact as children succeed. These ways of thinking tie in with the efforts to rescue "at-risk" students, discussed in the next section.

You may wish to explore preschool education through the following resources:

G. Robert Carlsen and Anne Sherrill. *Voices of Readers: How We Come to Love Books.* National Council of Teachers of English, 1988.

V. Hildebrand. *Introduction to Early Childhood Education.* Macmillan, 1986.

N. Peterson. *Early Intervention for Handicapped and At-Risk Children.* Love, 1987.

B. Spodel et al. *Foundations of Early Childhood Education.* Prentice-Hall, 1987.

Join the Early Childhood Education Network—Contact: S. M. Childs, Teaneck Public Schools; One Merrison St.; Teaneck NJ 07666.

The journal *Young Children* is published by the National Association for the Education of Young Children (NAEYC), 1834 Connecticut Ave., NW; Washington DC 20008.

Dimension is published quarterly by Southern Association on Children under Six (SACUS), Box 5403, Brady Station, Little Rock AR 72215.

Growing Concern for "At-Risk" Students

Within the past decade, various studies are pointing out that the United States faces an economic crisis. In the next century we will not have the educated workforce that we need in order to compete in the world. The reason is clear: A high percentage of our students are dropping out of school long before graduating from high school. Instead of a trained workforce, we will have a welfare-dependent segment of society that does not contribute to the nation's economy. Instead of contributing to society, these uneducated young people will drain the national income.

School districts and whole communities are addressing the problem of these "at-risk" students. This group includes the hundreds of thousands of young girls who become pregnant each year, the young adolescents on the streets involved in drugs and crime, and the little children who come into our schools with limited knowledge and experience. Multicultural education, with its emphasis on empathy, offers a hope of reaching the "at-risk" students before they drop out of school and out of mainstream society.

You may wish to explore this topic further in these resources:

Dianne Appleman and Johanna McClear. *Teacher, the Children Are Here.* Scott, Foresman, 1988.

Association for Supervision and Curriculum Development, 125 N. West St.,

Alexandria VA 22314. Audiocassette series; 5 tapes by educators from large urban school districts describe how they are handling this problem.

James S. Coleman. "Families and Schools." *Educational Researcher* (August/September 1987): 32–38.

Issues of *Educational Leadership,* February and March 1989.

Michael Harrington. *Who Are the Poor? A Profile of the Changing Faces of Poverty in the United States.* Justice for All, 1987.

U. S. Dept. of Labor. *Workforce 2000: Work and Workers for the 21st Century.* The Dept., 1987.

Issue of *Update,* March 1988.

Affirmative Action Efforts

Attempts to avoid discrimination based on race, ethnic background, gender, or age fit with the aims of multicultural education.

All employers are carefully avoiding discriminatory practices. They frequently collect data from potential employees using forms that begin with statements that usually read something like this:

> This university does not discriminate on the basis of race, color, national origin, religion, sex, or handicap in any of its policies, procedures, or practices. Nor does the university discriminate against any employees or applicants for employment on the basis of their age or because they are disabled veterans or veterans of the Vietnam Era, or because of their medical condition, their ancestry, or their marital status; nor does the university discriminate on the basis of citizenship, within the limits imposed by law or university policy. This nondiscrimination policy covers admission, access, and treatment in university programs and activities, and application for and treatment in university employment.

Voluntary information is requested from applicants for positions regarding sex, disability, and veteran status. Applicants are asked to identify their membership in one of the following groups:

Black/Afro-American
Chinese/Chinese American
Japanese/Japanese American
Pakistani/East Indian
Filipino/Philipino
Other Asian
American Indian/Native American
Latin American/Latino
Mexican/Mexican American/Chicano
Other Spanish/Spanish American
White

A shorter list includes:

White (Non-Hispanic)
Asian or Pacific Island
Black (Non-Hispanic)
American Indian or Alaskan Native
Hispanic

Such efforts demonstrate an awareness at the national level of the need to provide equity for all citizens.

You may wish to explore this topic further in the following resources:

C. J. Andersen, comp. *A Fact Book on Higher Education.* American Council on Education, 1986.

Carnegie Forum on Education and the Economy: Task Force on Teaching as a Profession. *A Nation Prepared: Teachers for the 21st Century.* The Carnegie Foundation, 1986.

National Commission on Excellence in Education. *A Nation at Risk: The Imperative for Educational Reform.* Department of Education, 1983.

National Education Association. *Teacher Supply and Demand.* NEA, 1986.

M. Trow. "Aspects of Diversity in American Higher Education," in *On the Making of Americans,* edited by H. Gans. University of Pennsylvania, 1979.

"Statistics You Can Use: Growth in Nontraditional Students, 1972–1982." *Higher Education and National Affairs,* June 18, 1984, p. 3.

Internationalization of Education

An executive speaking for the International Division of a large conglomerate includes the following among the projected corporate needs for the year 2000:

Employees who are not predominantly ethnocentric in their view of the world.

People who are able to work and live abroad effectively, who are comfortable with expatriation and repatriation and have the potential for linguistic success for studying foreign languages.

Employees who understand that the United States is competing on an even playing field in the next century . . . that the competition is as good as, often better than, that offered by U. S. organizations.

Employees who are willing to take risks – to try and maybe have setbacks, but who can get up, learn from adversity and try again. . . .

Employees who do not rely on English only sources of information. . . .[9]

This statement supports the need for educating students to live in a multicultural world. It extends the empathy we are trying to achieve among persons living in the United States to the global village that we share. Children who are brought up with limited perspectives of the world will be handicapped, unable to move beyond the narrow environs in which they were raised.

You may want to explore this topic further in the following:

Paulo Freire and Donaldo Macedo. *Literacy: Reading the Word and the World.* Bergin and Garvey, 1987.

June Jordan. *On Call: Political Essays.* South End Press, 1987.

M. Trow. "Comparative Reflections on Leadership in Higher Education." *Journal of Education* 20: 143–59.

M. Tsukada. "A Factual Overview of Education in Japan and the United States" in *Educational Policies in Crisis: Japanese and American Perspectives,* ed. by W. K. Cummings et al Praeger, 1986.

Summary

As we consider multicultural education, it is important to note progressive thinking and practices that stand out as exemplary. Across the country, teachers and school districts are making sincere efforts to reach multicultural goals from different perspectives. Grounded in self-esteem for all students and leading to understanding of others, these programs may address the needs of preschoolers or adolescent "at risk" students; they may be directed toward preparing the teacher; or they may deal directly with selection of content and methods of delivering the curriculum. Increasing support can be identified for multicultural education.

REFLECTIONS

As we reflect together on multicultural education, it might be well to remember the words of Kahlil Gibran in *The Prophet:*

> The teacher gives not of his wisdom,
> But rather of his faith and lovingness.

In designing and delivering a multicultural curriculum, we are concerned, of course, about content, but we are even more concerned about the young human beings who are molded by the school. As we coach them through our various courses, what are we teaching them? Are we teaching them the most important concepts that will guide them to lead inspired, stimulating lives? Do we have the courage to select what we truly believe is essential and dare to delete from our curriculum that which is trivial? As authors, we can only conclude: The choice is up to you. It always will be.

APPLICATIONS

1. Begin a clipping file of multicultural issues that appear in your local newspaper for a period of at least a month. Write a summary statement about multicultural concerns in your local area; these may reflect national or worldwide concerns.

2. Focus on one of the obstacles to the implementation of multicultural education enumerated in this chapter. Discuss this problem in a cooperative learning group. Share your group's thinking with the full class.

3. Begin interviewing local educators to identify exemplary practices related to multicultural education at any level. Write a review of this idea or program and attempt to obtain newspaper coverage for outstanding instructional practices.

4. Write a letter to the editor of your local newspaper. Point out the accomplishments of one minority group in your community.

Endnotes

1. John Dewey. *The School and Society.* University of Chicago, 1900.
2. National Council for Accreditation of Teacher Education. *Standards, Procedures, and Policies for the Accreditation of Professional Teacher Education Units.* NCATE, 1987.
3. William Bennett. *James Madison Elementary School: A Curriculum for American Students.* U.S. Government Printing Office, 1988.
4. Florence Heide. *Sound of Sunshine; Sound of Rain.* Parents, 1970.
5. Arthur Combs. Chair of the Committee, ASCD Yearbook, *Perceiving, Behaving, Becoming.* ASCD, 1962. Mario Fantini and Gerald Weinstein. *The Disadvantaged.* Harper, 1968. William Glasser. *Schools without Failure.* Harper, 1969.
6. Benjamin Bloom. *All Our Children Learning: A Primer for Parents, Teachers and Cther Educators.* McGraw, 1981.
7. James Moffett. *Student-Centered Language Arts and Reading Curriculum, K–13.* Houghton Mifflin, 1976.
8. The Bradley Commission. *Reforming the History Curriculum.* The Commission, 1989.
9. Michael Copeland. International Divisions, Procter & Gamble Company. Letter to Dr. Leon Boothe, President, Northern Kentucky University.

APPENDIX

A Literature Base for Multicultural Education

As you work with information presented in the ten chapters of *Multicultural Teaching,* you will find these extensive lists of books helpful as you develop units of study.

After you have completed this textbook, the lists will prove invaluable to you to support your teaching in any K–12 classroom.

EXTENDING YOUR RESOURCES

Using this well-organized basic list of resources, you will want to continue expanding the list in areas that particularly interest you. For example, if you plan a broad study of Japan and Japanese Americans, you will want to explore *Japanese Education Today,* a 1987 publication from the U.S. Department of Education. Each new publication that you locate will refer you to other resources to extend your knowledge.

MULTICULTURAL UNDERSTANDINGS: INTERGROUP RELATIONS, ETHNIC STUDIES, GLOBAL EDUCATION

The books listed here will extend your knowledge and understanding about the diverse cultures and groups that make up the population of the United States. At the same time, you will become aware of the universal concerns that transcend national borders. Multicultural education begins with a study of the individual and expands to a study of the world and its interdependent peoples.

James A. Banks. *Multiethnic Education: Theory and Practice.* 2nd ed. Allyn and Bacon, 1988.

James A. Banks. *Teaching Strategies for Ethnic Studies.* 4th ed. Allyn and Bacon, 1987. A good overview with many suggestions for the adult reader; suggests books that will provide information about specific ethnic groups.

Christine Bennett. *Comprehensive Multicultural Education: Theory and Practice.* Allyn and Bacon, 1986.

Francelia Butler and Richard W. Rotert. *The Triumph of the Spirit in Children's Literature.* Shoestring, 1986.

California State Dept. of Education. *Studies of Immersion Education: A Collection for U.S. Educators.* The Department, 1984.

Robert A. Carlson. *The Quest for Conformity: Americanization Through Education.* Wiley, 1975. Explains hostility toward nonconformity; gives historical perspective.

Ruth Kearney Carlson. *Emerging Humanity; Multi-Ethnic Literature for Children and Adolescents.* Brown, 1972. Describes values and criteria for multiethnic literature; suggestions for use.

H. T. Collins and S. B. Zakariya, eds. *Getting Started in Global Education.* NAESP, 1982. Good overview of this viewpoint.

Arthur Combs. *A Personal Approach to Teaching: Beliefs that Make a Difference.* Allyn and Bacon, 1982.

Francesco Cordasco, ed. *American Ethnic Groups: The European Heritage.* Arno, 1980.

CIBC. *Violence, the Ku Klux Klan and the Struggle for Equality.* Council on Interracial Books for Children, 1981. Information specific to this group and racism, with ideas for giving students an educated viewpoint.

CIBC Racism and Sexism Resource Center for Educators. *Human and Anti-Human Values in Children's Books: Guidelines for the Future.* The Council, 1976. Analyzes over 200 books and explores "hidden messages" transmitted to young readers.

Nina Gabelko and John Michaelis. *Reducing Adolescent Prejudice: A Handbook.* Teachers College, 1981.

Patrick Gallo, Jr. *Old Bread, New Wine: A Portrait of the Italian Americans.* Nelson, 1981.

Ricardo J. Garcia. *Education for Cultural Pluralism: Global Roots Stew.* Phi Delta Kappa, 1981.

_____. *Fostering a Pluralistic Society through Multi-Ethnic Education.* Phi Delta Kappa, 1978.

_____. *Teaching in a Pluralistic Society: Concepts, Models, Strategies.* Harper, 1982.

William Goodykoontz, ed. *Prejudice; The Invisible Wall.* Scholastic, 1968.

Andrew Greeley. *The Irish Americans: The Rise to Money and Power.* Harper, 1981.

Maxine Dunfee and Claudia Crump. *Teaching for Social Values in Social Studies.* Association for Childhood Education International, 1974.

Jack D. Forbes. *The Education of the Culturally Different: A Multi-Cultural Approach.* Far West Laboratory for Educational Research and Development, 1969. Explains educational disadvantages of monocultural orientation.

Merrill Harmin, Howard Kirschenbaum, and Sidney B. Simon. *Clarifying Values through Subject Matter: Applications for the Classroom.* Winston, 1973.

Robert C. Hawley and Isabel L. Hawley. *Human Values in the Classroom.* Hart, 1975.

J. Joseph Huthmacher. *A Nation of Newcomers: Ethnic Minority Groups in American History.* Dell, 1981.

R. Johansen. *The National Interest and the Human Interest.* Princeton University Press, 1980.

Charlotte Matthews Keating, comp. *Building Bridges of Understanding.* Palo Verde, 1967. An annotated bibliography of minority groups.

_____. *Building Bridges of Understanding Between Cultures.* Palo Verde, 1971. Annotations are listed by age level in each minority group; companion volume to above listing.

Ernece B. Kelly. *Searching for America. NCTE, 1972.* Contains critiques of twelve English textbooks; provides insights into distortions and exclusions in literature at all levels.

Louis Knowles and Kenneth Prewitt. *Institutional Racism in America.* Prentice, 1969. Explains ideological roots of racism; illustrates perpetuation of institutional racism.

Gil Loescher. *The World's Refugees: A Test of Humanity.* Harcourt, 1982. An overview suitable for older students.

Margaret MacDonald. *The Storyteller's Sourcebook: A Subject, Title, and Motif Index to Folklore Collections for Children.* Neal Shuman, 1982.

Joan Morrison and Charlotte Zabusky. *American Mosaic: The Immigrant Experience in the Words of those Who Lived It.* Dutton, 1981. Oral history.

John Naisbitt. *Megatrends.* Warner, 1984. Exciting ideas about future interdependence of all people.

J. Rosenau. *The Study of Global Interdependence.* Nichols Publishing Co., 1981.

William Ryan. *Blaming the Victim.* Pantheon, 1971. Exposes myths and racism and social science; well written.

Andrew Scott. *The Dynamics of Interdependence.* University of North Carolina Press, 1982.

Steven Steinberg. *The Ethnic Myth: Race, Ethnicity and Class in America.* Atheneum, 1981.

Melvin Steinfield. *Cracks in the Melting Pot: Racism and Discrimination in American History.* Glencoe, 1970. A collection of readings providing insight into racist practices at many levels.

Madelon D. Stent, William R. Hazard, and Harry N. Rivlin. *Cultural Pluralism in Education: A Mandate for Change.* Appleton, 1973. Excellent collection of papers given at a Chicago Conference by prominent educators and leaders from various cultural groups.

Robert W. Terry. *For Whites Only.* Eerdmans, 1970. Good analysis of the processes of racism; strategies for bringing about changes in the society.

Stephen Thernstrom, et al. *Encyclopedia of American Ethnic Groups.* Harvard University Press, 1980.

M. Donald Thomas. *Pluralism Gone Mad.* Phi Delta Kappa. 1981.

Pierre Van den Berghe. *The Ethnic Phenomenon.* Elsevier, 1981.

Eileen Tway, ed. *Reading Ladders for Human Relations.* 6th ed. National Council of Teachers of English, 1981. An outstanding annotated booklist on relevant themes; updated periodically.

David A. Welton and John T. Mallan. *Children and Their World: Teaching Elementary Social Studies.* Rand McNally, 1976.

Background Information about the World

If you are near a large city, visit the embassies of specific countries. If not, you can write on school stationery to request free information.

Africa

Ghana: Press Attaché, Embassy of Ghana, 2460 16th St., NW., Washington, D.C. 20009.

Tunisia: Embassy of Tunisia, 2408 Massachusetts Ave., NW., Washington, D.C. 20008.

Union of South Africa: Information Service of South Africa, 655 Madison Ave., New York, NY 10021.

Asia

Australia: Australian News and Information Bureau, 636 Fifth Ave., New York, NY 10020.

Burma: Embassy of the Union of Burma, 2300 S St., NW., Washington, D.C. 20008.

China: Embassy of the Republic of China, 552 National Press Building, Washington, D.C. 20004.

India: Information Service of India, 2107 Massachusetts Ave., NW., Washington, D.C. 20008.

Indonesia: Embassy of the Republic of Indonesia, 2020 Massachusetts Ave., NW., Washington, D.C. 20006.

Iraq: Embassy of the Republic of Iraq, 1801 P St., NW., Washington, D.C. 20036.

Israel: Consul General of Israel, 105 Montgomery St., San Francisco, CA 94104.

Japan: Information Section, Embassy of Japan, 2514 Massachusetts Ave., NW., Washington, D.C. 20008.

Jordan: Embassy of the Hashemite Kingdom of Jordan, 2319 Wyoming Ave., NW., Washington, D.C. 20008.

Korea: Embassy of Korea, 1145 19th St., NW., Suite 312, Washington, D.C. 20036.

Malaysia: Embassy of Malaysia, 2401 Massachusetts Ave., NW., Washington, D.C. 20008.

New Zealand: New Zealand Embassy, 19 Observatory Circle, NW., Washington, D.C. 20008.

Pakistan: Embassy of Pakistan, 2315 Massachusetts Ave., NW., Washington, D.C. 20008.

Sri Lanka: Embassy of Sri Lanka, 2148 Wyoming Ave., Washington, D.C. 20008.

Turkey: Turkey Tourism & Information Office, 500 5th Ave., New York, NY 10036.

U.S.S.R.: Embassy of the Union of Soviet Socialist Republics, 1706 18th St., NW., Washington, D.C. 20009.

Canada

Write the Canadian Government Travel Bureau, Ottawa, Ontario, Canada K1A OH6.

Alberta: Alberta Government Travel Bureau, 1629 Centennial Building, Edmonton, Alberta, Canada.

British Columbia: Dept. of Travel Industry, Govt. of British Columbia, 1019 Wharf St., Victoria, B.C., Canada V8W 2Z2.

Greater Vancouver Visitors and Convention Bureau, 650 Burrard St., Vancouver, B.C., Canada V6C 2L2.

Manitoba: Manitoba Tourist Branch, Dept. of Tourism and Recreation, Winnipeg 1, Manitoba, Canada.

Yukon: Yukon Tourism, Travel and Information Branch, Govt. of the Yukon, Box 2703, Whitehorse, Yukon, Canada.

Europe

Denmark: Danish Information Office, 280 Park Ave., New York, NY 10017.

Finland: Embassy of Finland, 1900 24th St., NW., Washington, D.C. 20008.

France: French Government Tourist Office, 972 Fifth Ave., New York, NY 10021.

Germany: German Information Center, 410 Park Ave., New York, NY 10022.

Ireland: Irish International Airlines, 564 Fifth Ave., New York, NY 10036.

Italy: Italian Government Travel Office-ENIT, 630 5th Ave., New York, NY 10020.

Netherlands: Royal Netherlands Embassy, 4200 Linnean Ave., NW., Washington, D.C. 20008.

Norway: Norwegian Embassy Information Service, 825 Third Ave., New York, NY 10022.

Portugal: Casa de Portugal, Portuguese National Tourist Office, 570 Fifth Ave., New York, NY 10036.

Spain: Spanish Embassy, Cultural Relations Office, 1629 Columbia Rd., NW., Washington, D.C. 20009.

Switzerland: Swiss National Tourist Office, 661 Market St., San Francisco, CA 94105.

Yugoslavia: Yugoslav State Tourist Office, 509 Madison Ave., New York, NY 10022.

South America

Colombia: Information Services Staff, Foreign Agricultural Information Division, U.S. Dept. of Agriculture.

Ecuador: Embassy of Ecuador, 2535 15th St., NW., Washington, D.C. 20009.

Venezuela: Embassy of Venezuela, Institute of Information and Culture, 2437 California St., NW., Washington, D.C. 20008.

Newsletters and Journals

Each month a number of newsletters and journals report promising practices related to multicultural education. These same periodicals often publish lists of books and other instructional materials of interest to teachers. Request sample copies and information about subscribing to those that have something to offer your staff.

The Booklist and Subscription Books Bulletin: A Guide to Current Books. American Library Association. 60 E. Huron St., Chicago, IL 60611.

Booknotes. World Affairs Council of Northern California, 312 Sutter St., Suite 200, San Francisco, CA 94108.

The Bulletin. Council in Interracial Books, CIBC Resource Center, Room 300, 1841 Broadway, New York, NY 10023.

Bulletin of the Center for Children's Books. University of Chicago Press, Box 37005, Chicago, IL 60637. Reviews new books and makes recommendations about purchasing; includes those you should not purchase.

Canadian Ethnic Studies. The University of Calgary, Calgary, Alberta, Canada.

Civil Rights Digest. United States Commission on Civil Rights, 1121 Vermont Avenue, NW, Washington, D.C. 20425.

Colloquy. School Program, World Affairs Council, 312 Sutter St., San Francisco, CA 94108. Excellent source of up-to-date information and publication lists.

Education and Society. Anti-Defamation League, 823 United Nations Plaza, New York, NY 10017.

Explorations in Ethnic Studies. Journal of the National Assn. of Interdisciplinary Ethnic Studies, California State Polytechnic University, 3801 W. Temple Ave., Pomona, CA 91768.

The Horn Book Magazine. Park Square Bld., Boston, MA 02116. Good articles; lists information about new books and authors.

Integrated education. Integrated Education Associates, School of Education, University of Massachusetts, Amherst, MA 01003.

Journal of Comparative Cultures. National Bilingual Education Assn., 9332 Vista Bonita, Cypress, CA 90630.

Journal of Ethnic Studies. Western Washington State University, Bellingham, WA 98225.

Journal of the National Association for Bilingual Education. 1201 16th St., NW., Washington, D.C. 20036.

Kirkus Reviews. 200 Park Ave. S, New York, NY 10003. (Bimonthly.)

Language Arts (with membership in NCTE). 1111 Kenyon Rd., Urbana, IL 61801. Articles on all aspects of language instruction; reviews books for children and professional materials; often features authors with full-page photo.

Melus: The Multi-Ethnic Literature of the United States. Dept. of English, University of Southern California, Los Angeles, CA 90007.

NABE: Journal of National Association of Bilingual Educators. Alma Flor Ada, ed. Los Angeles Publishing Co., 40–22 23rd St., Long Island City, New York, NY 11101. Subscription free with membership, quarterly publication.

The Negro Educational Review. Box 2895, General Mail Center, Jacksonville, FL 32203.

New York Times Book Review. 229 W. 43rd St., New York, NY 10036.

School Library Journal. 1180 Avenue of the Americas, New York, NY 10036.

Social Education. National Council for the Social Studies, 3501 Newark St., NW., Washington, D.C. 20016.

TESOL Newsletter; TESOL Quarterly. Teachers of English to Speakers of Other Languages, 455 Nevits, Georgetown University, Washington, D.C. 20057.

STUDYING SPECIFIC GROUPS

As we work with students in the classroom, we can develop units of study focused on one specific group. At that time students can read fiction and nonfiction to learn more about one part of our American culture.

Included here are lists of books for adults, information for students, bibliographies of available materials, and sources of additional up-to-date information and resources. Although these lists are not exhaustive, they do provide titles to get you started. Always consult your local librarians and the library card catalog to locate other materials. Also refer to such reference tools as *Children's Catalog, The High School Catalog, Education Index,* and *Reader's Guide to Periodical Literature* (all published by Wilson Publishing Company) to continue locating new books and articles that may help you.

Exploring the Backgrounds of Asian Americans

In this section we explore books and resources that provide information about Americans who have Chinese, Japanese, Korean, or Vietnamese backgrounds.

General Information

Frank Chin, et al., *Aiiieeeee! An Anthology of Asian-American Writers.* Howard University, 1974.

Russell Endo, et al. *Asian-Americans: Psychological Perspectives.* Science and Behavior Books, 1980.

Brett Melendy. *Asians in America: Filipines, Koreans, and East Indians.* Twayne, 1977.

Don Nasanishi, ed. *Asians and the American Educational Process.* Oryx Press, 1982.

Franklin Odo. *In Movement: A Pictorial History of Asian America.* Visual Communications, 1977.

Linda Perrin. *Coming to America.* Delacorte, 1980.

Amy Tachiki, et al., eds. *Roots: An Asian American Reader.* University of California at Los Angeles, 1971.

Periodicals

Amerasia Journal (irregular). Asian American Studies Center, 3232 Campbell Hall, UCLA, Los Angeles, CA 90024.

Asian American Review (irregular). Asian American Studies, 3407 Dwinelle Hall, Berkeley, CA 94720.

Bridge: An Asian American Perspective (quarterly). Box 477, Canal Station, New York, NY 10013.

Bulletin of Concerned Asian Scholars (quarterly). Box W, Charlemont, MA 01339.

Intercom (3–5 times a year). The Center for War/Peace Studies, 218 E. 18th St., New York, NY 10003. Articles on issues, resources, and guides for teachers on subjects related to Asia.

Additional Sources

Asia Society. 725 Park Avenue, New York, NY 10021.

Asian Writers' Project/Asian Media Project. *Soujourner.* Berkeley Unified School District.

Unicef. *Children of Asia.* 331 E. 38th St., New York, NY 10016.

Visual Communications. Asian American Studies Central, 1601 Griffith Park Blvd., Los Angeles, CA 90026.

Exploring the Backgrounds of Chinese Americans

General Resources

China Books & Periodicals, Inc. 2929 Twenty-Fourth Street, San Francisco, CA 94110. (Subscriptions to magazines published in China; English language).

China International Travel Service. 6 East Chang'an Avenue, Beijing, People's Republic of China.

The China Project (SPICE). Hoover Bldg., Rm. 200, Stanford University, Stanford, CA 94305.

East/West: The Chinese American Journal (weekly). 838 Grant Avenue, Suite 307, San Francisco, CA 94108.

U.S.-China Peoples Friendship Association. 50 Oak Street, San Francisco, CA 94102.

Bibliographies

Books for the Chinese-American Child; A Selected List. Comp. by Cecelia Mei-Chi Chen. Cooperative Children's Book Center, 1969. A list of books included for their literary quality and honesty.

The Chinese in Children's Books. Prepared by Anna Au Long et al. New York Public Library, 1973.

Arlene Posner and Arene J. deKeijzer, eds. *China: A Resource and Curriculum Guide.* University of Chicago Press, 1972. An annotated guide to books about China. Includes films, slides, tapes, records, periodicals, and organizations.

Teaching Materials

Center for Teaching about China. 407 So. Dearborn St., Suite 945, Chicago IL 60605.

The China Project. Hoover Bldg., Stanford University, Stanford, CA 94305.

Don Wong and Irene Collier. *Chinese Americans Past and Present: A Collection of Readings and Learning Activities.* Association of Chinese Teachers, San Francisco, 1977.

Ed Young and Hilary Beckett. *The Rooster's Horns.* World, 1978. (Directions for producing a puppet play.)

Fiction

Maxine Hong Kingston. *China Men.* Ballantine Books, 1980.

_____. *The Woman Warrior: Memoirs of a Girlhood among Ghosts.* Vintage, 1976.

Books for Students

You will also learn much by reading the books students read.

Fiction

Eve Bunting. *The Happy Funeral.* Harper, 1982.

Kathleen Chang. *The Iron Moonhunter.* Children's Book Press, 1977.

A.B. Chrisman. *Shen of the Sea: Chinese Stories for Children.* Dutton, 1968. Short stories.

M. DeJong. *The House of Sixty Fathers.* Harper & Row, 1956.

Demi. *Liang and the Magic Paintbrush.* Holt, 1980.

Eleanor Estes. *The Lost Umbrella of Kim Chu.* Atheneum, 1979.

M. Flack and K. Wiese. *The Story of Ping, A Duck Who Lived on a Houseboat on the Yangtze River*. Viking, 1933.

Julianna Foget. *Wesley Paul, Marathon Runner*. Lippincott, 1979.

Ina R. Friedman. *How My Parents Learned to Eat*. Houghton-Mifflin, 1984.

*T. Handforth. *Mei Li*. Doubleday, 1938.

*E. Lattimore. *Little Pear, The Story of a Little Chinese Boy*. Harcourt Brace Jovanovich, 1931.

E. Lewis. *Young Fu of the Upper Yangtze*. Rev. ed. Holt, Rinehart and Winston, 1973.

Bette Bao Lord. *In the Year of the Boar and Jackie Robinson*. Harper, 1984.

R. L. McCune. *Pie-Biter*. Design Enterprises of San Francisco, 1983.

J. Merrill. *The Superlative Horse*. Young Scott Books, 1961.

Manus Pinkwater. *Wingman*. Dodd, 1975.

Leo Politi. *Mr. Fong's Shop*. Scribner, 1979.

A. Ritchie. *The Treasure of Li-Po*. Harcourt Brace Jovanovich, 1949. Short stories.

C. Treffinger. *Li Lun, Lad of Courage*. Abingdon, 1947.

Jay Williams. *Everyone Knows What a Dragon Looks Like*. Four Winds, 1976.

Jade Snow Wong. *Fifth Chinese Daughter*. Harper, 1945.

Laurence Yep. *Dragonwings*. Harper, 1977.

_____. *Child of the Owl*. Harper, 1977.

_____. *Sea Glass*. Harper, 1979.

Jane Yolen. *The Seeing Stick*. Crowell, 1977.

Nonfiction

Gwenn Boardman. *Across the Bridge to China*. Nelson, 1979.

Jack Chen. *The Chinese of America*. New York: Harper and Row, 1980.

*Hou-tien Cheng. *The Chinese New Year*. Holt, 1976.

Frank Chin. *The Chicken Coop Chinaman: The Year of the Dragon: Two Plays*. University of Washington, 1981.

Laverne Mau Dicker. *The Chinese in San Francisco: A Pictoral History*. Dover, 1979.

Dorothy Dowdell. *The Chinese Helped Build America*. Messner, 1972.

Leonard Fisher. *The Great Wall of China*. Macmillan, 1986.

_____. *China Homecoming*. Putnam, 1985.

Jean Fritz. *Homesick: My Own Story*. Putnam, 1982.

Clarence Glick. *Sojourners and Settlers*. University of Hawaii, 1980.

Noel Gray. *Looking at China*. Lippincott, 1975.

Corrine Hoexter. *From Canton to California*. Four Winds, 1976.

Ellen Hsiao. *A Chinese Year*. Evans, 1970.

Claire Jones. *The Chinese in America*. Lerner, 1972.

*Suitable for primary grades.

Stanford Lyman. *Chinese Americans*. Random, 1974.

Pat Mauser. *A Bundle of Sticks*. Atheneum, 1982.

Ruthanne Lum McCunn. *An Illustrated History of the Chinese in America*. Design Enterprises of San Francisco, 1979.

Milton Meltzer. *The Chinese Americans*. Crowell, 1980.

Joe Molnar. *A Chinese-American Child Tells His Story*. Watts, 1973.

Victor Nee and Brett D. Nee, eds. *Longtime Californians: A Documentary Study of an American Chinatown*. Pantheon, 1972.

Margaret Rau. *Our World: The People's Republic of China*. Messner, 1974.

_____. *The People of New China*. Messner, 1978.

Seymour Reit. *Rice Cakes and Paper Dragons*. Dodd, 1973.

J. R. Roberson. *China from Manchu to Mao*. Atheneum, 1980.

M. Sasek. *This Is Hong Kong*. Macmillan, 1965.

Ruth Sidel. *Revolutionary China: People, Politics, and Ping-Pong*. Delacorte, 1974.

Cornelia Spencer. *The Yangtze, China's River Highway*. Garrard, 1963.

Stan Steiner. *Fusang: The Chinese Who Built America*. Harper, 1979.

Betty Lee Sung. *An Album of Chinese Americans*. Watts, 1977.

_____. *The Chinese in America*. Macmillan, 1972.

Kurt Wiese. *You Can Write Chinese*. Viking, 1945.

Ed Young. *High on a Hill: A Book of Chinese Riddles*. World, 1980.

Folklore

*Claire Bishop. *The Five Chinese Brothers*. Coward, 1938.

Frances Carpenter. *Tales of a Chinese Grandmother*. Doubleday, 1937.

Hou-tien Cheng. *Six Chinese Brothers*. Holt, 1979.

Dorothy Hoge. *The Black Heart of Indri*. Scribner, 1966.

Lotta Hume. *Favorite Children's Stories from China and Tibet*. Tuttle, 1962.

Carol Kendall and Yao-wen Li. *Sweet and Sour: Tales from China*. Seabury, 1982.

Jeanne Lee. *Legend of the Li River*. Holt, 1983.

_____. *Legend of the Milky Way*. Holt, 1982.

_____. *Toad Is the Uncle of Heaven*. Holt, 1985.

Adet Lin. *The Milky Way and Other Chinese Folk Tales*. Harcourt, 1961.

Ai-Ling Louie. *Yeh-Shen: A Cinderella Story from China*. Philomel, 1982.

Arlene Mosel. *Tikki Tikki Tembo*. Holt, 1968. (Illustrated by Blair Lent; film from Weston Woods.)

Neil Philip, ed. *The Spring of Butterflies and Other Folktales of China's Minority Peoples*. Lothrop, 1986.

Catherine Sadler. *Treasure Mountain: Folktales from Southern China*. Atheneum, 1982.

*Suitable for primary grades.

Diane Wolkstein. *White Wave: A Chinese Tale.* Crowell, 1982.

*Jane Yolen. *The Emperor and the Kite.* World, 1957.

Ed Young. *The Terrible Nung Gwama: A Chinese Tale.* Philomel, 1978.

Nathan Zimelman. *I Will Tell You of Peach Stone.* Lothrop, 1976.

Feenie Ziner. *Cricket Boy: A Chinese Tale Retold.* Doubleday, 1977.

Exploring the Backgrounds of Japanese Americans

General Resources

Japan Chronicle. The Pacific and Asian Affairs Council, Pacific House, 2004 University Ave., Honolulu, HI 96822.

Japan External Trade Organization (JETRO). 360 Post St., Suite 501, San Francisco, CA 94108.

Japan Information Service, 1737 Post St., Suites 4–5, San Francisco, CA 94115.

Japanese American Citizenship League. 224 So. San Pedro St., Room 506, Los Angeles, CA 90012.

Japanese American Curriculum Project. Box 367, San Mateo, CA 94401.

Nichi Bei Times (daily). 2211 Bush St., San Francisco, CA 94119 (in Japanese and English).

Social Studies Development Center. Indiana University, 2805 E. 10th St., Bloomington, IN 47405.

Stanford Program on International and Cross-Cultural Education: The Japan Project. Stanford University, Stanford, CA 94305.

Books for Adults

Frank Gibney. *Japan: The Fragile Superpower.* New American Library, 1985.

Akemi Kikumura. *Through Harsh Winters; The Life of a Japanese Immigrant Woman.* Chandler, 1981.

Harry Kitano. *Japanese Americans: The Evolution of a Subculture.* Prentice-Hall, 1976.

Joy Kogawa. *Obasan: A Novel.* Godine, 1982.

Gene Levine and Robert Rhodes. *The Japanese American Community: A Three-Generation Study.* Praeger, 1981.

Edwin Reishauer. *The Japanese.* Harvard, 1977.

Thomas Rohlen. *Japan's High Schools.* University of California, 1983.

Jared Taylor. *Shadows of the Rising Sun.* Morrow, 1983.

United States Department of Education. *Japanese Education Today.* U.S. Government Printing Office, 1987.

Robert Wilson and Bill Hosokawa. *East to Africa: A History of the Japanese in the United States.* Morrow, 1980.

*Suitable for primary grades.

Books for Students

Fiction

P. Buck. *The Big Wave*. Day, 1948 (new edition 1973).

Miriam Chaikin. *Yossi Asks the Angels for Help*. Harper, 1985.

E. Coatsworth. *The Cat Who Went to Heaven*. Macmillan, 1958.

*L. Hawkinson. *Dance, Dance Amy-Chan!* Whitman, 1964.

Hadley Irwin. *Kim/Kimi*. Macmillan, 1987.

Tetsuko Kuroyanagi. *Totto-Chan*. Harper, 1982.

*B. J. Lifton. *The Cock and the Ghost Cat*. Atheneum, 1965.

*_____. *The Dwarf Pin Tree*. Atheneum, 1963.

*Matsuno, M. *A Pair of Red Clogs*. Collins, 1963.

S. J. Myers. *The Enchanted Sticks*. Coward, 1979.

Katherine Paterson. *The Master Puppeteer*. Crowell, 1976.

_____. *Of Nightingales That Weep*. Crowell, 1974.

*Leo Politi. *Mieko*. Golden Gates, 1969.

Allen Say. *The Inn-keeper's Apprentice*. Harper, 1982.

*Yoshiko Uchida. *The Birthday Visitor*. Scribner's, 1975.

_____. *The Best Bad Thing*. Atheneum, 1983.

_____. *The Forever Christmas Tree*. Scribner's, 1963.

_____. *The Happiest Ending*. Atheneum, 1985.

_____. *Journey Home*. Atheneum, 1978.

_____. *Journey to Topaz*. Schribner's, 1971.

_____. *The Promised Year*. Harcourt, 1959.

_____. *The Rooster Who Understood Japanese*. Scribner's, 1976.

_____. *Samurai of Gold Hill*. Scribner's, 1972.

_____. *Sumi & the Goat & the Tokyo Express*. Scribner's, 1969.

_____. *Sumi's Prize*. Scribner's, 1964.

Yoko Kawashima Watkins. *So Far From the Bamboo Grove*. Lothrop, 1986.

Taro Yashima. *Crow Boy*. Viking, 1955.

_____. *The Golden Footprints*. World, 1960.

_____. *A Jar of Dreams*. Atheneum, 1981.

_____. *Seashore Story*. Viking, 1967.

_____. *Umbrella*. Viking, 1958.

Nonfiction

Gwynneth Ashby. *Looking at Japan*. Lippincott, 1969.

*Edith Battles. *What Does the Rooster Say, Yoshio?* Whitman, 1978.

*Suitable for primary grades.

Gwenn Boardman. *Living in Tokyo.* Nelson, 1970.

Maisie Conrat and Richard Conrat. *Executive Order 9066: The Internment of 110,000 Japanese Americans.* California Historical Society, 1972.

Jane Dallinger. *Swallowtail Butterflies.* Lerner, 1983 (originally published in Japan).

Daniel Davis. *Behind Barbed Wire.* Dutton, 1982.

Dorothy Dowdell. *The Japanese Helped Build America.* Messner, 1970.

Sam Epstein. *A Year of Japanese Festivals.* Garrard, 1974.

Budd Fukei. *The Japanese American Story.* Dillon, 1976.

Jane Goodsell. *Daniel Inouye.* Crowell, 1977.

Jeanne Wakatsuki Houston and James Houston. *Farewell to Manzanar.* Houghton Mifflin, 1973.

Estelle Ishigo. *Lone Heart Mountain.* Japanese American Curriculum Project.

Takeo Kaneshiro. *Internees War Relocation Center Memoirs and Diaries.* Vantage Press, 1976.

Noel Leathers. *The Japanese in America.* Lerner, 1967.

Toshi Maruki. *Hiroshima No Pika.* Lothrop, 1982.

Robert Masters. *Japan in Pictures.* Sterling, 1978.

Dennis Ogawa. *Jan Ken Po.* Japanese American Research Center, 1973.

Allen Say. *The Bicycle Man.* Parnassus, 1982.

Shizuye Takashima. *A Child in Prison Camp.* Tundra Brooks, 1971.

Tobi Tobias. *Isamu Noguchi: The Life of a Sculptor.* Crowell, 1974.

Josephine B. Vaughan. *The Land and People of Japan.* Lippincott, 1972.

*Taro Yashima. *The Village Tree.* Viking, 1953.

Folklore

Joanne Algarin. *Japanese Folk Literature: A Core Collection and Reference Guide.* Bowker, 1982.

Virginia Haviland. *Favorite Fairy Tales Told in Japan.* Little, 1967.

Margaret Hodges. *The Wave.* Houghton, 1964.

Jane Hori Ike. *The Japanese Fairy Tale.* Warne, 1982.

Nancy Luenn. *The Dragon Kite.* Harcourt, 1982.

Gerald McDermott. *The Stonecutter.* Viking, 1975.

Arlene Mosel. *The Funny Little Woman.* Dutton, 1972.

Patricia Newton. *The Five Sparrows.* Atheneum, 1982.

*Michelle Nikly. *The Emperor's Plum Tree.* Greenwillow, 1982.

Florence Sakade, ed. *Japanese Children's Favorite Stories.* Tuttle, 1958.

*Allen Say. *The Bicycle Man.* Houghton, 1982.

_____. *Once under the Cherry Blossom Tree.* Harper, 1974.

Yoshiko Uchida. *The Magic Listening Cap.* Harcourt, 1955.

*Suitable for primary grades.

Elizabeth Winthrop. *Journey to the Bright Kingdom*. Holiday, 1979.

*Taro Yashima. *Seashore Story*. Viking, 1967.

Kaethe Zemach. *The Beautiful Rat*. Four Winds, 1979.

Poetry

Virginia Olsen Baron, ed. *The Seasons of Time; Tanka Poetry of Ancient Japan*. Dial, 1968.

Harry Behn, comp. *Cricket Songs; Japanese Haiku*. Harcourt Brace Jovanovich, 1964.

_____. *More Cricket Songs; Japanese Haiku*. Harcourt Brace Jovanovich, 1971.

Sylvia Cassedy, comp. *Birds, Frogs, and Moonlight: Haiku*. Doubleday, 1967.

Richard Lewis, ed. *In A Spring Garden*. Dial, 1965. (Also on film; Weston Woods.)

_____. *The Moment of Wonder; A Collection of Chinese and Japanese Poetry*. Dial, 1964.

Exploring the Backgrounds of Korean Americans

General Information

Bong-youn Choy. *Koreans in America*. Nelson-Hall, 1979.

H. Brett Melendy. *Asians in America: Filipinos, Koreans, and East Indians*. Twayne. 1977.

Books for Students

Fiction

Elisabet McHugh. *Raising a Mother Isn't Easy*. Greenwillow, 1983.

Yoko Kawashima Watkins. *So Far from the Bamboo Grove*. Lothrop, 1986.

Nonfiction

Gene Gurney, *North & South Korea*. Watts, 1973.

Sylvia McNair. *Korea*. Children's Press, 1986.

Wayne Patterson. *The Koreans in America*. Lerner, 1977.

S.E. Solberg. *The Land and People of Korea*. Lippincott, 1973.

Folklore

So-un Kim. *The Story Bag: A Collection of Korean Folktales*. Tuttle, 1955.

Kathleen Seros. *Sun and Moon: Fairy Tales from Korea*. Holly, 1982.

Exploring the Backgrounds of Filipino Americans

This group is placed in the Asian-American section because of the location of the Philippines and because varied languages (Spanish is only one) are spoken by Filipinos.

*Suitable for primary grades.

General Information

Periodicals

Filipino American Herald (monthly). 508 Maynard Avenue, Seattle, WA 98108.

Philippines Mail. Filipino American Media of California, Box 1783, Salinas, CA 93901.

Adult Books

Carlos Bulosan. *America Is in the Heart.* University of Washington, 1973.

Hyung-chan Kim and Cynthia Mejia, eds. *The Filipinos in America.* Oceana Publications, 1976.

Teresita Laygo, ed. *Well of Time: Eighteen Short Stories from Philippine Contemporary Literature.* American Bilingual Center, 1977.

Alfredo Muñoz. *The Filipinos in America.* Mountainview Press, 1971.

Luís Teodoro. *Out of This Struggle: The Filipinos in Hawaii, 1906–1981.* The University of Hawaii, 1981.

Books for Students

Fiction

*Janet Bartosiak. *A Dog for Ramón.* Dial, 1966.

Carolos Bulosan. *The Laughter of My Father.* Harcourt, 1942.

Al Robles. *Looking for Ifugao Mountain.* Children's Book Press, 1977.

Nonfiction

Manuel Buaken. *I Have Lived with the American People.* Caxton, 1948.

John Nance. *The Land and People of the Philippines.* Lippincott, 1977.

Luis Taruc. *Born of the People.* International Publishers, 1953.

Folklore

Jose Aruego. *A Crocodile's Tale: A Philippine Folk Story.* Scholastic, 1975.

Elizabeth Sechrist. *Once in the First Times; Folk Tales from the Philippines.* Macrae, 1969.

Exploring the Backgrounds of Black Americans

General Information

James Banks and Cherry Banks. *March Toward Freedom: A History of Black Americans.* Fearon, 1978.

John H. Franklin. *From Slavery to Freedom: A History of Black Americans.* Vintage, 1980.

Alex Haley. *Roots: The Saga of an American Family.* Doubleday, 1976.

*Suitable for primary grades.

Vincent Harding. *There Is a River: The Black Struggle for Freedom in America*. Harcourt, 1981.

W. A. Low and Virgil Clift, eds. *Encyclopedia of Black America*. McGraw-Hill, 1981.

Nelson Mandela. *The Struggle Is My Life*. Pathfinder, 1986.

William Nelson and Charles Henry, eds. *Black Studies*. Ohio State, 1982.

Rudine Sims. *Shadow and Substance: Afro-American Experience in Contemporary Children's Fiction*. National Council of Teachers of Engish, 1982.

Geneva Smitherman. *Talkin and Testifyin: The Language of Black America*. Houghton Mifflin, 1977.

Dorothy Strickland. *Listen Children: An Anthology of Black Literature*. Bantam, 1982.

Periodicals

Africana Library Journal: A Quarterly Bibliography and Resource Guide. 101 Fifth Ave., New York, NY 10003. Evaluations of books on Africa published throughout the world; current bibliographies, information on African writers and scholars; children's books and AV materials, adult books.

The Black Scholar, P.O. Box 908, Sausalito, CA 94965. Highly influential black-oriented publication; contains valuable book review section.

Crisis. Organ of the National Association for the Advancement of Colored People. The Crisis Publishing Co., 1790 Broadway, New York, NY 10019.

Ebony. Johnson Publishing Co., 1820 S. Michigan Ave., Chicago, IL 60616.

Freedomways. Quarterly Review of the Negro Freedom Movement. Freedomway Associates, 799 Broadway, New York, NY 10013.

Jet. Johnson Publishing Co., 1820 S. Michigan Ave., Chicago, IL 60616.

Journal of Black Studies. 275 S. Beverly Dr., Beverly Hills, CA 90210.

The Journal of Negro History. Published quarterly by the Association for the Study of Negro Life and History, 1538 Ninth Street, NW., Washington, D.C. Contains scholarly articles on Negro culture and history, book reviews, important documents.

Negro-American Literature Forum for School and University Teachers. Indiana State University, Terre Haute, IN 47809.

Negro Heritage. P.O. Box 1057, Washington, D.C. 20013.

Negro History Bulletin. The Association for the Study of Negro Life and History, Inc., 1538 Ninth Street, NW., Washington, D.C. 20001.

Sepia. Sepia Publishing Co., 1220 Harding St., Fort Worth, TX 76102.

In addition, it is suggested that you read a sampling of literature by noted black writers, for example: Toni Morrison, Richard Wright, Maya Angelou, Gwendolyn Brooks, Alice Walker, and Langston Hughes.

Books for Young Readers

Read as many of these books as possible. You will learn as you read, and you can begin to plan lessons that are based on multicultural literature.

Fiction

C. S. Adler. *Always and Forever Friends*. Clarion, 1988.

Nana H. Agle. *Maple Street*. Seabury, 1970.

Martha Alexander. *Bobo's Dream*. Dial, 1970.

William H. Armstrong. *Sounder*. Harper, 1969.

Martha Bacon. *Sophia Scrooby Preserved*. Little, 1968.

Charlotte Baker. *Cockleburr Quarters*. Prentice-Hall, 1972.

Kathleen Benson. *Joseph on the Subway Trains*. Addison-Wesley, 1981.

Clayton Bess. *Story for a Black Night*. Houghton Mifflin, 1982.

Joan Blos. *A Gathering of Days*. Scribner, 1979.

Barbara Brenner. *Wagon Wheels*. Harper, 1978.

Clyde Bulla. *Charlie's House*. Crowell, 1983.

Peter Burchard. *Bimby*. Coward, 1968.

*Jeannette Caines. *Abby*. Harper, 1973.

*_____. *Just Us Women*. Harper, 1982.

Ann Cameron. *More Stories Julian Tells*. Knopf, 1986.

_____. *The Stories Julian Tells*. Pantheon, 1981.

Natalie Carlson. *Ann Aurelia and Dorothy*. Harper, 1968.

Peter Carter. *The Sentinels*. Oxford, 1982.

Alice Childress. *A Hero ain't nothin' but a Sandwich*. Coward, 1973.

Bess Clayton. *Story for a Black Night*. Houghton, 1982.

*Lucille Clifton. *Amifica*. Dutton, 1977.

*_____. *The Boy Who Didn't Believe in Spring*. Dutton, 1973.

_____. *The Lucky Stone*. Delacorte, 1979.

*_____. *My Friend Jacob*. Dutton, 1980.

*_____. *Three Wishes*. Viking, 1976.

Barbara Cohen. *Thank You, Jackie Robinson*. Lothrop, 1974.

James Collier. *Jump Ship to Freedom*. Delacorte, 1981.

Molly Cone. *The Other Side of the Fence*. Houghton, 1967.

Olivia Coolidge. *Come By Here*. Houghton, 1970.

*Pat Cummings. *Jimmy Lee Did It*. Lothrop, 1985.

Jane L. Curry. *The Daybreakers*. Harcourt, 1970.

Alexis Devereaux. *Na-Ni*. Harper, 1973.

Beth Engel. *Big Words*. Dutton, 1982.

*Tom Feelings and Eloise Greenfield. *Daydreams*. Dial, 1981.

Carol Fenner. *The Skates of Uncle Richard*. Random, 1978.

Dale Fife. *Who's in Charge of Lincoln?* Coward, 1965.

*Suitable for primary grades.

Louise Fitzhugh. *Nobody's Family Is Going to Change.* Farrar, 1974.

Paula Fox. *How Many Miles to Babylon?* White, 1967.

_____. *The Slave Dancer.* Bradbury, 1973.

*D. Freeman. *Corduroy.* Viking, 1968.

Jean Fritz. *Brady.* Coward, 1960.

Lorenz Graham. *North Town* (and other titles). Crowell, 1965.

Bette Greene. *Get on Out of Here, Philip Hall.* Dial, 1981.

_____. *Philip Hall Likes Me, I Reckon Maybe.* Dial, 1974.

*Eloise Greenfield. *Grandmamma's Joy.* Collins, 1980.

_____. *Me and Nessie.* Crowell, 1975.

_____. *She Come Bringing Me That Little Baby Girl.* Lippincott, 1974.

_____. *Sister.* Crowell, 1974.

_____. *Talk about a Family.* Lippincott, 1978.

Virginia Hamilton. *Arilla Sun Down.* Greenwillow, 1976.

_____. *House of Dies Drear.* Macmillan, 1968.

_____. *M.C. Higgins the Great.* Macmillan, 1974.

_____. *The Magical Adventures of Pretty Pearl.* Harper, 1983.

_____. *The Mystery of Drear House.* Greenwillow, 1987.

_____. *Time-ago Lost: More Tales of Jahdu.* Macmillan, 1973. Short stories.

_____. *The Time-ago Tales of Jahdu.* Macmillan, 1969. Short stories.

_____. *Zeely.* Macmillan. 1967.

Sarah Hayes. *Happy Christmas, Gemma.* Lothrop, 1986.

*Elizabeth Hill. *Evan's Corner.* Holt, 1967.

William Hooks. *Circle of Fire.* Atheneum, 1982.

Lila Hopkins. *Eating Crow.* Watts, 1988.

Kristin Hunter. *Soul Brothers and Sister Lou.* Scriber, 1968.

Belinda Hurmence. *A Girl Called Boy.* Clarion, 1982.

Hadley Irwin. *I Be Somebody.* Atheneum, 1984.

June Jordan. *Kimakao's Story.* Houghton, 1982.

_____. *New Life: New Room.* Crowell, 1975.

May Justus. *A New Home for Billy.* Hastings, 1966.

*Ezra Jack Keats. *The Snowy Day.* Viking, 1962. (Caldecott Award; see other books about Peter and his friends.)

Elaine Konigsburg. *Jennifer, Hecate, Macbeth, William McKinley, and Me, Elizabeth.* Atheneum, 1967.

Jill Krementz. *Sweet Pea: A Black Girl Growing up in the Rural South.* Harcourt, 1969.

Julius Lester. *This Strange New Feeling.* Dial, 1982.

*Suitable for primary grades.

*Joan Lexau. *Benjie.* Dial, 1964.

*_____. *I Should Have Stayed in Bed.* Harper, 1965.

*_____. *Me Day.* Dial, 1971.

*_____. *The Rooftop Mystery.* Harper, 1968.

_____. *Striped Ice Cream.* Lippincott, 1968.

*Lessie Little and Eloise Greenfield. *I Can Do It Myself.* Crowell, 1978.

Bette Bao Lord. *In the Year of the Boar and Jackie Robinson.* Harper, 1984.

*Patricia M. Martin. *The Little Brown Hen.* Crowell, 1960.

*Sharon Bell Mathis. *The Hundred Penny Box,* Viking, 1976.

_____. *Teacup Full of Roses.* Viking, 1972.

Walter Myers. *Fast Sam, Cool Clyde and Stuff.* Viking, 1975.

_____. *Mojo and the Russians.* Viking, 1977.

Ann Petry. *Tituba of Salem Village.* Crowell, 1964.

Harriette Robinet. *Ride the Red Cycle.* Houghton, 1980.

*Ann Scott. *Sam.* McGraw, 1967.

Ouida Sebestyen. *Words by Heart.* Little, 1979.

John Shearer. *I Wish I Had an Afro.* Cowles. 1970.

Louisa Shotwell. *Roosevelt Grady.* Collins, 1963.

Alfred Slote. *Jake.* Lippincott, 1971.

John Steptoe. *Marcia.* Viking, 1976.

_____. *Train Ride.* Harper, 1971.

*_____. *Stevie.* Harper, 1969.

_____. *Uptown.* Harper, 1970.

Mary Stolz. *A Wonderful Terrible Time.* Harper, 1967.

Eleanor Tate. *Just an Overnight Guest.* Dial, 1980.

Mildred Taylor. *Let the Circle Be Unbroken.* Dial, 1981.

_____. *Roll of Thunder, Hear My Cry.* Dial, 1976.

_____. *Song of the Trees.* Dial, 1975.

Theodore Taylor. *The Cay.* Doubleday, 1969.

Ianthe Thomas. *Hi, Mrs. Mallory.* Harper, 1979.

*_____. *Walk Home Tired, Billy Jenkins.* Harper, 1974.

*_____. *Willie Blows a Mean Horn.* Harper, 1981.

Janice Udry. *What Mary Jo Shared.* Whitman, 1966.

Cynthia Voight. *Come a Stranger.* Atheneum, 1986.

Jane Wagner. *J. T.* Dell, 1971.

Mildred Walter. *The Girl on the Outside.* Lothrop, 1982.

Karen Whiteside. *Brother Mouky and the Falling Sun.* Harper, 1980.

*Suitable for primary grades.

Brenda Wilkinson. *Ludell.* Harper, 1975.

_____. *Not Separate, Not Equal.* Harper, 1987.

Vera Williams. *Cherries and Cherry Pits.* Greenwillow, 1986.

Nonfiction

Ashley Bryan. *I'm Going to Sing: Black American Spirituals.* Vol. 2. Atheneum, 1982.

H. Buckmaster. *Flight to Freedom,* Crowell, 1958.

*Lucille Clifton. *The Black BC's.* Dutton, 1970.

Henry Commager. *The Great Proclamation.* Bobbs, 1960.

Burke Davis. *Black Heroes of the American Revolution.* Harcourt, 1976.

Eloise Greenfield. *Childtimes: A Three Generation Memoir.* Crowell, 1979.

J. H. Griffin. *A Time to Be Human.* Macmillan, 1977.

James Haskins. *Black Theater in America.* Crowell, 1982.

L. W. Ingraham. *Slavery in the United States.* Watts, 1968.

Florence Jackson. *The Black Man in America, 1932–1954.* Watts, 1979.

_____. *Blacks in America, 1954–1979.* Watts, 1980.

Jesse Jackson. *Blacks in America.* Messner, 1973.

Julius Lester. *To Be a Slave.* Dial, 1968.

Don Lawson. *South Africa.* Watts, 1986.

Milton Meltzer. *All Times, All Peoples: A World History of Slavery.* Harper, 1980.

_____. *In Their Own Words,* 3 vols. Crowell, 1964–67.

_____. *The Truth About the Ku Klux Klan.* Watts, 1982.

Christine Price. *Dance on the Dusty Earth.* Scribner, 1982.

Conrad Stein. *Kenya.* Childrens Press, 1985.

Dorothy Sterling. *Tear Down the Walls.* Doubleday, 1968.

_____. *The Trouble They Seen: Black People Tell the Story of Reconstruction.* Doubleday. 1976.

Hildegarde Swift. *North Star Shining.* Morrow, 1947.

Biography

David Adler. *Martin Luther King: Free at Last.* Holiday, 1986.

Arnold Adoff. *All the Colors of the Race.* Lothrop, 1986.

_____. *Black on Black.* Macmillan, 1968.

_____. *Malcolm X.* Crowell, 1970.

Rae Alexander. *Young and Black in America.* Random, 1970.

*Aliki. *A Week Is a Flower: The Life of George Washington Carver.* Prentice-Hall, 1965.

Jean H. Berg. *I Cry When the Sun Goes Down: The Story of Herman Wrice.* Westminster, 1975.

*Suitable for primary grades.

Jacqueline Bernard. *Journey toward Freedom: The Story of Sojourner Truth*. Norton, 1967.

Roland Bertol. *Charles Drew*. Crowell, 1970.

C. Bishop. *Martin de Porres, Hero*. Houghton, 1954.

Arna Bontemps. *Fredrick Douglass: Slave — Fighter — Freeman*. Knopf, 1959.

Susan Brownmiller. *Shirley Chisholm*. Doubleday, 1970.

Olive Burt. *Negroes in the Early West*. Messner, 1969.

Bradford Chambers. *Chronicles of Negro Protest*. Parents, 1968.

Elizabeth Chittenden. *Martin Luther King: Peaceful Warrior*. Prentice-Hall, 1968.

_____. *Profiles in Black and White*. Scribner, 1973.

James Collier. *Louis Armstrong: An American Success Story*. Macmillan, 1985.

Barbara Cohen. *Thank You, Jackie Robinson*. Lothrop, 1974.

Jean Cornell. *Louis Armstrong, Ambassador Satchmo*. Garrard, 1979.

Ossie Davis. *Langston: A Play*. Delacorte, 1982.

James De Kay. *Meet Martin Luther King, Jr.* Random, 1969.

Esther Douty. *Charlotte Forten: Free Black Teacher*. Garrard, 1971.

Ophelia Egypt. *James Weldon Johnson*. Crowell, 1974.

Mark Evans. *Scott Joplin and the Ragtime Years*. Dodd, 1976.

Doris Faber. *The Assassination of Martin Luther King, Jr.* Watts, 1978.

*Tom Feelings. *Black Pilgrimage*. Lothrop, 1972.

H. Felton. *Edward Rose: Negro Trail Blazer*. Dodd, 1967.

_____. *Mumbet: The Story of Elizabeth Freeman*. Dodd, 1970.

Franklin Folsom. *The Life and Legends of George McJunkin, Black Cowboy*. Nelson, 1973.

Florence Freedman. *Two Tickets to Freedom. The True Story of Ellen and William Craft, Fugitive Slaves*. Simon and Schuster, 1971.

Miriam Fuller. *Phyllis Wheatley: America's First Black Poet(ess)*. Garrard, 1971.

Berry Gordy. *Movin' Up*. Harper, 1979.

Shirley Graham. *Booker T. Washington*. Messner, 1955.

Eloise Greenfield. *Mary McLeod Bethune*. Crowell, 1977.

_____. *Paul Robeson*. Crowell, 1975.

_____. *Rosa Parks*. Crowell, 1973.

_____ and Lessie Jones Little. *Childtimes: A Three-Generation Memoir*. Crowell, 1982.

Virginia Hamilton. *Paul Robeson: The Life and Times of a Free Black Man*. Harper, 1974.

_____. *W. E. B. Du Bois*. Crowell, 1972.

Richard Hardwick. *Charles Richard Drew*. Scibner's, 1967.

James Haskins. *From Lew Alcindor to Kareem Abdul Jabbar*. Lothrop, 1972.

_____. *I'm Gonna Make You Love Me: The Story of Diana Ross*. Dial, 1980.

_____. *Katherine Dunham*. Coward, 1982.

*Suitable for primary grades.

_____. *The Life and Time of Martin Luther King, Jr.* Lothrop, 1977.

_____. *A Piece of the Power: Four Black Mayors.* Dial, 1972.

_____. *Shirley Chisholm.* Dial, 1975.

Robert Hayden. *Eight Black American Inventors.* Addison-Wesley, 1972.

_____, ed. *Kaleidoscope: Poems by American Negro Poets.* Harcourt, 1967.

_____. *Seven Black Scientists.* Addison-Wesley, 1970.

Dorothy Hoobler and Thomas Hoobler. *Nelson and Winnie Mandela.* Watts, 1987.

Genie Iverson. *Louis Armstrong.* Crowell, 1976.

Johanna Johnston. *A Special Bravery.* Dodd, 1967.

Hettie Jones. *Big Star Fallin' Mama: Five Women in Black Music.* Viking, 1974.

June Jordan. *Fannie Lou Hamer.* Crowell, 1972.

_____. *Harriet and the Runaway Book: The Story of Harriet Beecher Stowe.* Harper, 1977.

Mervyn Kaufman. *Jessie Owens.* Crowell, 1973.

Jacob Lawerence. *Harriet and the Promised Land.* Windmill, 1968.

Bill Libby. *Joe Louis, The Brown Bomber.* Lothrop, 1980.

_____. *The Reggie Jackson Story.* Lothrop, 1979.

Aletha Lindstrom. *Sojourner Truth.* Messner, 1980.

Robert Lipsyte. *Free to Be Muhammad Ali.* Harper, 1978.

Polly Longsworth. *Charlotte Forten: Black and Free.* Crowell, 1970.

Bette Bao Lord. *In the Year of the Boar and Jackie Robinson.* Harper, 1984.

Sharon Bell Mathis. *Ray Charles.* Crowell, 1973.

Ann McGovern. *Runaway Slave: The Story of Harriet Tubman.* Four Winds, 1965.

Patricia McKissack. *Mary McLeod Bethune: A Great American Educator.* Childrens, 1985.

Milton Meltzer. *Langston Hughes.* Crowell, 1968.

_____. *Winnie Mandela: The Soul of South Africa.* Viking, 1986.

Howard Meyer. *Colonel of the Black Regiment: The Life of Thomas Wentworth Higginson.* Norton, 1967.

Elizabeth Montgomery. *Duke Ellington: King of Jazz.* Garrard, 1972.

_____. *William C. Handy: Father of the Blues.* Garrard, 1968.

Carman Moore. *Somebody's Angel Child: The Story of Bessie Smith.* Crowell, 1970.

Elizabeth Myers. *Langston Hughes.* Garrard, 1970.

Shirlee Newman. *Marian Anderson.* Westminster, 1966.

Victoria Ortiz. *Sojourner Truth.* Lippincott, 1974.

Lillie Patterson. *Benjamin Banneker.* Abington, 1978.

_____. *Sure Hands, Strong Heart: The Life of Daniel Hale Williams.* Abington, 1981.

*Jackie Robinson. *Breakthrough to the Big League.* Harper, 1965.

Charlemae Rollins. *Famous American Negro Poets.* Dodd, 1965.

*Suitable for primary grades.

_____. *They Showed the Way: Forty American Negro Leaders.* Crowell, 1964.

Jeanne Rowe. *An Album of Martin Luther King, Jr.* Watts, 1970.

Robert Rubin. *Satchel Paige.* Putnam, 1974.

Kenneth Rudeen. *Jackie Robinson.* Crowell, 1971.

Pearle Schulz. *Paul Laurence Dunbar.* Garrard, 1974.

P. Sterling. *Four Took Freedom.* Doubleday, 1967.

_____. *Freedom Train: The Story of Harriet Tubman.* Doubleday, 1954.

Emma Gelders Sterne. *Mary McLeod Bethune.* Knopf, 1957.

Tobi Tobias. *Arthur Mitchell.* Crowell, 1975.

_____. *Marian Anderson.* Crowell, 1972.

Midge Turk. *Gordon Parks.* Crowell, 1971.

Alice Walker. *Langston Hughes, American Poet.* Crowell, 1974.

John A. Williams. *The Most Native of Sons.* Doubleday, 1970.

Diane Wolkstein. *The Cool Ride in the Sky.* Knopf, 1973.

Elizabeth Yates. *Amos Fortune: Free Man.* Dutton, 1950.

Bernice E. Young. *Harlem: The Story of a Changing Community.* Messner, 1972.

Margaret E. Young. *Black American Leaders.* Watts, 1969.

*_____. *The Picture Life of Ralph J. Bunche.* Watts, 1968.

Folk Literature

Verna Aardema. *Behind the Back of the Mountain.* Dial, 1973.

*_____. *Bimwili & the Zimibi; A Tale from Zanzibar.* Dial, 1985.

_____. *Black Folktales from Southern Africa.* Dial, 1973.

*_____. *Bringing the Rain to Kapiti Plain.* Dial, 1981.

*_____. *Half-a-ball-of kenki; An Ashanti Tale.* Warner, 1979.

_____. *Oh, Kojo! How Could You?* Dutton, 1984.

_____. *Tales from the Story Hat.* Coward, 1960.

_____. *What's So Funny, Ketu?* Dial, 1982.

_____. *Who's in Rabbit's House? A Masai Tail.* Dial, 1977.

_____. *Why Mosquitoes Buzz in People's Ears.* Dial, 1975. (Caldecott Award winner)

Joyce Arkhurst. *The Adventure of Spider; West African Tales.* Little, 1964.

Kathleen Arnott. *African Myths and Legends.* Oxford, 1962.

Ellen Babitt. *Jataka Tales.* Prentice-Hall, 1940.

Terry Berger. *Black Fairy Tales.* Atheneum, 1969.

Ashley Bryan. *The Adventures of Aku.* Atheneum, 1976.

Harold Courlander. *Beat the Story Drum, Pum, Pum.* Atheneum, 1980.

_____. *The Crest and the Hide and Other African Stories . . .* Coward, 1982.

*Suitable for primary grades.

_____. *The Hat-shaking Dance and Other Tales.* . . . Harcourt, 1957.

_____. *The King's Drum.* Harcourt, 1962.

_____. *Olade the Hunter.* Harcourt, 1968.

Elphinstone Dayrell. *Why the Sun and the Moon Live in the Sky.* Houghton, 1968.

William Faulkner. *The Day the Animals Talked.* Follett, 1977.

Harold Felton. *John Henry and His Hammer.* Knopf, 1950.

Mary Joan Gerson. *Why the Sky Is Far Away.* Harcourt, 1974.

Ann Grifalconi. *The Village of Round and Square Houses.* Little, 1986.

Gail Haley. *A Story, A Story.* Atheneum, 1970.

*Ezra Jack Keats. *John Henry.* Pantheon, 1965.

Julius Lester. *The Knee-high Man.* Dial, 1972.

Joan Lexau. *Crocodile and Hens.* Harper, 1969.

Gerald McDermott. *Anansi the Spider.* Holt, 1972.

Van Dyke Parks. *Jump! The Adventures of Brer Rabbit.* Harcourt, 1986.

Adjai Robinson. *Singing Tales of Africa.* Scribner, 1974.

Peter Seeger. *Abiyoyo.* Macmillan, 1986.

Philip Sherlock. *Anansi, the Spider Man.* Crowell, 1954 (Also on film; Weston Woods).

Poetry

Arnold Adoff. *All the Colors of the Races.* Lothrop, 1982.

_____. *Big Sister Tells Me I'm Black.* Holt, 1976.

_____. *Black Out Loud: An Anthology of Modern Poetry.* Macmillan, 1970.

_____. *I Am the Darker Brother.* Macmillan, 1968.

_____. *I Am the Running Girl.* Harper, 1979.

_____, ed. *My Black Me: A Big Book of Poetry.* Dutton, 1974.

_____. *Under the Early Morning Trees.* Dutton, 1978.

Arna Bontemps. *Golden Slippers. An Anthology.* . . . Harper, 1941.

Gwendolyn Brooks. *Bronzeville Boys and Girls.* Harper, 1956.

Lucille Clifton. *Everett Anderson's Friend.* Holt, 1976. (See other books about Everett Anderson.)

Paul Dunbar. *I Greet the Dawn.* Antheneum, 1978.

*Nikki Giovanni. *Spin a Soft Black Song.* Hill & Wang, 1971.

Eloise Greenfield. *Daydreamers.* Dial, 1981.

_____. *Honey, I Love, and Other Love Poems.* Crowell, 1978.

Nikki Grimes. *Something on My Mind.* Dial, 1978.

Langston Hughes. *Don't You Turn Back.* Knopf, 1970.

_____. *The Dream Keeper and Other Poems.* Knopf, 1986.

*Suitable for primary grades.

June Jordan. *Who Look at Me?* Crowell, 1969.

Jacob Lawrence. *Harriet and the Promised Land.* Simon & Schuster, 1968.

Exploring the Backgrounds of Hispanics

The largest group that falls in this category are the Americans with Mexican backgrounds. However, we also need to be aware of such other groups as Filipino, Cuban, Puerto Rican, and Spanish (from Spain) Americans.

General Resources

Patricia Beilke and Frank Sciara. *Selecting Materials for and about Hispanic and East Asian Children and Young People.* Shoestring, 1986.

Daniel Duran. *Latino Materials: A Multimedia Guide for Children and Young Adults. American Bibliographic Center—CLIO Press,* 1979.

A. J. Jaffee, et al. *The Changing Demography of Spanish Americans.* Academic Press, 1980.

Milton Meltzer. *The Hispanic Americans.* Crowell, 1982 (For students also.)

National Hispanic University. 225 East 14th Street, Oakland, CA 94606.

Febe Orozco. "A Bibliography of Hispanic Literature." *English Journal* (November 1982).

Isabel Schon. *Basic Collection of Children's Books in Spanish.* Scarecrow, 1986.

_____. *Books in Spanish for Children and Young Adults.* Scarecrow, 1985.

_____. *A Hispanic Heritage.* Scarecrow Press, 1980.

Shirley Wagoner. "Mexican-Americans in Children's Literature Since 1970." *The Reading Teacher* (December 1982).

Exploring the Backgrounds of Mexican Americans/Chicanos

Nearly six million Americans have Mexican backgrounds, and this number is growing. These Americans tend to be located in the large cities of California and the southwestern states that border Mexico.

General Background

Rodolfo Acuña. *Occupied America: A History of Chicanos.* Harper, 1981.

Rudolfo Anaya. *Bless Me Última.* Tonatiuh, 1972.

Livie Duran and Bernard Russell, eds. *Introduction to Chicano Studies.* Macmillan, 1982.

Matt Meier and Feliciano Rivera, eds. *Dictionary of Mexican American History.* Greenwood Press, 1981.

Margarita Melville, ed. *Twice a Minority: Mexican American Women.* Mosby, 1980.

Isabel Schon. *A Bicultural Heritage: Themes for the Exploration of Mexican and Mexican-American Culture in Books for Children and Adolescents.* Scarecrow, 1978.

James Vigil. *From Indian to Chicanos: A Sociocultural History.* Mosby, 1980.

Periodicals

Aztlán: International Journal of Chicano Studies Research. Campbell Hall, Rm. 3122, University of California, Los Angeles, CA 90024.

Bronze. 1560 34th Avenue, Oakland, CA 94601.

Carta Editorial. P.O. Box 54624, Terminal Annex, Los Angeles, CA 90054.

Chicano Student Movement. P.O. Box 31322, Los Angeles, CA 90031.

Compass. 1209 Egypt Street, Houston, TX 77009. (Free)

El Gallo. 1265 Cherokee Street, Denver, CO 80204.

El Grito del Norte. Rt. 2, Box 5, Española, NM 87532.

El Hispanoamericano. 630 Ninth Street, Sacramento, CA 95825.

Inside Eastside. P.O. Box 63273, Los Angeles, CA 90063.

Lado. 1306 N. Western Avenue, Chicago, IL 60622.

El Macriado. P.O. Box 130, Delano, CA 93215.

Mexican American Sun. 319 North Soto St., Los Angeles, CA 90033.

La Opinión. 1426 S. Main Street, Los Angeles, CA 90015.

La Prensa Libre. 2973 Sacramento Street, Berkeley, CA 94702.

Provyecto Leer Bulletin, 1736 Columbia Road, NW., St. 107, Washington, D.C. 20009.

La Raza. 2445 Gates Street, Los Angeles, CA 90031.

Times of the Americas. P.O. Box 1173, Coral Gables, FL 33134.

La Verdad. P.O. Box 13156, San Diego, CA 92113.

Books for Students

Fiction

Ruth Adams. *Fidelia.* Lothrop, 1970.

Anne Alexander. *Trouble on the Treat Street.* Atheneum, 1974.

Lorraine Babbit. *Pink Like the Geranium.* Children's Press, 1974.

*Jan Balet. *The Fence.* Delacorte, 1969.

Laura Bannon. *Manuela's Birthday.* Whitman, 1972.

Patricia Beatty. *Lupita Manana.* Morrow, 1982.

*Harry Behn. *The Two Uncles of Pablo.* Harcourt Brace Jovanovich, 1959.

Frank Bonham. *Viva Chicano.* Dutton, 1970.

Rose Blue. *We Are Chicanos.* Watts, 1974.

Clyde Robert Bulla. *The Poppy Seeds.* Crowell, 1955.

Hila Colman. *Chicano Girl.* Morrow, 1973.

Mary Dunne. *Reach Out, Ricardo.* Abelard, 1971.

*Marie Hall Ets. *Bad Boy, Good Boy.* Crowell, 1967.

*Suitable for primary grades.

*_____. *Nine Days to Christmas.* Viking, 1959. (Easy)

Bob Fitch and Lynne Fitch. *Soy Chicano; I am Mexican-American.* Creative Education, 1971.

Marjorie Flack and Karl Larrson. *Pedro.* Macmillan, 1940.

Aylesa Forsee. *Too Much Dog.* Lippincott, 1957.

Ed Foster. *Tejanos.* Hill and Wang, 1970.

Suzanne Fulle. *Lanterns for Fiesta.* Macrae, 1973.

Claire Galbraithe. *Victor.* Little, 1971.

Helen Garrett. *Angelo, the Naughty One.* Viking, 1944.

Marian Garthwaite. *Tomás and the Red-Haired Angel.* Messner, 1966.

Maurine Gee. *Chicano Amigo.* Morrow, 1972.

Loren Good. *Panchito.* Coward, 1955.

Dorothy Hamilton. *Anita's Choice.* Herald, 1971.

Kathryn Hitte and William B. Hayes. *Mexicali Soup.* Parents', 1970.

Carl Kidwell. *Arrow in the Sun.* Viking, 19611.

Joseph Krumgold. *And Now Miguel.* Crowell, 1970.

Evelyn S. Lampman. *Go Up the Road.* Atheneum, 1972.

Marion Lay. *Wooden Saddles: The Adventures of a Mexican Boy in His Own Land.* Morrow, 1939.

*Thomas P. Lewis. *Hill of Fire.* Harper & Row, 1971.

Claudia Mills. *Luisa's American Dream.* Four Winds, 1981.

Joe Molnar, ed. *Graciela: A Mexican-American Child Tells Her Story.* Watts, 1972.

Grace Moon. *Tita of México.* Stokes. 1934.

Elizabeth Morrow. *The Painted Pig.* Knopf, 1930.

Iris Noble. *Tingambatu: Adventure in Archaeology.* Messner, 1983.

James Norman. *Charro: Mexican Horseman.* Putnam, 1970.

Scott O'Dell. *The Black Pearl.* Houghton Mifflin, 1967.

_____. *Carlotta.* Houghton, 1977.

_____. *The King's Fifth.* Houghton Mifflin, 1966.

Helen Rand Parish. *Estebáncio.* Viking, 1974.

Paula Paul. *You Can Hear a Magpie Smile.* Nelson, 1980.

*Leo Politi. *Juanita.* Scribner's, 1948.

*_____. *The Mission Bell.* Scribner's, 1953.

*_____. *Pedro, the Angel of Olvera Street.* Scribner's, 1946.

*_____. *Rosa.* Scribner's, 1963.

*_____. *Three Stalks of Corn.* Scribner's, 1978.

Barbara Ritchie. *Ramón Makes a Trade: Los Cambios de Ramón.* Parnassus, 1959.

Jessie Ruiz, *El Gran Cesar.* Education Consulting, 1973.

*Suitable for primary grades.

Ruth Sawyer. *The Least One.* Viking, 1941.

*Byrd Baylor Schweitzer. *Amigo.* Macmillan, 1963.

Nancy Smith. *Josie's Handful of Quietness.* Abingdon, 1975.

*Barbara Todd. *Juan Patricio.* Putnam, 1972.

Elizabeth Borton de Treviño. *Nacar, the White Deer.* Farrar, Straus, & Giroux, 1963.

Dorothy Witton. *Crossroads for Chela.* Messner, 1956.

Nonfiction

Rudy Acuña. *Cultures in Conflict.* Charter School Books, 1970.

Bernadine Bailey. *Famous Latin American Liberators.* Dodd, Mead, 1960.

_____. *Picture Book of New Mexico.* Whitman, 1960.

Patricia Beatty. *Lupita Mañana.* Morrow, 1981.

Jacqueline Bernard. *Voices from the Southwest.* Scholastic, 1972.

Sonia Blecker. *The Aztec: Indians of Mexico.* Morrow, 1963.

_____. *The Maya: Indians of Central America.* Morrow, 1961.

Rose Blue. *We Are Chicano.* Watts, 1973.

Susan Carver and Paula McGuire. *Coming to North America: From Mexico, Cuba, and Puerto Rico.* Delacorte, 1981.

Harold Coy. *Chicano Roots Go Deep.* Dodd, 1975.

Mark Day. *Forty Acres: César Chavez and the Farm Workers.* Praeger, 1971.

Patricia de Garza. *Chicanos: The Story of Mexican Americans.* Messner, 1973.

Discovers of the New World, by the editors of American Heritage. American Heritage, 1960.

Arnold Dobrin. *The New Life—La Vida Nueva.* Dodd, 1971.

Sam Epstein. *The First Book of Mexico.* Watts, 1967.

Ruth Franchere. *César Chavez.* Crowell, 1970.

Shirley Glubok. *The Art of Ancient Mexico.* Harper & Row, 1968.

Delia Goetz. *Neighbors to the South.* Harcourt Brace Jovanovich.

Clara Louise Grant. *Mexico, Land of the Plumed Serpent.* Garrard, 1968.

Dorothy Childs Hogner. *Children of Mexico.* Heath, 1942.

Robert Jackson. *Supermax: The Lee Trevino Story.* Walck, 1973.

W. J. Jacobs. *Hernando Cortés.* Watts, 1974.

William Loren Katz. *Modern America, 1957 to the Present.* Watts, 1975.

_____. *Years of Strife, 1929–1956.* Watts, 1975.

Rebecca B. Marcus and Judith Marcus. *Fiesta Time in Mexico.* Garrard, 1974.

Albert Marrin. *Aztecs and Spaniards: Cortés and the Conquest of Mexico.* Atheneum, 1986.

Patricia M. Martin. *Chicanos: Mexicans in the United States.* Parents, 1971.

May McNeer. *The Mexican Story.* Ariel, 1953.

*Suitable for primary grades.

Marie Neurath. *They Lived Like This in Ancient Mexico.* Watts, 1971.

Clarke Newlon. *Famous Mexican-Americans.* Dodd, 1972.

Jane Pinchott. *The Mexicans in America.* Lever, 1973.

Patricia Rose. *Let's Read about Mexico.* Fideler, 1955.

Elizabeth Hough Sechrist. *Christmas Everywhere.* Macrae Smith, 1962.

_____. *It's Time for Brotherhood.* Macrae Smith, 1973.

Ronald Syme. *Cortés of Mexico.* Morrow, 1951.

_____. *Juárez: The Founder of Modern Mexico.* Morrow, 1972.

Sandra Weiner. *Small Hands, Big Hands.* Pantheon, 1970.

Florence White. *César Chavez: Man of Courage.* Garrard, 1973.

Barbara Kerr Wilson. *Fairy Tales of Mexico.* Casell, (London)-Dutton, 1960.

Bernard Wolf. *In This Proud Land: The Story of a Mexican American Family.* Lippincott, 1979.

Folklore

John Bierhorst, ed. *The Hungry Woman: Myths and Legends of the Aztecs.* Morrow, 1984.

Anita Brenner. *The Boy Who Could Do Anything & Other Mexican Folk Tales.* Young Scott, 1942.

Camilla Campbell. *Star Mountain, and Other Legends of Mexico.* McGraw-Hill, 1968.

Patricia F. Ross. *In Mexico They Say.* Knopf, 1942.

B. Traven. *The Creation of the Sun and the Moon.* Hill & Wang, 1968.

Poetry

Toni De Gerez. *2-Rabbit, 7-Wind.* Viking, 1971.

Richard Lewis, ed. *Still Waters of the Air: Poems by Three Modern Spanish Poets.* Dial, 1970.

Alastair Reid and Anthony Kerrigan. *Mother Goose in Spanish/Poesías de la Madre Oca.* Crowell, 1968.

Exploring the Backgrounds of Puerto Ricans

General Resources

Kenneth Aran, et al. *Puerto Rican History and Culture: A Study Guide and Curriculum Outline.* United Federation of Teachers.

A Handbook for Teaching Portuguese-Speaking Students. California State Dept. of Education, 1983.

Patricia Beilke and Frank Sciara. *Selecting Materials for and about Hispanic and East Asian Children and Young People.* Shoestring, 1986.

Diane Herrera, ed. *Puerto Ricans and Other Minority Groups in the Continental United States.* Blaine Ethridge, 1979.

Adult Books

María Theresa Babin and Stan Steiner, eds. *Borinquen: An Anthology of Puerto Rican Literature*. Vintage, 1974.

Joseph Fitzpatrick. *Puerto Rican Americans: The Meaning of Migration to the Mainland*. Prentice-Hall, 1971.

Clifford Haubert. *Puerto Rico and Puerto Ricans: A Study of Puerto Rican History and Immigration in the United States*. Hippocrene Books, 1974.

Karl Wagenheim. *Cuentos: An Anthology of Short Stories from Puerto Rico*. Shocken Books, 1978.

_____, ed. *Puerto Rico: A Profile*. Praeger, 1975.

Books for Students

Fiction

Robert Barry. *The Musical Palm Tree*. McGraw, 1968.

*Edna Barth. *The Day Luís Was Lost*. Little, 1971.

Pura Belpré. *Santiago*. Warne, 1969.

Rose Blue. *I Am Here; Yo Estoy Aquí*. Watts, 1971.

Lois Bouchard. *The Boy Who Wouldn't Talk*. Doubleday, 1969.

Nardi Campion. *Casa Means Home*. Holt, 1970.

Arthur Getz. *Tar Beach*. Dial, 1979.

Gloria Gonzalez. *Gaucho*. Knopf, 1977.

Lynn Hall. *Danza!* Scribner, 1981.

Ezra Jack Keats and Pat Cherr. *My Dog Is Lost!* Crowell, 1960.

Myron Levoy. *A Shadow Like a Leopard*. Harper, 1981.

Peggy Mann. *The Street of Flower Boxes*. Coward, 1966.

Nicholasa Mohr. *El Bronx Remembered*. Harper, 1975.

_____. *Felita*. Dial, 1979.

_____. *Nilda*. Harper, 1973.

Louisa Shotwell. *Magdalena*. Viking, 1971.

Ruth Sonneborn. *Friday Night Is Papa Night*. Viking, 1970.

Piri Thomas. *Stories from El Barrio*. Knopf, 1978.

Sandra Weiner. *They Call Me Jack: The Story of a Boy from Puerto Rico*. Pantheon, 1973.

Nonfiction

Stuart Brahs. *An Album of Puerto Ricans in the United States*. Watts, 1973.

Peter Buckley. *I Am from Puerto Rico*. Simon, 1971.

*Antonio J. Colorado. *The First Book of Puerto Rico*. Watts, 1978.

*Suitable for primary grades.

Morton Golding. *A Short History of Puerto Rico.* Watts, 1978.

Wendy Kesselman. *Joey.* Hill, 1972.

Arlene Kurtis. *Puerto Ricans.* Messner, 1969.

Ronald Larsen. *The Puerto Ricans in America.* Lerner, 1973.

Barry Levine. *Benjy Lopez. A Picaresque Tale of Emigration and Return.* Basic Books, 1980.

Jack Manning. *Young Puerto Rico.* Dodd, 1962.

Cruz Martel. *Yagua Days.* Dial, 1976.

Robin McKown. *The Image of Puerto Rico: Its History and Its People: On the Island — On the Mainland.* McGraw, 1973.

Joe Molnar. *Elizabeth: A Puerto Rican-American Child Tells Her Story.* Watts, 1974.

Lila Perl. *Puerto Rico: Island between Two Worlds.* Morrow, 1979.

Geraldo Rivera. *Puerto Rico: Island of Contrasts.* Parents, 1973.

Warren Schloat, Jr. *María and Ramón: A Girl and Boy of Puerto Rico.* Knopf, 1966.

Elizabeth Sechrist. *It's Time for Brotherhood.* Macrae, 1973.

Julia Singer. *We All Come from Puerto Rico Too.* Atheneum, 1977.

Philip Sterling and Maria Brau. *The Quiet Rebels.* Doubleday, 1968.

Morris Weeks, Jr. *Hello, Puerto Rico.* Grosset, 1972.

Biography

Paul Allyn. *The Picture Life of Herman Badilla.* Watts, 1972.

Alfredo Matilla and Ivan Silen, eds. *The Puerto Rican Poets: Los Poétas Puertorriqueños.* Bantam, 1972.

Clarke Newlon. *Famous Puerto Ricans.* Dodd, 1975.

Philip Sterling and Maria Brau. *The Quiet Rebels.* Doubleday, 1968.

Folklore

Ricardo Alegría. *The Three Wishes.* Harcourt, 1969.

Pura Belpré. *Dance of the Animals.* Warne, 1972.

_____. *Once in Puerto Rico.* Warne, 1973.

_____. *Oté.* Pantheon, 1969.

_____. *Perez and Martina.* Warne, 1961.

_____. *The Rainbow-colored Horse.* Warne, 1978.

_____. *The Tiger and the Rabbit.* Lippincott, 1965.

Exploring the Backgrounds of Cuban Americans

As you can see, the material is limited for this group. Check the *Reader's Guide* for articles in magazines.

General Resources

Esther Gonzales. *Annotated Bibliography on Cubans in the United States 1960–1976.* Florida International University, 1977.

Adult Books

Richard Fagan et al. *Cubans in Exile.* Stanford University Press, 1968.

Geoffrey Fox. *Working-class Emigrés from Cuba.* R. E. Research Associates, 1979.

Irving Horowitz. *Cuban Communism.* Transaction, 1984.

William Mackey and Von Beebe. *Bilingual Schools for a Bicultural Community.* Newburg House, 1977.

Rafael Probías and Lourdes Casal. *The Cuban Minority in the U.S.* Florida Atlantic University, 1973.

Eleanor M. Rogg. *The Assimilation of Cuban Exiles: The Role of Community and Class.* Aberdeen, 1974.

Hugh Thomas. *Cuba—The Pursuit of Freedom.* Harper, 1971.

_____. *The Cuban Revolution.* Westview, 1984.

Books for Students

Margaretta Curtin. *Cubanita in a New Land: Cuban Children of Miami.* Miami Press, 1974.

Virginia Ortiz. *The Land and People of Cuba.* Lippincott, 1973.

Lorin Philipson and Rafael Llerena. *Freedom Flights.* Random, 1980.

Exploring the Backgrounds of Indochinese Americans

The number of persons coming from Indochina to the United States is increasing, but the literature is still scarce.

General Resources

Duong Thanh Binh. *A Handbook for Teachers of Vietnamese Students: Hints for Dealing with Cultural Differences in Schools.* Center for Applied Linguistics, 1975.

Tam Thi Dang Wei. *Vietnamese Refugee Students: A Handbook for School Personnel.* National Assessment and Dissemination Center for Bilingual/Bicultural Education, 1980.

Adult Books

Charles Anderson. *Vietnam: The Other War.* Presidio Press, 1982.

Center for Applied Linguistics. *Vietnamese Refugee Education Series.* The Center, 1975.

Frances Fitzgerald. *Fire in the Lake: The Vietnamese and the Americans in Vietnam.* Vintage, 1972.

Bruce Grant, ed. *The Boat People*. Penguin, 1979.

Gail P. Kelly. *From Vietnam to America: A Chronicle of Vietnamese Immigration to the United States*. Westview, 1977.

Stephen Wright. *Meditations in Green*. Scribner, 1983. (fiction)

Books for Students

Fiction

Ann Nolan Clark. *To Stand Against the Wind*. Viking, 1978.

Helen Coutant. *First Snow*. Knopf, 1974.

Marylois Dunn. *The Absolutely Perfect Horse*. Harper, 1983.

Katherine Paterson. *Park's Quest*. Dutton, 1988.

Nonfiction

Hal Buell. *Vietnam, Land of Many Dragons*. Dodd, 1968.

Joseph Buttinger. *A Defiant Dragon: A Short History of Vietnam*. Praeger, 1972.

John Caldwell. *Let's Visit Vietnam*. Day, 1966.

Mace Goldfarb. *Fighters, Refugees, Immigrants: A Story of the Hmong*. Carolrhoda, 1982.

Peter Goldman and Tony Fuller. *What Vietnam Did to Us*. Morrow, 1983.

James Haskins. *The New Americans: Vietnamese Boat People*. Enslow, 1980.

_____. *The War and the Protest: Vietnam*. Doubleday, 1973.

Don Lawson. *An Album of the Vietnam War*. Watts, 1986.

Robert Mason. *Chickenhawk*. Viking, 1983.

Bernard Newman. *Let's Visit Vietnam*. Burke, 1983.

Huynh Quang Nhuong. *The Land I Lost: Adventures of a Boy in Vietnam*. Harper, 1982.

Jon Nielson. *Artist in South Vietnam*. Messner, 1969.

Tim Page. *Tim Page's Vietnam*. Knopf, 1983.

Vuong Thuy. *Getting to Know the Vietnamese and Their Culture*. Ungar, 1976.

Lynda Van Devanter. *Home Before Morning: The Story of an Army Nurse in Vietnam*. Beaufort, 1983.

Folklore

Ann Nolan Clark. *In the Land of Small Dragon: A Vietnamese Folktale*. Viking, 1979.

Mark Taylor. *The Fisherman and the Goblin*. Golden Gate, 1971.

L. D. Vuong. *The Brocaded Slipper and Other Vietnamese Tales*. Addison-Wesley, 1982.

Exploring the Backgrounds of Native Americans

Background Information for the Teacher

Howard M. Bahr, Bruce A. Chadwick, and Robert C. Day. *Native Americans Today: Sociological Perspectives*. Harper, 1972.

Russell Barsh and James Henderson. *The Road: Indian Tribes and Political Liberty*. University of California, 1980.

William M. Beauchamp. *A History of the New York Iroquois*. Friedman, 1968.

Dee Brown. *Bury My Heart at Wounded Knee*. Holt, 1970.

_____. *Creek Mary's Blood*. Holt, 1971.

_____. *Killdeer Mountain*. Holt, 1972.

Robert Burnette and John Koster. *The Road to Wounded Knee*. Bantam, 1974. Analysis of events leading up to Wounded Knee, 1973.

Mary Gloyne Byler. *American Indian Authors for Young Readers*. Association on American Indian Affairs, 432 Park Ave., South, New York, NY 10016. An annotated bibliography.

The Council on Interracial Books for Children. *Chronicles of American Indian Protest*. A collection of documents recounting the American Indian's struggle for survival. Offers supplemental reading assignments for classes.

John Lane Deer and Richard Erdoes. *Lame Deer, Seeker of Visions*. Washington Square, 1984.

Vine Deloria, Jr. *Custer Died for Your Sins*. Avon, 1970.

_____. *God Is Red*. Laurel, 1979.

David Edmunds, ed. *American Indian Leaders: Studies in Diversity*. University of Nebraska Press, 1980.

William N. Fenton, ed. *Parker on the Iroquois*. Syracuse University Press, 1968.

Zane Grey. *The Vanishing American*. Washington Square, 1984.

Barbara Graymont. *The Iroquois in the American Revolution*. Syracuse U. Press, 1972.

William T. Hagan. *American Indians*. University of Chicago Press, 1961.

Jamake Highwater. *The Primal Mind*. Harper, 1981.

Alvin Josephy, Jr. *Now That the Buffalo's Gone*. Knopf, 1981.

Frank LaPointe. *The Sioux Today*. Macmillan, 1972. Stories of young Indians.

R. J. Lenarcic. *Pre-Columbian Indians: New Perspectives*. Community College Social Science Assoc., 1974.

Peter Navakov, ed. *Native American Testimony*. Crowell, 1978.

Wendell H. Oswalt. *This Land Was Theirs*. Wiley, 1966. Pre-Columbian cultural aspects.

Francis Paul Prucha. *American Indian Policy in the Formative Years*. University of Nebraska Press, 1962. Trade and Intercourse Acts, 1790–1834.

Anna Lee Strensland. *Literature By and About the American Indian: An Annotated Bibliography for Jr. and Sr. High School Students*. NCTE, 1978.

William Sturtevant, ed. *Handbook of North American Indians*. U.S. Government, 1981.

Dale Van Every. *Disinherited*. Morrow, 1966. Removal of the Cherokee.

Alan Velie. *American Indian Literature*. Harper, 1980.

Frank Waters. *The Man Who Killed the Deer*. Swallow, 1970.

Edmund Wilson. *Apologies to the Iroquois*. Vintage, 1959. Historical and contemporary problems.

Journals

AAIA. 432 Park Ave., New York, NY 10016. General and legislative information; newsletter.

Akwesasne Notes: Mohawk Nation via Roosevelt Town, NY 13683. Indian paper; current events and activities. Donation, publishes calendar.

American Indian Culture and Research Journal. 3220 Campbell Hall, University of California, Los Angeles CA 90004.

American Indian Media Directory. American Indian Press Association, Room, 206, 1346 Connecticut Ave., NW., Washington, D.C. 20036. Listing press, radio, TV/video, film, theater.

Warpath. United Native Americans, Inc. Box 26149, San Francisco, CA 94126.

Wassaja. American Indian Historical Society, 1451 Masonic Ave., San Francisco, CA 94117. Monthly newspaper; significant events.

Sources of Materials

Alaska Rural School Project. Univ. of Alaska, College, AK 99701.

American Indian Education Handbook. California State Dept. of Education, 1982.

Navajo Curriculum Center. Rough Rock Demonstration School, Rough Rock, AZ.

Navajo Social Studies Project. College of Education. The Univ. of New Mexico, Albuquerque, NM 87106.

Senate Committee on Labor and Public Welfare, Washington, D.C.

South Central Regional Ed. Lab. Corp., 408 National Old Line Bldg., Little Rock, AR 72201.

Nonprint Media

Bibliography of Nonprint Instructional Materials on the American Indian prepared by the Instructional Development Program for the Institute of Indian Services and Research, Brigham Young University. Brigham Young University Printing Service, Provo, Utah 84601, 1972. A 220-page publication including films of all types, slides, recordings, varied visual teaching aids, and multimedia kits. Entries are annotated and indexed with a reference to the grade level.

Books for Children

Fiction

Betty Baker. *And One Was a Wooden Indian*. Macmillan, 1970.

Olaf Baker. *Where the Buffaloes Begin*. Warne, 1981.

Carol Ann Bales. *Kevin Cloud; Chippewa Boy in the City*. Reilly & Lee, 1972.

Lynne Banks. *The Return of the Indian*. Doubleday, 1986.

Byrd Baylor. *When Clay Sings*. Scribner's, 1972.

Patricia Beatty. *The Bad Bell of San Salvador*. Morrow, 1973.

Denton Bedford. *Tsali*. Indian Historian Press, 1972.

*Nathaniel Benchley. *Small Wolf.* Harper & Row, 1972.

Clyde Bulla. *Conquista!* Crowell, 1978.

Patricia Calvert. *The Hour of the Wolf.* Scribner's, 1983.

Elizabeth Cleaver. *The Enchanted Caribou.* Atheneum, 1985.

Eth Clifford. *The Year of the Three-Legend Deer.* Houghton Mifflin, 1972.

Eleanor Clymer. *The Spider, the Cave and the Pottery Bowl.* Atheneum, 1971.

Belle Coate. *Mak.* Parnassus, 1982.

*Alice Dagliesh. *The Courage of Sarah Noble.* Scribner's, 1954.

T. A. Dyer. *A Way of His Own.* Houghton, 1981.

Dale Fife. *Ride the Crooked Wind.* Coward, 1973.

James Forman. *The Life and Death of Yellow Bird.* Farrar, Straus & Giroux, 1973.

Jean Craighead George. *The Talking Earth.* Harper, 1983.

Paul Goble and Dorothy Goble. *The Friendly Wolf.* Bradbury, 1975.

*_____. *The Girl Who Loved Wild Horses.* Bradbury, 1978.

*_____. *Lone Bull's Horse Raid.* Bradbury, 1973.

*_____. *Red Hawk's Account of Custer's Last Battle.* Pantheon, 1970.

Arnold A. Griese. *At the Mouth of the Luckiest River.* Crowell, 1973.

Janet Hale. *The Owl's Song.* Avon, 1976.

Danita Haller. *Not Just Any Ring.* Knopf, 1982.

Virginia Hamilton. *Arilla Sun Down.* Greenwillow, 1976.

Christie Harris. *Raven's Cry.* Atheneum, 1966.

James Houston. *Eagle Mask.* Harcourt, 1966.

_____. *Ghost Paddle.* Harcourt, 1966.

Weyman Jones. *Edge of Two Worlds.* Dial, 1968.

Ruth Karen. *Feathered Serpent: The Rise and Fall of the Aztecs.* Four Winds, 1982.

Evelyn Sibley Lampman. *Squaw Man's Son.* Atheneum, 1975.

_____. *White Captives.* Atheneum, 1978.

_____. *The Year of Small Shadow.* Harcourt, 1971.

*Gerald McDermott. *Arrows to the Sun: A Pueblo Indian Tale.* Viking, 1974.

D'Arcy McNickle. *The Surrounded.* University of New Mexico, 1978.

_____. *Wind from an Enemy Sky.* Harper, 1978.

*F. N. Monjo. *Indian Summer.* Harper & Row, 1968.

Scott O'Dell. *The Amethyst Ring.* Houghton Mifflin, 1983.

_____. *Island of the Blue Dolphins.* HOughton Mifflin, 1960.

_____. *Sing Down the Moon.* Houghton Mifflin, 1970.

_____. *Streams to the River, River to the Sea: A Novel of Sacagawea.* Harper, 1986.

Harry Paige. *Johnny Stands.* Warne, 1982.

*Suitable for primary grades.

Katy Peake. *The Indian Heart of Carrie Hodges*. Viking, 1972.

William Sleator. *The Angry Moon*. Little, Brown, 1970.

Virginia Driving Hawk Sneve. *Betrayed*. Holiday House, 1974. Fictional account of historical episode.

Elizabeth Speare. *The Sign of the Beaver*. Houghton Mifflin, 1983.

Hyemeyohsts Storm. *Seven Arrows*. Harper, 1972.

*Betty Waterton. *A Salmon for Simon*. Atheneum, 1981.

Barbara Williams. *The Secret Name*. Harcourt Brace Jovanovich, 1972.

Bernard Wolf. *Tinker and the Medicine Man: The Story of a Navajo Boy of Monument Valley*. Random House, 1973.

Nonfiction

Terry Allen, ed. *The Whispering Wind*. Doubleday, 1972. Poetry written by young Eskimo, Aleut, and American Indian students.

Aline Amon. *The Earth Is Sore; Nature Americans on Nature*. Atheneum, 1981.

Virginia Irving Armstrong, ed. *I Have Spoken*. Sage Books, 1971.

Brent Ashabranner. *Morning Star, Black Sun: The Northern Cheyenne Indians and America's Energy Crisis*. Dodd, 1982.

_____. *Children of the Maya; A Guatemalan Indian Odyssey*. Dodd, 1986.

White Deer Autumn. *Ceremony In the Cirlce of Life*. Carnival, 1982.

Paul D. Bailey. *Ghost Dance Messiah*. Westernlore, 1970.

Betty Baker. *At the Center of the World*. Macmillan, 1973. Based on Papago and Pima myths; includes six myths about the Arizona Indians.

_____. *Settlers and Strangers*. Macmillan, 1977.

Gordon C. Baldwin. *The Apache Indians: Raiders of the Southwest*. Four Winds, 1978.

_____. *How Indians Really Lived*. Putnam, 1967.

Byrd Baylor. *Before You Came This Way*. Dutton, 1969.

_____. *They Put on Masks*. Scribner's, 1974.

_____. *When Clay Sings*. Scribner's, 1972.

Alex W. Bealer. *Only the Names Remain: The Cherokee and the Trail of Tears*. Little, Brown, 1972.

William M. Beauchamp. *A History of the New York Iroquois*. Friedman, 1968.

Barbara L. Beck. *The First Book of the Aztecs*. Watts, 1966.

John Bierhorst, ed. *A Cry from the Earth: Music of the North American Indians*. Four Winds, 1978.

_____. *In the Trail of the Wind; American Indian Poems and Ritual Orations*. Farrar, Straus & Giroux, 1971.

Sonia Bleeker. *The Cherokee: Indians of the Mountains*. Morrow, 1952.

_____. *The Crow Indians: Hunters of the Northern Plains*. Morrow, 1951.

*Suitable for primary grades.

_____. *The Delaware Indians: Eastern Fishermen and Farmers.* Morrow, 1953.

_____. *Indians of the Longhouse: The Story of the Iroquois.* Morrow, 1950.

_____. *The Maya.* Morrow, 1961.

_____. *The Mission Indians of California.* Morrow, 1956.

_____. *The Navajo: Herders, Weavers and Silversmiths. Morrow, 1958.*

_____. *The Sioux Indians: Hunters and Warriors of the Plains.* Morrow, 1962.

Charles Blood. *The Goat in the Rug.* Parents, 1976.

Victor Boesen. *Edward S. Curtis, Photographer of the North American Indian.* Coward, 1977.

Mary Bringle. *Eskimos.* Watts, 1973.

Dee Brown. *Bury My Heart at Wounded Knee.* Holt Rinehart and Winston, 1970.

Clyde Bulla. *Pocahontas and the Strangers.* Crowell, 1971.

Jesse Clifton Burt. *Indians of the Southeast: Then and Now.* Abingdon, 1973.

Ann Nolan Clark. *Circle of Seasons.* Farrar, Straus & Giroux, 1970. Describes ceremonies of the Pueblo Indians.

John Collier. *The Indians of the Americas.* Norton, 1947.

Peter Collier. *When Shall They Rest? The Cherokees' Long Struggle with America.* Holt, Rinehart and Winston, 1970.

Harold Coy. *Man Comes to America.* Little Brown, 1973.

Margaret Crary. *Susette La Flesche: Voice of the Omaha Indians.* Hawthorne, 1973.

Chief Eagle Dallas. *Winter Count.* Golden Bell, 1968.

Janet D'Amato. *Algonquian and Iroquois Crafts for You to Make.* Messner, 1979.

_____. *American Indian Craft Inspirations.* Evans, 1972.

Walter M. Daniels, ed. *American Indians.* Wilson, 1957.

Russell David and Brent Ashabranner. *Chief Joseph, War Chief of the Nez Percé.* McGraw-Hill, 1962.

Vine Deloria. *Indians of the Pacific Northwest.* Doubleday, 1977.

Edith Dorian. *Hokahey! American Indians Then and Now.* McGraw-Hill, 1957.

Charles A. Eastman. *Indian Boyhood.* Dover, 1971.

Amy Ehrlich. *Wounded Knee: An Indian History of the American West.* Holt, Rinehart and Winston, 1974.

Paul Elliott. *Eskimos of the World.* Messner, 1976.

Mary Elting. *The Hopi Way.* Evans, 1969.

Richard Erdoes. *The Pueblo Indians.* Young Readers' Indian Library, 1967.

_____. *The Native Americans: Navajos.* Sterling, 1978.

_____. *The Rain Dance People: The Pueblo Indians.* Knopf, 1976.

_____. *The Sun Dance People.* Knopf, 1972.

Norma Farber. *Mercy Short.* Dutton, 1982.

William N. Fenton, ed. *Parker on the Iroquois.* Syracuse University Press, 1968.

Franklin Folsom. *Red Power on the Rio Grande: The Nature of the American Revolution of 1680.* Follett, 1973.

Grant Foreman. *Indian Removal.* University of Oklahoma Press, 1932.

George Fronval. *Indian Signs and Signals.* Sterling, 1978.

Frieda Gates. *North American Indian Masks: Craft and Legend.* Walker, 1982.

Shirley Glubok. *The Art of Ancient Mexico.* Harper & Row, 1964.

_____. *The Art of the North American Indian.* Harper & Row, 1964.

_____. *The Art of the Northwest Coast Indians.* Macmillan, 1975.

_____. *The Art of the Southwest Indians.* Macmillan, 1971.

Bruce Grant. *American Indians Yesterday and Today.* Dutton, 1958.

Barbara Graymont. *The Iroquois in the American Revolution.* Syracuse University Press, 1972.

Marion E. Gridley. *American Indian Women.* Hawthorne, 1974. Describes the lives of 19 women ranging over a period of 300 years.

_____. *Indian Tribes of America.* Hubbard, 1973.

Miriam Gurko. *Indian America: The Black Hawk War.* Crowell, 1970.

William T. Hagan. *American Indians.* University of Chicago Press, 1961.

Charles Hamilton. *Cry of the Thunderbird.* Macmillan, 1950.

Mary Sayre Haverstock. *Indian Gallery.* Four Winds, 1973. A bibliography of artist George Catlin who traveled among the Indian tribes painting Indian subjects and collecting materials for an Indian museum.

Wilma P. Hays. *Foods the Indians Gave Us.* Washburn, 1973.

S. Carl Hirsch. *Famous American Indians of the Plains.* Rand McNally, 1973.

Charles Hofmann. *American Indians Sing.* Day, 1967.

Robert Hofsinde. *Indian Arts.* Morrow, 1971.

_____. *The Indian and His Horse.* Morrow, 1960.

_____. *The Indian Medicine Man.* Morrow, 1966.

_____. *Indian Music Makers.* Morrow, 1967.

_____. *Indian Sign Language.* Morrow, 1956.

_____. *Indian Warriors and Their Weapons.* Morrow, 1965.

_____. *Indians at Home.* Morrow, 1964.

W. Ben Hunt. *The Complete Book of Indian Crafts and Lore.* Golden, 1976.

Indian Culture Series. Montana Reading Publications, Level 4, Stapleton Building, Billings, MT 59101. Series written and illustrated by Indian children for Indians.

Daniel Jacobson. *Great Indian Tribes.* Hammond, 1970.

Johanna Johnston. *The Indians and the Strangers.* Dodd, Mead, 1972.

Jayne Clark Jones. *The American Indian in America.* Lerner, 1973.

_____. *The Patriot Chiefs.* Viking, 1958.

_____. *Red Power: The American Indians' Fight for Freedom.* American Heritage Press, 1971.

Alvin Josephy. *The Nez Percé Indians and the Opening of the Northwest.* Yale University Press, 1965.

William Loren Katz. *Early America, 1492–1812.* Watts, 1974.

Ruth Kirk. *David, Young Chief of the Quileutes: An American Indian Today.* Harcourt Brace Jovanovich, 1967.

_____. *Hunters of the Whale*. Morrow, 1974.

Theodora Kroeber. *Ishi: Last of His Tribes*. Parnassus, 1964.

Oliver La Farge. *The American Indian*. Golden, 1960.

_____. *Pictorial History of the American Indian*. Crown, 1956.

Sigmund Lavine. *The Games the Indians Played*. Dodd, 1974.

_____. *Indian Corn and Other Gifts*. Dodd, 1974.

R. J. Lenarcic. *Pre-Columbian Indians: New Perspectives*. Community College Social Science Assoc., 1974.

Grant Lyons. *The Creek Indians*. Messner, 1978.

Richard Lytle. *People of the Dawn*. Atheneum, 1980.

David Mangurian. *Children of the Incas*. Four Winds, 1979.

Rebecca Marcus. *The First Book of the Cliff Dwellers*. Watts, 1968.

Alice Marriott. *The First Comers*. Longman's, 1960.

_____. *Indians on Horseback*. Crowell, 1968. © 1948.

May McNeer. *The American Indian Story*. Ariel, 1963.

J. Walker McSpadden. *Indian Heroes*. Crowell, 1950.

Patricia Miles Martin. *Indians, the First Americans*. Parents', 1970.

Sherry Mathers, et al. *Our Mother Corn*. Daybreak, 1981.

Emerson N. Matson. *Legends of the Great Chiefs*. Nelson, 1972. Focuses on the Pacific Coastal tribes.

Julian May. *Before the Indians*. Holiday, 1969.

N. Scott Momaday. *The Way to Rainy Mountain*. Ballantine, 1970. A poetic mixture of retellings of Kiowa tales, stories for the history of the Kiowa, and the author's memories of his grandmother.

Dorothy Morrison. *Chief Sarah. Sarah Winnemullen's Fight for Indian Rights*. Atheneum, 1980.

Gerald Newman. *The Changing Eskimos*. Watts, 1979.

Ethel Nurge, ed. *The Modern Sioux*. University of Nebraska Press, 1970.

Peggy Parish. *Let's Be Indians*. Harper & Row, 1962.

Arthur C. Parker. *Skunny Wundy: Seneca Indian tales*. Whitman, 1970. Useful for practicing creative storytelling for students of all ages.

Elizabeth Payne. *Meet the North American Indians*. Random House, 1965.

Tillie S. Pine. *The Indians Knew*. McGraw-Hill, 1957.

Peter Pitseolak. *Peter Pitseolak's Escape from Death*. Delacorte, 1978.

Hermina Poatgieter. *Indian Legacy*. Messner, 1981.

C. Fayne Porter. *Our Indian Heritage: Profiles of 12 Great Leaders*. Chilton, 1964.

William K. Powers. *Here Is Your Hobby: Indian Dancing and Costumes*. Putnam, 1966.

Seymour Reit. *Child of the Navajos*. Dodd, Mead, 1971.

Thomas L. Robertson. *The Yellow Cane*. Steck, 1956.

Maudie Robinson. *Children of the Sun: The Pueblos, Navajos, and Apaches of New Mexico*. Messner, 1973.

Glen Rounds. *Buffalo Harvest.* Holiday Harvest. Holiday House, 1952.

William E. Scheele. *The Mound Builders.* World, 1960.

Charles and Martha Shapp. *Let's Find Out About Indians.* Watts, 1962.

Sally Sheppard. *Indians of the Eastern Woodlands.* Watts, 1975.

Paul Showers. *Indian Festivals.* Crowell, 1969.

Beatrice Siegel. *Indians of the Woodland Before and After the Pilgrims.* Walker, 1972.

Nancy Simon. *American Indian Habitats.* McKay, 1978.

William O. Steele. *Talking Bones.* Harper, 1978.

Stan Steiner. *The Tiguas: The Lost Tribe of Indians.* Collier, 1972.

Craig Kev Strete. *When Grandfather Journeys into Winter.* Greenwillow, 1979.

Alfred Tamarin. *Ancient Indians of the Southwest.* Doubleday, 1975.

––––––. *We Have Not Vanished.* Follet, 1974.

Tobi Tobias. *Maria Tallchief.* Crowell, 1970.

Edwin Tunis. *Indians.* Crowell, 1979.

Dale Van Every. *Disinherited.* Morrow, 1966.

Olivia Vlahos. *New World Beginnings, Indian Cultures in the Americas.* Viking, 1970.

Betsy Warren. *Indians Who Lived in Texas.* Steck, 1970.

Charles Morrow Wilson. *Gerónimo.* Dillon, 1973.

Edmund Wilson. *Apologies to the Iroquois.* Vantage, 1959.

Shirley Hill Witt. *The Tuscaroras.* Crowell-Collier, 1972.

Nancy Wood. *Hollering Sun.* Simon and Schuster, 1972.

The World of the American Indian. National Geographic Society, Washington, D.C., 1974.

Edgar Wyatt. *Cochise, Apache Warrior and Statesman.* McGraw-Hill, 1973.

Rosebud Yellow Robe. *An Album of the American Indian.* Watts, 1969.

Charlotte Yue. *The Pueblo.* Houghton Mifflin, 1986.

––––––. *The Tipi: A Center of Native American Life.* Knopf, 1984.

Folklore

Betty Baker. *And Me, Coyote!* Macmillan, 1982.

––––––. *Rat Is Dead and Ant Is Sad.* Harper, 1981.

Byrd Baylor. *A God on Every Mountain Top.* Scribner, 1981.

––––––. *Moon Song.* Scribner, 1982.

Natalia Belting. *Our Fathers Had Powerful Songs.* Dutton, 1974.

––––––. *Whirlwind Is a Ghost Dancing.* Dutton, 1974.

Margery Bernstein and Janet Kobrin. *The Summer Maker.* Scribner, 1977.

Charles Blood. *The Goat in the Rug.* Parents, 1976.

Henry Chafetz. *Thunderbird and Other Stories.* Pantheon, 1964.

Elizabeth Cleaver. *The Enchanted Caribou.* Atheneum, 1985.

Jane Louise Curry. *Down from the Lonely Mountain.* Harcourt, 1964.

Edward Curtis. *The Girl Who Married a Ghost.* Four Winds, 1978.

Tomie DePaola. *The Legend of the Bluebonnet.* Putnam, 1983.

Dorothy DeWit, ed. *The Talking Stone: An Anthology of Native American Tales and Legends.* Greenwillow, 1979.

Anne B. Fisher. *Stories California Indians Told.* Parnassus, 1957.

Mirra Ginsburg. *The Proud Maiden, Tungak, and the Sun.* Macmillan, 1974.

*Paul Goble. *The Great Race of the Birds and Animals.* Bradbury, 1985.

_____. *Star Boy.* Bradbury, 1983.

_____ and Dorothy Goble. *The Gift of the Sacred Dog.* Bradbury, 1980.

George Grinnell. *The Whistling Skeleton, American Indian Tales of the Supernatural.* Four Winds, 1982.

Christie Harris. *Mouse Woman and the Mischief-makers.* Atheneum, 1977.

_____. *Mouse Woman and the Muddleheads.* Atheneum, 1977.

_____. *Mouse Woman and the Vanished Princesses.* Atheneum, 1976.

_____. *Once More upon a Totem.* Atheneum, 1982.

_____. *The Trouble with Adventurers.* Atheneum, 1982.

_____. *The Trouble with Princesses.* Atheneum, 1980.

Virginia Haviland, ed. *North American Legends.* Collins, 1978.

Jamake Highwater. *Anpao: An American Indian Odyssey.* Lippincott, 1977.

Hilda M. Hooke. *Thunder in the Mountains: Legends of Canada.* Oxford, 1947.

Alice Marriott and Carol Rachlin. *American Indian Mythology.* Crowell, 1968.

D'Arcy McNickle. *Runner in the Sun: A Story of Indian Maize.* Holt, 1954.

*Jane Mobley. *The Star Husband.* Doubleday, 1979.

Gail Robinson. *Raven the Trickster. Legends of the North American Indians.* Atheneum, 1982.

Ann Siberell. *Whale in the Sky.* Dutton, 1982.

William Toye. *The Fire Stealer.* Oxford, 1980.

Alex Whitney. *Stiff Ears: Animal Folktales of the North American Indian.* Walck, 1974.

Rosebud Yellow Robe. *Tonweya and the Eagles and Other Lakota Indian Tales.* Dial, 1978.

Poetry

Terry Allen. *The Whispering Wind.* Doubleday, 1972. Poetry. Poetry by young American Indians.

Aline Amon. *The Earth Is Sore: Native Americans on Nature.* Atheneum, 1981.

Natalia Belting. *Our Fathers Had Powerful Songs.* Dutton, 1974.

John Bierhorst. *In the Trail of the Wind.* Farrar, Straus & Giroux, 1971. American Indian poems and ritual orations.

*Jamake Highwater. *Moonsong Lullaby.* Lothrop, 1981.

*Suitable for primary grades.

James Houston. *Songs of the Dream People.* Atheneum, 1972. Chants and images from the Indians and Eskimos of North America.

Hettie Jones. *The Trees Stand Shining.* Dial, 1971. Poetry of the North American Indians.

Henry Wadsworth Longfellow. *The Song of Hiawatha.* Dutton, 1960.

Ramaho Navajo Students. *Reflections on Illusion—Reality.* Pine Hill Media Center, 1981.

Judith Ullom, comp. *Folklore of the North American Indians: An Annotated Bibliography.* Library of Congress, 1969.

Nancy Wood. *War Cry on a Prayer Feather.* Colorado Centennial Commission.

Biography

Ingri d'Aulaire and Edgar P. d'Aulaire. *Pocahontas.* Doubleday, 1946.

Russell Davis. *Chief Joseph: War Chief of the Nez Percé.* McGraw, 1962.

Mary Gardner. *Mary Jemison: Seneca Captive.* Harcourt, 1966.

Marion Gridley. *American Indian Women.* Hawthorn, 1974.

Johanna Johnston. *The Indians and the Strangers.* Dodd, 1972.

Lois Lenski. *Indian Captive: The Story of Mary Jemison.* Lippincott, 1941.

William Steele. *The Wilderness Tattoo: A Narrative of Juan Ortiz.* Harcourt, 1972.

Ronald Syme. *Osceola. Seminole Leader.* Morrow, 1976.

Exploring the Backgrounds of Jewish Americans

Crossing ethnic and national lines throughout the world, the Jews have probably suffered from more prejudice and stereotyping than any other group. Students will benefit from reading fiction and nonfiction about the history of the Jews and their contemporary life, a complex study that covers broad issues and concerns.

General Information

Nathan Belth. *A Promise to Keep: A Narrative of the American Encounter with Anti-Semitism.* New York Times, 1979.

Max Dimont. *The Jews in America: The Roots, History and Destiny of American Jews.* Simon & Schuster, 1978.

Nathan Glazer. *American Judaism.* University of Chicago Press, 1972.

Sidney Goldstein and Calvin Goldschieder. *Jewish-Americans: Three Generations in a Jewish Community.* Prentice-Hall, 1968.

Irving Howe. *World of Our Fathers: The Journey of the East European Jews to America and the Life They Found and Made.* Simon & Schuster, 1976.

_____ and Kenneth Libo. *How We Lived: A Documentary History of Immigrant Jews in America, 1880–1930.* Richard Marek, 1979.

Anita L. Lebeson. *Pilgrim People: A History of the Jews in America from 1492 to 1974.* Minerva Press, 1975.

Milton Meltzer. *Never to Forget: The Jews of the Holocaust*. Harper, 1976.

_____. *Taking Root: Jewish Immigrants in America*. Farrar, 1976.

Chain Potok. *The Chosen*. Simon & Schuster, 1967.

_____. *My Name Is Asher Lev*. Knopf, 1972.

_____. *The Promise*. Knopf, 1976.

Jerome Rothenberg, ed. *A Big Jewish Book: Poems and Other Visions of the Jews from Tribal Times to the Present*. Doubleday, 1978.

Books for Students

Fiction

Tamar Bergman. *The Boy from Over There*. Houghton, 1988.

Marge Blaine. *Dvora's Journey*. Holt, 1979.

Miriam Chaiken. *Finders Weepers*. Harper, 1980.

_____. *Getting Even*. Harper, 1982.

_____. *I Should Worry, I Should Care*. Harper, 1979.

_____. *Yossi Asks the Angels for Help*. Harper, 1985.

Eth Clifford. *The Remembering Box*. Houghton Mifflin, 1985.

Barbara Cohen. *Bitter Herbs and Honey*. Lothrop, 1976.

_____. *The Carp in the Bathtub*. Lothrop, 1972.

Gloria Goldreich. *Lori*. Holt, 1976.

_____. *Season of Discovery*. Nelson, 1976.

_____. *A Treasury of Jewish Literature*. Holt, 1982.

Bette Greene. *Summer of My German Soldier*. Dial, 1973.

Anita Heyman. *Exit from Home*. Crown, 1977.

*Marilyn Hirsh. *Ben Goes into Business*. Holiday, 1973.

Anne Holm. *North to Freedom*. Harcourt, 1965.

Johanna Hurwitz. *Once I Was a Plum Tree*. Morrow, 1980.

Naomi Karp. *Turning Point*. Harcourt, 1976.

Phyllis Krasilovsky. *L. C. Is the Greatest*. Nelson, 1975.

Sonia Levitin. *Journey to America*. Atheneum, 1970.

_____. *A Sound to Remember*. Harcourt, 1976.

Harry Mazer. *The Last Mission: A Novel*. Delacorte, 1979.

Marietta Moskin. *Waiting for Mama*. Coward, 1975.

Emily Neville. *Berries Goodman*. Harper, 1965.

I. L. Peretz. *The Case Against the Wind and Other Stories*. Macmillan, 1975.

*Mildred Phillips. *The Sign on Mendel's Window*. Macmillan, 1985.

Shalom Rabinowitz. *Holiday Tales of Sholom Aleichem*. Scribner, 1979.

*Suitable for primary grades.

Lois Ruby. *Two Truths in My Pocket.* Viking, 1982.

Marilyn Sachs. *Mary.* Doubleday, 1970.

Alezra Shevin. *Holiday Tales of Sholom Aleichem.* Scribner, 1976.

Carol Snyder. *Ike and Mama and the Block Wedding.* Coward, 1979.

Fannie Steinberg. *Birthday in Kishenev.* Jewish Publication Society, 1976.

*Sadie Weilerstein. *The Best of K'tonton.* Jewish Publication Society, 1960.

Nonfiction

Chana Abells. *The Children We Remember.* Kav-Ben Copies, 1983.

*David Adler. *A Picture Book of Hanukkah.* Holiday, 1982.

Mary Antin. *The Promised Land.* Houghton Mifflin, 1969.

Joanne E. Bernstein. *Dmitry: A Young Soviet Immigrant.* Ticknor & Fields, 1981.

Deborah Brodie. *Stories My Grandfather Should Have Told Me.* Hebrew Publishers, 1977.

Miriam Chaikin. *Ask Another Question; The Story and Meaning of Passover.* Clarion, 1985.

_____. *Sound the Shofar; The Story and Meaning of Rosh Hashanah and Yom Kippur.* Clarion, 1986.

Hila Coleman. *Rachel's Legacy.* Morrow, 1978.

Norman Finkelstein. *Remember Not to Forget.* Watts, 1985.

Howard Greenfeld. *Rosh Hashanah and Yom Kippur.* Holt, 1979.

Arlene Kurtis. *The Jews Helped Build America.* Messner, 1970.

Milton Meltzer, ed. *The Jewish Americans: A History in Their Own Words 1650–1950.* Crowell, 1982.

Bert Merter. *Bar Mitzvah, Bar Mitzvah: How Jewish Boys & Girls Come of Age.* Houghton, 1984.

Shirley Milgrim. *Haym Salomon: Liberty's Son.* Jewish Publications Society, 1976. (Biography).

Susan Purdy. *Jewish Holiday Cookbook.* Watts, 1979.

Johanna Reiss. *The Upstairs Room.* Crowell, 1972.

Ellen N. Stern. *Embattled Justice: The Story of Louis Dembitz Brandeis.* Jewish Publication Society, 1971. (Biography)

Folklore

Barbara Cohen. *Yussel's Prayer.* Lothrop, 1981.

Florence Freedman. *Brothers; A Hebrew Legend.* Harper, 1985.

Marilyn Hirsh. *Could Anything Be Worse? A Yiddish Tale.* Holiday, 1974.

Uri Shulevitz. *The Magician.* Macmillan, 1973.

Isaac B. Singer. *The Golem.* Farrar, 1982.

_____. *Mazel and Shlimazel.* Farrar, 1967.

_____. *When Shlemiel Went to Warsaw & Other Stories.* Farrar, 1968.

*Suitable for primary grades.

_____. *Zlateh, the Goat, and Other Stories.* Harper, 1966.

Margot Zemach. *It Could Always Be Worse: A Yiddish Folk Tale Retold.* Farrar, 1976.

Exploring Additional National Origins

In addition to the more detailed lists of books for children for important minority groups presented in the preceding pages, here are recommended books about specific countries or areas of the world.

Explore in both public and college libraries for additional information about any group you are studying. Check both adult and children's sections under the following categories:

Card catalog—subject entry

305.8	Racial, ethnic, and national groups
398.2	Folklore
808.8	Literature collections
811	American poetry
900	Geography and history; numbered according to specific groups
92,920	Biographies

Some books deal with immigration of groups, for example:

Gladys Nadler. *Coming to America: Immigrants from Southern Europe.* Delacorte, 1982.

Albert Robbins. *Coming to America: Immigrants from Northern Europe.* Delacorte, 1982.

Australia, New Zealand, and Tasmania

*Pamela Allen. *Who Sank the Boat?* Coward, 1983.

Patricia Beatty. *Jonathan Down Under.* Morrow, 1982.

Godfrey Blunden. *The Land and People of Australia.* Lippincott, 1972.

Diane Hebley, comp. *Off the Shelf: Twenty-One Years of New Zealand Books for Children.* Associated Books Publishers, Ltd.

W. F. Henderson. *Looking at Australia.* Lippincott, 1977.

Edna M. Kaula. *The Land and People of New Zealand.* Lippincott, 1972.

National Geographic Society. *Amazing Animals of Australia.* The Society, 1984.

Ruth Park. *Playing Beatie Bow.* Atheneum, 1982.

Joyce Powzyk. *Tasmania, A Wildlife Journey.* Lothrop, 1987.

Marilyn Sachs. *Call Me Ruth.* Doubleday, 1982.

*Suitable for primary grades.

Austria and Lichtenstein

Carol Greene. *Austria.* Children's Press, 1986.

Egypt

Aliki. *Mummies Made in Egypt.* Crowell, 1977.

Norma Katan. *Hieroplyphs: The Writing of Ancient Egypt.* Atheneum, 1981.

*Lise Maniche. *The Prince Who Knew His Fate.* Philomel, 1982.

England

Joan Aiken. *The Shadow Guests.* Delacorte, 1980.

Rachel Anderson. *The Poacher's Son.* Oxford, 1983.

Mitsumasa Anno. *Anno's Britain.* Philomel, 1982.

Shirley Blumenthal. *Coming to America: Immigrants from the British Isles.* Delacorte, 1980.

Nancy Bond. *Country of Broken Stone.* Atheneum, 1980.

John Branfield. *The Fox in White.* Atheneum, 1982.

Alan Hamilton. *Queen Elizabeth II.* Hamilton Hamish, 1983.

Barbara Hill. *Cooking the English Way.* Lerner, 1982.

Gene Kemp. *The Turbulent Term of Tyke Tiler.* Faber, 1977.

Penelope Lively. *Fanny's Sister.* Dutton, 1980.

Richard Mabey. *Oak and Company.* Greenwillow, 1983.

Michelle Magorian. *Good Night, Mr. Tom.* Harper, 1982.

Alison Morgan. *Paul's Kite.* Atheneum, 1982.

Ann Schlee. *Ask Me No Questions.* Holt, 1982.

Rosemary Sutcliff. *Frontier Wolf.* Dutton, 1981.

———. *Song for a Dark Queen.* Crowell, 1982.

France

Lilian J. Bragdon. *The Land and People of France.* Lippincott, 1972.

Walter Buehr. *The French Explorers in America.* Putnam, 1961.

Vivian Grey. *The Chemist Who Lost His Head: The Story of Antoine Lavoisier.* Coward, 1983.

Virginia Haviland. *Favorite Fairy Tales Told in France.* Little, 1959.

Virginia Kunz. *The French in America.* Lerner, 1966.

Robert Lexalt. *Sweet Promised Land.* Harper, 1957.

Robert C. Sieur de Syme. *La Salle of the Mississippi.* Morrow, 1953.

*Suitable for primary grades.

Germany

Margot Benary-Isbert. *The Ark*. Harcourt, 1953.

Lee Cooper. *Fun with German*. Little, 1965.

T. Degens. *The Visit*. Viking, 1982.

John Dornberg. *The Two Germanys*. Dial, 1974.

Bathold Fles. *East Germany*. Watts, 1973.

Robert Goldston. *The Life and Death of Nazi Germany*. Bobbs, 1967.

Evert Hartman. *War without Friends*. Crown, 1982.

Mara Kay. *In Face of Danger*. Crown, 1977.

Ilse Koehn. *My Childhood in Nazi Germany*. Greenwillow, 1972.

Virginia Kunz. *The Germans in America*. Lerner, 1966.

Otfried Preussler. *The Satanic Mill*. Macmillan, 1973.

Hans Richter. *Friedrich*. Holt, 1970.

Julia Singer. *Impressions. A Trip to the German Democratic Republic*. Atheneum, 1979.

Ellen Switzer. *How Democracy Failed*. Atheneum, 1975.

Raymond Wohlrabe. *The Land and the People of Germany*. Lippincott, 1972.

Greece

A study of Greek-American backgrounds fits well with mythology and the Olympics.

Isaac Asimov. *The Greeks: A Great Adventure*. Houghton, 1965.

Olivia Coolidge. *The Golden Days of Greece*. Crowell, 1968.

Julie Delton. *My Uncle Nikos*. Crowell, 1983.

Theodore Giankoulis. *The Land and People of Greece*. Lippincott, 1972.

Margaret Hodges. *The Avenger*. Scribner, 1982.

Norma Johnston. *The Days of the Dragon's Seed*. Atheneum, 1983.

Winifred Madison. *The Party That Lasted All Summer*.

Charles Robinson. *The First Book of Ancient Greece*. Watts, 1960.

Jonathan Rutland. *See Inside an Ancient Greek Town*. Warwick, 1979.

Miroslav Sasek. *This Is Greece*. Macmillan, 1966.

Janet Van Duyn. *The Greeks: Their Legacy*. McGraw, 1972.

Jill P. Walsh. *Children of the Fox*. Farrar, 1978.

Ruth Warren. *Modern Greece*. Watts, 1979.

Jane Yolen. *The Boy Who Had Wings*. Crowell, 1974.

India and Pakistan (Sri Lanka)

Mulk Raj Arand. *Indian Fairy Tales*. Bombay: Bhatkal, 1966. Colorful tales; good illustrations.

*Ellen C. Babbitt. *The Jatakas, Tales of India*. Appleton, 1940. Animal stories from India.

*Suitable for primary grades.

Leona Bagai. *The East Indians and the Pakistanis in America*. Lerner, 1967.

Astrid Bergman Sucksdorff. *Chendru*. Harcourt, 1960.

Jean Bothwell. *The First Book of India*. Watts, 1978.

Joseph Gaer. *Fables of India*. Little, 1955.

Madhur Jaffrey. *Seasons of Splendour: Tales, Myths, and Legends of India*. Atheneum, 1985.

Rudyard Kipling. *The Jungle Book and Just So Stories*. Varied editions.

Robert Lang. *The Land and People of Pakistan*. Lippincott, 1974.

Daulat Panday. *The Tales of India*. India: Ashram, 1963. Descriptive text; good illustrations.

Barbara Leonie Picard. *The Story of Rama and Sita*. London: Harrap, 1960. Exciting legend; good color illustrations.

F. W. Rawding. *Gandhi and the Struggle for India's Independence*. Lerner, 1982.

Ireland

Karen Bransom. *Streets of Gold*. Putnam, 1981.

Rhoda Fagen. *Ireland in Pictures*. Sterling, 1978.

Patricia Giff. *The Gift of the Pirate Queen*. Delacorte, 1982.

James Johnson. *The Irish in America*. Lerner, 1976.

Sondra Langford. *Red Bird of Ireland*. Atheneum, 1983.

Joan L. Nixon. *The Gift*. Macmillan, 1983.

Elinor O'Brien. *The Land and People of Ireland*. Lippincott, 1972.

Miroslav Sasek. *This Is Ireland*. Macmillan, 1965.

Catherine Sefton. *Island of the Strangers*. Harcourt, 1985.

Mary Tannen. *The Lost Legend of Finn*. Knopf, 1982.

Margaret Wetterer. *The Giant's Apprentice*. Atheneum, 1982.

Italy

Penrose Colyer. *I Can Read Italian: My First English-Italian Word Book*. Watts, 1983.

*Tomie De Paola. *Big Anthony and the Magic Ring*. Harcourt, 1979.

Sam Epstein. *The First Book of Italy*. Watts, 1972.

Ronald Grossman. *The Italians in America*. Lerner, 1966.

Erik Haugaard. *The Little Fishes*. Houghton, 1967.

Virginia Haviland. *Favorite Fairy Tales Told in Italy*. Little, 1965.

Frances Winwar. *The Land and People of Italy*. Lippincott, 1972.

Middle East

Aramco World Magazine. 1800 Augusta Dr., Suite 300, Houston TX 77057. Wonderful photoggraphy and informative articles; request free subscription.

*Suitable for primary grades.

Barbara Cohen and Bahija Lovejoy. *Seven Daughters and Seven Sons.* Atheneum, 1982.

Russell Davis and Brent Ashabranner. *Ten Thousand Desert Swords.* Little, Brown, 1960. 158 pp. Good adventure story.

*Olga Economakis. *Oasis of the Stars.* Coward, McCann & Geoghegan, 1965. Text vague and derogatory, nonfactual; good illustrations.

L. E. Leipold. *Folktales of Arabia.* Denison, 1973. Six of the best-known Arabian tales are retold in a simplified form.

Arthur Scholey, comp. *The Discontented Dervishes and Other Persian Tales.* Deutsch, 1982.

William Spencer. *Islamic States in Conflict.* Watts, 1983.

*Virginia A. Tashjian. *Three Apples Fell from Heaven.* Little, Brown, 1971. Entertaining stories; excellent illustrations.

*Barbara K. Walker. *The Courage of Kazan.* Crowell, 1970. Well-written story; beautiful illustrations.

Persia

Arthur Scholey, comp. *The Discontented Dervishes and Other Persian Tales.* Deutsch, 1982.

Poland

Anne Pellowski. *Winding Valley Farm: Annie's Story.* Philomel, 1982.

Cass Sandak. *Poland.* Watts, 1986.

Christine Szambelan-Stravinsky. *Dark Hour of Noon.* Lippincott, 1983.

Portugal

Esther Cross. *Portugal.* Childrens Press, 1986.

Scandinavia

Ulla Andersen. *We Live in Denmark.* Watts, 1984.

Peter Asbjørnsen. *East of the Sun and West of the Moon.* Doubleday, 1977.

James Bowman. *Tales from A Finnish Tupa.* Whitman, 1936.

Patricia Coombs. *The Magic Pot.* Lothrop, 1977.

Mary Hatch. *13 Danish Tales.* Harcourt, 1947.

Virginia Haviland. *Favorite Fairy Tales Told in Denmark.* Little, 1971.

_____. *Favorite Fairy Tales Told in Norway.* Little, 1961.

_____. *Favorite Fairy Tales Told in Sweden.* Little, 1966.

Martin Hintz. *Sweden.* Childrens Press, 1985.

Anita Lobel. *King Rooster, Queen Hen.* Greenwillow, 1975.

*_____. *The Pancake.* Greenwillow, 1978.

*Suitable for primary grades.

Sylvia Munsen. *Cooking the Norwegian Way.* Lerner, 1982.

Elsa Olenius, comp. *Great Swedish Fairy Tales.* Delacorte, 1973.

Kari Olsson. *Sweden: A Good Life for All.* Dillon, 1983.

Joan Sandin. *The Long Way to a New Land.* Harper, 1981.

Otto Svend. *The Giant Fish and Other Stories.* Larousse, 1983.

Scotland

Susan Cooper. *The Selkie Girl.* McElderry, 1986.

Thailand

Fiction

Astrid Lindgren. *Noy Lives in Thailand.* Macmillan, 1967.

Judith Spiegelman. *Galong, River Boy of Thailand.* Messner, 1970.

Nonfiction

Frederick Poole. *Thailand.* Watts, 1973.

Union of Soviet Socialists Republic

E. M. Almedingen. *Land of Muscovy: The History of Early Russia.* Farrar, 1972.

Bonnie Carey. *Baba Yaga's Geese and Other Russian Stories.* Indiana University Press, 1973.

Kornei Chukovsky. *The Silver Crest: My Russian Boyhood.* Holt, 1976.

Barbara Cohen. *Molly's Pilgrims.* Lothrop, 1983.

Guy Daniels. *Ivan the Fool and Other Tales of Leo Tolstory;* tr. by the author. Macmillan, 1966.

Nancy Eubank. *The Russians in America.* Lerner, 1973.

Virginia Haviland (retold by). *Favorite Fairy Tales Told in Russia.* Little, 1961.

Philip Hewitt. *Looking at Russia.* Lippincott, 1977.

Cynthia Jameson. *The Clay Pot Boy.* Coward-McCann, 1973.

Kathryn Lasky. *The Night Journey.* Warne, 1981.

Albert Likhanov. *Shadows across the Sun;* tr. from the Russian by Richard Lourie. Harper, 1983.

Miriam Morton. *Pleasures and Palaces: The After-school Activities of Russian Children.* Atheneum, 1972.

Alexander Nazaroff. *The Land and People of Russia.* Lippincott, 1972.

Tamara Talbot Rice. *Finding Out about the Early Russians.* Lothrop, 1964.

James Riordan. *Tales from Tartary.* Viking, 1977.

Uri Shulevitz. *Soldier and Tsar in the Forest.* Farrar, 1972.

Ernest Small. *Baba Yaga.* Houghton Mifflin, 1966.

Alke Zei. *The Sound of the Dragon's Feet.* Dutton, 1979.

United States

In addition to the many books already listed under special categories, here are a few additional resources that will be helpful.

Kathryn Cusick and Faye Morrison. *Golden Poppies: An Annotated Bibliography of California Historical Fiction and Non-Fiction for Young Readers.* Shoestring, 1986.

Elva Harman and Anna Milligan. *Reading for Young People: The Southwest.* American Library Association, 1982.

Barbara Immroth. *Texas in Children's Books: An Annotated Bibliography.* Shoestring, 1986.

Appalachia

George Ella Lyon. *Borrowed Children.* Watts, 1988.

Katherine Paterson. *Come Sing, Jimmy Jo.* Dutton, 1985.

Doris B. Smith. *Return to Bitter Creek: A Novel.* Viking, 1986.

Cajun (Acadia and Louisiana)

Berthe Amoss. *The Loup Garou.* Pelican, 1979.

John Bergeron. *Cajun Folklore.* Bergeron, 1980.

Muriel Fontenot Blackwell. *The Secret Dream.* Broadman, 1981.

Marguerite Bougere. *Louisiana Stories for Boys and Girls.* Louisiana University Press, 1966.

Allan Carpenter. *Louisiana.* Children's Press, 1967.

Elaine C. Crump. *Chinaberry Beads.* Pelican, 1978. (poetry)

*Alice Durio. *Cajun Columbus.* Pelican, 1975.

Tim Edler. *The Adventures of Crawfish-Man.* Little Cajun Books, 1979.

_____. *Dark Gator, Villain of the Atchafalaya.* Little Cajun Books, 1980.

_____. *Maurice the Snake and Gaston the Near-Sighted Turtle.* Little Cajun Books, 1977.

_____. *Santa's Cajun Christmas Adventure.* Little Cajun Books, 1981.

_____. *T-Boy, The Little Cajun.* Little Cajun Books, 1978.

_____. *T-Boy in Mossland.* Little Cajun Books, 1978.

_____. *T-Boy and the Trial for Life.* Little Cajun Books, 1978.

Zelma Engelhardt. *Beyond the Bayous.* Clarios, 1962. (poetry)

*Mary Alice Fontenot. *Clovis and E. Excargat.* Acadiana, 1979.

_____. *Clovis Crawfish and Curious Crapaud.* Acadiana, 1970.

_____. *Clovis Crawfish and His Friends.* Acadiana, 1962.

_____. *Clovis Crawfish and Michelle Mantis.* Acadiana, 1976.

_____. *Clovis Crawfish and Spinning Spider.* Acadiana, 1968.

_____. *Clovis Crawfish and the Big Betail.* Acadiana, 1963.

_____. *Clovis Crawfish and the Singing Cigales.* Pelican, 1981.

*Suitable for primary grades.

_____. *Ghost of Bayou Tigre.* Clairos, 1965.

Lois Lenski. *Bayou Suzette.* Lippincott, 1943.

*James Rice. *Cajun Alphabet.* Pelican, 1976.

_____. *Gaston Goes to Mardi Gras.* Pelican, 1977.

_____. *Gaston Lays an Off-shore Pipeline.* Pelican, 1979.

Corrine L. Saucier. *Folktales from French Louisiana.* Clarios, 1962.

George Smith. *Bayou Boy and the Wolf Dog.* Quality Books, 1973

Isadore L. Sonnier. *Cajun Boy.* Exposition Press, 1980.

Robert Tallant. *Evangeline and the Acadians.* Random, 1957.

*Trosclair. *Cajun Night before Christmas.* Pelican. 1974.

Eskimos

Carolyn Meyer. *Eskimos: Growing up in a Changing Culture.* Atheneum, 1977.

Peter Pitseolak. *Peter Pitseolak's Escape from Death.* Delacorte. 1978.

CHILDREN'S BOOKS IN OTHER LANGUAGES

As you conduct studies of other groups, children will be especially interested in books published in different languages. These books can be obtained in the original language, or they may be found in translation. There is a value in having both, but English translations are more easily obtained.

Translations

Notice that these translations have been published by American publishing companies.

Afrikaans

Sam Hobson and George Hobson. *The Lion of the Kalahari.* Greenwillow.

Danish

Ole Lund Kirkegaard. *Otto Is a Rhino.* Addison-Wesley.

Ib Spang Olsen. *The Little Locomotive.* Coward.

Thorsteinn Stefansson. *The Golden Future.* Nelson.

Dutch

Thea Beckman. *Crusade in Jeans.* Scribner's.

Margriet Heymans. *Cats and Dolls.* Addison-Wesley.

*Suitable for primary grades.

Flemish

Gommaar Timmermans. *The Great Balloon Race.* Addison-Wesley.

_____. *The Little White Hen and the Emperor of France.* Addison-Wesley.

Willy Vandersteen. *The Circus Baron.* Hiddigeigei Books.

_____. *An Island Called Hoboken.* Hiddigeigei Books.

_____. *The Merry Musketeers.* Hiddigeigei Books.

_____. *The Tender-hearted Matador.* Hiddigeigei Books.

French

Paul Jacques Bonzon. *The Runaway Flying Horse.* Parents'.

Laurent de Brunhoff. *Barbar's French Lessons.* Random.

Nancy Gurney. *The King, The Mice and the Cheese.* Beginner Books.

Hergé (4th series). *The Adventures of Tintin.* Atlantic—Little Brown.

Sesyle Joslin. *There Is a Dragon in My Bed. . .* Harcourt.

Tanobe Miyuki. *Québec: Je t'aime. . . .* Tundra.

Dr. Seuss. *The Cat in the Hat.* Random.

Edward Smith. *The Frogs Who Wanted a King . . .* Four Winds.

German

Hans Baumann. *The Hare's Race.* Morrow.

Max Bollinger. *The Giant's Feast.* Addison-Wesley.

Achim Broger. *Outrageous Kasimir.* Morrow.

Hans and Monique Dossenbach. *Animal Babies of East Africa.* Putnam.

Hans Isenbart and Hanns-Jorg Anders. *The Foal Is Born.* Putnam.

Luis Murschetz. *A Hamster's Journey.* Prentice-Hall.

_____. *Mister Mole.* Prentice-Hall.

Hannelore Valencak. *When Half-Gods Go.* Morrow.

Japanese

Chiyoko Nakatani. *My Teddy Bear.* Crowell.

Hiroyuki Takahaski. *The Foxes of Chironupp Island.* Windmill/Dutton.

Polish

Jerzy Ficowski. *Sister of the Birds and Other Gypsy Tales.* Abingdon.

Russian

Kornei Chukovsky. *The Silver Crest: My Russian Boyhood.* Holt, Rinehart and Winston.

Mirra Ginsburg, ed. *The Air of Mars and Other Stories of Time and Place.* Macmillan.

_____, ed. *Pamalche of the Silver Teeth.* Crown.

Spanish

John Bierhorst, ed. *Black Rainbow* (Inca Legends and Peruvian Myths). Farrar.

Thomas Blanco. *The Child's Gifts.* Westminster.

Doris Dana. *The Elephant and His Secret.* Atheneum.

P. D. Eastman. *Are You My Mother?* Beginner Books.

Antonio Frasconi. *The Snow and the Sun.* Harcourt.

Nancy Guerney. *The King, The Mice and the Cheese.* Beginner Books.

Sesyle Joslin. *There Is a Bull on My Balcony* . . . Harcourt.

Anne Rockwell. *El Toro Pinto, and Other Songs in Spanish.* Macmillan.

Isabel Schon. *Basic Collection of Children's Books in Spanish.* Scarecrow, 1986.

———. *Books in Spanish for Children and Young Adults.* Scarecrow, 1985.

Dr. Seuss. *The Cat in the Hat.* Random.

Swedish

Bo Carpelan. *Dolphins in the City.* Delacorte/Seymour Lawrence.

Stig Ericson. *Dan Henry in the Wild West.* Delacorte/Seymour Lawrence.

Maria Gripe. *Elvis and His Friends.* Delacorte/Seymour Lawrence.

———. *Elvis and His Secret.* Delacorte/Seymour Lawrence.

———. *In the Time of the Bells.* Delacorte/Seymour Lawrence.

Astrid Lindgren. *Pippi on the Run.* Viking.

Lists of Books Published Abroad

Country	Name, Language, and Frequency of List	Order From
Australia	*Reading Time,* Publication No. 1, "Book of the Year and Picture Book Awards 1946–1976," a 16-page pamphlet listing the winners, highly commended and commended titles for these awards since the inception of the awards program.	*Reading Time,* Children's Book Council of Australia, c/o Library Services, 35 Mitchell St., North Sydney 2060, Australia
Brazil	"Separata" within the quarterly *Boletim Informativo,* with annotated reviews of recommended new books arranged by age level. (Portuguese)	Fundação Nacional do Livro Infantil e Juvenil, rua Voluntãrios da Pãtria 107, ZC-02 Rio de Janeiro, Brazil
France	Annual selection of best children's books appears as part of the last issue each year of *Bulletin d'analyses de lvres pour enfants,* published six times a year. Annual subscription is 45 francs; single issue is 8 francs. (French)	la Joie par les Livres, Centre de documentation, 4, rue di Louvois, 75002 Paris, France

Country	Name, Language, and Frequency of List	Order From
Great Britain	"Poetry Books for Children: A *Signal* Booklist," a 32-page annotated selection of over 100 poetry books from the earliest books to the midteens. Alan Tucker. Illustrations.	The Thimble Press, Lockwood Station R., South Woodchester, STROUD, Glos.5EQ, England
Israel	"Books from Israel: Suggestions for Publication Abroad," a 1976 catalog prepared for the Frankfurt Book Fair (Children's books pp. 15–23). (English)	International Promotion and Literary Rights Dept., Book Publishers Assn. of Israel, 29 Carlebach St., Tel-Aviv 67-132, Israel (Free)
Sweden	"Vi läser på fritid: Basta bocker for barn och ungdom." Eight-page pamphlet containing annotated listings of approximately 80 best children's books of the year. Illustrations. Published annually in November. (Swedish)	Children's Booklists Ed. Bibliotekstjänst AB, Fack 221 01 Lund, Sweden.
	"Boknyheter: Barnbocker," an annual annotated selection of books for libraries, schools and youth organizations. (Swedish)	Address as above.
Switzerland	"Zürcher Klassenleseserien der Schweizerischen Volksbibliothek 1976/77," an annotated listing of under 200 recommended children's books. (German)	Mr. A. Lüthi (Schweizerischer Bund für Jugendliteratur) Newdorfstr. 29 CH 8820 Wädenswil. Switzerand (Free; limited supply)

NOTE: Booklist, a library buying guide published by the American Library Association, features such lists regularly. Address inquiries to: 50 E. Huron St., Chicago, IL 60611.

EXPLORING SPECIAL IDENTITY GROUPS

Although identity groups could be included, we have selected only three major groups: (1) the aged, (2) the disabled, and (3) women and girls.

Aging and the Aged

Anne E. Baldwin. *Sunflowers for Tina.* Four Winds, 1978.

Gunnel Beckman. *That Early Spring.* Viking, 1977.

Lenore Blegvard. *Moon-Watch Summer.* Harcourt, Brace & Jovanovich, 1972.

Rose Blue. *Grandma Didn't Wave Back.* Watts, 1972.

Pearl Buck. *The Beach Tree.* John Day, 1955.

Clyde Robert Bulla. *The Sugar Pear Tree.* Crowell, 1961.

Robert Burch. *Two That Were Tough.* Viking, 1976.

_____. *The House of Wings.* Viking, 1972.

Betsy Byars. *Trouble River* Viking, 1969.

Vera Cleaver. *Queen of Hearts.* Lippincott, 1978.

Vera and Bill Cleaver. *The Whys and Wherefores of Litta Belle Lee.* Atheneum, 1974.

Eth Clifford. *The Rocking Chair Rebellion.* Houghton Mifflin, 1978.

Barbara Corcoran. *The Faraway Island.* Atheneum, 1977.

Tomie de Paola. *Nana Upstairs & Nana Downstairs.* Putnam & Sons, 1973.

_____. *Now One Foot, Now the Other.* Putnam's Sons, 1981.

_____. *Watch Out for the Chicken Feet in Your Soup.* Prentice Hall, 1974.

Norma Farber. *How Does It Feel to be Old?* Dutton, 1979.

Patricia Lee Gauch. *Grandpa & Me.* McGann, 1972.

Rumer Goden. *The Fairy Doll.* Viking, 1956.

Susan Goldman. *Grandma Is Somebody Special.* Whitman, 1976.

Phyllis Green. *Mildred Murphy, How Does Your Garden Grow?* Dell, 1977.

Constance Greene. *The Unmaking of Rabbit.* Dell, 1972.

Lucille Heins. *My Very Special Friend.* Judson, 1974.

Kevin Henkes. *Grandpa & Bo.* Greenwillow, 1986.

Charlotte Herman. *Our Snowman Had Olive Eyes.* Dutton, 1977.

Edith T. Hurd. *I Dance in My Red Pajamas..* Harper & Row, 1982.

Mildred Kantrowitz. *Maxie.* Parents Magazine Press, 1970.

Dayal K. Khalsa. *Tales of a Gambling Grandma.* New York: Potter, 1986.

Barbara Kirk. *Grandpa, Me, & Our House in the Tree.* MacMillan, 1976.

Kathryn Lasky. *I Have Four Names for My Grandfather.* Little Brown, 1976.

_____. *My Island Grandma.* Warne, 1979.

Gen LeRoy. *Emma's Dilemma.* Harper and Row, 1975.

Joan Lexau. *Benjie on His Own.* Dial, 1970.

Sharon Bell Mathis. *The Hundred Penny Box.* Viking, 1975.

Norma Fox Mazer. *A Figure of Speech.* Delacourt, 1973.

J. F. Mearian. *Someone Slightly Different.* Dial, 1980.

Miska Miles. *Annie and the Old One.* Little Brown, 1971.

Elaine Moore. *Grandma's House.* Lothrop, Lee & Shepard, 1985.

Evaline Ness. *Josefina February.* Scribner's Sons, 1963.

Melinda Pollowitz. *Cinnamon Cane.* Harper and Row, 1977.

Fran Pratt. *Understanding Aging.* Conant School, 1982.

Jean Robinson. *The Secret Life of T. K. Dearing.* Seabury, 1973.

Eleanor Schick. *Peter and Mr. Brandon.* Macmillan, 1973.

Leisel Skorpen. *Mandy's Grandmother.* Dial, 1975.

Ruth Sonneborn. *I Love Gram.* Viking, 1971.

Susan Varley. *Badger's Parting Gifts.* Lothrop, Lee & Shepard, 1984.

Elizabeth Winthrop. *Walking Away.* Harper & Row, 1973.

Sally Wittman. *A Special Trade.* Harper & Row, 1978.

Charlotte Zolotow. *I Know A Lady.* Greenwillow, 1984.

_____. *My Grandson Lew.* Harper & Row, 1974.

Positive Images of the Elderly

Primary Grades

Josephine Aldridge. *Fisherman's Luck.* Parnassus, 1966.

Martha Alexander. *The Story Grandmother Told.* Dial, 1969.

Edward Ardizzone. *Tim of the Lighthouse.* Walck, 1968.

Jeannie Baker. *Grandmother.* Deutsch, 1978.

Jennifer Bartoli. *Nona.* Harvey, 1975.

Barbara Borack. *Grandpa.* Harper, 1967.

Kay Chorao. *Lester's Overnight.* Dutton, 1977.

Helen Constant. *The Gift.* Knopf, 1983.

Tomie de Paola. *Nana Upstairs and Nana Downstairs.* Putnam's 1973.

_____. *Watch Out for Chicken Feet in Your Soup.* Prentice, 1974.

Arnold Dobrin. *Scat!* Four Winds, 1971.

James Flora. *Grandpa's Farm.* Harcourt, 1965.

Patricia Lee Gauch. *Grandpa and Me.* Coward, 1972.

M.B. Goffstein. *Fish for Supper.* Dial, 1976.

Susan Goldman. *Grandma Is Somebody Special.* Whitman, 1978.

_____. *Grandpa and Me Together.* Whitman, 1979.

Lucille Heins. *My Very Special Friend.* Judson, 1974.

Russell Hoban. *How Tom Beat Captain Najork and His Hired Sportsman.* Atheneum, 1974.

Louise A. Jackson. *Grandpa Had a Windmill, Grandma Had a Churn.* Parent, 1977.

Mildren Kantrowitz. *Maxie.* Parent, 1970.

Eleanor J. Lapp. *The Mice Came in Early This Year.* Whitman, 1976.

Kathryn Lasky. *I Have Four Names for My Grandfather.* Little Brown, 1976.

Joan M. Lexau. *Benjie and His Own.* Dial, 1970.

Jan Loof. My Grandpa Is a Pirate. Harper, 1968.

Max Lundgren. *Matt's Grandfather.* Putnam, 1972.

Miska Miles. *Annie and the Old One.* Little Brown, 1971.

Evaline Ness. *Josefina February.* Scribner, 1963.

Shirley P. Newman. *Tell Me, Grandpa; Tell Me, Grandma.* Houghton, 1979.

Steven Palay. *I Love My Grandma.* Raintree, 1977.

Dorka Raynor. *Grandparents Around the World.* Whitman, 1977.

Eleanor Schick. *Peter and Mr. Brandon*. Macmillan, 1974.

Liesel Moak Skorpen. *Mandy's Grandmother*. Dial, 1975.

_____. *Old Arthur*. Harper, 1972.

William Sleator. *The Angry Moon*. Little Brown, 1970.

Ianthe Thomas. *Hi, Mrs. Mallory*. Harper, 1979.

Tobi Tobias. *Jane Wishing*. Viking, 1977.

Janice May Udry. *Mary Jo's Grandmother*. Whitman, 1970.

Barbara Williams. *Kevin's Grandma*. Dutton, 1975.

Sally Wittman. *A Special Trade*. Harper, 1978.

Joyce Wood. *Grandmother Lucy Goes on a Picnic*. World, 1970.

Charlotte Zolotow. *My Grandson Lew*. Harper, 1974.

_____. *William's Doll*. Harper, 1972.

Books for Older Students

Patricia Beatty. *The Coach That Never Came*. Morrow, 1985.

Mem Fox. *Wilfrid Gordon McDonald Partridge*. Miller, 1985.

Nancy Smiler Levinson. *The Ruthie Greene Show*. Lodestar, 1985.

The Disabled

General Information

Barbara Adams. *Like It Is: Facts and Feelings about Handicaps from Kids Who Know*. Walker, 1979. Photographs.

Gilda Berger. *Physical Disabilities*. Watts, 1979.

Tricia Brown. *Someone Special, Just Like You*. Holt, 1984. Photographs.

Lorraine Henriod. *Special Olympics and Paralympics*. Watts, 1979.

Theodore Huebener. *Special Education Careers: Training the Handicapped Child*. Watts, 1977.

Richard Lyttle. *Challenged by Handicap: Adventures in Courage*. Reilly, 1971.

*Mary Ellen Powers. *Our Teacher's in a Wheelchair*. Whitman, 1986.

Margaret Pursell. *A Look at Physical Handicaps*. Lerner, 1976. Photographs.

Ron Roy. *Move Over, Wheelchairs Coming Through: Seven Young People in Wheelchairs Talk about Their Lives*. Clarion, 1985.

Autism

Ruth Arthur. *Portrait of Margarita*. Atheneum, 1968.

Phyllis Gold. *Please Don't Say Hello*. Human Science Press. 1975.

*Suitable for primary grades.

Blindness/Problems with Eyesight

James Garfield. *Follow My Leader*. Viking, 1957.

_____. *Smith*. Pantheon, 1967.

Florence Heide. *Sound of Sunshine, Sound of Rain*. Parents, 1972.

Virginia Jensen and Dorca Haller. *What's That?* World, 1977. A book that blind children can read, too.

Madeleine L'Engle. *The Young Unicorns*. Farrar, Straus, 1968. The training of a mime who becomes expert.

Ramona Maher. *The Blind Boy and the Loon and Other Eskimo Myths*. Day, 1969.

Sharon Mathis. *Listen for the Fig Tree*. Viking, 1974.

*Ellen Raskin. *Spectacles*. Atheneum, 1978.

Glen Rounds. *The Blind Colt*. Holiday, 1969.

Aimee Sommerfelt. *The Road to Agra*. Criterion, 1961.

Theodore Taylor. *The Cay*. Doubleday, 1969.

William Thomas. *The New Boy Is Blind*. Thomas, 1980.

Malcolm Weiss. *Seeing Through the Dark: Blind and Sighted—A Vision Shared*. Harcourt, 1976.

Bernard Wolf. *Connie's New Eyes*. Lippincott, 1976.

Brain Damage

Daniel Keyes. *Flowers for Algernon*. Harcourt, 1966.

Kim Platt. *Hey, Dummy*. Dell, 1971.

C. L. Rinaldo. *Dark Dreams*. Harper, 1974.

Cerebral Palsy

*Joan Fassler. *Howie Helps Himself*. Whitman, 1975.

Jean Little. *Mine for Keeps*. Little, 1962.

Jan Slepian. *The Alfred Summer*. Macmillan, 1980.

*Sara Stein. *About Handicaps: An Open Family Book for Parents and Children Together*. Walker, 1974.

Deaf/Blind

Margaret Davidson. *Helen Keller*. Hastings, 1969.

Francene Sabin. *The Courage of Helen Keller*. Troll Associates, 1982.

Deafness

Remy Charlip, et al. *Handtalk: An ABC of Finger Spelling & Sign Language*. Parent's, 1974.

*Suitable for primary grades.

Olivia Coolidge. *Come by Here.* Houghton, 1970.

Elaine Costello. *Signing: How to Speak with Your Hands.* Bantam, 1983.

Etta DeGering. *Gallaudet: Friend of the Deaf.* McKay, 1964.

Meindert DeJong. *Journey from Peppermint Street.* Harper, 1968.

Judith Greenberg. *What Is the Sign for Friend?* Lothrop, 1985.

Edna Levine. *Lisa and Her Soundless World.* Human Sciences Press, 1974.

Mary Riskind. *Apple Is My Sign.* Houghton, 1981.

Veronica Robinson. *David in Silence.* Philadelphia, 1966.

Eleanor Spence. *The Nothing Place.* Harper, 1972.

Lou Walker. *Amy: The Story of a Deaf Child.* Lodestar, 1985.

Maia Wojciechowska. *A Single Light.* Bantam, 1968.

Deformity

Frederich Drimmer. *The Elephant Man.* Putnam, 1985.

Down's Syndrome

Elaine Ominsky. *Jon O: A Special Boy.* Prentice, 1977.

Dwarfism

M. E. Kerr. *Little Little.* Harper, 1981.

Susan Kuklin. *Thinking Big; The Story of a Young Dwarf.* Lothrop, 1986.

Dyslexia

Margot Marek. *Different, Not Dumb.* Watts, 1985.

Michele Murray. *Nellie Cameron.* Seabury, 1971.

Emotional Problems/Mental Illness

Virginia Axline. *Dibs in Search of Self: Personality Development in Play Therapy.* Houghton, 1964.

Eve Bunting. *One More Flight.* Warne, 1976.

Beverly Butler. *Feather in the Wind.* Dodd, 1965.

Carol Carrick. *Stay Away from Simon.* Clarion, 1985.

Joanne Greenberg. (Hannah Green). *I Never Promised You a Rose Garden.* Holt, 1964.

Virginia Hamilton. *The Planet of Junior Brown.* Macmillan, 1971.

Deborah Hautizig. *Second Star to the Right.* Greenwillow, 1981.

Florence Heide. *Secret Dreamer, Secret Dreams.* Lippincott, 1978.

M. E. Kerr. *Dinky Hocker Shoots Smack!* Dell, 1972.

Norma Klein. *It's Not What You Expect.* Pantheon, 1973.

John Langone. *Goodby to Bedlam: Understanding Mental Illness and Retardation*. Little, 1974.

Mary MacCracken. *A Circle of Children*. Lippincott, 1973.

Phyllis Naylor. *The Keeper*. Atheneum, 1986.

John Newfeld. *Lisa, Bright and Dark*. Phillips, 1969.

Zibby O'Neal. *The Language of Goldfish*. Viking, 1980.

Virginia Sorensen. *Miracles on Maple Hill*. Harcourt, 1956.

Patricia Windsor. *The Summer Before*. Harper, 1973.

Epilepsy

Ellen Howard. *Edith Herself*. Atheneum, 1987.

General Health Problems

Alice Bach. *Waiting for Johnny Miracel*. Harper, 1980. Cancer.

Virginia Lee. *The Magic Moth*. Seabury, 1972. Heart defect.

Elizabeth Winthrop. *A Little Demonstration of Affection*. Harper, 1975. Asthma.

Learning Disabled

*Joe Lasker. *He's My Brother*. Whitman, 1974.

Marilyn Levinson. *And Don't Bring Jeremy*. Holt, 1985.

*Muriel Stanek. *Left, Right; Left, Right!* Whitman, 1969.

Missing Limbs

Cynthia Voigt. *Izzy, Willy-Nilly*. Atheneum, 1986.

Bernard Wolf. *Don't Feel Sorry for Paul*. Lippincott, 1974. Photographs.

Orthopedic Impairment

James Aldridge. *A Sporting Proposition*. Little, 1973.

Harold Courlander. *The Son of the Leopard*. Crown, 1974.

Marguerite DeAngeli. *The Door in the Wall*. Doubleday, 1949.

Meindert DeJong. *The Wheel on the School*. Harper, 1954.

Ester Forbes. *Johnny Tremain*. Houghton, 1971.

Isabelle Holland. *Heads You Win, Tails I Lose*. Lippincott, 1973.

Irene Hunt. *No Promises in the Wind*. Follett, 1970.

Mollie Hunter. *The Stronghold*. Harper, 1974.

Sulamith Ish-Kishor. *Our Eddie*. Pantheon, 1969.

*Suitable for primary grades.

Katherine Paterson. *Of Nightingales That Weep*. Crowell, 1974.

Doris Smith. *Tough Chauncey*. Morrow, 1974.

Elizabeth Speare. *The Witch of Blackbird Pond*. Houghton, 1958.

Phillis Whitney. *Nobody Likes Trina*. New American Library, 1976.

Retardation

Frank Bonham. *Mystery of the Fat Cat*. Dutton, 1968.

Betsy Byars. *Summer of the Swans*. Viking, 1970.

Vera Cleaver and Bill Cleaver. *Me, Too*. Lippincott, 1973.

Lucille Clifton. *My Friend Jacob*. Dutton, 1980.

Barthe DeClements. *6th Grade Can Really Kill You*. Viking, 1985.

Robert Dunbar. *Mental Retardation*. Watts, 1978.

Maria Farrai. *A Look at Mental Retardation*. Lerner, 1976. Photographs.

*Joan Fassler. *One Little Girl*. Human Sciences, 1969.

Sharon Grollman. *More Time to Grow: Explaining Mental Retardation to Children, A Story*. Beacon, 1977.

Lynn Hall. *Sticks and Stones*. Follett, 1972.

Irene Hunt. *Up a Road Slowly*. Grosset, 1966.

Edwin Kaplan. *No Other Love*. Bantam, 1979.

Gerda Klein. *The Blue Rose*. Hill, 1974.

Earlene Luis and Barbara Millar. *Listen, Lissa: A Candy Striper Meets the Biggest Challenge*. Dodd, 1968.

Marlene Shyer. *Welcome Home, Jellybean*. Schribner, 1978.

Gene Smith. *The Hayburners*. Delacorte, 1974.

Ivan Southall. *Hill's End*. Macmillan, 1962.

Susan Wexler. *The Story of Sandy*. Bobbs-Merrill, 1970.

Patricia Wrightson. *A Racecourse for Andy*. Harcourt, 1968.

Speech Impediments

Rebecca Caudill. *A Certain Small Shepherd*. Holt, 1965.

Julia Cunningham. *Burnish Me Bright*. Pantheon, 1970.

Joan Fassler. *Won't Worry, Dear*. Human Sciences, 1971.

Marguerite Henry. *King of the Wind*. Rand, 1948.

Breaking Down Stereotypes of Women

Readers of all ages need to read books that present positive images of women engaged in varied lifestyles and careers. From fantasy to nonfiction, books can support

*Suitable for primary grades.

the self-esteem of the girls who are reading, and they can provide an enlightened perspective of women for male readers. This potpourri is grouped by difficulty levels.

Primary Grades

Arlene Alda. *Sonya's Mommy Works.* Simon, 1982. A photographic essay of a contemporary family in which mother has a career.

Roshyn Banesh. *I Want to Tell You about My Baby.* Wingbow Press, 1982. Black and white photos tell story of preparation for new baby.

Jeanette Caines. *Daddy.* Harper, 1977. Story of child's special relationship with father who is separated from Mother.

Norma Klein. *Girls Can Be Anything.* Dutton, 1973. Marina lets her kindergarten pal, Adam, know that "girls can be anything."

Mercer Mayer. *Liza Lou and the Yeller Belly Swamp.* Four Winds, 1976. How Liza Lou outwits the swamp devil.

Eve Merrian. *Mommies at Work.* Scholastic, 1973. Picture book showing all kinds of mommies at all kinds of jobs.

Harlow Rockell. *My Doctor.* Picture book of female doctor who removes child's fears of visiting the doctor.

Miriam Schlein. *The Girl Who Would Rather Climb Trees.* About a tomboy who receives a doll and what she does with it.

Amy Schwartz. *Bea and Mr. Jones.* Puffin, 1982. A kindergartener and her father change places.

John Steptoe. *Daddy is a Monster . . . Sometimes.* Lippincott, 1980. Story of a single, loving parent and his two children.

_____. *My Special Best Words.* Viking, 1974. A delightful picture book about Bweela, age 3, Javaka, age 1, and their father.

Middle Grades

Sue Alexander. *Nadia the Willful.* Pantheon, 1983. Nadia, daughter of sheik Tarik, deals with her brother's death.

Caroline Bauer. *My Mom Travels a Lot.* Warne, 1982. Story about good and bad situations caused by mother's many absences from home.

Vera and Bill Cleaver. *Hazel Rye.* Lippincott, 1983. The struggles between an 11-year-old girl and her father.

Barbara Cohen and Bahija Lovejoy. *Seven Daughters and Seven Sons.* Atheneum, 1982. Buran, the daughter of Malik, is educated as though she were a son and later poses as a man. Set in ancient Baghdad.

Walter de la Mare. *Molly Whuppie.* Farrar, 1983. An old tale retold; a girl outwits a giant.

Madeline L'Engle. *A Wrinkle in Time.* Ariel, 1962.

Ruth Meyers and Beryle Banfield. *Embers: Stories for a Changing World.* Feminist Press, 1983. Includes fiction, biography, poetry, and oral history portraying people struggling to overcome barriers of sex, race, and disability.

Tamora Pierce. *Alanna, The First Adventure.* Atheneum, 1983. Lord Alan's twin daughter, Alanna, and son, Thom, trade places. Alanna trains to be a knight, and Thom trains to be a sorcerer.

Robert Peck. *Trig.* Little, 1982. An independent girl chooses a name to fit her new gun.

Barbara Robinson. *The Best Christmas Pageant Ever.* Harper, 1972. Story of family of six children who wreak havock on the town's annual Christmas pageant.

Cynthia Voight. *Homecoming.* Atheneum, 1981. Dicey, a 13-year-old girl, cares for her brothers and sisters after they are abandoned. See also *Dicey's Song, The Calandar Papers,* and *Solitary Blue* by the same author.

Jay Williams. *Petronella.* Parents, 1973. Petronella, third child who turns out to be a girl, sets out with brothers to seek her fortune and find a prince.

_____. *The Practical Princess.* Parents, 1978. Princess Bedelia fights dragons and rescues a prince.

Young Adults

Carol Brink. *Caddie Woodlawn.* Macmillan, 1970. Caddie, who lives in the Wisconsin frontier, is an adventurous tomboy who resists accepting her sex role.

Barbara Cohen. *Seven Daughters and Seven Sons.* Atheneum, 1982. Buran of Baghdad disguises herself as a boy to help her family.

Lois Duncan. *Daughters of Eve.* Little, 1979. Thriller about a club of teenage girls who decide to rebel against the dominating men in their lives.

Norma Klein. *Give and Take,* Viking, 1985. The summer before Spence enters college provides unexpected experiences with women. See also *Lovers, Angel Face, the Swap,* and *Beginners' Love* by the same author.

_____. *Mom, the Wolf Man and Me.* Pantheon, 1972. Brett's unmarried mother decides to marry without asking her daughter's permission.

Norma Fox Mazer. *Dear Bill, Remember Me?* Delacorte, 1977. Collection of eight short stories in which young girls break away from conventional female role.

Robin McKinley. *The Blue Sword.* Greenwillow, 1983. Harry, a teenage girl, exhibits courage in this story of magic and fantasy.

Marilyn Sachs. *Call Me Ruth.* Doubleday, 1982. Rifka (Ruth) and her mother, Faigel, are Russian immigrants. Ruth is torn between the old and new ways.

Folktales with Active Heroines

"Atlanta" in *Free to Be . . . You and Me.* Marlo Thomas, conceiver. McGraw, 1974.

"Baba Yaga" in *Old Peter's Russian Tales.* Arthur Ransome and Nelson, 1916. Out of print; Dover reprint.

"The Barber's Clever Wife" in *Tales from the Punjab.* Flora A. Steele. Macmillan, 1894. Out of print; *Fools and Funny Fellows.* Phyllis Fenner. Knopf, 1947.

"The Betrothal Gifts" in *Czechoslovak Fairy Tales.* Parker Fillmore. Harcourt, 1919.

"The Bigger Giant" retold by Nancy Green. Follett, 1963.

"The Black Bull of Norroway" in *More English Folk and Fairy Tales*. Joseph Jacobs. Putnam, 1904.

"Boadicea . . . The Warrior Queen" in *The World's Great Stories: 55 Legends That Live Forever*. Louis Untermeyer. Lippincott, 1964.

"Cap O' Rushes" in *English Folk and Fairy Tales*. Joseph Jacobs. Putnam, 1904. Dover reprint as *English Fairy Tales; Womenfolk and Fairy Tales*. Rosemary Minard. Houghton, 1975.

"Chinese Red Riding Hoods" in *Chinese Fairy Tales*. Isabelle C. Chang. Barre, 1965.

"Clever Grethel" in *Tales Told Again*. Walter de la Mare. Knopf, 1927. Dover reprint as *English Fairy Tales; Womenfolk and Fairy Tales*. Rosemary Minard. Houghton, 1975.

"Clever Kadra" in *African Wonder Tales*. Frances Carpenter. Doubleday, 1963.

"Clever Manka" in *The Shepherd's Nosegay*. Parker Fillmore. Harcourt, 1920. o.p.; *Fools and Funny Fellows*. Phyllis Fenner. Knopf, 1947. Dover reprint as *English Fairy Tales; Womenfolk and Fairy Tales*. Rosemary Minard. Houghton, 1975.

"Clever Ooagh" in *William Mayne's Book of Giants*. Dutton, 1969.

"The Dragon's Revenge" in *Magic Animals of Japan*. Davis Pratt. Parnassus, 1967.

East of the Sun and West of the Moon. P. C. Asbjounsen. Dover reprint as *English Fairy Tales; Womenfolk and Fairy Tales*. Rosemary Minard. Houghton, 1975.

"The Feather of Finist the Falcon" in *Russian Wonder Tales*. Post Wheeler. Thomas Yoseloff, 1957.

"Fin M'Coul and Cucullin" in *A Book of Giants*. Ruth Manning-Sanders. Dutton, 1963.

The Forest Princess. Harriet Herman. Rainbow Press, 1974.

"The Forty Thieves" in *The Blue Fairy Book*. Andrew Lang. Longmans, 1889. Dover reprint as *English Fairy Tales; Womenfolk and Fairy Tales*. Rosemary Minard. Houghton, 1975.

"A Fox Who Was Too Sly" in *Magic Animals of Japan*. Davis Pratt. Parnassus, 1967.

"The Gnome Maiden" in *Piskey Folk, a Book of Cornish Legends*. Elizabeth Yates. John Day, 1940.

"Gyda's Saucy Message" in *Viking Tales*. Jennie Hall. McNally, 1902.

The Handsome Prince. Nancy Schimmel. Franciscan Films, 1975.

"The Husband Who Was to Mind the House" in *East of the Sun and West of the Moon*. P. C. Asbjornsen. Dover reprint as *English Fairy Tales; Womenfolk and Fairy Tales*. Rosemary Minard. Houghton, 1975.

"Kate Crackernuts" in *English Folk & Fairy Tales*. Joseph Jacobs. Putnam, 1904. Dover reprint as *English Fairy Tales; Womenfolk and Fairy Tales*. Rosemary Minard. Houghton, 1975.

"The Lass Who Went Out at the Cry of Dawn" in *Thistle and Thyme*. Sorche Nic Leodhas. Holt, 1962. Dover reprint as *English Fairy Tales; Womenfolk and Fairy Tales*. Rosemary Minard. Houghton, 1975.

The Little Red Hen. Janina Domanska, adapt. and illus. Macmillan, 1973. Paul Galdone, Seabury, 1973.

"Luck and Wit" in *Rumanian Folk Tales*. Jean Ure. Watts, 1960.

"Mr. Fox" in *More English Folk and Fairy Tales*. Dover reprint as *English Fairy Tales; Womenfolk and Fairy Tales*. Rosemary Minard. Houghton, 1975.

"Mollie Whuppie" in *English Folk & Fairy Tales*. Joseph Jacobs. Putnam, 1904. *Tales Told*

Again. Walter de la Mare. Knopf, 1927. Dover reprint as *English Fairy Tales; Womenfolk and Fairy Tales.* Rosemary Minard. Houghton, 1975.

Molly and the Giant. Retold by Kurt Werth and Mabel Watts. Parents, 1973.

"Mutsmag" in *Grandfather Tales.* Richard Chase. Houghton, 1948.

"The Old Woman and Her Dumpling" in *Japanese Fairy Tales.* Lafcadio Hearn. Pauper, 1948. Dover reprint as *English Fairy Tales; Womenfolk and Fairy Tales.* Rosemary Minard. Houghton, 1975.

Petronella. Jay Williams. Parents, 1973.

The Practical Princess. Jay Williams. Parents, 1969.

"Rabbit and Hedgehog" in *American Negro Folktales.* Richard M. Dorson. Fawcett, 1967.

"The Salt at Dinner" in *Rumanian Folk Tales.* Jean Ure. Watts, 1960.

The Silver Whistle. Jay Williams. Parents, 1971.

"The Skull" in *The Book of Ghosts and Goblins.* Ruth Manning Sanders. Dutton, 1973.

"The Squire's Bride" in *True and Untrue, and Other Norse Tales.* Sigrid Undset. Knopf, 1945.

"The Stolen Bairn and the Sidh" in *Thistle and Thyme.* Sorche Nic Leodhas. Holt, 1962.

"Tamlane" in *More English Folk and Fairy Tales..*

This Time, Tempe Wick? Patricia Gauch. Coward, 1974.

"Three Sisters Who Were Entrapped into a Mountain" in *English Fairy Tales; Womenfolk and Fairy Tales.* Rosemary Minard. Houghton, 1975.

Three Strong Women: A Tall Tale From Japan. Claus Stamm. Viking, 1962. Dover reprint as *English Fairy Tales; Womenfolk and Fairy Tales.* Rosemary Minard. Houghton, 1975.

Turnabout; A Norwegian Tale. William Wiesner. Seabury, 1972.

"Twelve Brothers" in *Household Stories from the Collection of the Brothers Grimm.* Lucy Crane, trans. Dover reprint as *English Fairy Tales; Womenfolk and Fairy Tales.* Rosemary Minard. Houghton, 1975.

"The Two Old Women's Bet" in *Grandfather Tales.* Richard Chase. Houghton, 1948.

"Umai" in *The Inland Whale.* Theodore Kroeber. Indiana U. Press; U. of California Press, 1959.

"Unanana and the Elephant" in *African Myths and Legends.* Kathleen Arnott. Walck, 1962.

"The Wise Wife" in *Eurasian Folk and and Fairy Tales.* I. F. Balatkin. Abelard, 1965.

The Wolf and the Seven Little Kids. Brothers Grimm. Harcourt out of print in the *Arbuthnot Anthology of Children's Literature.*

The Wolf Who Had a Wonderful Dream: A French Tale. Anne Rockwell, ret. Crowell, 1973.

Index